Hindi, Urdu & Bengali

lonely planet

phrasebooks

and

Richard Delacy & Shahara Ahmed

Hindi, Urdu & Bengali phrasebook
4th edition – September 2011

Published by Lonely Planet Publications Pty Ltd
ABN 36 005 607 983

Lonely Planet Offices
Australia Locked Bag 1, Footscray, Victoria 3011
USA 150 Linden St, Oakland CA 94607
UK 2nd fl, 186 City Rd, London, EC1V 2NT

Contact
talk2us@lonelyplanet.com.au
lonelyplanet.com/contact

Cover Illustration Andy Lewis

ISBN 978 1 74220 306 5

10 9 8 7 6 5 4 3 2 1

Printed in China

acknowledgments

Editor Branislava Vladisavljevic would like to thank the following people for their contributions to this phrasebook:

Richard Delacy for translating the Hindi and Urdu content in this book. Richard has studied and taught Hindi and Urdu formally at tertiary institutions in Australia and the US for several years. He has been travelling to India since the early 1990s and has also been to Pakistan. He continues to travel to India annually and has many friends there. Richard would like to thank Shahara Ahmed for typing in all the Urdu phrases, Sudha Joshi for invaluable advice on the translations and all those friends and acquaintances in the subcontinent who have taught him so much about the complexities of Hindi and Urdu.

Shahara Ahmed for translating the Bengali words and phrases in this book and for patiently keying in the Urdu script. Shahara is originally from Dhaka and now lives in Melbourne and works for Lonely Planet as a managing cartographer. She still considers Bangladesh her home and visits as often as she can. Besides her Bengali expertise, she has a degree in architecture and takes particular interest in the art, architecture, cuisine and culture of the subcontinent. Shahara would like to thank her father for his advice and guidance and her husband and children for their support.

Richard and Shahara would like to thank Ben and Branislava at Lonely Planet for their guidance and forbearance working with two authors, three languages and as many crazy scripts.

John Mock for proofing the Hindi and Urdu and providing additional translations at the last minute.

Tanveer Ahmed and Latifa Khanum for proofing the Bengali.

Lonely Planet Language Products

Associate Publisher: Tali Budlender
Commissioning Editor: Ben Handicott
Editor: Branislava Vladisavljevic
Assisting Editor: Jodie Martire
Managing Editor: Annelies Mertens
Layout Designers: David Kemp, Kerrianne Southway
Managing Layout Designers: Chris Girdler, Jane Hart
Cartographer: Wayne Murphy
Internal Illustrations: Wendy Wright
Series Designer: Yukiyoshi Kamimura
Production Support: Mark Germanchis

make the most of this phrasebook ...

Anyone can speak another language! It's all about confidence. Don't worry if you can't remember your school language lessons or if you've never learnt a language before. Even if you learn the very basics (on the inside covers of this book), your travel experience will be the better for it. You have nothing to lose and everything to gain when the locals hear you making an effort.

finding things in this book

This book is divided into a Hindi/Urdu part and a Bengali part – for ease of navigation, both are subdivided into the same sections. The Tools chapters are the ones you'll thumb through time and again. The Practical sections cover basic travel situations like catching transport and finding a bed. The Social sections give you conversational phrases and the ability to express opinions – so you can get to know people. Food has a section all of its own: gourmets and vegetarians are covered and local dishes feature. Safe Travel equips you with health and police phrases, just in case. Remember the colours of each section and you'll find everything easily; or use the comprehensive Index. Otherwise, check the two-way traveller's Dictionaries for the word you need.

being understood

Throughout this book you'll see coloured phrases on each page. They're phonetic guides to help you pronounce the language – you don't even need to look at the language if you're not familiar with the Hindi, Urdu or Bengali script. The pronunciation for Hindi and Urdu words and phrases is generally the same, but where they differ we've given a different pronunciation guide for each, preceded by ⓗ for Hindi and ⓤ for Urdu. The pronunciation chapter in Tools will explain more, but you can feel confident that if you read the coloured phrase slowly, you'll be understood.

communication tips

Body language, ways of doing things, sense of humour – all have a role to play in every culture. 'Local talk' boxes show you common ways of saying things, or everyday language to drop into conversation. 'Listen for ...' boxes supply the phrases you may hear and 'signs' boxes show you signs you might encounter.

Hindi & Urdu

hindi & urdu

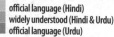

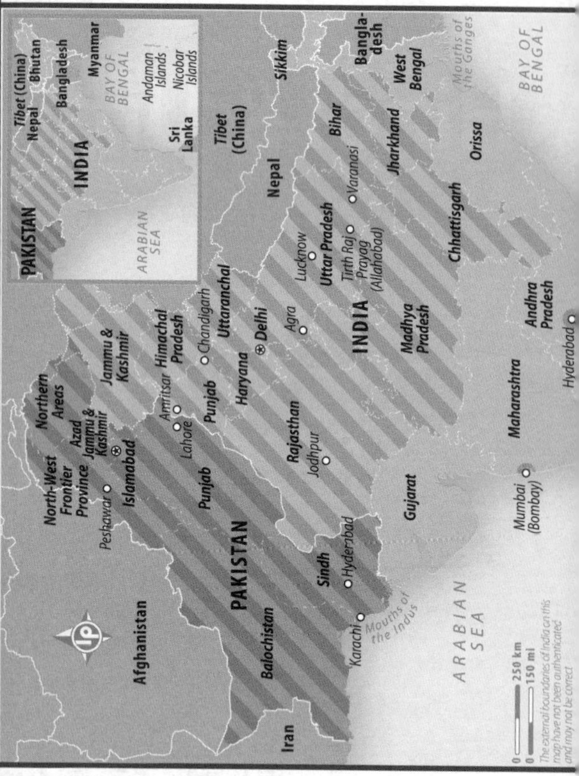

official language (Hindi)
widely understood (Hindi & Urdu)
official language (Urdu)

For more details, see the **introduction**, page 11.

INTRODUCTION

भूमिका • پیش لفظ

Hindi and Urdu are generally considered to be one spoken language with two different literary traditions. This means that Hindi and Urdu speakers who shop in the same markets (and watch the same Bollywood films) have no problems understanding each other – they'd both say yeh *kit*·ne kaa hay for 'How much is it?' – but the written form for Hindi will be यह कितने का है? and the Urdu one will be یہ کتنے کا ہے؟

Hindi is written from left to right in the Devanagari script, and is the official language of India, along with English. Urdu, on the other hand, is written from right to left in the Nastaliq script (a modified form of the Arabic script) and is the national language of Pakistan. It's also one of the official languages of the Indian states of Bihar and Jammu & Kashmir. Considered as one, these tongues constitute the second most spoken language in the world, sometimes called Hindustani. In their daily lives, Hindi and Urdu speakers communicate in their 'different' languages without major problems. The greatest variations between the two appear at academic and philosophical levels – this is because the majority of the 'intellectual' vocabulary in Hindi comes directly from Sanskrit, while Urdu relies on the Arabic and Persian ancestry of its writing system.

Both Hindi and Urdu developed from Classical Sanskrit, which appeared in the Indus Valley (modern Pakistan and northwest India) at about the start of the Common Era. The first old Hindi (or Apabhransha)

at a glance …

language name: Hindi, Urdu

name in language:
हिन्दी *hin*·dee
اردو *ur*·doo

language family: the Indo-Aryan family of Indo-European languages

approximate number of speakers : 600 million

close relatives: Nepali, Punjabi, Sanskrit

donations to English: cheesy, cheetah, chutney, cowry, cummerbund, dinghy, hookah, jungle, khaki, loot, pyjama, shampoo, tandoori, thug, veranda

poetry was written in the year 769AD, and by the European Middle Ages it became known as 'Hindvi'. Muslim Turks invaded the Punjab in 1027 and took control of Delhi in 1193. They paved the way for the Islamic Mughal Empire, which ruled northern India from the 16th century until it was defeated by the British Raj in the mid-19th century. It was at this time that the language of this book began to take form, a mixture of Hindvi grammar with Arabic, Persian and Turkish vocabulary. The Muslim speakers of Hindvi began to write in Arabic script, creating Urdu, while the Hindu population incorporated the new words but continued to write in Devanagari script.

During their rule, the British Raj used Hindi, Urdu and English to administer India, bringing these languages to prominence across the subcontinent. In 1947 Britain gave up its rule and India and Pakistan were divided into two nations. In the years leading up to this act, known as the Partition, Britain's India saw violent tensions between Muslims and Hindus, and the question of language was intimately linked to religious and cultural pride. Urdu was seen as a Muslim-only language, and Hindi was considered a non-Muslim language which could govern most of India. Accordingly, Urdu was chosen as Pakistan's national language, and Hindi became one of India's two official languages, with 21 other languages recognised in the Constitution. Issues of language, religion and culture continue to cause tension, and often violence, within both countries.

Today, Urdu is the national language of Pakistan, yet it's only spoken as a first language by 11% of the population. Within India, 180 million people speak Hindi as a first or second language, and around 50 million speak Urdu.

This book gives you the practical phrases you need to get by in Hindi and Urdu, as well as all the fun, spontaneous phrases that can lead to a better understanding of its speakers. Once you've got the hang of how to pronounce the language, the rest is just a matter of confidence. Local knowledge, new relationships and a sense of satisfaction are on the tip of your tongue. So don't just stand there, say something!

abbreviations used in this book

a	adjective	int	intimate	pl	plural
adv	adverb	lit	literal translation	pol	polite
dir	direct (case)	m	masculine	sg	singular
f	feminine	n	noun	v	verb
inf	informal	obl	oblique (case)		

TOOLS > pronunciation

उच्चारणें • تلّفظ

Many of the Hindi and Urdu sounds are also found in English. As ever, no book will replace listening to the language, but as a guide it can get you started.

vowel sounds

The length of a vowel is distinctive, so work on getting the differences between short vowels (like a) and long vowels (like aa) right.

vowel sounds		
symbol	english equivalent	hindi/urdu example
a	run	*pa*·ti
aa	father	pi·*taa*
ai	aisle	sa·*mai*
ay	day	*pay*·se
au	cow	*au*·rat
e	bed	de·*kaa*
ee	bee	pat·*nee*
i	bit	*mil*·naa
o	go	*bol*·naa
oo	fool	dood
u	put	*sun*·naa

consonant sounds

There's a difference between 'aspirated' consonants (pronounced with a strong puff of air, like saying 'h' after the sound) and 'unaspirated' ones. There are also 'retroflex' consonants, where you bend your tongue backwards to make the sound. Our simplified pronunciation guide doesn't include these distinctions – however, you'll be understood just fine if you follow our system.

consonant sounds		
symbol	english equivalent	hindi/urdu example
b	big	boo
ch	cheat	chat
d	doubt	dost
f	frog	fayl
g	go	geet
h	hit	hosh
j	juggle	jag
k	skin	kaam
l	loud	laal
m	man	man
n	no	naa
ng	king (nasal sound)	ka·*haang*
p	spit	pul
r	run (but slightly trilled)	rel
s	so	saal
sh	show	shaam
t	talk	taal
v	van	van
y	yes	yaa
z	zero	za·*raa*

syllables & word stress

In our coloured pronunciation guide, words are divided into syllables separated by a dot (eg *kam*·raa room) to help you pronounce them. Word stress in Hindi and Urdu is very light, and the rules are quite complex – we've indicated the stressed syllables in italics. Until you begin to learn some words yourself, just follow our pronunciation guide.

reading & writing

hindi

Hindi is written in the Devanagari script, just like Sanskrit, Nepali and Marathi. The script has 46 characters in the primary forms – 35 for consonants and 11 for vowels – and is written from left to right. Devanagari is mostly phonetic, so each symbol represents only one sound. Vowels are traditionally listed first in the alphabet, followed by the consonants. These are arranged according to where the sound comes from in your mouth (from the throat to the lips). Each consonant is 'naturally' pronounced with an a sound. You'll notice that in our pronunciation guide some consonants are pronounced the same way as we don't distinguish aspirated and retroflex sounds.

hindi vowels										
a अ	aa आ	i इ	ee ई	u उ	oo ऊ	ri ऋ	e ए	ay ऐ	o ओ	au औ

hindi consonants						
ka क	ka ख	ga ग	ga घ	na ङ		
cha च	cha छ	ja ज	ja झ	na ञ		
ta ट	ta ठ	da ड	da ढ	na ण	ra ड़	ra ढ़
ta त	ta थ	da द	da ध	na न		
pa प	pa फ	ba ब	ba भ	ma म		
ya य	ra र	la ल	va व			
sha श	sha ष	sa स				
ha ह						

A line across the top of all letters indicates the length of a word in Devanagari script. The vertical line at the end of a sentence (।) is equivalent to a full-stop. Other punctuation marks are the same as in English. If you'd like to learn how to read and write Devanagari script, get a copy of Rupert Snell's *Teach Yourself Beginner's Hindi Script*.

urdu

In both India and Pakistan, Urdu is traditionally written in a modified form of the Persio-Arabic script called nas·*taa*·lik. The script used in this book is an alternative script called nashk which is also used to write Arabic. Both scripts are written from right to left, but in nas·*taa*·lik words slant diagonally from the top to the bottom of the line, while words in nashk run along the line. In Urdu there are 35 letters in their basic form. The consonants are phonetic (ie each symbol represents only one sound), but the vowel symbols can be pronounced in several ways. Also, each letter can have a different written form depending on whether it appears at the beginning, middle or end of a word, but in the table below we've only provided the full form.

urdu alphabet					
a·lif ا	be ب	pe پ	te ت	te ٹ	se ث
jim ج	che چ	*ba*·ri he ح	khe خ	dal د	dal ڈ
zal ذ	re ر	re ڑ	ze ز	zhe ژ	sin س
shin ش	svad ص	zad ض	*to*·e ط	*zo*·e ظ	ain ع
ghain غ	fe ف	qaf ق	kaf ک	gaf گ	lam ل
mim م	nun ن	vao و	*cho*·ti he ہ	ye ی	

Individual words in Urdu can be hard to identify as the letters are often joined together to form hybrid characters, but sentences are separated by a horizontal stroke (۔) equivalent to a full stop. Commas (،) and question marks (؟) are the mirror image of English ones. All other punctuation marks are the same as in English. If you'd like to learn how to read and write nas·*taa*·lik, get a copy of Richard Delacy's *Teach Yourself Beginner's Urdu Script*.

contents

The index below shows which grammatical structures you need to say what you want. Look under each function – in alphabetical order – for information on how to build your own phrases. For example, to tell the taxi driver where your hotel is, look for **giving directions/orders** in the index below, which then directs you to information on **case**, **postpositions**, **verbs** etc. A glossary of grammatical terms is included at the end of this book to help you (see page 297). The abbreviations dir and obl in the literal translations for each example refer to the case of the noun – this is explained in the **glossary** and in **case**. The scripts for Hindi and Urdu are not included in this chapter.

adjectives & adverbs

describing people/things • doing things

Adjectives come before the noun they go with. Adjectives which end in ·aa in the masculine form change for number and gender to agree with the noun they qualify (as shown in the table below), but all other adjectives have only one form. Adverbs have only one form and can come at the start of a sentence or before the verb.

noun	singular		plural	
masculine	-aa	*ach*·chaa *kam*·raa nice room	-e	*ach*·che *kam*·re nice rooms
feminine	-ee	*ach*·chee *lar*·kee nice girl	-ee	*ach*·chee *lar*·ki·yaang nice girls

cheap ticket m	*sas*·taa ti·*ket*	(lit: cheap ticket)
Go straight.	*see*·de *jaa*·o	(lit: straight go)

See also **case** and **gender**.

articles

describing people/things • naming people/things

Hindi and Urdu don't have equivalents for 'a/an' and 'the'. The words ek (one) and *ko*·ee (anyone/someone) can act as 'a/an', and the personal pronoun voh (he/she/it/that) can act as 'the'.

a man m	ek/*ko*·ee *aad*·mee	(lit: one/someone man)
the man m	voh *aad*·mee	(lit: that man)

be

describing people/things • doing things • possessing

The verb *ho*·naa (be) is irregular in most tenses, as the forms don't always reflect gender and number of the subject of the sentence, as other verbs do (see **verbs**).

ho·naa (be) - present tense			
I	am	mayng	hoong
you sg int	are	too	hay
you sg inf	are	tum	ho
you sg pol	are	aap	hayng
he/she/it/this (near) inf	is	yeh	hay
he/she/it/this (near) pol	is	ye	hayng
he/she/it/that (far) inf	is	voh	hay
he/she/it/that (far) pol	is	vo	hayng
we	are	ham	hayng
you pl inf	are	tum	ho
you pl pol	are	aap	hayng
they/these (near)	are	ye	hayng
they/those (far)	are	vo	hayng

He's British.
voh *an*·grez hay (lit: he-inf-far English is)

See also **negatives, personal pronouns** and **possession**.

case

describing people/things • giving directions/orders • indicating location • naming people/things • possessing

Hindi and Urdu are 'case' languages, which means that nouns, pronouns, adjectives and demonstratives change their endings to show their role and relationship to other elements in the sentence.

In this **phrasebuilder**, the case of each noun has been given to show when to use the direct (dir) or the oblique case (obl) within a sentence. Nouns found in the **dictionary** and the word lists in this phrasebook are in the direct case. You can use the direct case in any phrase and be understood just fine, even though it won't always be completely correct grammatically.

direct case dir – used for the subject of the sentence	
This room is full. yeh *kam*·raa ba·*raa* hay	(lit: this-dir room-dir full is)
oblique case obl – used for all roles other than the subject of the sentence	
Place it in this room. is *kam*·re meng ra·ki·*ye*	(lit: this-obl room-obl in place)

The endings for cases in Hindi and Urdu are laid out in the next table:

	direct case		oblique case	
type of noun	singular	plural	singular	plural
masculine ending in -aa	-aa *kam*·raa room	-e *kam*·re rooms	-e *kam*·re room	-ong *kam*·rong rooms
masculine not ending in -aa	ma·*kaan* house	ma·*kaan* house	ma·*kaan* house	-ong ma·*kaa*·nong houses
feminine ending in -ee	-ee *pat*·nee wife	-i·yaang *pat*·ni·yaang wives	-ee *pat*·nee wife	-i·yong *pat*·ni·yong wives
feminine not ending in -ee	*baa*·shaa language	-eng baa·*shaa*·eng languages	*baa*·shaa language	-ong baa·*shaa*·ong languages

See also **adjectives**, **gender**, **possession** and **postpositions**.

demonstratives

describing people/things • naming people/things • pointing things out

Demonstratives in Hindi and Urdu can come before a noun or they can be used on their own. They take different forms for direct and oblique case.

this hotel	yeh *ho*·tal	(lit: this hotel)
those ones	voh	(lit: those ones)

	with direct case nouns	with oblique case nouns
this	yeh	is
that	voh	us
these	ye	in
those	vo	un

What's that?
voh kyaa hay (lit: that-dir what is)

How much does this coat cost?
ⓗ is kot kaa daam kyaa hay (lit: this-obl coat-obl of price-dir what is)
ⓤ is kot kee *kee*·mat kyaa hay (lit: this-obl coat-obl of price-dir what is)

See also **case**, **gender** and **word order**.

gender

describing people/things • naming people/things

Nouns in Hindi and Urdu are either 'masculine' or 'feminine'. For people and animals, grammatical gender matches physical gender. For all other nouns, you need to learn the gender when you learn the noun. Plural and case endings are added in different ways, depending on what type of masculine and feminine noun a word is (as shown in the table below). Nouns in the **dictionary** and in word lists in this phrasebook have their gender marked where applicable. See also **adjectives & adverbs**, **case** and **verbs**.

masculine nouns			feminine nouns		
ending in -aa	sg	-aa *kam*·raa (room)	ending in -ee	sg	-ee *pat*·nee (wife)
	pl	-e *kam*·re (rooms)		pl	-i·yaang pat·ni·*yaang* (wives)
not ending in -aa	sg	ma·*kaan* (house)	not ending in -ee	sg	-i·yaa chi·ri·*yaa* (bird)
	pl	ma·*kaan* (houses)		pl	-i·yaang chi·ri·*yaang* (birds)

negatives

doing things • negating

Place the word na, naa or na·*heeng* directly before the verb to make it negative. These words translate as both 'no' and 'not'.

She works.
voh kaam *kar*·tee hay (lit: she-inf-far work do-f is)

She doesn't work.
voh kaam na·*heeng kar*·tee (lit: she-inf-far work not do-f)

See also **verbs** and **word order**.

personal pronouns

doing things • naming people/things

Personal pronouns are listed below. There are three forms for 'you': the intimate too (used only with very close friends and kids), the informal tum (used with younger people and friends) and the polite aap (used for older people and strangers). There's only one word for 'he', 'she' and 'it' as the gender is shown in the verb ending (see **verbs**). There are different forms, however, depending on whether the person or thing is 'near' or 'far' and whether it's referred to in the informal or polite way. Note that the plural forms for the third person (they) are also used as polite singular forms. Throughout this book, we've used the forms appropriate for the context.

personal pronouns			
I	mayng	**we**	ham
you sg int	too	**you** pl inf	tum
you sg inf	tum		
you sg pol	aap	**you** pl pol	aap
he/she/it/this (near) inf	yeh	**they/these (near)**	ye
he/she/it/this (near) pol	ye		
he/she/it/that (far) inf	voh	**they/those (far)**	vo
he/she/it/that (far) pol	vo		

plurals

There's no easy rule for forming plurals in Hindi and Urdu – plural forms change according to the case and gender of the noun. See **case** and **gender** for more.

possession

describing people/things • naming people/things • possessing

To show possession in Hindi and Urdu, place one of the possessive pronouns from the table below (shown in the direct case only) in front of the thing which is owned, depending on whether it's masculine singular or plural, or feminine.

my bag	*me*·raa beg	(lit: my bag)
your bags	*te*·re beg	(lit: your bags)

	masculine sg	masculine pl	feminine
my	*me*·raa	*me*·re	*me*·ree
your sg int	*te*·raa	*te*·re	*te*·ree
your sg inf	tum·*haa*·raa	tum·*haa*·re	tum·*haa*·ree
your sg pol	*aap*·kaa	*aap*·ke	*aap*·kee
his/her/its/of this (near) inf	*is*·kaa	*is*·ke	*is*·kee
his/her/its/of these (near) pol	*in*·kaa	*in*·ke	*in*·kee
his/her/its/of that (far) inf	*us*·kaa	*us*·ke	*us*·kee
his/her/its/of that (far) pol	*un*·kaa	*un*·ke	*un*·kee
our	ha·*maa*·raa	ha·*maa*·re	ha·*maa*·ree
your pl inf	tum·*haa*·raa	tum·*haa*·re	tum·*haa*·ree
your pl pol	*aap*·kaa	*aap*·ke	*aap*·kee
their/of these (near)	*in*·kaa	*in*·ke	*in*·kee
their/of those (far)	*un*·kaa	*un*·ke	*un*·kee

Both Hindi and Urdu use the verb 'be' instead of 'have' to express possession. To talk about people or nonmovable possessions (like in the first example below), the structure is 'your X is'. For a movable possession (as in example two), say 'X is near you'.

He has two sisters.
us·kee do *be*·ha·neng hayng (lit: his-inf-far two sisters-dir are)

We have three tickets.
ha·*maa*·re paas teen ti·*ket* hayng (lit: our near three tickets-dir are)

See also **be, case, gender** and **postpositions**.

postpositions

giving directions/orders • indicating location

Hindi and Urdu use a system of postpositions to show the relationship between words in a sentence. They perform the same function as English prepositions do (eg 'at', 'to'), except that they come after the noun or pronoun they refer to. Most postpositions come after a noun in the oblique case. Here are some useful postpositions:

postpositions			
at	par	**of**	kaa/ke/kee m sg/m pl/f
by/from	se	**outside**	ke *baa*·har
for	ke li·*ye*	**to/on/at (time & space)**	ko
in	meng	**until/up to**	tak
inside	ke *an*·dar	**with**	ke saat

from London *lan*·dan se (lit: London-obl from)
at the airport ha·*vaa*·ee *ad*·de meng (lit: airport-obl in)

What are you doing on Saturday night?
sha·ni·*vaar* kee raat ko aap kyaa *kar*·ne·*vaa*·le hayng (lit: Saturday-obl of night-obl on you what will-do are)

See also **case** and **possession**.

questions

asking questions • making requests

You can change a statement into a yes/no question by raising your voice towards the end of a sentence or adding the word kyaa at the beginning. When kyaa appears directly before the verb, it means 'what'.

This room is free.
yeh *kam*·raa *kaa*·lee hay (lit: this room-dir free is)

Is this room free?
kyaa yeh *kam*·raa *kaa*·lee hay (lit: kyaa this room-dir free is)

You can also use the question words listed in the table below:

question words			
how	*kay*·se	what	kyaa
how much/many	*kit*·naa m sg	when	kab
	kit·ne m pl	where	ka·*haang*
	kit·nee f	which	*kaun*·saa
what kind	*kay*·saa m sg	who	kaun
	kay·se m pl	why	kyong
	kay·see f		

How did this happen?
yeh *kay*·se hu·*aa* (lit: this-inf-near how happened)

What kind of man is he?
voh *kay*·saa *aad*·mee hay (lit: he-inf-far what-kind man-dir is)

To make a polite request, take the verb stem (ie the dictionary form of the verb minus the ·naa ending) and add ·i·ye:

come *aa*·naa
Can you please come? *aa*·i·ye

See also **verbs** and **word order**.

there is/are

indicating location • pointing things out

To say 'there is/are', use the appropriate form of the verb 'be' – hay for singular and hayng for plural. The word na·*heeng* (not) is used before the verb for negation.

There's a telephone in the station.
ste·shan meng fon hay (lit: station-obl in phone-dir is)

There are no telephones in the station.
ste·shan meng fon na·*heeng* hay (lit: station-obl in phone-dir not is)

See also **be, negatives** and **verbs.**

verbs

doing things • giving directions/orders • making requests • negating

The dictionary forms of Hindi and Urdu verbs all end in ·naa. Removing the suffix ·naa leaves the verb stem, which is used to form all verb tenses. Be careful – in Hindi and Urdu it's the verbs, not the pronouns 'he' or 'she', which show whether the subject of the sentence is masculine or feminine, ie whether a male or female is doing the action. The gender of the different forms is marked in this phrasebook where appropriate.

The structure of the present simple tense is given in the next table, using the verb *bol*·naa (speak). You need the verb stem – in this case bol· – then add a suffix which shows the gender and number of the subject (·taa m sg, ·te m pl or ·tee f), and then the appropriate present tense form of the verb 'be' (hoong/hay/ho/hayng). The suffix agrees in gender and number with the subject of the verb, while the verb 'be' agrees in person and number with the subject of the verb.

		masculine	feminine
I	speak	*bol*·taa hoong	*bol*·tee hoong
you sg int		*bol*·taa hay	*bol*·tee hay
you sg inf		*bol*·te ho	*bol*·tee ho
you sg pol		*bol*·te hayng	*bol*·tee hayng
he/she/it sg inf	speaks	*bol*·taa hay	*bol*·tee hay
he/she/it sg pol		*bol*·te hayng	*bol*·tee hayng
we	speak	*bol*·te hayng	*bol*·tee hayng
you pl inf		*bol*·te ho	*bol*·tee ho
you pl pol		*bol*·te hayng	*bol*·tee hayng
they		*bol*·te hayng	*bol*·tee hayng

I speak Hindi.
mayng *hin*·dee *bol*·taa/*bol*·tee hoong (lit: I Hindi-dir speak-m/f am)

See also **be**, **gender**, **negatives** and **word order**.

word order

asking questions • giving directions/orders • doing things

Word order in Hindi and Urdu is generally subject-object-verb, even for questions and negative sentences.

Are you studying Hindi?
kyaa aap *hin*·dee *par*·te/*par*·tee hayng (lit: kyaa you-sg-pol Hindi-dir study-m/f are)

I'm studying Urdu.
mayng *ur*·doo *par*·taa/*par*·tee hoong (lit: I Urdu-dir study-m/f am)

See also **negatives** and **questions**.

language difficulties

समझने में दिक़्क़तें • سمجھنے میں دقّت

Do you speak (English)?
क्या आपको (अंग्रेज़ी) आती है? — kyaa aap ko (an·*gre*·zee) *aa*·tee hay
کیا آپ کو (انگریزی) آتی ہے؟

Does anyone speak (English)?
क्या किसीको (अंग्रेज़ी) आती है? — kyaa ki·*see* ko (an·*gre*·zee) *aa*·tee hay
کیا کسی کو (انگریزی) آتی ہے؟

Do you understand?
क्या आप समझे? — kyaa aap *sam*·je
کیا آپ سمجھے؟

Yes, I understand.
जी हाँ मैं समझ गया/गयी। — jee haang mayng sa·*maj* ga·*yaa*/ga·*yee* m/f
جی ہاں میں سمجھ گیا/گئی۔

No, I don't understand.
मैं नहीं समझा/समझी। — mayng na·*heeng* *sam*·jaa/*sam*·jee m/f
میں نہیں سمجھا/ سمجھی۔

I speak (English).
मुझे (अंग्रेज़ी) आती है। — *mu*·je (an·*gre*·zee) *aa*·tee hay
مجھے (انگریزی) آتی ہے۔

I don't speak (Hindi/Urdu).
मुझे (हिन्दी/उर्दू) नहीं आती। — *mu*·je (*hin*·dee/*ur*·doo) na·*heeng* *aa*·tee
مجھے (ہندی/اردو) نہیں آتی۔

two languages or one?

Although Hindi and Urdu are written in different scripts, they share a common core vocabulary. Therefore, most phrases in this book will be understood by both Hindi and Urdu speakers. Where phrases differ, however, you'll find the following signs before their pronunciation guides: ⓗ for Hindi and ⓤ for Urdu. The difference will generally be the substitution of a word of Sanskrit origin in the case of Hindi with a synonymous word of either Persian or Arabic origin in the case of Urdu.

I speak a little.

मुझे थोड़ा आता है।
مجھے تھوڑا آتا ہے۔
mu·je to·*raa aa*·taa hay

What does 'bu·*rad*' mean?

बुरा का क्या मतलब है?
برا کا کیا مطلب ہے؟
bu·*raa* kaa kyaa *mat*·lab hay

How do you say this?

यह कैसे कहते हैं?
یہ کیسے کہتے ہیں؟
yeh *kay*·se *keh*·te hayng

How do you write this?

यह कैसे लिखते हैं?
یہ کیسے لکھتے ہیں؟
yeh *kay*·se *lik*·te hayng

Could you please ...?

कृपया ...
ⓗ kri·pa·*yaa* ...

مہربانی کرکے ...
ⓤ me·har·*baa*·nee *kar*·ke ...

repeat that	फिर से कहिये	پھر سے کہئے	pir se ka·*hi*·ye
speak more slowly	धीरे बोलिये	دھرے بولئے	*dee*·re bo·*li*·ye
write it down	यह लिखिये	یہ لکھئے	yeh li·*ki*·ye

indian english

Under the British Raj (1858–1947) English was used as the official language of administration throughout India. In independent India, Hindi and English have equal status as the two official languages and are also widely used as a lingua franca throughout the country (although a number of other languages predominate in Southern India). At first you might find it challenging to understand the 'Indian English' pronunciation, affected as it is by the sound systems of native languages. Grammar and vocabulary on the subcontinent can also vary from standard English, so listen carefully – of course, if you don't understand something, politely ask the speaker to repeat it.

numbers & amounts
संख्या और मात्राएँ • شمار اور گنتی

cardinal numbers

संख्य • اعداد

0	शून्या	صفر	ⓗ *shoon*·yaa ⓤ *si*·far
1	एक	ایک	ek
2	दो	دو	do
3	तीन	تین	teen
4	चार	چار	chaar
5	पाँच	پانچ	paanch
6	छह	چھ	chay
7	सात	سات	saat
8	आठ	آٹھ	aat
9	नौ	نو	nau
10	दस	دس	das
11	ग्यारह	گیارہ	*gyaa*·rah
12	बारह	بارہ	*baa*·rah
13	तेरह	تیرہ	*te*·rah
14	चौदह	چودہ	*chau*·dah
15	पंद्रह	پندرہ	*pan*·drah
16	सोलह	سولہ	*so*·lah
17	सत्रह	سترہ	*sat*·rah
18	अठारह	اٹھارہ	a·*taa*·rah
19	उन्नीस	انیس	*un*·nees
20	बीस	بیس	bees
30	तीस	تیس	tees
40	चालीस	چالیس	*chaa*·lees
50	पचास	پچاس	pa·*chaas*
60	साठ	ساٹھ	saat
70	सत्तर	سترّ	*sat*·tar
80	अस्सी	اسّی	*as*·see
90	नब्बे	نبّے	*nab*·be
100	सौ	سو	sau
200	दो सौ	دو سو	do sau

1,000	एक हज़ार	ایک ہزار	ek ha·*zaar*
100,000	एक लाख	ایک لاکھ	ek laak
10,000,000	एक करोड़	ایک کروڑ	ek ka·*ror*

For Hindi and Urdu numerals, see the box **learn to count**, page 72.

ordinal numbers

क्रमबद्ध संख्या • عدد ترتیبی

1st	पहला	پہلا	*peh*·laa
2nd	दूसरा	دوسرا	*doos*·raa
3rd	तीसरा	تیسرا	*tees*·raa
4th	चौथा	چوتھا	*chau*·taa
5th	पाँचवाँ	پانچواں	*paanch*·vaang

fractions

भिन्न • جزوقلیل

a quarter	एक चौथाई	ایک چوتھائی	ek *chau*·taa·ee
a third	एक तिहाई	ایک تہائی	ek ti·*haa*·ee
a half	आधा	آدھا	*aa*·daa
three-quarters	तीन चौथाई	تین چوتھائی	teen chau·*taa*·e

useful amounts

उपयोगी मात्राएँ • مفید مقدار

a little	ज़रा	زرا	za·*raa*
less	कम	کم	kam
many/much	बहुत	بہت	ba·*hut*
more	ज़्यादा	زیادہ	*zyaa*·daa
some	कुछ	کچھ	kuch

time & dates

टाइम और तारीख़ • ٹائم اور تاریخ

telling the time

टाइम बताना • ٹائم بتنا

What time is it?
टाइम क्या है?
ٹائم کیا ہے؟
taa·im kyaa hay

It's (ten) o'clock.
(दस) बजे हैं।
(دس) بجے ہیں۔
(das) ba·*je* hayng

Five past (ten).
(दस) बज कर पाँच मिनट हैं।
(دس) بج کر پانچ منٹ ہیں۔
(das) baj kar paanch mi·*nat* hayn

Quarter past (ten).
सवा (दस)।
سوا (رس)۔
sa·*vaa* (das)

Half past (ten).
साढ़े (दस)।
ساڑھے (دس)۔
saa·re (das)

Quarter to (ten).
पौने (दस)।
پونے (دس)۔
pau·ne (das)

Twenty to (ten).
(दस) बजने में बीस मिनट।
(دس) بجنے میں بیس منٹ۔
(das) ba·*je* meng bees mi·*nat*

At what time ...?
कितने बजे ...?
کتنے بجے ...؟
kit·ne ba·*je* ...

At 7.57pm.
आठ बजने में तीन मिनट।
آٹھ بجنے میں تین منٹ۔
aat ba·*je* meng teen mi·*nat*

am	सुबह	صبح	su·*bah*
pm	शाम	شام	shaam

the calendar

कैलेंडर • کیلینڈار

days

Monday	सोमवार	پیر	ⓗ *som*·vaar ⓤ peer
Tuesday	मंगलवार	منگل	ⓗ man·*gal*·vaar ⓤ *man*·gal
Wednesday	बुधवार	بدھ	ⓗ *bud*·vaar ⓤ bud
Thursday	गुरुवार	جمعرات	ⓗ gu·ru·*vaar* ⓤ ju·*me*·raat
Friday	शुक्रवार	جمع	ⓗ *shuk*·ra·vaar ⓤ ju·*maa*
Saturday	शनिवार	ہفتہ	ⓗ sha·ni·*vaar* ⓤ *haf*·taa
Sunday	रविवार	اتوار	ⓗ ra·vi·*vaar* ⓤ *it*·vaar

months

January	जनवरी	جنوری	*jan*·va·ree
February	फरवरी	فروری	*far*·va·ree
March	मार्च	مارچ	maarch
April	अप्रैल	اپریل	a·*prayl*
May	मई	مئی	ma·*ee*
June	जून	جون	joon
July	जुलाई	جلائی	ju·*laa*·ee
August	अगस्त	اگست	a·*gast*
September	सितम्बर	ستمبر	si·*tam*·bar
October	अक्टूबर	اکتوبر	ak·*too*·bar
November	नवम्बर	نومبر	na·*vam*·bar
December	दिसम्बर	دسمبر	di·*sam*·bar

dates

What date is it today?

आज क्या तारीख़ है?
آج کیا تاریخ ہے؟
aaj kyaa *taa*·reek hay

It's (18 October).

आज (अठारह अक्टूबर) है।
آج (اٹھارہ اکتوبر) ہے۔
aaj (a·*taa*·rah ak·*too*·bar) hay

seasons

spring m	वसंत	وسنت	va·*sant*
summer m pl	गरमी के दिन	گرمی کے دن	*gar*·mee ke din
autumn m	पतझड़	پتجھڑ	*pat*·jar
winter f	सरदी	سردی	*sar*·dee

time is relative

You might say that the concept of time is more relative in India than in the Western culture, at least if language is anything to go by. In Hindi and Urdu, there's only one word for both 'yesterday' and 'tomorrow' – kal (कल کل). Not only that, but 'the day before yesterday' and 'the day after tomorrow' are both described with the same word – *par*·song (परसों پرسوں).

present

वर्तमान • حال

today	आज	آج	aaj
tonight	आज रात	آج رات	aaj raat

this ...

morning	आज सुबह	آج صبح	aaj su·*bah*
afternoon	आज दोपहर	آج دوپہر	aaj *do*·pa·har
week	इस हफ़्ते	اس ہفتے	is *haf*·te
month	इस महीने	اس مہینے	is ma·*hee*·ne
year	इस साल	اس سال	is saal

past

भूत • ماضی

last …	पिछले …	پچھلے …	*pich*·le …
week	हफ़्ते	ہفتے	*haf*·te
month	महीने	مہینے	ma·*hee*·ne
year	साल	سال	saal
yesterday …	कल …	کل …	kal …
morning	सुबह	صبح	su·*bah*
afternoon	दोपहर	دوپہر	*do*·pa·har
evening	शाम	شام	shaam
last night	कल रात	کل رات	kal raat
since (May)	(मई) से	(مئی) سے	(ma·*ee*) se

future

भविष्य • مستقبل

next …	अगले …	اگلے …	*ag*·le …
week	हफ़्ते	ہفتے	*haf*·te
month	महीने	مہینے	ma·*hee*·ne
year	साल	سال	saal
tomorrow …	कल …	کل …	kal …
morning	सुबह	صبح	su·*bah*
afternoon	दोपहर	دوپہر	*do*·pa·har
evening	शाम	شام	shaam
until (June)	(जून) तक	(جون) تک	(joon) tak

PRACTICAL > transport
सवारी • سواری

getting around
किस सवारी से • کس سوای سے

Which … goes to (Karachi)?
कौनसी … (कराची) जाती है? *kaun*·see … (ka·*raa*·chee) *jaa*·tee hay
کونسی ... (کراچی) جاتی ہے؟

bus	बस	بس	bas
train	ट्रेन	ڑرین	tren
tram	ट्राम	ڑرام	traam

Is this the … to (Agra)?
क्या यह … (आगरा) जाता है? kyaa yeh … (*aag*·raa) *jaa*·taa hay
کیا یہ ... (آگرہ) جاتا ہے؟

boat	जहाज़	جہاز	ja·*haaz*
ferry	फ़ेरी	فیری	*fe*·ree
plane	हवाई जहाज़	ہوائ جہاز	ha·*vaa*·ee ja·*haaz*

When's the … (bus)?
… (बस) कब जाती है? … (bas) kab *jaa*·tee hay
... (بس) کب جاتی ہے؟

first	पहली	پہلی	*peh*·lee
next	अगली	اگلی	*ag*·lee
last	आख़िरी	آخری	*aa*·ki·ree

What time does it leave?
कितने बजे जाता/जाती है? *kit*·ne ba·*je* *jaa*·taa/*jaa*·tee hay m/f
کتنے بجے جاتا/جاتی ہے؟

How long will it be delayed?
उसे कितनी देर हुई है? u·*se* *kit*·nee der hu·*ee* hay
اسے کتنی دیر ہوئ ہے؟

Is this seat available?
क्या यह सीट ख़ाली है? kyaa yeh seet *kaa*·lee hay
کیا یہ سیٹ خالی ہے؟

That's my seat.

वह मेरी सीट है। — voh *me*·ree seet hay

وہ میری سیٹ ہے۔

Please tell me when we get to (Islamabad).

जब (इसलामाबाद) आता है, मुझे बताइये। — jab (is·laa·*maa*·baad) *aa*·taa hay mu·*je* ba·*taa*·i·ye

جب (اسلامآباد) آتا ہے،
مجھے بتائے۔

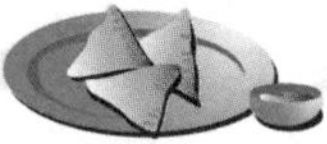

tickets

टिकट • ٹکٹ

Where do I buy a ticket?

टिकट कहाँ मिलता है? — ti·*kat* ka·*haang* *mil*·taa hay

ٹکٹ کہاں ملتا ہے؟

Where's the booking office for foreigners?

विदेशियों का बुकिंग ऑफिस कहाँ है? — ⓗ vi·de·*shi*·yong kaa bu·*king* *aa*·fis ka·*haang* hay

غیر ملکوں کا بکنگ
آفس کہاں ہے؟ — ⓤ gair mul·*ki*·yong kaa bu·*king* *aa*·fis ka·*haang* hay

Do I need to book well in advance?

जाने से बहुत पहले बुकिंग होनी चाहिये? — *jaa*·ne se ba·*hut* *peh*·le bu·*king* *ho*·nee *chaa*·hi·ye

جانے سے بہت پہلے
بکنگ ہونی چاہئے؟

Is there a waiting list?

वेटलिस्ट है? — *vet*·list hay

ویٹلسٹ ہے؟

Can I get a stand-by ticket?

क्या स्टेंड बाई का टिकट मिलेगा? — kyaa stend *baa*·ee kaa ti·*kat* mi·*le*·gaa

کیا سٹینڈ بائ
کا ٹکٹ ملیگا؟

A … ticket to (Kanpur).

(कानपुर) के लिये … टिकट दीजिये। — (*kaan*·pur) ke li·*ye* … ti·*kat dee*·ji·ye

(کانپر) کے لئے ...
ٹکٹ دیجئے۔

1st-class	फ़र्स्ट क्लास	فرسٹ کلاس	farst klaas
2nd-class	सेकंड क्लास	سیکنڈ کلاس	se·*kand* klaas
child's	बच्चे का	بچّے کا	*bach*·che kaa
one-way	एक तरफ़ा	ایک طرفہ	ek ta·ra·*faa*
return	आने जाने का	آنے جانے کا	*aa*·ne *jaa*·ne kaa
student	छात्र का	چھاتر کا	*chaa*·tra kaa

I'd like a/an … seat.

मुझे … सीट चाहिये। — mu·*je* … seet *chaa*·hi·ye

مجھے ... سیٹ چاہئے۔

aisle	किनारे	کنارے	ki·*naa*·re
nonsmoking	नॉन स्मोकिंग	نان سموکنگ	naan *smo*·king
smoking	स्मोकिंग	سموکنگ	*smo*·king
window	खिड़की के पास	کھڑکی کے پاس	*kir*·kee ke paas

Is there (a) …?

क्या … है? — kyaa … hay

کیا ... ہے؟

air conditioning	ए० सी०	اے-سی	e see
blanket	कम्बल	کمبل	*kam*·bal
sick bag	सिक बेग	سک بیگ	sik beg
toilet	टाइलेट	ٹائلیٹ	*taa*·i·let

How long does the trip take?

जाने में कितनी देर लगती है? — *jaa*·ne meng *kit*·nee der *lag*·tee hay

جانے میں کتنی دیر لگتی ہے؟

Is it a direct route?

क्या सीधे जाते हैं? — kyaa *see*·de *jaa*·te hayng

کیا سیدھے جاتے ہیں؟

What time should I check in?

कितने बजे चेक इन करना चाहिये? — *kit*·ne ba·*je* chek in *kar*·naa *chaa*·hi·ye

کتنے بجے چیک ان کرنا چاہئے؟

I'd like to … my ticket, please.

मुझे टिकट … है।			mu·*je* ti·*kat* … hay
مجھے ٹکٹ … ہے۔			
cancel	कैंसल कराना	کینسل کرانا	*kayn*·sal ka·*raa*·naa
change	बदलना	بدلنا	ba·*dal*·naa
confirm	कंफर्म कराना	کنفرم کرانا	*kan*·farm ka·*raa*·naa

For chair cars, sleeper cars, and other specific requests, see **train**, page 42.

luggage

सामान • سامان

My luggage has been …

मेरा सामान … गया है।			*me*·raa *saa*·man … ga·*yaa* hay
میرا سامان … گیا ہے۔			
damaged	ख़राब हो	خراب ہو	ka·*raab* ho
lost	खो	کھو	ko
stolen	चोरी हो	چوری ہو	*cho*·ree ho

Where can I find the …?

… कहाँ है?			… ka·*haang* hay
… کہاں ہے؟			
baggage claim	बेगेज क्लैम	بیگیج کلیم	*be*·gej klaym
luggage lockers	सामान के लाकर	سامان کے لاکر	*saa*·maan ke *laa*·kar

Can I have some coins/tokens?

क्या मुझे कुछ सिक्के/ टोकन देंगे?

کیا مجھے کچھ سکّے/ ٹوکن دینگے؟

kyaa mu·*je* kuch *sik*·ke/ *to*·kan *deng*·ge

PRACTICAL

plane

हवाई जहाज़ • ہوائی جہاز

Where does flight number (12) arrive/depart?

फ्लाइट नम्बर (बारह) कहाँ उतरती/उड़ती है?

فلائٹ نمبر (بارہ) کہاں اترتی/اڑتی ہے؟

flaa·it *nam*·bar (*baa*·rah) ka·*haang* u·*tar*·tee/*ur*·tee hay

Where's (the) ...?

... कहाँ है?

... کہاں ہے؟

... ka·*haang* hay

airport shuttle	एयरपोर्ट शटल	ائرپورٹ شٹل	e·*yar*·port sha·*tal*
arrivals hall	आगमन	آمد	ⓗ *aa*·ga·man ⓤ *aa*·mad
departures hall	प्रस्थान	روانگی	ⓗ pras·*thaan* ⓤ ra·*vaa*·na·gee
duty-free shop	ड्यूटी फ़्री	ڈیوٹی فری	*dyoo*·tee free
gate (three)	गेट (तीन)	گیٹ (تین)	get (teen)

bus & coach

बस और कोच • بس اور کوچ

Does it stop at (Benaras)?

क्या (बनारस) में रुकती है?

کیا (بنارس) میں رکتی ہے؟

kyaa (ba·*naa*·ras) meng *ruk*·tee hay

I'd like to get off at (Allahabad).

मुझे (इलाहाबाद) में उतरना है।

مجھے (الّہآباد) میں اترنا ہے۔

mu·*je* (i·laa·*haa*·baad) meng u·*tar*·naa hay

What's the next stop?

अगला स्टॉप क्या है?

اگلا سٹاپ کیا ہے؟

ag·laa staap kyaa hay

Where's the queue for female passengers?

औरतों के लिये क्यू कहाँ है? — *aur*·tong ke li·*ye* kyoo ka·*haang* hay

عورتوں کے لئے کیو کہاں ہے؟

Where are the seats for female passengers?

औरतों के लिये सीट कहाँ है? — *aur*·tong ke li·*ye* seet ka·*haang* hay

عورتوں کے لئے سیٹ کہاں ہے؟

… bus f	… बस	… بس	… bas
city	शहर की	شہر کی	sha·*har* kee
intercity	इंटर सिटी	انٹر سٹی	*in*·tar si·*tee*
local	लोकल	لوکل	lo·*kal*
express	एक्स्प्रेस	ایکسپریس	*ek*·spres

train

ट्रेन • ٹرین

What station is this?

यह कौन सा स्टेशन है? — yeh kaun saa *ste*·shan hay

یہ کون سا سٹیشن ہے؟

What's the next station?

अगला स्टेशन क्या है? — *ag*·laa *ste*·shan kyaa hay

اگلا سٹیشن کیا ہے؟

Do I need to change?

क्या खुले पैसे चाहिये? — kyaa ku·*le pay*·se *chaa*·hi·ye

کیا کھلے پیسے چاہئے؟

Is it (a) …?

क्या वह … है? — kyaa voh … hay

کیا وہ … ہے؟

2-tier	टू टीर	ٹو ٹیر	too teer
3-tier	थ्री टीर	تھری ٹیر	tree teer
air-conditioned	ए० सी०	اۓ-سی	e see
chair car	चैयर कार	چیر کار	*chay*·yar kaar
direct	सीधे जाती	سیدھے جاتی	*see*·de *jaa*·tee
express	एक्स्प्रेस	ایکسپریس	*ek*·spres
sleeper car	स्लीपर	سلیپر	*slee*·par

PRACTICAL

Which carriage is (for) ...?

कौन सा डिब्बा ... है?
كون سا دبّا ... ہے؟
kaun saa *dib*·baa ... hay

(Jhansi)	(झांसी) के लिये	(جھانسی) کے لئے	(*jaan*·see) ke li·*ye*
1st class	फ़र्स्ट क्लास	فرسٹ کلاس	farst klaas
dining	खाने के लिये	کھانے کے لئے	*kaa*·ne ke li·*ye*

taxi

टैक्सी • ٹیکسی

I'd like a taxi ...

मुझे ... टैक्सी चाहिये।
مجھے ... ٹیکسی چاہئے۔
mu·*je* ... *tayk*·see *chaa*·hi·ye

at (9am)	(सुबह नौ) बजे	(صبح نو) بجے	(su·*bah* nau) ba·*je*
now	अभी	ابھی	a·*bee*
tomorrow	कल	کل	kal

Is this taxi available?

क्या यह टैक्सी ख़ाली है?
کیا یہ ٹیکسی خالی ہے؟
kyaa yeh *tayk*·see *kaa*·lee hay

How much is it to (Lahore)?

(लाहौर) तक कितने रुपये लगते हैं?
(لاہور) تک کتنے روپیہ لگتے ہیں؟
(*laa*·haur) tak *kit*·ne ru·pa·*ye* *lag*·te hayng

Can I see the fare chart?

चार्ट दिखाना।
چارٹ دکھانا۔
chaart di·*daa*·naa

Please put the meter on.

मीटर लगाना।
میٹر لگانا۔
mee·tar la·*gaa*·naa

We need ... seats.

हमें ... सीटें चाहिये।
ہمیں ... سیٹیں چاہئے۔
ha·*meng* ... *see*·teng *chaa*·hi·ye

Please take me to …
… ले जाइये।
… لے جائے۔
… le *jaa*·i·ye

Slow down.	धीरे चलिये।	دھیرے چلئے۔	*dee*·re cha·li·*ye*
Stop here.	यहाँ रुकिये।	یہاں رکئے۔	ya·*haang* ru·ki·*ye*
Wait here.	यहाँ इंतज़ार कीजिये।	یہاں انتظار کیجئے۔	ya·*haang* *in*·ta·zaar *kee*·ji·ye

car & motorbike

कार और मोटर साइकिल • کار اور موٹر سائکل

hire

I'd like to hire a/an …
मुझे … किराये पर लेना है।
مجھے ... کرائے پر لینا ہے۔
mu·*je* … ki·*raa*·ye par *le*·naa hay

4WD	फ़ोर व्हील ड्राइव	فور وہیل ڈرایو	for vheel *draa*·iv
automatic	आटोमेटिक	آٹومیٹک	aa·to·*me*·tik
car	कार	کار	kaar
manual	मेन्यूल	مینیول	*men*·yool
motorbike	मोटर साइकिल	موٹر سائکل	*mo*·tar *saa*·i·kil

with (a) …
… के साथ
… کے ساتھ
… ke saat

air conditioning	ए० सी०	اے-سی	e see
driver	ड्राइवर	ڈرایور	*draa*·i·var

How much for … hire?
… के लिये किराया कितना है?
… کے لئے کرایا کتنا ہے؟
… ke li·*ye* ki·*raa*·yaa *kit*·naa hay

daily	एक रोज़	ایک روز	ek roz
weekly	हफ़्ते	ہفتے	*haf*·te

Does that include insurance/mileage?
उस में बीमा/दूरी शामिल हैं?
اس میں بیما/دوری شامل ہے؟
us meng *bee*·maa/*doo*·ree *shaa*·mil hay

PRACTICAL

road signs			
प्रवेश	اندر	ⓗ *pra*·vesh ⓤ an·dar	**Entrance**
निकास	نکاس	ni·*kaas*	**Exit**
अन्दर आना मना है	اندر آنا منع ہے	*an*·dar *aa*·naa ma·*naa* hay	**No Entry**
एक तरफ़ा	ایک طرفہ	ek ta·ra·*faa*	**One-way**
ठहरिये	ٹھہریے	*theh*·ri·ye	**Stop**
चुंगी	چنگی	*chun*·gee	**Toll**

on the road

What's the speed limit?
गतिसीमा क्या है? — ⓗ ga·ti·*see*·maa kyaa hay
رفتار کی انتہا کیا ہے؟ — ⓤ *raf*·taar kee *in*·ta·haa kyaa hay

Is this the road to (Ajmer)?
क्या यह (अजमीर) का रास्ता है? — kyaa yeh (*aj*·meer) kaa *raas*·taa hay
کیا یہ (اجمیر) کا راستہ ہے؟

Can I park here?
यहाँ पार्क कर सकता/सकती हूँ? — ya·*haang* paark kar
یہاں پارک کر سکتا/سکتی ہوں؟ — *sak*·taa/*sak*·tee hoong m/f

Where's a petrol station?
पेट्रोल पम्प कहाँ है? — *pet*·rol pamp ka·*haang* hay
پیٹرول پمپ کہاں ہے؟

Can you check the ...?
... देखिये। — ... de·ki·*ye*
... دیکھیے۔

oil	तेल	تیل	tel
tyre pressure	टायर का प्रेशर	ٹایر کا پریشر	*taa*·yar kaa *pre*·shar
water	पानी	پانی	*paa*·nee

problems

I've had an accident.
दुर्घटना हुई है। — ⓗ dur·*gat*·naa hu·*ee* hay
حادثہ ہو گیا ہے۔ — ⓤ *haad*·saa ho ga·*yaa* hay

I need a mechanic.

मुझे मरम्मत करने वाला चाहिये। — mu·*je* ma·*ram*·mat *kar*·ne *vaa*·laa *chaa*·hi·ye

مجھے مرمّت کرنے والا چاہئے۔

The car/motorbike has broken down (at Lucknow).

कार/मोटर साइकिल (लखनऊ में) ख़राब हो गयी है। — kaar/*mo*·tar *saa*·i·kil (*lakh*·na·oo meng) ka·*raab* ho ga·*yee* hay

کار/موٹر سائکل (لکھنو میں) خراب ہو گئ ہے۔

I have a flat tyre.

टायर पंक्चर हो गया है। — *taa*·yar *pank*·char ho ga·*yaa* hay

ٹایر پنکچر ہو گیا ہے۔

I've lost my car keys.

चाबी खो गयी है। — *chaa*·bee ko ga·*yee* hay

چابی کھو گئ ہے۔

I've run out of petrol.

पेट्रोल ख़त्म हो गया है। — *pet*·rol katm ho ga·*yaa* hay

پٹرول ختم ہو گیا ہے۔

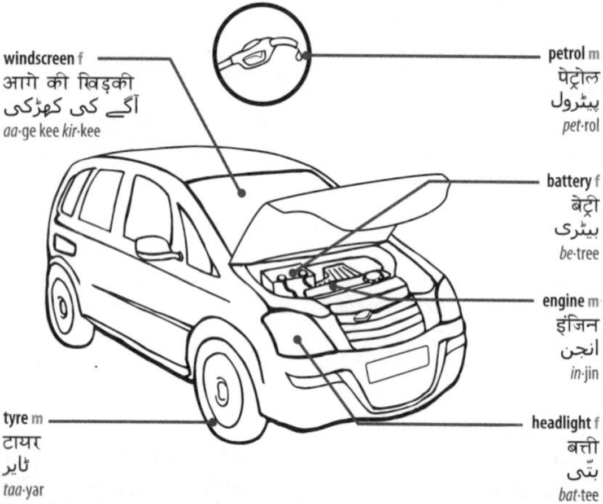

bicycle

साइकिल • سائکل

I'd like …

मुझे साइकिल … है।
مجھے سائکل ... ہے۔

mu·je saa·i·kil … hay

my bicycle repaired	की मरम्मत करानी	کی مرمّت کرانی	kee ma·*ram*·mat ka·*raa*·nee
to buy a bicycle	ख़रीदनी	خریدنی	ka·*reed*·nee
to hire a bicycle	किराये पर लेनी	کرائے پر ینی	ki·*raa*·ye par *le*·nee

I'd like a … bike.

मुझे … बाइक चाहिये।
مجھے ... بائک چاہئے۔

mu·je … baa·ik chaa·hi·ye

mountain	माउण्टन	ماؤنٹن	maa·*un*·tan
racing	रेसिंग	ریسنگ	*re*·sing
second-hand	पुरानी	پرانی	pu·*raa*·nee

I have a puncture.

पंक्चर हो गया है।
پنکچر ہو گیا ہے۔

pank·char ho ga·yaa hay

local transport

लोकल सवारी • لوکل سواری

Where can I find a scooter-taxi?

आटो कहाँ मिलेगा?
آٹو کہاں ملیگا؟

aa·to ka·haang mi·le·gaa

Are there any shared jeeps?

क्या एक सीट जीप में मिलेगी?
کیا ایک سیٹ جیپ میں ملیگی؟

kyaa ek seet jeep meng mi·le·gee

I'd like to get a cycle-rickshaw.

मुझे साइकिल रिक्शा चाहिये।
مجھے سائکل رکشہ چاہئے۔

mu·je saa·i·kil rik·shaa chaa·hi·ye

I'd like to get an auto-rickshaw.

मुझे आटो चाहिये।
مجھے آٹو چاہئے۔

mu·je aa·to chaa·hi·ye

Can we agree on a fare?

पहले से किराया तय करें?
پہلے سے کرایا طے کریں؟
peh·le se ki·*raa*·yaa tai ka·*reng*

I'll pay when we get there.

पहुँचने पर पैसा देता/देती हूँ।
پہنچنے پر پیسا دیتا/دیتی ہوں۔
pa·*hunch*·ne par *pai*·saa *de*·taa/*de*·tee hoong **m/f**

Can we share a ride?

हम साथ साथ चलें?
ہم ساتھ ساتھ چلیں؟
ham saat saat cha·*leng*

Are you waiting for more people?

क्या आप किसी और का इंतज़ार कर रहे हैं?
کیا آپ کسی اور کا انتظار کر رہے ہیں؟
kyaa aap ki·*see* aur kaa *in*·ta·zaar kar ra·*he* hayng

Can you take us around the city, please?

क्या आप हमें शहर में घुमा देंगे?
کیا آپ ہمیں شہر میں گھما دینگے؟
kyaa aap ha·*meng* sha·*har* meng gu·*maa deng*·ge

Please go straight to this address.

इसी जगह को फ़ौरन जाइए।
اسی جگہ کو فورا جائے۔
is·ee *ja*·gah ko *fau*·ran *jaa*·i·ye

Please continue.

जारी रखिए।
جاری رکھئے۔
jaa·ree ra·*kee*·ye

This is not the place I wanted to go to.

मैं इस जगह नहीं आना चाहता/चाहती हूँ।
|میں اس جگہ نہیں آنا چاہتا/چاہتیہ ہوں۔
maing is *ja*·gah na·*heeng* *aa*·naa *chaah*·taa/*chaah*·tee hoong **m/f**

I don't want to stop at the carpet shop.

मैं क़ालीन की दुकान पर नहीं रुकना चाहता/चाहती हूँ।
میں قالین کی دکان پر نہیں رکنا چاہتا/چاہتی ہوں۔
maing *kaa*·leen kee du·*kaan* par na·*heeng ruk*·naa *chaah*·taa/*chaah*·tee hoong **m/f**

PRACTICAL

border crossing

सीमा पार करना • سرحد پار کرنا

border crossing

सीमा-पार करना • سرحد پار کرنا

I'm here for (three) ...
मैं (तीन) ... के लिये आया/आयी हूँ।
میں (تین) ... کے لئے آیا/آئ ہوں۔
mayng (teen) ... ke li·*ye* *aa*·yaa/*aa*·yee hoong m/f

days	दिन	دن	din
months	महीने	مہینے	ma·*hee*·ne
weeks	हफ़्ते	ہفتے	*haf*·te

I'm in transit.
मैं रास्ते में हूँ।
میی راستے میں ہوں۔
mayng *raa*·ste meng hoong

I'm on business.
मैं व्यापार करने आया/आयी हू।
میی کاروبار کرنے آیا/آئ ہوں۔
Ⓗ mayng *vyaa*·paar *kar*·ne *aa*·yaa/*aa*·yee hoong m/f
Ⓤ mayng *kaa*·ro·baar *kar*·ne *aa*·yaa/*aa*·yee hoong m/f

I'm on holiday.
मैं छुट्टी मनाने आया/आयी हू।
میی چھٹی منانے آیا/آئ ہوں۔
mayng *chut*·tee ma·*naa*·ne *aa*·yaa/*aa*·yee hoong m/f

I'm going to (Karachi).
मैं (कराची) जा रहा/रही हूँ।
میی (کراچی) جا رہا/رہی ہوں۔
mayng (ka·*raa*·chee) jaa ra·*haa*/ra·*hee* hoong m/f

I'm staying at (the Awadh Hotel).
मैं (अवध होटल) में ठहरा/ठहरी हूँ।
میں (اودھ ہوٹل) میں ٹھرا/ٹھری ہوں۔
mayng (*a*·wad ho·*tel*) meng *teh*·raa/*teh*·ree hoong m/f

Do I need a special permit?

क्या मुझे विशेष परमिट चाहिये?
کیا مجھے خاص پرمٹ چاۓ؟

ⓗ kyaa mu·*je* vi·*shesh* *par*·mit *chaa*·hi·ye
ⓤ kyaa mu·*je* kaas *par*·mit *chaa*·hi·ye

Is it a restricted area?

क्या वहाँ जाना मना है?
کیا وہاں جانا منع ہے؟

kyaa va·*haang* *jaa*·naa ma·*naa* hay

at customs

सीमाधिकार • کسٹمس

I have nothing to declare.

कुछ डिक्लेर करने के लिये नहीं है।
کچھ ڈکلیر کرنے کے لۓ نہیں ہے۔

kuch dik·*ler* *kar*·ne ke li·*ye* na·*heeng* hay

That's (not) mine.

वह मेरा (नहीं) है।
وہ میرا (نہیں) ہے۔

voh *me*·raa (na·*heeng*) hay

I didn't know I had to declare it.

मुझे मालूम नहीं था कि यह दिखाना चाहिये था।
مجھے معلوم نہیں تھا کہ یہ دکھانا چاۓ تھا۔

mu·*je* *maa*·loom na·*heeng* taa ki yeh di·*kaa*·naa *chaa*·hi·ye taa

signs

कस्टम्स	کسٹمس	*kas*·tam	**Customs**
ड्यूटी-फ़्री	ڈیوٹی فری	*dyoo*·tee free	**Duty-Free**
सीमाधिकार	امگریشن	ⓗ see·*maa*·di·kaar ⓤ i·mi·*gre*·shan	**Immigration**
पासपोर्ट कंट्रोल	پاسپورٹ کنٹرول	*paas*·port *kan*·trol	**Passport Control**
क्वारेंटीन	کوارینٹین	kvaa·*ren*·teen	**Quarantine**

directions

किस तरफ़ चलें • کس طرف چلیں

Where's a/the …?
… कहाँ है?
… کہاں ہے؟
… ka·*haang* hay

bank	बैंक	بینک	baynk
market	बाज़ार	بازار	*baa*·zaar
tourist office	टूरिस्ट ऑफ़िस	ٹورسٹ آفس	*too*·rist *aa*·fis

It's …
वह … है।
وہ … ہے۔
voh … hay

behind …	… के पीछे	… کے پیچھے	… ke *pee*·che
close	नज़दीक	نزدیک	*naz*·deek
here	यहाँ	یہاں	ya·*haang*
in front of …	… के सामने	… کے سامنے	… ke *saam*·ne
near …	… के पास	… کے پاس	… ke paas
next to …	… के पास	… کے پاس	… ke paas
on the corner	कोने पर	کونے پر	*ko*·ne par
opposite …	… के सामने	… کے سامنے	… ke *saam*·ne
straight ahead	सीधे	سیدھے	*see*·de
there	वहाँ	وہاں	va·*haang*

Turn …
… मुड़िये।
… مڑئے۔
… mu·ri·*ye*

at the corner	कोने पर	کونے پر	*ko*·ne par
at the traffic lights	सिगनल पर	سگنل پر	*sig*·nal par
left	लेफ़्ट	لیفٹ	left
right	राइट	رائٹ	*raa*·it

by bus	बस से	بس سے	bas se
by taxi	टैक्सी से	ٹیکسی سے	*tayk*·see se
by train	ट्रेन से	ٹرین سے	tren se
on foot	पैदल	پیدل	*pay*·dal

How far is it?

वह कितनी दूर है? — voh *kit*·nee door hay

وہ کتنی دور ہے؟

Can you show me (on the map)?

(नक्शे में) दिखा सकते है? — (*nak*·she meng) di·*kaa sak*·te hayng

(نقشے میں) دکھا سکتے ہیں؟

What's the address?

पता क्या है? — pa·*taa* kyaa hay

پتہ کیا ہے؟

north m	उर	شمال	ⓗ *ut*·tar ⓤ shu·*maal*
south m	दक्षिण	جنوب	ⓗ *dak*·shin ⓤ ja·*noob*
east m	पूर्व	مشرق	ⓗ poorv ⓤ *mash*·rik
west m	पश्चिम	مغرب	ⓗ *pash*·chim ⓤ *mag*·rib

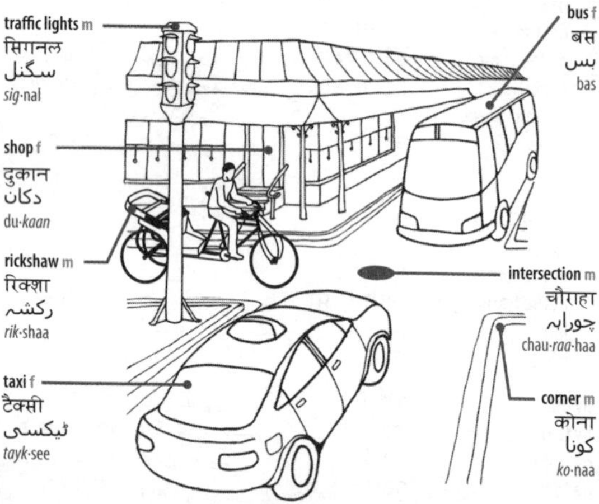

accommodation

ठहरने की जगह • ٹھہرنے کی جگہ

finding accommodation

जगह ढूँढना • جگہ ڈھونڈھنا

Where's a ...?

... कहाँ है? — ... ka·*haang* hay

... کہاں ہے؟

guesthouse	गेस्ट हाउस	گیسٹ ہاوس	gest *haa*·us
hotel	होटल	ہوٹل	*ho*·tal
tourist bungalow	टूरिस्ट बंगला	ٹورسٹ بنگلا	*too*·rist *ban*·glaa
youth hostel	यूथ हास्टल	یوتھ ہاسٹل	yoot *haas*·tal

Can you recommend somewhere ...?

... जगह का पता दे सकते हैं? — ... ja·*gah* kaa pa·*taa* de *sak*·te hayng

... جگہ کا پتہ دے سکتے ہیں؟

cheap	सस्ती	سستی	*sas*·tee
good	अच्छी	اچّھی	*ach*·chee
nearby	पास की	پاس کی	paas kee

What's the address?

पता क्या है? — pa·*taa* kyaa hay

پتہ کیا ہے؟

For responses, see **directions**, page 51.

booking ahead & checking in

बुकिंग और चेक इन • بکنگ اور چیک ان

I'd like to book a room, please.

मुझे कमरा चाहिये। — mu·*je* *kam*·raa *chaa*·hi·ye

مجھے کمرہ چاہئے۔

I have a reservation.

बुकिंग तो है। — bu·*king* to hay

بکنگ تو ہے۔

Do you have a … room?

क्या … कमरा है? — kyaa … *kam*·raa hay

کیا … کمرہ ہے؟

double	डबल	ڈبل	da·*bal*
single	सिंगल	سنگل	*sin*·gal

How much is it per …?

… के लिय कितने पैसे लगते हैं? — … ke li·*ye kit*·ne *pay*·se *lag*·te hayng

… کے لئے کتنے پیسے لگتے ہیں؟

night	एक रात	ایک رات	ek raat
person	हर व्यक्ति	ہر شخص	ⓗ har *vyak*·ti ⓤ har shaks
week	एक हफ्ते	ایک ہفتے	ek *haf*·te

Can I see it?

क्या मैं देख सकता/सकती हूँ? — kyaa mayng dek *sak*·taa/*sak*·tee hoong **m/f**

کیا میں دیکھ سکتا/سکتی ہوں؟

I'll take it.

ले लूँगा/लूँगी। — le *loong*·gaa/*loong*·gee **m/f**

لے لوں گا/ لوں گی۔

My name's …

मेरा नाम … है। — *me*·raa naam … hay

میرا نام … ہے۔

For (three) nights/weeks.

(तीन) दिन/हफ्ते के लिये। — (teen) din/*haf*·te ke li·*ye*

(تین) دن/ہفتے کے لئے۔

From (2 July) to (6 July).

(दो जुलाई) से (छहै जुलाई) तक। — (do ju·*laa*·ee) se (chay ju·*laa*·ee) tak

(دو جلائ) سے (چھ جلائ) تک۔

Do I need to pay upfront?

क्या अभी पैसे देने हैं? — kyaa a·*bee pay*·se *de*·ne hayng

کیا ابھی پیسے دینے ہیں؟

Can I pay by ...?

क्या मैं ... से पैसे दे सकता/सकती हूँ?	کیا میں ... سے پیسے دے سکتا/سکتی ہوں؟	kyaa mayng ... se *pay*·se de *sak*·taa/*sak*·tee hoong m/f	
credit card	क्रेडिट कार्ड	کریڈٹ کارڑ	*kre*·dit kaard
travellers cheque	ट्रेवलर्स चेक	ٹریولرس چیک	*tra*·va·lars chek

For other methods of payment, see **money & banking**, page 71.

signs

बाथरूम	باتھ روم	*baat*·room	**Bathroom**
कमरा ख़ाली नहीं है	کمرہ خالی نہیں ہے	*kam*·raa *kaa*·lee na·*heeng* hay	**No Vacancy**
कमरा ख़ाली है	کمرہ خالی ہے	*kam*·raa *kaa*·lee hay	**Vacancy**

requests & queries

माँगना और पूछना • مانگنا اور پوچھنا

When/Where is breakfast served?

नाश्ता कब/कहाँ होता है?
ناشتہ کب/کہاں ہوتا ہے؟
naash·taa kab/ka·*haang* *ho*·taa hay

Please wake me at (seven).

मुझे (सात बजे) उठाइये।
مجھے (سات بجے) اٹھائے۔
mu·*je* (saat ba·*je*) u·*taa*·i·ye

Can I use the ...?

क्या मैं ... का इस्तेमाल कर सकता/सकती हूँ?	کیا میں ... کا استعمال کر سکتا/سکتی ہوں؟	kyaa mayng ... kaa is·*te*·maal kar *sak*·taa/*sak*·tee hoong m/f	
kitchen	रसोई	رسوئی	ra·*so*·ee
laundry	लांड्री	لانڑری	*laan*·dree
telephone	फ़ोन	فون	fon

Is there…?

क्या … है?			kyaa … hay
کیا ... ہے؟			
air conditioning	ए० सी०	اۓ سی	e see
heating	हीटिंग	ہیٹنگ	*hee*·ting
hot water	गर्म पानी	گرم پانی	garm *paa*·nee
running water	चौबीस घंटे पानी	جوبیس گھنٹے پانی	*chau*·bees *gan*·te *paa*·nee

Do you have a/an …?

क्या यहाँ … है?			kyaa ya·*haang* … hay
کیا یہاں ... ہے؟			
elevator	लिफ्ट	لفٹ	lift
safe	तिजोरी	تجوری	ti·*jo*·ree
washerman	धोबी	دھوبی	do·*bee*

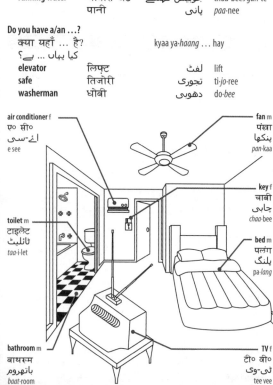

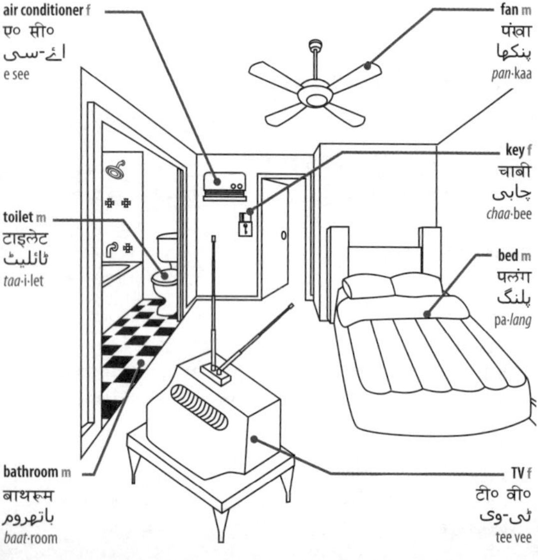

PRACTICAL

Is the bathroom …?
क्या बाथरूम … है?
کیا باتھروم ... ہے؟
kyaa *baat*·room … hay

communal	कॉमुनल	کامیونل	*kaa*·mu·nal
private	कमरे में	کمرے میں	*kam*·re meng

Are the toilets…?
क्या टाइलेट … है?
کیا ٹائلیٹ ... ہے؟
kyaa *taa*·i·let … hay

Indian-style	भारतीय शैली का	ہندوستانی ڈھنگ کا	ⓗ *baa*·ra·teey *shay*·lee kaa ⓤ hin·du·*staa*·nee dang kaa
Western-style	पश्चिमी शैली का	مغربی ڈھنگ کا	ⓗ *pash*·chi·mee *shay*·lee kaa ⓤ *mag*·ri·bee dang kaa

Could I have a/an …, please?
क्या … मिलेगा/मिलेगी?
کیا ... ملیگا/ملیگی؟
kyaa … mi·*le*·gaa/mi·*le*·gee m/f

extra blanket	एक और कम्बल	ایک اور کمبل	ek aur *kam*·bal
mosquito net	मसहरी	مچھردانی	ⓗ *mas*·ha·ree ⓤ ma·*char daa*·nee
receipt	रसीड	رسید	ra·*seed*

Could I have my key, please?
चाबी दीजिये।
چابی دیجئے۔
chaa·bee *dee*·ji·ye

complaints

शिकायतें • شکائتیں

It's too …
ज़्यादा … है।
زیارہ ... ہے۔
zyaa·daa … hay

cold	ठंडा	ٹھنڑا	*tan*·daa
dark	अंधेरा	اندھیرا	an·*de*·raa
noisy	शोर गुल	شورغل	shor gul
small	छोटा	چھوٹا	*cho*·taa

The … doesn't work.

… ख़राब है। … ka·*raab* hay

... خراب ہے۔

air conditioner	ए० सी०	اۓ-سی	e see
fan	पंखा	پنکھا	*pan*·kaa
toilet	टाइलेट	ٹائلیٹ	*taa*·i·let

This (pillow) isn't clean.

(तकिया) साफ़ नहीं है। (ta·ki·*yaa*) saaf na·*heeng* hay

(تکیا) ساف نہیں ہے۔

checking out

कमरा ख़ाली करना • کمرہ خالی کرنا

What time is checkout?

कितने बजे कमरा ख़ाली करना है? *kit*·ne ba·*je kam*·raa *kaa*·lee *kar*·naa hay

کتنے بجے کمرہ خالی کرنا ہے ؟

Can I leave my bags here?

क्या मैं यहाँ सामान छोड़ सकता/सकती हूँ? kyaa mayng ya·*haang saa*·maan chor *sak*·taa/*sak*·tee hoong m/f

کیا میں یہاں سامان چھوڑ سکتا/سکتی ہوں؟

Could I have my …, please?

… दे दीजिये। … de *dee*·ji·ye

... دے دیجئے۔

deposit	डिपासिट	ڈپاسٹ	di·*paa*·sit
passport	पासपोर्ट	پاسپورٹ	*paas*·port
valuables	बेशक़ीमती चीज़ें	بیشقیمتی چیزیں	besh·*keem*·tee *chee*·zeng

I'll be back …

मैं … वापस आऊँगा/आऊँगी। mayng … *vaa*·pas aa·*oong*·gaa/aa·*oong*·gee m/f

میں ... واپس آؤں گا/ آؤں گی۔

in (three) days	(तीन) दिन बाद	(تین) دن بعد	(teen) din baad
on (Tuesday)	(मंगलवार) को	(منگلوار) کو	(man·*gal*·vaar) ko

looking for ...

... ढूँढना • ... ڈھونڈھنا

Where's a/the ...?
... कहाँ है?
... کہاں ہے؟
... ka·*haang* hay

***khadi* shop**	खादी की दुकान	کھادی کی دکان	*kaa*·dee kee du·*kaan*
market	बाज़ार	بازار	*baa*·zaar
supermarket	सुपरमार्केट	سپرمارکیٹ	su·par·*maar*·ket

Where can I buy (a padlock)?
(ताला) कहाँ मिलेगा/मिलेगी?
(تالا) کہاں ملیگا/ملیگی؟
(*taa*·laa) ka·*haang* mi·*le*·gaa/mi·*le*·gee **m/f**

For responses, see **directions**, page 51.

making a purchase

ख़रीदना • خرید نا

I'm just looking.
सिर्फ़ देखने आया/आयी हूँ।
صرف دیکھنے آیا/آیی ہوں-
sirf *dek*·ne *aa*·yaa/*aa*·yee hoong **m/f**

I'd like to buy (an adaptor plug).
मुझे (अडप्टर प्लग) चाहिये।
مجھے (اڈپٹر پلگ) چاہئے-
mu·*je* (a·*dap*·tar plag) *chaa*·hi·ye

Can I look at it?
दिखाइये।
دکھائے-
di·*kaa*·i·ye

Do you have any others?
दूसरा है?
دوسرا ہے؟
doos·raa hay

How much is it?

कितने का है?
کتنے کا ہے؟
kit·ne kaa hay

Can you write down the price?

दाम काग़ज़ पर लिखिये?
دام کاغز پر لکھئے؟
daam *kaa*·gaz par li·ki·*ye*

Do you accept ...?

क्या आप ... लेते/लेती हैं?
کیا آپ ... لیتے/لیتی ہیں؟
kyaa aap ... *le*·te/*le*·tee hayng m/f

credit cards	क्रेडिट कार्ड	کریڈٹ کارڈ	*kre*·dit kaard
debit cards	डेबिट कार्ड	ڈیبٹ کارڈ	*de*·bit kaard
travellers cheques	ट्रेवलर्स चेक	ٹریولرس چیک	*tre*·va·lars chek

Could I have it wrapped?

क्या आप बाँध सकते/सकती हैं?
کیا آپ باندھ سکتے/سکتی ہیں؟
kyaa aap baangd *sak*·te/*sak*·tee hayng m/f

Does it have a guarantee?

क्या यह गरैंटी के साथ आता/आती है?
کیا یہ گرینٹی کے ساتھ آتا/آتی ہے؟
kyaa yeh ga·*rayng*·tee ke saat *aa*·taa/*aa*·tee hay m/f

Can I have it sent overseas?

क्या आप बाहर भिजवा देंगे/देंगी?
کیا آپ باہر بھجوا دیں گے/دیں گی؟
kyaa aap *baa*·har *bij*·vaa *deng*·ge/*deng*·gee m/f

Can you order it for me?

क्या आप मेरे लिये मंगवा सकते/सकती हैं?
کیا آپ میرے لئے منگوا سکتے/سکتی ہیں؟
kyaa aap *me*·re li·*ye mang*·vaa *sak*·te/*sak*·tee hayng m/f

Can I pick it up later?

क्या मैं बाद में ले जा सकता/सकती हूँ?
کیا میں بعد میں لے جا سکتا/سکتی ہوں؟
kyaa mayng baad meng le jaa *sak*·taa/*sak*·tee hoong m/f

It's faulty.

यह ख़राब है।

یہ خراب ہے۔

yeh ka·*raab* hay

I'd like to return this.

मुझे यह वापस करना है।

مجھے یہ واپس کرنا ہے۔

mu·*je* yeh *vaa*·pas *kar*·naa hay

I'd like ..., please.

मुझे ... चाहिये।

مجھے ... چاہئے۔

mu·*je* ... *chaa*·hi·ye

my change	बाक़ी पैसे	باقی پیسے	*baa*·kee *pay*·se
a receipt	रसीद	رسید	ra·*seed*
a refund	पैसे वापस	پیسے واپس	*pay*·se *vaa*·pas

local talk

baksheesh f	बख़्शिश	بخشش	*bak*·shish
to bargain	मोलतोल करना	مولتول کرنا	*mol*·tol *kar*·naa
fixed-price shop f	एक दाम की दुकान	ایک دام کی دکان	ek daam kee du·*kaan*
to rip off	ज़्यादा दाम लगाना	زیادہ دام لگانا	*zyaa*·daa daam la·*gaa*·naa
specials f	ख़ास छूट	خاص چھوٹ	kaas choot

bargaining

मोलतोल करना • مولتول کرن

That's too expensive.

यह बहुत महंगा/महंगी है।

یہ بہت مہنگا/مہنگی ہے۔

yeh ba·*hut* ma·*han*·gaa/ma·*han*·gee hay m/f

Can you lower the price?

क्या आप दाम कम करेंगे?

کیا آپ دام کم کریں گے؟

kyaa aap daam kam ka·*reng*·ge

Do you have something cheaper?

इस से सस्ता नहीं है? | is se *sas*·taa na·*heeng* hay

اس سے سستہ نہیں ہے؟

I don't have much money.

मेरे पास बहुत पैसे नहीं हैं। | *me*·re paas ba·*hut pay*·se na·*heeng* hayng

میرے پاس بہت پیسے نہیں ہیں۔

I'll think about it.

मैं सोच लूँगा/लूँगी। | mayng soch *loong*·gaa/*loong*·gee m/f

میں سوچ لوں گا/لوں گی۔

I'll give you (30 rupees).

मैं (तीस रुपये) दूँगा/दूँगी। | mayng (tees ru·pa·*ye*) *doong*·gaa/*doong*·gee m/f

میں (تیس روپیہ) دوں گا/دوں گی۔

bargain bazaar

Bargaining is a fundamental part of shopping in India, though at times it could almost be viewed as entertainment. The entertainment ends only in larger shops, where you'll often see the sign:

एक दाम है। ایک دام ہے۔ ek daam hay **Fixed Prices**

books & reading

किताबें और पढ़ना • کتابیں اور پڑھنا

Do you have a/an ...?

क्या आप के पास ... है? | kyaa aap ke paas ... hay

کیا آپ کے پاس ... ہے؟

book by (Rabindranath Tagore)	(रवींद्रनाथ ठाकुर) की कोई किताब	(رویندرناتھ ٹھاکر) کی کوئ کتاب	(ra·veen·*dra*·naat *taa*·kur) kee *ko*·ee ki·*taab*
entertainment guide	एंटरटैंमेंट गाइड	اینٹرٹینمینٹ گائڈ	en·tar·*tayn*·ment *gaa*·id

Is there an English-language ...?

क्या अंग्रेज़ी ... है?
کیا انگریزی ... ہے؟
kyaa an·*gre*·zee ... hay

bookshop	किताबों की दुकान	کتابوں کی دکان	kee·*taa*·bong kee du·*kaan*
section	का हिस्सा	کا حصّہ	kaa *his*·saa

I'd like a ...

मुझे ... चाहिये।
مجھے ... چاہئے۔
mu·*je* ... *chaa*·hi·ye

dictionary	कोश	لغت	ⓗ kosh ⓤ lu·*gat*
newspaper (in English)	(अंग्रेज़ी) अख़बार	(انگریزی) اخبار	(an·*gre*·zee) *ak*·baar

clothes

कपड़े • کپڑے

My size is ...

मेरी साइज़ ... है।
میرے سائز ... ہے۔
me·ree *saa*·iz ... hay

(40)	(चालीस)	(چالیس)	*chaa*·lees
small	छोटी	چھوٹی	*cho*·tee
medium	बीच की	بیچ کی	beech kee
large	बड़ी	بڑی	ba·*see*

Can I try it on?

पहनकर देखूँ?
پہنکر دیکھوں؟
pehn·kar de·*koong*

It doesn't fit.

यह साइज़ ठीक नहीं है।
یہ سائز ٹھیک نہیں ہے۔
yeh *saa*·iz teek na·*heeng* hay

For clothing items and colours, see the **dictionary**.

hairdressing

बाल काटना • بال کاٹنا

I'd like a shave.
दाढ़ी बनाइये।
داڑھی بنائے۔
daa·ree ba·*naa*·i·ye

I'd like a haircut.
बाल काटिये।
بال کاٹئے۔
baal *kaa*·ti·ye

Please cut only a little.
थोड़ा ही काटिये।
تھوڑا ہی کاٹئے۔
tho·raa hee *kaa*·ti·ye

Please colour it.
रंग लगाइये।
رنگ لگائے۔
rang la·*gaa*·i·ye

Please use a new blade.
नया ब्लैड लगाइये।
نیا بلیڈ لگائے۔
na·*yaa* blayd la·*gaa*·i·ye

music

संगीत • موسیقی

I'd like a …
मुझे … चाहिये।
مجھے … چاہئے۔
mu·*je* … *chaa*·hi·ye

blank tape	ख़ाली टेप	خالی ٹیپ	*kaa*·lee tep
CD	सी० डी०	سی-ڈی	see dee
DVD	डी० वी० डी०	ڈی-وی-ڈی	dee vee dee
video	विडियो	وڈیو	vi·di·*yo*

I'm looking for something by (Abeda Parveen).
मुझे (अबिदा परवीन) का संगीत चाहिये।
ⓗ mu·*je* (a·*bi*·daa *par*·veen) kaa *san*·geet *chaa*·hi·ye
مجھے (عبدا پروین) کی موسیقی چاہئے۔
ⓤ mu·*je* (a·*bi*·daa *par*·veen) kee moo·*see*·kee *chaa*·hi·ye

What's their best recording?

उन की सब से अच्छी
रिकोर्डिंग क्या है?
اس کی سب سے اچھے
رکورڈنگ کیا ہے؟

us kee sab se *ach*·chee
ri·*kor*·ding kyaa hay

Can I listen to this?

क्या मैं यह सुन सकता/सकती हूँ?
کیا میں یہ سن سکتا/سکتی ہوں؟

kyaa mayng yeh sun
sak·taa/*sak*·tee hoong m/f

photography

फोटो • فوٹو

I need a/an … film for this camera.

मुझे इस कैमरे के लिये एक
… रील चाहिये।
مجھے اس کیمرے کے لئے ایک
... ریل چاہئے۔

mu·*je* is *kaym*·re ke li·*ye* ek
… reel *chaa*·hi·ye

APS	ए० पी० एस०	اۓ-پی-ایس	e pee es
B&W	ब्लैक एंड व्हाइट	بلیک اینڈ وہائٹ	blayk end *vhaa*·it
colour	रंगीन	رنگین	*ran*·geen
slide	स्लाइड	سلائڈ	*slaa*·id
… speed	… स्पीड	... سپیڈ	… speed

Do you have … for this camera?

क्या इस कैमरे के लिये
आप के पास … है?
کیا اس کیمرے کے لئے
آپ کے پاس ... ہے؟

kyaa is *kaym*·re ke li·*ye*
aap ke paas … hay

batteries	सेल	سیل	sel
memory cards	मेमरी कार्ड	میمری کارڈ	*mem*·ree kaard

Can you transfer photos from my camera to CD?

क्या आ मेरे कैमरे की फोटो
सी० डी० पर लगा सकते हैं?
کیا آپ میرے کیمرے کی فوٹو
سی ڈی پر لگا سکتے ہیں؟

kyaa aap *me*·re *kaim*·re kee foto
see dee par la·*gaa* *sak*·te hayng

Can you recharge the battery for my digital camera?

क्या आप मेरे डिजिटल कैमरे का सेल रिचार्ज कर सकते/सकती हैं?
کیا آپ میرے ڈجٹل کیمرے کا سیل رچارج کر سکتے/سکتی ہیں؟
kyaa aap *me*·re *di*·ji·tal *kaym*·re kaa sel ri·*chaarj* kar *sak*·te/*sak*·tee hayng m/f

Can you develop this film?

क्या आप यह रील धो सकते/सकती हैं?
کیا آپ یہ ریل دھو سکیے/سکتی ہیں؟
kyaa aap yeh reel do *sak*·te/*sak*·tee hayng m/f

repairs

मरम्मत कराना • مرمّت کرانا

Can I have my … repaired here?

यहाँ … की मरम्मत होती है?
یہاں … کی مرمت ہوتی ہے؟
ya·*haang* … kee ma·*ram*·mat *ho*·tee hay

backpack	बेकपेक	بیکپیک	*bek*·pek
camera	कैमरा	کیمرا	*kaym*·raa
shoes	जूते	جوتے	*joo*·te
glasses	चश्मे	چشمہ	*chash*·me

When will it be ready?

कब तैयार होगा/होगी?
کب تیار ہو گا/ہو گی؟
kab *tay*·yaar *ho*·gaa/*ho*·gee m/f

souvenirs			
bangles f	चूड़ियाँ	چوڑیاں	*choo*·ri·yaang
incense f	अगरबत्ती	اگربتّی	a·gar·*bat*·tee
papier-mâché m	पेपर माशे	پیپر ماشے	*pe*·par *maa*·she
rugs f	कालीन	کالین	*kaa*·leen
sandals f	चप्पलें	چپّلیں	*chap*·pa·leng
saris f	साड़ियाँ	ساڑیاں	*saa*·ri·yaang
sitars m	सितार	ستار	si·*taar*

the internet

इंटरनेट • انٹرنیٹ

Where's the local Internet café?

इंटरनेट कैफ़े कहाँ है?
انٹرنیٹ کیفے کہاں ہے؟
in·*tar*·net *kay*·fe ka·*haang* hay

I'd like to ...

मुझे ... है।
مجھے ... ہے۔
mu·*je* ... hay

check my email	ई-मेल देखनी	اےمیل دیکھنی	ee·mayl *dek*·nee
get Internet access	इंटरनेट देखना	انٹرنیٹ دیکھنا	in·*tar*·net *dek*·naa
use a printer	कॉपी निकालनी	کاپی نکالنی	*kaa*·pee ni·*kaal*·nee
use a scanner	कुछ स्कैन करना	کچھ سکین کرنا	kuch skayn *kar*·naa

Do you have (a) ...?

क्या आप के पास ... है?
کیا ـپ کے پاس ... ہے؟
kyaa aap ke paas ... hay

Macs	मैक	میک	mayk
PCs	पी० सी०	پی-سی	pee see
Zip drive	ज़िप ड्राइव	زپ ڈرایو	zip *draa*·iv

How much per ...?

... कितने पैसे लगते हैं?
... کتنے پیسے لگتے ہیں؟
... *kit*·ne *pay*·se *lag*·te hayng

hour	प्रति घंटे	ہر گھنٹے	ⓗ *pra*·ti *gan*·te ⓤ har *gan*·te
page	एक पेजे के लिय	ایک پیج کے لئے	ek pej ke li·*ye*

How do I log on?

लोग ओन कैसे करते हैं?
لوگ اون کیسے کرتے ہیں؟
log on *kay*·se *kar*·te hayng

Please change it to the English-language setting.

इसे अंग्रेज़ी में बदल दीजिये। — i·*se* an·*gre*·zee meng ba·*dal* *dee*·ji·ye

اسے انگریزی میں بدل دیجئے۔

It's crashed.

क्रैश हो गया है। — kraysh ho ga·*yaa* hay

کریش ہو گیا ہے۔

I've finished.

मेरा काम हो गया है। — *me*·raa kaam ho ga·*yaa* hay

میرا کام ہو گیا ہے۔

mobile/cell phone

सेल फ़ोन • سیل فون

I'd like a …

मुझे … चाहिये। — mu·*je* … *chaa*·hi·ye

مجھے ... چاہئے۔

charger for	फ़ोन का	فون کا	fon kaa
my phone	चार्जर	چارجر	*chaar*·jar
mobile/cell	सेल फ़ोन	سیل فون	sel fon
phone for hire	किराये पर	کرائے پر	ki·*raa*·ye par
prepaid mobile/	प्रीपैड	پریپیڈ	*pree*·payd
cell phone	सेल फ़ोन	سیل فون	sel fon
SIM card	आप के	آپ کے	aap ke
for your	नेटवर्क के लिये	نیٹورک کے لئے	*net*·vark ke li·*ye*
network	सिम कार्ड	سم کارڈ	sim kaard

What are the rates?

दर क्या है? — dar kyaa hay

در کیا ہے؟

(30 rupees) per minute.

हर मिनट के लिये (तीस रुपये)। — har mi·*nat* ke li·*ye* (tees ru·pa·*ye*)

ہر منٹ کے لئے (تیس روپیہ)۔

Is roaming available?

क्या रोमिंग भी है? — kyaa ro·*ming* bee hay

کیا رومنگ بھی ہے؟

phone

फ़ोन • فون

Where's the nearest public phone?

यहाँ पी० सी० ओ० कहाँ है? — ya·*haang* pee see o ka·*haang* hay

یہاں پی-سی-او کہاں ہے؟

What's your phone number?

आप का नम्बर क्या है? — aap kaa *nam*·bar kyaa hay

آپ کا نمبر کیا ہے؟

The number is …

नम्बर … है। — *nam*·bar … hay

نمبر ... ہے۔

I want to …

मैं … चाहता/चाहती हूँ। — mayng … *chaah*·taa/*chaah*·tee hoong m/f

میں ... چاہتا/چاہتی ہوں۔

buy a phonecard	फ़ोनकार्ड ख़रीदना	فون کارڈ خریدنا	*fon*·kaard ka·*reed*·naa
call (Singapore)	(सिंगापुर को) फ़ोन करना	(سنگاپر کو) فون کرنا	(sin·*gaa*·pur ko) fon *kar*·naa
make a (local) call	(लोकल) कॉल करना	(لوکل) کال کرنا	(lo·*kal*) kaal *kar*·naa
reverse the charges	रिवर्स चार्जेज़ करना	رورس چارجز کرنا	ri·*vars chaar*·jez *kar*·naa
speak for (three) minutes	(तीन) मिनट के लिये बोलना	(تین) منٹ کے لئے بولنا	(teen) mi·*nat* ke li·*ye bol*·naa

How much does … cost?

… कितना लगता है? — … *kit*·naa *lag*·taa hay

... کتنا لگتا ہے؟

a (three)-minute call	(तीन) मिनट बात करने के लिये	(تین) منٹ بات کرنے کے لئے	(teen) mi·*nat* baat *kar*·ne ke li·*ye*
each extra minute	हरेक अतिरिक्त मिनट के लिये	اوپر سے ہرایک منٹ کے لئے	ⓗ ha·*rek* a·ti·*rikt* mi·*nat* ke li·*ye* ⓤ *oo*·par se ha·*rek* mi·*nat* ke li·*ye*

post office

डाकख़ाना • ڈاکخانہ

I want to send a/an …

मुझे … भेजना है।

مجھے ... بھیجنا ہے۔

mu·*je* … *bej*·naa hay

fax	फ़ैक्स	فیکس	fayks
letter	पत्र	خط	ⓗ pa·*tra* ⓤ kat
parcel	पार्सल	پارسل	*paar*·sal
postcard	पोस्टकार्ड	پوسٹ کارڈ	*post*·kaard

I want to buy a/an …

मुझे … दीजिये।

مجھے ... دیجئے۔

mu·*je* … *dee*·ji·ye

aerogram	हवाई पत्र	ہوائی خط	ⓗ ha·*vaa*·ee pa·*tra* ⓤ ha·*vaa*·ee kat
envelope	लिफ़ाफ़ा	لفافہ	li·*faa*·faa
stamp	टिकट	ٹکٹ	ti·*kat*

snail mail

airmail f	एयर मेल	ایر میل	a·*yar* mayl
express mail f	एक्स्प्रेस मेल	ایکسپریس میل	ek·*spres* mayl
registered mail f	रेजिस्टड मेल	ریجسٹڈ میل	re·*jis*·tad mayl
surface mail f	सर्फ़स मेल	سرفس میل	*sar*·fas mayl

Please send it by airmail to (Australia).

उसे एयर मेल से (ऑस्ट्रेलिया) को भेजिये।

اسے ایر میل سے (آسٹریلیا) کو بھیجئے۔

i·*se* a·*yar* mayl se (aas·*tre*·li·yaa) ko *be*·ji·ye

money & banking

पैसे और बैंक का काम • پیسے اور بینک کا کام

What time does the bank open?

बैंक कितने बजे खुलता है? — baynk *kit*·ne ba·*je kul*·taa hay

بینک کتنے بجے کھتا ہے؟

Where's ...?

... कहाँ है? — ... ka·*haang* hay

... کہاں ہے؟

an automated teller machine	ए० टी० एम०	اے-ٹی-ایم	e tee em
a foreign exchange office	फ़ॉरेन एक्स्चेंज ऑफ़िस	فارین ایکسچینج آفس	*faa*·ren *eks*·chenj *aa*·fis

I'd like to ...

मैं ... चाहता/चाहती हूँ। — mayng ... *chaah*·taa/*chaah*·tee hoong m/f

میں ... چاہتا/چاہتی ہوں۔

cash a cheque	चेक कैश करना	چیک کیش کرنا	chek kaysh *kar*·naa
change money	पैसे बलदना	پیسے بدلنا	*pay*·se ba·*dal*·naa
change a travellers cheque	ट्रेवलर्स चेक कैश करना	ٹریولرس چیک کیش لینا	*tre*·va·lars chek kaysh *kar*·naa
withdraw money	पैसे निकालना	پیسے نکالنا	*pay*·se ni·*kaal*·naa

What's the ...?

... क्या है? — ... kyaa hay

... کیا ہے؟

charge for that	उस के लिये चार्ज	اس کے لئے چارج	us ke li·*ye* chaarj
exchange rate	एक्स्चेंज रेट	ایکسچینج ریٹ	*eks*·chenj ret

Do you accept ...?

क्या आप ... लेते हैं? — kyaa aap ... *le*·te hayng

کیا آپ ... لیتے ہیں؟

credit cards	क्रेडिट कार्ड	کریڈٹ کارڈ	*kre*·dit kaard
debit cards	डेबिट कार्ड	ڈیبٹ کارڈ	*de*·bit kaard
travellers cheques	ट्रेवलर्स चेक्स	ٹریولرس چیکس	*tre*·va·lars cheks

I'd like ..., please.

मुझे ... चाहिये।
مجھے ... چاہئے-

mu·*je* ... *chaa*·hi·ye

my change	बाक़ी पैसे	باقی پیسے	*baa*·kee *pay*·se
a refund	पैसे वापस	پیسے واپس	*pay*·se *vaa*·pas

How much is it?

यह कितने का है?
یہ کتنے کا ہے؟

yeh *kit*·ne kaa hay

Can you write down the price?

इस का दाम लिखिये।
اس کا دام لکھئے-

is kaa daam li·*ki*·ye

It's free.

यह मुफ़्त है।
یہ مفت ہے-

yeh muft hay

It's (300) rupees.

यह (तीन सौ) रुपये है।
یہ (تین سو) روپیہ ہے-

yeh (teen sau) ru·pa·*ye* hay

Can you give me some change?

क्या आप खुले पैसे
दे सकते/सकती हैं?
کیا آپ کھلے پیسے
دے سکتے/سکتی ہیں؟

kyaa aap ku·*le* *pay*·se
de *sak*·te/*sak*·tee hayng m/f

learn to count

The numerals used in English (in the first column) developed from the Sanskrit numbers (in the second column), which are also used in Hindi. You can come across both in India, along with a third set of characters, Perso-Arabic in origin (in the third column), which are used as numerals in Urdu. If all this is too confusing, you can always use your fingers to count to 10.

1	१	١	ek	6	६	٦	chay
2	२	٢	do	7	७	٧	saat
3	३	٣	teen	8	८	٨	aat
4	४	٤	chaar	9	९	٩	nau
5	५	٥	paanch	10	१०	١٠	das

sightseeing

घूमना • گھومنا

I'd like a/an …

मुझे … चाहिये।			mu·*je* … *chaa*·hi·ye
مجھے ... چاہئے۔			
audio set	ऑडियो सेट	آڈیو سیٹ	*aa*·di·yo set
catalogue	कैटेलॉग	کیٹیلاگ	kay·*te*·laag
guide	गाइड	گائڈ	*gaa*·id
guidebook in English	अंग्रेज़ी में गाइडबुक	انگریزی میں گائڈبک	an·*gre*·zee meng *gaa*·id·buk
(local) map	(लोकल) नक्शा	(لوکل) نقشہ	(*lo*·kal) *nak*·shaa

Do you have information on … sights?

क्या आप के पास … साइट्स की कुछ सूचना है?			Ⓗ kyaa aap ke paas … *saa*·its kee kuch *sooch*·naa hay
کیا آپ کے پاس ... سائٹس کی کچھ معلومات ہے؟			Ⓤ kyaa aap ke paas … *saa*·its kee kuch maa·loo·*maat* hay
cultural	सांस्कृतिक	تہزیب کی	Ⓗ saan·*skri*·tik Ⓤ *teh*·zeeb kee
historical	ऐतिहासिक	تاریخی	Ⓗ ay·ti·*haa*·sik Ⓤ taa·*ree*·kee
religious	धार्मिक	مزہبی	Ⓗ *daar*·mik Ⓤ *maz*·ha·bee

I'd like to see …

मैं … देखना चाहता/चाहती हूँ।			mayng … *dek*·naa
میں ... دیکھنا چہتا/چاہتی ہوں۔			*chaah*·taa/*chaah*·tee hoong m/f
deserted cities	खंडहर	کھنڈہر	*kan*·da·har
forts	क़िले	قلعہ	ki·*le*
mosques	मस्जिद	مسجد	*mas*·jid
temples	मंदिर	مندر	*man*·dir
tombs	मक़बरे	مقبرے	*mak*·ba·re

What's that?

वह क्या है?

وہ کیا ہے؟

voh kyaa hay

Who made it?

किसने यह बनवाया?

کس نے یہ بنوایا؟

kis·ne yeh ban·*vaa*·yaa

How old is it?

वह कितना पुराना है?

وہ کتنا پرانا ہے؟

voh *kit*·naa pu·*raa*·naa hay

Could you take a photo of me?

क्या आप मेरा फ़ोटो लेंगे/लेंगी?

کیا آپ میرا فوٹو لیں گے/ لیں گی؟

kyaa aap *me*·raa *fo*·to *leng*·ge/*leng*·gee m/f

Can I take a photo (of you)?

क्या मैं (आप का) फ़ोटो ले सकता/सकती हूँ?

کیا میں (آپ کا) فوٹو لے سکتا/ سکتی ہوں؟

kyaa mayng (aap kaa) *fo*·to le *sak*·taa/*sak*·tee hoong m/f

I'll send you the photo.

मैं आपको फ़ोटो भेजूँगा/भेजूँगी।

میں آپ کو فوٹو بھیجوں گا/بھیجوں گی۔

mayng *aap*·ko *fo*·to be·*joong*·gaa/be·*joong*·gee m/f

getting in

प्रवेश करना • اندر جانا

What time does it open?

कितने बजे खुलता है?

کتنے بجے کھلتا ہے؟

kit·ne ba·*je* *kul*·taa hay

What time does it close?

कितने बजे बंद होता है?

کتنے بجے بند ہوتا ہے؟

kit·ne ba·*je* band *ho*·taa hay

What's the admission charge?

अंदर जाने का क्या दाम लगता है?
اندر جانے کی کیا قیمت لگتی ہے؟

ⓗ *an*·dar *jaa*·ne kaa kyaa daam *lag*·taa hay
ⓤ *an*·dar *jaa*·ne kee kyaa *kee*·mat *lag*·tee hay

Is there a discount for ...?

क्या ... के लिय विशेष छूट है?
کیا ... کے لئے خاص چھوٹ ہے؟

ⓗ kyaa ... ke li·*ye* vi·*shesh* choot hay
ⓤ kyaa ... ke li·*ye* kaas choot hay

children	बच्चों	بچّوں	*bach*·chong
families	परिवार	خاندان	ⓗ pa·ri·*vaar* ⓤ *kaan*·daan
groups	दल	گروہ	ⓗ dal ⓤ gur·*oh*
older people	वयोवृद्धों	بزرگوں	ⓗ va·yo·*vrid*·dong ⓤ bu·*zur*·gong
students	छात्रों	طالب عام	ⓗ *chaa*·trong ⓤ *taa*·li·be ilm

tours

घूमना • گھومنا

Can you recommend a ...?

... के बारे में बताइये।
... کے بارے میں بتائے۔

... ke *baa*·re meng ba·*taa*·i·ye

When's the next ...?

अगला/अगली ... कब है?
اگلا ... کب ہے؟

ag·laa/*ag*·lee ... kab hay m/f

boat trip	नाव की यात्रा	ناو کا سفر	ⓗ naav kee *yaa*·traa f ⓤ naav kaa sa·*far* m
day trip	एक दिन की यात्रा	ایک دن کا سفر	ⓗ ek din kee *yaa*·traa f ⓤ ek din kaa sa·*far* m
tour m	टूर	ٹور	toor

Is … included?

क्या … भी शामिल है? — kyaa … bee *shaa*·mil hay

کیا ... بھی شامل ہے؟

accommodation	रहना	رہنا	*reh*·naa
food	खाना	کھانا	*kaa*·naa
transport	आना जाना	آنا جانا	*aa*·naa *jaa*·naa

The guide will pay.

गाइड पैसे देगा। — *gaa*·id *pay*·se de·*gaa*

گائڈ پیسے دیگا۔

The guide has paid.

गाइड ने पैसे दिये हैं। — *gaa*·id ne *pay*·se di·*ye* hayng

گائڈ نے پیسے دئے ہیں۔

How long is the tour?

टूर कितनी देर की है? — toor *kit*·nee der kee hay

ٹور کتنی دیر کی ہے؟

What time should we be back?

हमें कितने बजे वापस आना चाहिये? — ha·*meng* *kit*·ne ba·*je* *vaa*·pas *aa*·naa *chaa*·hi·ye

ہمیں کتنے بجے واپس آنا چاہئے؟

I'm with them.

मैं इन के साथ हूँ। — mayng in ke saat hoong

میں ان کے ساتھ ہوں۔

I've lost my group.

मैं अपने साथियों से अलग हो गया/गयी हूँ। — mayng *ap*·ne *saa*·ti·yong se a·*lag* ho ga·*yaa*/ga·*yee* hoong m/f

میں اپنے ساتھیوں سے الگ ہو گیا/گئی ہوں۔

male or female?

Verbs in Hindi and Urdu change their form according to the gender of the subject in the sentence. It's the verbs – not the pronouns 'he' or 'she' – which show if a male or female is doing the action. Throughout this book, we've given both forms where required (ie where the subject could be either masculine or feminine) – the two forms of the verb are marked m/f in our pronunciation guides.

Where's the ...?

... कहाँ है?
... کہاں ہے؟

... ka·*haang* hay

business centre	बिज़नेस सेंटर	بزنیس سینٹر	*biz*·nes *sen*·tar
conference	कॉन्फ़्रेंस	کانفرینس	*kaan*·frens
meeting	मीटिंग	میٹنگ	*mee*·ting

I'm attending a ...

मैं एक ... में हिस्सा लेने आया/आयी हूँ।
میں ایک ... میں حصّہ لینے آیا/آئی ہوں۔

mayng ek ... meng *his*·saa *le*·ne *aa*·yaa/*aa*·yee hoong m/f

course	कोर्स	کورس	kors
trade fair	ट्रेड फ़ेयर	ٹریڈ فیر	tred *fe*·yar

I'm with my colleague(s).

मैं अपने सहयोगियो के साथ हूँ।
میں اپنے ہمجولیوں کے ساتھ ہوں۔

ⓗ mayng *ap*·ne seh·*yo*·gi·yong ke saat hoong
ⓤ mayng *ap*·ne ham·*jo*·li·yong ke saat hoong

I'm with (two) others.

मैं (दो) अन्य लोगों के साथ हूँ।
میں (دو) اور لوگوں کے ساتھ ہوں۔

ⓗ mayng (do) *an*·ya *lo*·gong ke saat hoong
ⓤ mayng (do) aur *lo*·gong ke saat hoong

I'm alone.

मैं अकेला/अकेली हूँ।
میں اکیلا/اکیلی ہوں۔

mayng a·*ke*·laa/a·*ke*·lee hoong m/f

I have an appointment with ...

... के साथ मेरा अॅपाइंटमेंट है।
... کے ساتھ میرا اپائنٹمینٹ ہے۔

... ke saat *me*·raa aa·paa·*int*·ment hay

I'm staying at …, room …

मैं … में ठहरा/ठहरी हूँ,
… नम्बर कमरे मैं।
میں … میں ٹھہرا/ٹھہری ہوں،
… نمبر کمرے میں۔

mayng … meng *teh*·raa/*teh*·ree hoong
… *nam*·bar *kam*·re meng **m/f**

I'm here for (two days).

मैं (दो दिन) के लिये
आया/आयी हूँ।
میں (دو دن) کے لئے
آیا/آئ ہوں۔

mayng (do din) ke li·*ye*
aa·yaa/*aa*·yee hoong **m/f**

Here's my business card.

मेरा बिज़नेस कार्ड लीजिये।
میرا بزنیس کارڈ لیجیئے۔

me·raa *biz*·nes kaard *lee*·ji·ye

What's your …?

आप का … क्या है?
آپ کا … کیا ہے؟

aap kaa … kyaa hay

address	पता	پتہ	pa·*taa*
email address	ई-मेल एड्रेस	ایمیل ایدریس	*ee*·mayl e·*dres*
fax number	फ़ैक्स नम्बर	فیکس نمبر	fayks *nam*·bar

I need a/an …

मुझे … चाहिये।
مجھے … چاہئے۔

mu·*je* … *chaa*·hi·ye

computer	कम्प्यूटर	کمپیوٹر	kam·*pyoo*·tar
Internet connection	इंटरनेट कनेक्शन	انٹرنیٹ کنیکشن	in·*tar*·net ka·*nek*·shan
interpreter	दूभाषिया	ترجمان	ⓗ du·*baa*·shi·yaa ⓤ *tar*·ja·maan

That went very well.

वह बहुत अच्छा हुआ।
وہ بہت اچّھا ہوا۔

voh ba·*hut ach*·chaa hu·*aa*

Thank you for your time.

आपके समय देने
के लिये थैंक्यू।
آپ کے وقت دینے
کے لئے شکریہ۔

ⓗ aap ke sa·*mai de*·ne
ke li·*ye thayn*·kyoo
ⓤ aap ke vakt *de*·ne
ke li·*ye shuk*·ri·yah

senior & disabled travellers

वयोवृद्ध और विकलांग यात्री • بزرگ اور اپاہج مسافر

I have a disability.

मैं विकलांग हूँ।	ⓗ mayng vi·ka·*laangg* hoong
میں اپاہج ہوں۔	ⓤ mayng a·*paa*·hij hoong

Is there wheelchair access?

क्या व्हीलचैयर के लिये अन्दर जाने का रास्ता है?	kyaa vheel·*chay*·yar ke li·*ye* *an*·dar *jaa*·ne kaa *raas*·taa hay
کیا وہیلچیر کے لئے اندر جانے کا راستہ ہے؟	

Is there a lift?

क्या लिफ़्ट है?	kyaa lift hay
کیا لفٹ ہے؟	

Are there disabled toilets?

क्या विकलांगों के लिये टॉइलेट है?	ⓗ kyaa vi·ka·*laang*·gong ke li·*ye* *taa*·i·let hay
کیا اپاہجوں کے لئے ٹائلیٹ ہے؟	ⓤ kyaa a·*paa*·hi·jong ke li·*ye* *taa*·i·let hay

Are there rails in the bathroom?

क्या बाथरूम में रेल है?	kyaa *baat*·room meng rel hay
کیا باتھروم میں ریل ہے؟	

Are guide dogs permitted?

क्या गाइड डॉग जा सकता है?	kyaa *gaa*·id daag jaa *sak*·taa hay
کیا گائڈ ڈاگ جا سکتا ہے؟	

Could you help me cross the street safely?

क्या आप मुझे सड़क के उस पार पहुँचा देंगे?	kyaa aap mu·*je* sa·*rak* ke us paar pa·hun·*chaa* *deng*·ge
کیا آپ مجھے سڑک کے اس پار پہنچا دینگے؟	

women travellers

महिला यात्री • خواتین مسافر

Travelling in India is hugely enjoyable, but like anywhere, cultural misunderstandings can arise. 'Eve teasing' – unwanted attention or hassle from men towards foreign and local women alike – can be limited by dressing modestly, not returning stares and not engaging in inane conversations with men, which can all be seen as a bit of a turn on. If, despite this, your intentions are misinterpreted, clearly express your needs and concerns – be firm but polite in response to unwanted attention, and leave the scene if you can.

Leave me alone!	छोड़ो मुझे!	چھوڑو مجھے!	*cho*·ro mu·*je*
Go away!	जाओ!	جاؤ!	*jaa*·o

You're annoying.

तुम मुझे बहुत परेशान कर रहे/रही हो।
تم مجھے بہت پریشان کر رہے/رہی ہو۔
tum mu·*je* ba·*hut* pa·*re*·shaan kar ra·*he*/ra·*hee* ho m/f

Shall I call the police?

मैं पुलिस को बुलाऊँ?
میں پولیس کو بلاؤں؟
mayng pu·*lis* ko bu·*laa*·oong

travelling with children

बच्चों के साथ यात्रा करना • بچّوں کے ساتھ سفر کرنا

Are there any good places to take children around here?

यहाँ के आसपास बच्चों के लिये कोई अच्छी जगह है?
یہاں کے آس پاس بچّوں کے لئے کوئ اچّھی جگہ ہے؟
ya·*haang* ke *aas*·paas *bach*·chong ke li·*ye* *ko*·ee *ach*·chee ja·*gah* hay

Are children allowed?

क्या बच्चे जा सकते हैं?
کیا بچّے جا سکتے ہیں؟
kyaa *bach*·che jaa *sak*·te hayng

Is there a …?

क्या … है?

کیا ... ہے؟

kyaa … hay

baby change room	शिशु के कपड़े बदलने का कमरा	بچّہ کے کپڑے بدلنے کا کمرہ	ⓗ *shi*·shu ke *kap*·re ba·*dal*·ne kaa *kam*·raa ⓤ *bach*·chong ke *kap*·re ba·*dal*·ne kaa *kam*·raa
child-minding service	बच्चे की देखभाल करने की सेवा	بچّے کی دیکھبھال کرنے کی خدمت	ⓗ *bach*·che kee *dek*·baal *kar*·ne kee *se*·vaa ⓤ *bach*·che kee *dek*·baal *kar*·ne kee *kid*·mat
discount for children	बच्चे के लिये छूट	بچّے کے لئے چھوٹ	*bach*·che ke li·*ye* choot
family room	परिवार के लिये कमरा	خاندان کے لئے کمرہ	ⓗ pa·ri·*vaar* ke li·*ye kam*·raa ⓤ *kaan*·daan ke li·*ye kam*·raa
family ticket	परिवार का टिकट	خاندان کا ٹکٹ	ⓗ pa·ri·*vaar* kaa ti·*kat* ⓤ *kaan*·daan kaa ti·*kat*

I need a/an …

मुझे … चाहिये।

مجھے ... چاہئے۔

mu·*je* … *chaa*·hi·ye

baby seat	शिशु के लिये विशेष कुरसी	چھوٹے بچّے کے لئے خاص کرسی	ⓗ *shi*·shu ke li·*ye* vi·*shesh kur*·see ⓤ *cho*·te *bach*·che ke li·*ye* kaas *kur*·see
(English-speaking) babysitter	(अंग्रेज़ी बोलने वाली) आया	(انگریزی بولنے والی) آیا	(an·*gre*·zee *bol*·ne *vaa*·lee) *aa*·yaa
highchair	ऊँची कुरसी	اونچی کرسی	*oon*·chee *kur*·see

Do you sell ...?

क्या आप ... बेचते/बेचती हैं?			kyaa aap ... *bech*·te/*bech*·tee hayng **m/f**
کیا آپ ... بیچتے/بیچتی ہیں؟			
baby wipes	बेबी व्हाइप्स	بیبی وہائپس	*be*·bee *vhaa*·ips
nappies	नैपी	نیپی	*nay*·pee
painkillers for infants	शिशु के लिये दर्द की दवा	بچّے کے لئے درد کی دوا	ⓗ *shi*·shu ke li·*ye* dard kee da·*vaa* ⓤ *bach*·chong ke li·*ye* dard kee da·*vaa*

Do you hire out ...?

क्या आप ... किराये पर देते/देती हैं?			kyaa aap ... ki·*raa*·ye par *de*·te/*de*·tee hayng **m/f**
کیا آپ ... کرائے پر دیتے/دیتی ہیں؟			
prams	प्रैम	پریم	praym
strollers	स्ट्रोलर्स	سٹرولرس	*stro*·lars

If your child is sick, see **health**, page 133.

kids' talk

When's your birthday?

तुम्हारा जन्मदिन कब है? — ⓗ tum·*haa*·raa *janm*·din kab hay

تمہاری سال گرہ کب ہے؟ — ⓤ tum·*haa*·ree *saal*·gi·rah kab hay

Do you go to school?

क्या तुम स्कूल में जाते/जाती हो? — kyaa tum skool meng *jaa*·taa/*jaa*·tee ho **m/f**

کیا تم سکول میں جاتے/جاتی ہو؟

Do you like sport?

क्या तुमको खेल अच्छा लगता है? — kyaa tum ko kel *ach*·chaa *lag*·taa hay

کیا تم کو کھیل اچّھا لگتا ہے؟

Do you learn English?

क्या तुम अंग्रेज़ी सीखते/सीखती हो? — kyaa tum an·*gre*·zee *seek*·te/*seek*·tee ho **m/f**

کیا تم انگریزی سیکھتے/سیکھتی ہو؟

PRACTICAL

SOCIAL > meeting people

लोगों से मिलना • لوگوں سے ملنا

basics

आम बातें • عام باتیں

Yes.	जी हाँ।	جی ہاں۔	jee haang
No.	जी नहीं।	جی نہیں۔	jee na·*heeng*
Please …	कृपया …	مہربانی کرکے …	ⓗ kri·pa·*yaa* … ⓤ me·har·*baa*·nee kar ke …
Thank you.	थैंक्यू।	شکریہ۔	ⓗ *thayn*·kyoo ⓤ *shuk*·ri·yah
You're welcome.	कोई बात नहीं।	کوئ بات نہیں۔	*ko*·ee baat na·*heeng*
Excuse me. (to get attention)	सुनिये।	سنئے۔	su·ni·*ye*
Excuse me. (to get past)	रास्ता दे दीजिये।	راستہ دے دیجیے۔	*raas*·taa de *dee*·ji·ye
Sorry.	माफ़ कीजिये।	معاف کیجئے۔	maaf *kee*·ji·ye

male or female?

Verbs in Hindi and Urdu change their form according to the gender of the subject in the sentence. It's the verbs – not the pronouns 'he' or 'she' – which show if a male or a female is doing the action. Throughout this book, we've given both forms where required (ie where the subject could be either masculine or feminine) – the two forms of the verb are marked **m/f** in our pronunciation guides:

How are you?

आप कैसे/कैसी हैं?
آپ کیسے/کیسی ہیں؟
aap *kay*·se/*kay*·see hayng **m/f**

greetings & goodbyes

हेलो और टाटा • ہیلو اور ٹاٹا

When greeting, Hindus fold their hands in front of their chest, while Muslims raise one hand to their forehead. Some Hindus touch the feet of elders as a sign of respect – they bend from the waist and use the right hand (or both hands) and sometimes bring it to their chest after touching the feet. If you're a woman, it's best to shake hands with people only if they extend theirs first. Kissing isn't a part of the greeting ritual for the majority of people on the subcontinent and is likely to embarass.

Hello.

नमस्ते।	ⓗ na·ma·*ste*
السلام عالیکم۔	ⓤ *as*·sa·laam a·*lay*·kum

Good morning.

सुप्रभात।	ⓗ su·*pra*·bhaat
السلام عالیکم۔	ⓤ *as*·sa·laam a·*lay*·kum

Good afternoon/evening.

नमस्ते।	ⓗ na·ma·*ste*
السلام عالیکم۔	ⓤ *as*·sa·laam a·*lay*·kum

How are you?

आप कैसे/कैसी हैं?	aap *kay*·se/*kay*·see hayng **m/f**
آپ کیسے/کیسی ہیں؟	

Fine. And you?

मैं ठीक हूँ। आप सुनाइये।	mayng teek hoong aap su·*naa*·i·ye
میں ٹھیک ہوں۔ آپ سنائے۔	

What's your name?

आप का नाम क्या है?	aap kaa naam kyaa hay
آپ کا نام کیا ہے؟	

My name is ...

मेरा नाम ... है।	*me*·raa naam ... hay
میرا نام ... ہے۔	

I'd like to introduce you to ...

... से मिलिये।	... se mi·li·*ye*
... سے ملئے۔	

This is my …

यह मेरा/मेरे … है।

یہ میرا/میری ... ہے۔

yeh *me*·raa/*me*·ree … hay m/f

colleague m&f	सहयोगी	ہمجولی	ⓗ seh·*yo*·gee ⓤ ham·*jo*·lee
daughter	बेटी	بیٹی	*be*·tee
friend m&f	दोस्त	دوسپ	dost
husband	पति	شوہر	ⓗ *pa*·ti ⓤ *shau*·har
son	बेटा	بیٹا	*be*·taa
wife	पत्नी	بیوی	ⓗ *pat*·nee ⓤ *bee*·vee

For other family members, see **family**, page 90, and the **dictionary**.

I'm pleased to meet you.

आपसे मिलकर
बहुत ख़ुशी हुई।

آپ سے ملکر
بہت خوشی ہوی۔

aap se *mil*·kar
ba·*hut* ku·*shee* hu·*ee*

A pleasure to meet you, too.

मुझे भी।

مجھے بھی۔

mu·*je* bee

See you later.	फिर मिलेंगे।	پھر ملیں گے۔	pir mi·*leng*·ge
Goodbye.	नमस्ते।	خدا حافظ۔	ⓗ na·ma·*ste* ⓤ ku·*daa haa*·fiz
Good night.	शुभ रात्रि।	شب بخیر۔	ⓗ shub *raa*·tri ⓤ sha·*baa* kair
Bon voyage!	शुभ यात्रा।	سہی سلامت جائے۔	ⓗ shub *yaa*·traa ⓤ sa·*hee* sa·*laa*·mat *jaa*·i·ye

addressing people

लोगों से संबोधन करना • لوگوں سے مخاتب ہونا

Hindi equivalents of terms such as 'Mr' and 'Mrs' can be used before someone's family name. In Urdu, they're also used after the name or simply on their own. It's best to only use the two terms to address a Muslim woman, *be*·gam and *saa*·hi·baa, if you're invited to do so. The term *bay*·yaa (brother) is informal and shows a certain warmth towards the person addressed – it can be used for people who are doing a task for you. The word yaar (mate) is only used among good friends and is very informal.

Mister/Sir	श्रीमन/सर	صاحب/جناب	ⓗ *shree*·man/sar ⓤ *saa*·hab/ja·*naab*
Mrs/Madam	श्रीमती/मैडम	بیگم/صاحبہ	ⓗ *shree*·ma·tee/*may*·dam ⓤ *be*·gam/*saa*·hi·baa
Ms/Miss	मिस/कुमारी	بیبی/مس	ⓗ mis/ku·*maa*·ree ⓤ *bee*·bee/mis

who are you, again?

The word 'you' has three forms in Hindi and Urdu – intimate (too), informal (tum) and polite (aap). The polite form is used to show respect or formality when addressing someone. If you're invited to be more informal, you can use the word tum. The too form is used in intimate situations only and should be avoided as it could show too much intimacy or be seen as disrespectful. The form appropriate for the context has been used for all phrases throughout this book.

making conversation

बातचीत करना • باتچیت کر نا

What's happening?
क्या हो रहा है?
کیا ہو رہا ہے؟
kyaa ho ra·*haa* hay

How's it all going?
सब कुछ कैसा चल रहा है?
سب کچھ کیسا چل رہا ہے؟
sab kuch *kay*·saa chal ra·*haa* hay

SOCIAL

How long are you here for?

आप कितने दिन के लिये आये/आयी हैं?
آپ کتنے دن کے لئے آئے/آئی ہیں؟
aap *kit*·ne din ke li·*ye aa*·ye/*aa*·yee hayng m/f

I'm here for (four) weeks.

मैं (चार) हफ़्ते के लिये आया/आयी हूँ।
میں (چار) ہفتے کے لئے آیا/آئی ہوں۔
mayng (chaar) *haf*·te li·*ye aa*·yaa/*aa*·yee hoong m/f

I'm here ...

मैं ... आया/आयी हूँ।
میں ... آیا/آئی ہوں۔
mayng ... *aa*·yaa/*aa*·yee hoong m/f

for a holiday	छुट्टी मनाने	چھٹّی منانے	*chut*·tee ma·*naa*·ne
on business	व्यापार करने	کاروبار کرنے	ⓗ *vyaa*·paar *kar*·ne ⓤ kaa·*ro*·baar *kar*·ne
to study	पढ़ने	پڑھنے	*par*·ne

nationalities

देश और क़ौम की बात • دیش اور قوم کی بات

Where are you from?

आप कहाँ के/की हैं?
آپ کہاں کے/کی ہیں؟
aap ka·*haang* ke/kee hayng m/f

I'm from ...

मैं ... का/की हूँ।
میں ... کا/کی ہوں۔
mayng ... kaa/kee hoong m/f

Australia	आईस्ट्रेलिया	آسٹریلیا	aas·*tre*·li·yaa
Canada	कनडा	کنڈا	ka·na·*daa*
England	इंग्लैंड	انگلینڈ	*in*·glaynd
Germany	जर्मनी	جرمنی	*jar*·ma·nee
Netherlands	नैदरलैंड्स	نیدرلینڈس	nay·*dar*·lands
Singapore	सिंगापुर	سنگاپر	sin·*gaa*·pur
USA	अमरीका	امریکا	am·*ree*·kaa

age

उम्र • عمر

How old is/are ...?

... की क्या उम्र है?

... کی کیا عمر ہے؟

... kee kyaa u·*mar* hay

you	आप	آپ	aap
your son	आपके बेटे	آپکے بیٹے	*aap*·ke *be*·te
your daughter	आपकी बेटी	آپکی بیٹی	*aap*·kee *be*·tee

I'm ... years old.

मैं ... साल का/की हूँ।

میں ... سال کا/کی ہوں۔

mayng ... saal kaa/kee hoong **m/f**

He/She is ... years old.

वह ... साल के/की हैं।

وہ ... سال کے/کی ہیں۔

voh ... saal ke/kee hayng **m/f**

For your age, see **numbers & amounts**, page 31.

occupations & studies

काम और पढ़ाई • کام اور پڑھائی

What's your occupation?

आप क्या करते/करती हैं?

آپ کیا کرتے/کرتی ہیں؟

aap kyaa *kar*·te/*kar*·tee hayng **m/f**

I'm a ...

मैं ... हूँ।

میں ... ہوں۔

mayng ... hoong

chef	खाना बनानेवाला/ बनानेवाली	کھانا بنانے والا/ بنانے والی	*kaa*·naa ba·*naa*·ne·*vaa*·laa/ ba·*naa*·ne·*vaa*·lee **m/f**
journalist	पत्रकार	اخبارنویس	ⓗ *pat*·ra·kaar **m&f** ⓤ *ak*·baar na·*vees* **m&f**
teacher	टीचर	ٹیچر	*tee*·char **m&f**

I work in …

मैं … में काम
करता/करती हूँ।
میں ... میں کام
کرتا/کرتی ہوں۔

mayng … meng kaam
kar·taa/*kar*·tee hoong **m/f**

administration	प्रशासन	نوکرشاہی	ⓗ pra·*shaa*·san ⓤ *nau*·kar *shaa*·hee
health	स्वास्थ्य के क्षेत्र	ہیلتھ	ⓗ *svaas*·tya ke *kshe*·tra ⓤ helt
sales & marketing	सेल्स और मार्केटिंग	سیلس اور مارکیٹنگ	sels aur *maar*·ke·ting

I'm …

मैं … हूँ।
میں ... ہوں۔

mayng … hoong

retired	रिटायर	رٹایر	ri·*taa*·yar **m&f**
self-employed	अपने लिये काम करता/करती	آپنے لئے کام کرتا/کرتی	*ap*·ne li·*ye* kaam *kar*·taa/*kar*·tee **m/f**
unemployed	बेरोज़गार	بیروزگار	be·*roz*·gaar **m&f**

What are you studying?

आप क्या पढ़ते/पढ़ती हैं?
آپ کیا پڑھتے/ پڑھتی ہیں؟

aap kyaa *par*·te/*par*·tee hayng **m/f**

I'm studying …

मैं … पढ़ता/पढ़ती हूँ।
میں ... پڑھتا/پڑھتی ہوں۔

mayng … *par*·taa/*par*·tee hoong **m/f**

Bengali	बंगला	بنگلا	*ban*·glaa
Hindi	हिन्दी	ہندی	*hin*·dee
humanities	ह्यूमैनिटीज़	ہیومینٹیز	hyu·*may*·ni·tees
science	साइंस	سائنس	*saa*·ins
Urdu	उर्दू	اردو	*ur*·doo

For more occupations and studies, see the **dictionary**.

family

परिवार • خاندان

Are you married?

क्या आप की शादी हुई है?
کیا آپ کی شادی ہوئ ہے؟

kyaa aap kee *shaa*·dee hu·*ee* hay

I'm married.

मेरी शादी हुई है।
میری شادی ہوئ ہے۔

me·ree *shaa*·dee hu·*ee* hay

I'm single.

मेरी शादी नहीं हुई।
شادی نہیں ہوئ۔

me·ree *shaa*·dee na·*heeng* hu·*ee*

Do you have a brother?

क्या आप का (भाई) है?
کیا آپ کا (بھائ) ہے؟

kyaa aap kaa *baa*·ee hay

I (don't) have a sister.

मेरी बहन (नहीं) है।
میری بہن (نہیں) ہے۔

me·ree ba·*han* (na·*heeng*) hay

farewells

विदाई • رخصت

Here's my phone number.

यह मेरा फ़ोन नम्बर है।
یہ میرا فون نمبر ہے۔

yeh *me*·raa fon *nam*·bar hay

What's your email address?

आप का ई-मेल
का पता क्या है?
آپ کا ایمیل کا پتہ کیا ہے؟

aap kaa *ee*·mayl
kaa pa·*taa* kyaa hay

common interests

आम रुचियाँ • عام شوق

Do you like …?

क्या आपको … पसंद है?

کیا آپ کو … پسند ہے؟

kyaa *aap*·ko … pa·*sand* hay

I (don't) like …

मुझे … पसंद (नहीं) है।

مجھے … پسند (نہیں) ہے۔

mu·*je* … pa·*sand* (na·heeng) hay

meditation	ध्यान लगाना	دھیان لگانا	dyaan la·*gaa*·naa
puppetry	कठपुतलियाँ	پتلیوں کا تماشہ	ⓗ kat·*put*·li·yaang ⓤ *put*·li·yong kaa ta·*maa*·shaa
Sanskrit theatre	संस्कृत नाटक	سنسکرت ناٹک	*sans*·krit *naa*·tak
yoga	योगासन	یوگاسن	yo·*gaa*·san

For sporting activities, see **sport**, page 94.

music

संगीत • موسیقی

Do you …?

क्या आप … हैं?

کیا آپ … ہیں؟

kyaa aap … hayng

go to concerts	कॉन्सर्ट के लिये जाते/जाती	کانسرٹ کے لئے جاتے/جاتی	*kaan*·sart ke li·*ye* *jaa*·te/*jaa*·tee m/f
play an instrument	बाजा बजाते/ बजाती	باجا بجاتے/ بجاتی	*baa*·jaa ba·*jaa*·te/ ba·*jaa*·tee m/f
sing	गाते/गाती	گاتے/گاتی	*gaa*·te/*gaa*·tee m/f

Planning to go to a concert? See **tickets**, page 38, and **going out**, page 99.

cinema & theatre

सिनेमा/नाटक • سنیما/ڈرامہ

What's showing at the cinema tonight?
आज कौनसी फ़िल्म लगी है?
آج کونسی فلم لگی ہے؟
aaj *kaun*·see film la·*gee* hay

What's showing at the theatre tonight?
आज कौनसा नाटक लगा है?
آج کونسا ڈرامہ لگا ہے؟
Ⓗ aaj *kaun*·saa *naa*·tak la·*gaa* hay
Ⓤ aaj *kaun*·saa *draa*·maa la·*gaa* hay

Does it have subtitles?
सबटायटल्स हैं?
سبٹائٹلس ہیں؟
sab·*taay*·tals hayng

I feel like going to a ...
... का मन हो रहा है।
... کا من ہو رہا ہے۔
... kaa man ho ra·*haa* hay

Do you feel like going to a ...?
क्या आप का ... देखने का मन हो रहा है?
کیا آپ کا ... دیکھنے کا من ہو رہا ہے؟
kyaa ap kaa ... *dek*·ne kaa man ho ra·*haa* hay

ballet	बैले	بیلے	*bay*·le
film	फ़िल्म	فلم	film
play	नाटक	ڈرامہ	Ⓗ *naa*·tak Ⓤ *draa*·maa

I (don't) like ...
मुझे ... पसंद (नहीं) है।
مجھے ... پسند (نہیں) ہے۔
mu·*je* ... pa·*sand* (na·*heeng*) hay

action movies	एक्शन फिल्में	ایکشن فلمیں	*ek*·shan *fil*·meng
comedies	कामेडी	کامیڈی	kaa·*me*·dee
drama	नाटक	ڈرامہ	Ⓗ *naa*·tak Ⓤ *draa*·maa
(Indian) cinema	(इंडियन) फ़िल्में	(انڈین) فلمیں	(*in*·di·yan) *fil*·meng

art

कलाएँ • فن

When's the museum open?

संग्रहालय कब खुलता है? — ⓗ san·gra·*haa*·lai kab *kul*·taa hay

عجائبگھر کب کھلتا ہے؟ — ⓤ a·*jaa*·ib·gaar kab *kul*·taa hay

When's the gallery open?

गैलरी कब खुलती है? — *gay*·la·ree kab *kul*·tee hay

گیلری کب کھلتی ہے؟

What kind of art are you interested in?

आपको कौनसी कला अच्छी लगती है? — ⓗ *aap*·ko *kaun*·see ka·*laa* *ach*·chee *lag*·tee hay

آپکو کونسا فن اچھا لگتا ہے؟ — ⓤ *aap*·ko *kaun*·saa fan *ach*·chaa *lag*·taa hay

It's an exhibition of …

यह … की प्रदर्शनी है। — ⓗ yeh … kee pra·*dar*·sha·nee hay

یہ ... کی نمائش ہے۔ — ⓤ yeh … kee nu·*maa*·ish hay

I'm interested in …

मुझे … की रुचि है। — ⓗ mu·*je* … kee *ru*·chi hay

مجھے ... کا شوق ہے۔ — ⓤ mu·*je* … kaa shauk hay

architecture	वास्तुकला	تعمیرت کا فن	ⓗ *vaa*·stu·ka·*laa* f ⓤ taa·*mee*·raat kaa fan m
art	कला	فن	ⓗ ka·*laa* f ⓤ fan m
ceramics m	मिट्टी का काम	مٹّی کا کام	*mit*·tee kaa kaam
embroidery f	कढ़ाई	کڑھائی	ka·*raa*·ee
painting (canvas) f	तस्वीर	تصویر	*tas*·veer
period m	युग	زمانہ	ⓗ yug ⓤ za·*maa*·naa
sculpture f	शिल्पकला	سنگ تراشی	ⓗ shilp·ka·*laa* ⓤ sang·ta·*raa*·shee
style f	शैली	طریقہ	ⓗ *shay*·lee ⓤ ta·*ree*·kaa
woodwork m	लकड़ी का काम	لکڑی کا کام	*lak*·ree kaa kaam

sport

खेल-कूद • کھیل کود

What sport do you play?

आप कौनसा खेल खेलते/खेलती हैं?	aap *kaun*·saa kel *kel*·te/*kel*·tee hayng m/f
آپ کونسا کھیل کھیلتے/کھیلتی ہیں؟	

What sport do you follow?

आपको किस खेल का शौक़ है?	*aap*·ko kis kel kaa shauk hay
آپکو کس کھیل کا شوق ہے؟	

I play/do ...

मैं ... खेलता/खेलती हूँ।	mayng ... *kel*·taa/*kel*·tee hoong m/f
میں ... کھیلتا/کھیلتی ہوں۔	

I follow ...

मुझे ... का शौक़ है।	mu·*je* ... kaa shauk hay
مجھے ... کا شوق ہے۔	

athletics	एथलेटिक्स	ایتھلیٹکس	et·*le*·tiks
basketball	बास्केटबॉल	باسکیٹبال	*baas*·ket·baal
cricket	क्रिकेट	کرکیٹ	*kri*·ket
football (soccer)	फुटबाईल	فٹ بال	*fut*·baal
hockey	हॉकी	ہاکی	*haa*·kee
polo	पोलो	پولو	*po*·lo
scuba diving	स्कूबा डाइविंग	سکوبا ڈائونگ	*skoo*·baa *daa*·i·ving
table tennis	टेबल टेनिस	ٹیبل ٹینس	*te*·bal *te*·nis
tennis	टेनिस	ٹینس	*te*·nis
volleyball	वॉलीबॉल	والی بال	*vaa*·lee baal
wrestling	कुश्ती लड़ना	کشتی لڑنا	*kush*·tee *lar*·naa

on a sticky wicket

A very popular children's game in India is called *gul*·lee *dan*·daa (गुल्ली डंडा گلّی ڈنڈا). It's played with two wooden sticks. The aim is to hit the smaller stick with the larger one so that it spins up into the air and then hit it again in mid-air as far as possible. If it's caught, the player's out – if not, it's a point.

feelings & opinions

भावनाएँ और राय • جز بات اور رائے

feelings

भावनाएँ • جز بات

Are you ...?
क्या आपको ...? — kyaa *aap*·ko ...
کیاآپ کو ...؟

I'm (not) ...
मुझे ... (नहीं) ... है। — mu·*je* ... (na·*heeng*) ... hay
موجھے ... (نہیں) ... ہے۔

cold	ठंड ... लग रही	سردی ... لگ رہی	ⓗ tand ... lag ra·*hee* ⓤ sar·*dee* ... lag ra·*hee*
embarrassed	शर्म ... आयी	شرم ... آئ	sharm ... *aa*·yee
hot	गर्मी ... लग रही	گرمی ... لگ رہی	*gar*·mee ... lag ra·*hee*
hungry	भूख ... लगी	بھوک ... لگی	book ... la·*gee*
thirsty	प्यास ... लगी	پیاس ... لگی	pyaas ... la·*gee*
tired	थकान ... हुई	تھکان ... ہوئ	ta·*kaan* ... hu·*ee*

Are you OK?
क्या आपकी तबीयत ठीक है? — kyaa *aap*·kee ta·bi·*yat* teek hay
کیا آپ کی طبیعت ٹھیک ہے؟

I'm OK.
मैं ठीक हूँ। — mayng teek hoong
میں ٹھیک ہوں۔

If you're not feeling well, see **health**, page 133.

anything you say

The all-purpose word *ach*·chaa (lit: good) is almost the Indian equivalent of 'OK'. You can use it to answer a general enquiry or express agreement, approval or understanding. Depending on the context and your tone of voice, it can mean 'as you wish', 'I understand', 'I agree', 'right' or 'really?'

politics & social issues

राजनैतिक और सामाजिक मुद्दे • سیاست اور سماجی مسائل

Kashmir is always a sensitive issue both in India and Pakistan, and shouldn't be broached lightly as a subject of conversation. Hindu-Muslim conflict in general is also a fairly sensitive topic.

Did you hear about ...?
क्या आपने ... के बारे में सुना है? — kyaa *aap*·ne ... ke *baa*·re meng su·*naa* hay
کیا آپنے ... کے بارے میں سنا ہے؟

Do you agree with it?
क्या आप उससे सहमत हैं? — ⓗ kyaa aap *us*·se *seh*·mat hayng
کیاآپ کواس سے اتفاق ہے؟ — ⓤ kyaa *aap*·ko *us*·se i·ti·*faak* hay

How do people feel about ...?
... के बारे में लोग क्या सोचते हैं? — ... ke *baa*·re meng log kyaa *soch*·te hayng
... کے بارے میں لوگ کیا سوچتے ہیں؟

the caste system f	वर्ण-व्यवस्था	زاتپات	ⓗ varn·*vya*·va·staa ⓤ *zaat*·paat
child labour f	बालमज़दूरी	بالمزدوری	baal·maz·*doo*·ree
crime m	अपराध	جرم	ⓗ *ap*·raad ⓤ jurm
the dispute over Kashmir m	कश्मीर का विवाद	کشمیر کا مسلہ	ⓗ *kash*·meer kaa vi·*vaad* ⓤ *kash*·meer kaa *mas*·laa
the economy f	अर्थ-व्यवस्था	اقتسادی	ⓗ art·*vya*·va·staa ⓤ ik·ti·*saa*·dee
education f	शिक्षा	تعلیم	ⓗ *shik*·shaa ⓤ *taa*·leem
feminism	नारी अधिकार	تانشیات	ⓗ *naa*·ree a·di·*kaar* m ⓤ *taan*·ni·si·yat f
human rights m	मानवाधिकार	انسانی حقوق	ⓗ maa·na·*vaa*·di·kaar ⓤ in·*saa*·nee hu·*kook*

SOCIAL

pilgrimage	तीर्थ यात्रा	حج	ⓗ teert *yaa*·traa f ⓤ haj m
poverty f	ग़रीबी	غریبی	ga·*ree*·bee
racism	जातिवाद	نسلپرستی	ⓗ *jaa*·ti·vaad m ⓤ nasl·pa·ra·*stee* f
religious extremism f	धार्मिक कट्टरता	مزہبی انتہا پسندی	ⓗ *daar*·mik kat·*tar*·taa ⓤ *maz*·ha·bee *in*·ta·haa pa·*san*·dee
terrorism	आतंकवाद	دہشت پسندی	ⓗ aa·*tank*·vaad m ⓤ *deh*·shat pa·*san*·dee f
unemployment f	बेरोज़गारी	بیروزگاری	be·roz·*gaa*·ree
the war in ...	... में युद्ध	... میں جنگ	ⓗ ... meng yudd m ⓤ ... meng jang f

being polite

There are many ways to show politeness in Hindi and Urdu. To address someone in this fashion, use the formal 'you' form (aap) – we've used it in this book as appropriate for the context. You can also call men *bay*·yaa (brother) when you're asking nicely for something. If you hear the words kri·pa·*yaa* ⓗ or me·har·*baa*·nee kar ke ⓤ (please) you'll know the speaker is asking a really special favour of you ...

the environment

पर्यावरण • ماحول

Is there a ... problem here?

क्या यहाँ ... की समस्या है?	ⓗ kyaa ya·*haang* ... kee sa·*mas*·yaa hay
کیا یہاں ... کا مسئلہ ہے؟	ⓤ kyaa ya·*haang* ... kaa *mas*·laa hay

What should be done about ...?

... के बारे में क्या करना चाहिये? ... کے بارے میں کیا کرنا چاہئے؟	... ke *baa*·re meng kyaa *kar*·naa *chaa*·hi·ye

deforestation f	वन कटाई	جنگل کی کٹائی	ⓗ van ka·*taa*·ee ⓤ *jan*·gal kee ka·*taa*·ee
drought m	अकाल	سوکھا	ⓗ a·*kaal* ⓤ *soo*·kaa
flood	बाढ़	سیلاب	ⓗ baar f ⓤ *se*·laab m
hunting m	शिकार खेलना	شکار کھیلنا	shi·*kaar kel*·naa
hydroelectricity f	जलविद्युत	پن بجلی	ⓗ jal·*vid*·yut ⓤ pan *bij*·lee
irrigation f	सिंचाई	سنچائی	sin·*chaa*·ee
nuclear energy f	परमाणु ऊर्जा	ایٹمی توانائی	ⓗ par·*maa*·nu *oor*·jaa ⓤ *ay*·ta·mee ta·vaa·*naa*·ee
nuclear testing m	परमाणु परीक्षण	ایٹمی امتحان	ⓗ par·*maa*·nu pa·*reek*·shan ⓤ *ay*·ta·mee *im*·ta·haan
pesticides f	कीड़े मारने की दवा	کیڑے مارنے کی دوا	*kee*·re *maar*·ne kee da·*vaa*
pollution	प्रदूषण	آلودگی	ⓗ pra·*doo*·shan m ⓤ aa·loo·*daa*·gee f
recycling m	पुनर्प्रयोग	بازگردانی کرنا	ⓗ pu·nar·*pra*·yog ⓤ baaz·gar·*daa*·nee *kar*·naa
water supply f	पानी की आपूर्ति	پانی کی سپلائی	ⓗ *paa*·nee kee *aa*·poor·ti ⓤ *paa*·nee kee sa·*plaa*·ee

keeping a distance

In Hindi and Urdu, the word for 'he' and 'she' is yeh and the word for 'they' is ye – these are used when talking about people that are 'nearby', physically or in terms of context. To refer to people that are 'far away', both contextually and spacially, use voh (he/she) and vo (they). The plural forms (ye/vo) can be used to refer to one person – 'he' or 'she' – out of formality or as a sign of respect.

going out

बाहर जाना • باہر جانا

where to go

किधर जायें • کدھر جائیں

What's on ...?

... कोई शो होनेवाला है? ... *ko*·ee sho *ho*·ne·*vaa*·laa hay

... کوئی شو ہونے والا ہے؟

locally	यहाँ	یہاں	ya·*haang*
this weekend	इस वीक-एंड	اس ویکاینڈ	is *veek*·end
today	आज	آج	aaj
tonight	आज रात को	آج رات کو	aaj raat ko

I feel like going to a ...

... जाने का मन हो रहा है। ... *jaa*·ne kaa man ho ra·*haa* hay

... جانے کا من ہو راہا ہے۔

ballet	बैले	بیلے	*bay*·le
café	कैफ़े	کیفے	*kay*·fe
concert	कॉन्सर्ट	کانسرٹ	*kaan*·sart
film	फ़िल्म	فلم	film
folk theatre performance	नौटंकी	علاقائی ڈرامہ شو	ⓗ nau·*tan*·kee ⓤ i·laa·*kaa*·ee *draa*·maa sho
karaoke bar	करेओके	کاریوکے	ka·re·*o*·ke
nightclub	नाइट क्लब	نائٹ کلاب	*naa*·it klab
party	पार्टी	پارٹی	*paar*·tee
play	नाटक	ناٹک	*naa*·tak
puppet theatre	कठपुतली का शो	پتھلیوں کا شو	ⓗ kat·*put*·lee kaa sho ⓤ *put*·li·yong kaa sho
regional music performance	लोकगीत का कार्यक्रम	علاقائی موسیق شو	ⓗ *lok*·geet kaa *kaar*·ya·kram ⓤ i·laa·*kaa*·ee moo·*see*·kee sho
traditional dance performance	लोकनृत्य	لوک ناچ	ⓗ lok·*nrit*·ya ⓤ lok naach

Where can I find ...?

... कहाँ मिलेगा? | ... ka-*haang* mi-*le*-gaa
... کہاں ملیگا ؟

bars	बार	بار	baar
places to eat	रेस्टोरेंट	ریسٹورینٹ	res-*to*-rent

Is there a local ... guide?

क्या ... का गाइड है? | kyaa ... kaa *gaa*-id hay
کیا ... کا گائڈ ہے؟

entertainment	एंटरटेंमेंट	اینٹرٹینمینٹ	en-tar-*ten*-ment
film	फ़िल्मों	فلموں	*fil*-mong

For more on eateries, bars and drinks, see **eating out**, page 109.

invitations

निमंत्रण • دعاوت

Would you like to go (for a) ...?

क्या आप ... के लिये जाना चाहते/चाहती हैं? | kyaa aap ... ke li-*ye* *jaa*-naa *chaah*-te/*chaah*-tee hayng m/f
کیا آپ ... کے لئے
جانا چاہتے/چاہتی ہیں؟

I feel like going (for a) ...

मैं ... के लिये जाना चाहता/चाहती हूँ। | mayng ... ke li-*ye* *jaa*-naa *chaah*-taa/*chaah*-tee hoong m/f
میں ... کے لئے جانا
چاہتا/چاہتی ہوں۔

dancing	नाचने	ناچنے	*naach*-ne
drink	कुछ पीने	کچھ پینے	kuch *pee*-ne
meal	खाना खाने	کھانا کھانے	*kaa*-naa *kaa*-ne
walk	घूमने	گھومنے	*goom*-ne

SOCIAL

responding to invitations

निमंत्रण का उत्तर • دعاوت کا جواب

Yes, I'd love to.

जी हाँ, मुझे बहुत अच्छा लगेगा।

جی ہاں، مجھے بہت اچّھا لگیگا۔

jee haang mu·*je* ba·*hut* *ach*·chaa la·*ge*·gaa

No, I'm afraid I can't come.

माफ़ कीजिये, मैं आ नहीं सकता/सकती।

معاف کیجئے، میں آ نہیں سکتا/سکتی۔

maaf *kee*·ji·ye mayng aa na·*heeng* *sak*·taa/*sak*·tee m/f

For other responses, see **women travellers**, page 80.

arranging to meet

मिलने का प्रबंध • ملنے کا انتظام

What time will we meet?

हम कितने बजे मिलें?

ہم کتنے بجے ملیں؟

ham *kit*·ne ba·*je* mi·*leng*

Where will we meet?

हम किधर मिलें?

ہم کدھر ملیں؟

ham ki·*dar* mi·*leng*

body language

- Whistling, winking and pointing with your finger is considered rude. To beckon, point your hand with the palm down and your fingers scooped in.
- The common Indian gesture of rotating the head can show agreement, doubt or dismissal, or it may simply mean they're mulling over what you're saying.
- Feet are considered unclean, so if your feet or shoes accidentally touch someone else, you should apologise straight away. Pointing the soles of your feet at someone is also offensive.

Let's meet at …

क्या हम … मिलें? — kyaa ham … mi·*leng*

کیا ہم ... ملیں؟

(eight) o'clock	(आठ) बजे	(آٹھ) بجے	(aat) ba·*je*
the entrance	प्रवेश द्वार के पास	اندر جانے کے دروازے کے پاس	ⓗ *pra*·vesh dvaar ke paas ⓤ *an*·dar *jaa*·ne ke dar·*vaa*·ze ke paas

drugs

I don't take drugs.

मैं नशीली दवाओं का सेवन नहीं करता/करती। — ⓗ mayng na·*shee*·lee da·*vaa*·ong kaa se·van na·*heeng kar*·taa/*kar*·tee **m/f**

میں نشیلی دواؤں کا استعمال نہیں کرتا/کرتی۔ — ⓤ mayng na·*shee*·lee da·*vaa*·ong kaa *is*·te·maal na·*heeng kar*·taa/*kar*·tee **m/f**

I take … occasionally.

मैं … कभी-कभी लेता/लेती हूँ। — mayng … ka·*bee* ka·*bee* *le*·taa/*le*·tee hoong **m/f**

میں ... کبھی کبھی لیتا/لیتی ہوں۔

Do you want to have a smoke?

क्या आप दम लगाना चाहतेधचाहती हैं? — kyaa aap dam la·*gee*·naa *chaah*·te/*chaah*·tee hayng **m/f**

کیا آپ دم لگانا چاہتے/چاہتی ہیں؟

Do you have a light?

माचिस है? — *maa*·chis hay

ماچس ہے؟

I'm high.

नशा चढ़ गया है। — na·*shaa* char ga·*yaa* hay

نشا چڑھ گیا ہے۔

If the police are talking to you about drugs, see **police**, page 130.

beliefs & cultural differences

स्था और संस्कृतिक विभिन्नता • عقده اور تہزیب اختلاف

religion

धर्म • مزہب

What's your religion?

आप का क्या मज़हब है? — aap kaa kyaa *maz*·hab hay
آپ کا مزہب کیا ہے؟

I'm not religious.

मेरा कोई मज़हब नहीं है। — *me*·raa *ko*·ee *maz*·hab na·*heeng* hay
میرا کوی مزہب نہیں ہے۔

I'm (a) …

मैं … हूँ। — mayng … hoong
میں … ہوں۔

agnostic	नास्तिक	ناستک	*naas*·tik
Buddhist	बौद्ध धर्म का/की अनुयायी	بودھ مزہب کا/کی پیرو	ⓗ baud darm kaa/kee a·nu·*yaa*·yee m/f ⓤ baud *maz*·hab kaa/kee *pay*·rav m/f
Catholic	कैथोलिक	کیتھولک	kay·*to*·lik
Christian	ईसाई	عیسئ	ee·*saa*·ee
Hindu	हिन्दू	ہندو	*hin*·doo
Jain	जैन	جین	jayn
Jewish	यहूदी	یہودی	ya·*hoo*·dee
Muslim	मुसलमान	مسلمان	mu·*sal*·maan
Sikh	सिक्ख	سکّھ	sik
Zoroastrian	पारसी	پارسی	*paar*·see

mr & ms pilgrim

The meaning of the word *haa*·jee (Haji) is 'one who has been on the Haj' (the pilgrimage to Mecca and Medina). It's often used among Muslims in place of 'Mr' as a term of respect. The word for a Muslim woman (less frequently used), is haa·ji·*yaa*·nee. Hindi pilgrims (both men and women) are called teert·*yaat*·ree.

cultural differences

संस्कृतिक विभिन्नता • تہزیبی اختلاف

Is this a local or national custom?

क्या यह लोकल या राष्ट्रीय प्रथा है? — ⓗ kyaa yeh *lo*·kal yaa *raash*·treey *pra*·taa hay

کیا یہ لوکل یا قومی روائت ہے؟ — ⓤ kyaa yeh *lo*·kal yaa *kau*·mee ri·*vaa*·yat hay

I'm sorry, it's against my …

माफ़ कीजिये, यह मेरे … के विरुद्ध है। — ⓗ maaf *kee*·ji·ye yeh *me*·re … ke vi·*rud* hay

معاف کیجئے، یہ میری … کے خلاف ہے۔ — ⓤ maaf *kee*·ji·ye yeh *me*·re … ke ki·*laaf* hay

beliefs	सिद्धांत	اصول	ⓗ *sid*·daant ⓤ u·*sool*
religion	मज़हब	مزہب	*maz*·hab

I didn't mean to do/say anything wrong.

माफ़ कीजिये, जानबूझकर मैं ने यह नहीं किया/कहा। — maaf *kee*·ji·ye jaan·*booj*·kar mayng ne yeh na·*heeng* ki·*yaa*/ka·*haa*

معاف کیجئے، جانبوجھ کر میں نے نہیں کیا/کہا۔

what's in the food

- Foods conducive to serenity and spirituality, in Hindu beliefs, are called 'sustaining foods' (*saat*·tvik *kaa*·naa सात्त्विक खाना ساتوک کھنا). They include milk and its products, honey, fruit and vegetables.
- Bitter, sour, salty, pungent or hot foods, believed among Hindus to induce restlessness, are known as 'vitalising foods' (*raa*·ja·sik *kaa*·naa राजसिक खाना راجسک کھانا).

hiking

हाइकिंग • ہائکنگ

Where can I buy supplies?
मुझे सप्लाई कहाँ मिलेगी?
مجھے سپلائ کہاں ملیگی؟
mu·*je* sap·*laa*·ee ka·*haang* mi·*le*·gee

Where can I find someone who knows this area?
मुझे कोई ऐसा आदमी कहाँ मिलेगा जो यह इलाक़ा अच्छी तरह जानता है?
مجھے کوئ ایسا آدمی کہاں ملیگا جو یہ علاقہ اچھّی طرح جانتا ہے؟
mu·*je* *ko*·ee *ay*·saa *aad*·mee ka·*haang* mi·*le*·gaa jo yeh i·*laa*·kaa *ach*·chee ta·*rah* *jaan*·taa hay

Where can I get a map?
मुझे नक्शा कहाँ मिलेगा?
مجھے نقشہ کہاں ملیگا؟
mu·*je* *nak*·shaa ka·*haang* mi·*le*·gaa

Where can I hire hiking gear?
मुझे हाइकिंग का सामान किराये पर कहाँ मिलेगा?
مجھے ہائکنگ کا سامان کرائے پر کہاں ملیگا؟
mu·*je* *haa*·i·king kaa *saa*·maan ki·*raa*·ye par ka·*haang* mi·*le*·gaa

Do we need a guide?
क्या हमको गाइड की ज़रूरत होगी?
کیا ہمکو گائڈ کی ضرورت ہوگی؟
kyaa *ham*·ko *gaa*·id kee za·*roo*·rat *ho*·gee

How high is the climb?
चढ़ाई कितनी ऊँची है?
چڑھائ کتنی اونچی ہے؟
cha·*raa*·ee *kit*·nee *oon*·chee hay

How long is the trail?
रास्ता कितना लम्बा है?
راستہ کتنا لمبا ہے؟
raas·taa *kit*·naa *lam*·baa hay

Which is the … route?

कौनसा रास्ता सब से … है?
کونسا راستہ سب سے ... ہے؟
kaun·saa *raas*·taa sab se … hay

easiest	आसान	آسان	*aa*·saan
most interesting	रुचिकर	دلچسپ	ⓗ ru·*chi*·kar ⓤ *dil*·chasp
shortest	छोटा	چھوٹا	*cho*·taa

Where can I find the …?

… किधर मिलेगा?
... کدھر ملیگا؟
… ki·*dar* mi·*le*·gaa

camping ground	कैम्पिंग ग्राउंड	کیمپنگ گراونڈ	*kaym*·ping *graa*·und
nearest village	सब से नज़दीक गाँव	سب سے نزدیک گاؤں	sab se *naz*·deek gaangv
showers	नहाने की जगह	نہانے کی جگہ	na·*haa*·ne kee ja·*gah*
toilets	टाइलेट	ٹائلیٹ	*taa*·i·let

Does this path go to …?

क्या यह … जाने का रास्ता है?
کیا یہ ... جانے کا راستہ ہے؟
kyaa yeh … *jaa*·ne kaa *raas*·taa hay

I'm lost.

मैं खो गया/गयी हूँ।
میں کھو گیا/گئ ہوں۔
mayng ko ga·*yaa*/ga·*yee* hoong m/f

Is this water safe to drink?

क्या यह पानी साफ़ है?
کیا یہ پانی صاف ہے؟
kyaa ye *paa*·nee saaf hai

sacred water

The water from the river Ganges, or *gan*·gaa jal (गंगा जल گنگا جل), is considered pure and sacred. Orthodox Hindus will always keep a supply at home because it's a necessary element for the last rites.

SOCIAL

weather

मौसम • موسم

What's the weather like?
मौसम कैसा है?
موسم کیسا ہے؟
mau·sam *kay*·saa hay

What will the weather be like tomorrow?
कल मौसम कैसा होगा?
کل موسم کیسا ہوگا؟
kal *mau*·sam *kay*·saa *ho*·gaa

It's …	… है।	… ہے۔	… hay
cloudy	बादल	بادل	*baa*·dal
cold	ठंड	ٹھنڈ	tand
dry	सूखा	سوکھا	*soo*·kaa
dusty	धूल	دھول	dool
freezing	बहुत ठंड	بہت ٹھنڈ	ba·*hut* tand
hot	बहुत गर्मी	بہت گرمی	ba·*hut gar*·mee
humid	उमस	امس	u·*mas*
muddy	कीचड़	کیچڑ	*kee*·char
raining	बारिश	بارش	*baa*·rish
snowing	बर्फ़ पड़ रही	برف پڑ رہی	barf par ra·*hee*
sunny	धूप	دھوپ	doop
warm	गर्मी	گرمی	*gar*·mee
windy	बहुत हवा	بہت ہوا	ba·*hut* ha·*vaa*
… season	… का मौसम	… کا موسم	… kaa *mau*·sam
cool	सर्दी	سردی	*sar*·dee
harvesting	फ़सल काटने	فصل کاٹنے	fa·*sal kaat*·ne
hot	गर्मी	گرمی	*gar*·mee

drought m	अकाल	اکال	a·*kaal*
flood	बाढ़	سیلاب	ⓗ baar f ⓤ *se*·laab m
monsoon f	बरसात	برسات	*bar*·saat

flora & fauna

पौधे और जानवर • نباتات اور حیوانات

What ... is that?

वह कौन-सा ... है?		voh *kaun*·saa ... hay	
وہ کونسا ... ہے؟			
animal	जानवर	جنور	*jaan*·var
flower	फूल	پھول	pool
plant	पौधा	پودوں	*pau*·daa
tree	पेड़	پیڑ	per

local flora & fauna

banyan tree m	बरगद	برگد	*bar*·gad
camel m	ऊँट	اونٹ	oongt
crocodile m	मगरमच्छ	مگرمچھ	ma·*gar*·mach
elephant m	हाथी	ہاتھی	*haa*·tee
leopard m	तेंदुआ	چیتا	ⓗ *ten*·du·aa ⓤ *chee*·taa
rhinoceros m	गैंडा	گینڈا	*gayn*·daa
tiger m	बाघ	شیر	ⓗ baag ⓤ sher

SOCIAL

basics

आम बातें • عام باتیں

breakfast m	नाश्ता	ناشتہ	*naash*·taa
lunch m	दिन का खाना	دن کا کھانا	din kaa *kaa*·naa
dinner m	रात का खाना	رات کا کھانا	raat kaa *kaa*·naa
snack m	नाश्ता	ناشتہ	*naash*·taa
to eat	खाना	کھانا	*kaa*·naa
to drink	पीना	پینا	*pee*·naa

finding a place to eat

हम कहाँ खाएँ • ہم کہاں کھایں

Can you recommend a ...?

क्या आप ... का नाम बता सकते/सकती हैं?
کیا آپ ... کا نام بتا سکتے/سکتی ہیں؟
kyaa aap ... kaa naam ba·*taa sak*·te/*sak*·tee hayng m/f

bar	एक बार	ایک بار	ek baar
café	कैफ़े	کیفے	*kay*·fe
dhaba (local eatery)	ढाबा	ڈھابا	*daa*·baa
restaurant	रेस्टोरेंट	ریسٹورینٹ	*res*·to·rent

Where would you go for ...?

आप ... खाने के लिय कहाँ जाते/जाती हैं?
آپ ... کھانے کے لئے کہاں جاتے/جاتی ہیں؟
aap ... *kaa*·ne ke li·*ye* ka·*haang jaa*·te/*jaa*·tee hayng m/f

a cheap meal	सस्ता खाना	سستہ کھانا	*sas*·taa *kaa*·naa
local specialities	लोकल खाना	لوکل کھانا	*lo*·kal *kaa*·naa

I'd like to reserve a table for …

मैं … के लिये बुकिंग
कराना चाहता/चाहती हूँ।
میں ... کے لئے بکنگ
کرنا چاہتا/چاہتی ہوں۔

mayng … ke li·*ye* bu·*king*
ka·*raa*·naa *chaah*·taa/*chaah*·tee hoong m/f

(two) people	(दो) लोगों	(دو) لوگوں	(do) lo·*gong*
(eight) o'clock	(आठ) बजे	(آٹھ) بجے	(aat) ba·*je*

I'd like the …, please.

मुझे … चाहिये।
مجھے ... چاہئے۔

mu·*je* … *chaa*·hi·ye

bill	बिल	بل	bil
drink list	पीने का मेन्यू कार्ड	پینے کا مینیو کارڈ	*pee*·ne kaa *men*·yoo kaard
menu	मेन्यू	مینیو	*men*·yoo
nonsmoking section	नॉन-स्मोकिंग	نان سموکنگ	naan *smo*·king

listen for …

band hay	**We're closed.**
ja·*gah* na·*heeng* hay	**We're full.**
men·yoo kaard na·*heeng* hay	**There's no menu, only meals.**

restaurant

रेस्टॉरेंट • ریسٹورینٹ

What would you recommend?

आपके ख़्याल में
क्या अच्छा होगा?
آپ کے خیال میں
کیا اچّھا ہو گا؟

aap ke kyaal meng
kyaa *ach*·chaa *ho*·gaa

FOOD

I'd like it with …

मुझे … के बिना चाहिये।	ⓗ mu·*je* … ke bi·*naa chaa*·hi·ye
مجھے … کے بغیر چاہئے۔	ⓤ mu·*je* … ke ba·*gay chaa*·hi·ye

I'd like it without …

मुझे … के साथ चाहिये।	mu·*je* … ke saat *chaa*·hi·ye
مجھے … کے بغیر چاہئے۔	

chilli	मिर्च	مرچ	mirch
garlic	लहसुन	لہسن	*leh*·sun
oil	तेल	تیل	tel
pepper	काली मिर्च	کالی مرچ	*kaa*·lee mirch
salt	नमक	نمک	na·*mak*
spices	मिर्च मसाला	مرچ مسالہ	mirch ma·*saa*·laa
vinegar	सिरका	سرکا	*sir*·kaa

For other specific meal requests, see **vegetarian & special meals**, page 119.

look for …

शुरू में	شورع میں	shu·*roo* meng	**Appetisers**
रोटी नान	روٹی نان	*ro*·tee naan	**Breads**
सूप	سوپ	soop	**Soups**
आँट्रे	آنٹرے	*aan*·tre	**Entrées**
सलाद	سلاد	sa·*laad*	**Salads**
दूध से बनी चीज़ें	دودھ سے بنی چیزیں	dood se ba·*nee* *chee*·zeng	**Dairy**
दाल	دال	daal	**Lentils**
चावल	چاول	*chaa*·val	**Rice Dishes**
गोश्त	گوشت	gosht	**Meat Dishes**
मछली	مچھلی	*mach*·lee	**Fish & Seafood**
सब्ज़ी	سبزی	*sab*·zee	**Vegetables**
चटनी और अचार	چٹنی اور اچار	*chat*·nee aur a·*chaar*	**Chutneys & Relishes**
रायता वग़ैरह	رائتا وغیرہ	*raai*·taa va·*gay*·rah	**Side Dishes**
मीठा	میٹھا	*mee*·taa	**Desserts**
पीने की चीज़ें	پینے کی چیزیں	*pee*·ne kee *chee*·zeng	**Drinks**

For more words you might find on a menu, see the **culinary reader**, page 121.

at the table

मेज़ पर • میز پر

Please bring a/the …

… लाइये। … *laa*·i·ye

… لائیے۔

ashtray	एशट्रे	ایشٹرے	*esh*·tre
bill	बिल	بل	bil
serviette	नैपकिन	نیپکن	*nayp*·kin
wineglass	शराब का ग्लास	شراب کا گلاس	sha·*raab* kaa glaas

I didn't order this.

यह मैं ने ऑडर नहीं किया। yeh mayng ne *aa*·dar na·*heeng* ki·*yaa*

یہ میں نے آرڈر نہیں کیا۔

There's a mistake in the bill.

बिल में गलती है। bil meng *gal*·tee hay

بل میں غلطی ہے۔

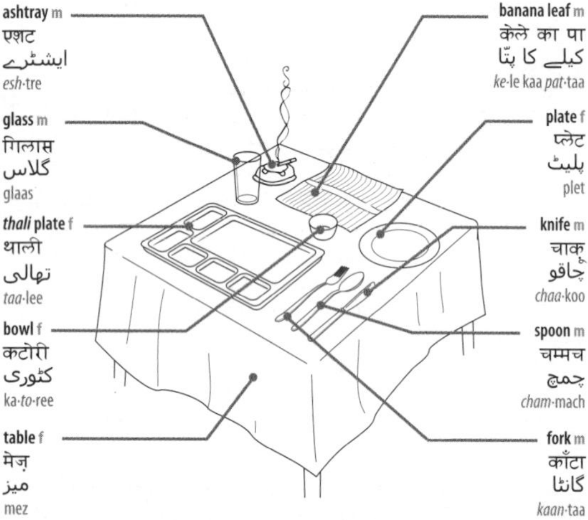

FOOD

talking food

खाने की बातें करना • کھانے کی باتیں کرنا

This is …
यह … है।
یہ … ہے۔
yeh … hay

(too) cold	(बहुत) ठंडा	(بہت) ٹھنڈا	(ba·*hut*) *tan*·daa
oily	बहुत तेल	بہت تیل	ba·*hut* tel
spicy	बहुत तीखा	بہت تیکھا	ba·*hut tee*·kaa
superb	बढ़िया	بڑھیا	ba·ri·*yaa*
sweet	मीठा	میٹھا	*mee*·taa

That was delicious.
बहुत मज़ेदार हुआ।
بہت مزےدار ہوا۔
ba·*hut* ma·ze·*daar* hu·*aa*

methods of preparation

बनाने के तरीके • بنانے کا طریقہ

I'd like it …
मुझे … चाहिये।
مجھے … چاہئے۔
mu·*je* … *chaa*·hi·ye

I don't want it …
मुझे … हुआ नहीं चाहिये।
مجھے … ہوا نہیں چاہئے۔
mu·*je* … hu·*aa* na·*heeng chaa*·hi·ye

boiled	उबला	ابلا	*ub*·laa
fried	तला	تلا	ta·*laa*
medium	कम पका	کم پکا	kam pa·*kaa*
rare	बहुत कम पका	بہت کم پکا	ba·*hut* kam pa·*kaa*
steamed	भाप से पका	بھاپ سے پکا	baap se pa·*kaa*
well-done	अच्छी तरह पका	اچّھی طرح پکا	*ach*·chee ta·*rah* pa·*kaa*

nonalcoholic drinks

सॉफ़्ट ड्रिंक्स • سافٹ ڈرنکس

boiled water m	उबला हुआ पानी	ابلا ہوا پانی	*ub*·laa hu·aa *paa*·nee
hot water m	गर्म पानी	گرم پانی	garm *paa*·nee
mineral water m	मिनरल वाटर	منرل واٹر	*min*·ral *vaa*·tar
orange juice m	ओरेंज जूस	اورینج جوس	*o*·renj joos
soda water m	सोडा वाटर	سوڈا واٹر	*so*·daa *vaa*·tar
soft drink m	सॉफ़्ट ड्रिंक्स	سافٹ ڈرنکس	saaft drink
water m	पानी	پانی	*paa*·nee

(cup of) coffee ...
(एक कप) काईफ़ी ... — (ek kap) *kaa*·fee ...
(ایک کپ) کافی ...

(cup of) tea ...
(एक कप) चाय ... — (ek kap) chaai ...
(ایک کپ) چائے ...

with (milk)	(दूध) के साथ	(دودھ) کے ساتھ	(dood) ke saath
without (sugar)	(चीनी) के बिना	(چینی) کے بغیر	ⓗ (*chee*·nee) ke bi·*naa* ⓤ (*chee*·nee) ke ba·*gayr*

local drinks

नारियल का पानी	ناریل کا پانی	*naa*·ri·yal kaa *paa*·nee	**green coconut juice**
दूध बादाम	دودھ بادام	dood *baa*·daam	**milk flavoured with almonds**
गन्ने का रस	گنّے کا رس	*gan*·ne kaa ras	**sugar-cane juice**
शरबत	شربت	*shar*·bat	**drink made of sugar & fruit**
लस्सी	لسّی	*las*·see	**yogurt drink**

FOOD

alcoholic drinks

दारू • دارو

Drinking alcohol is less socially acceptable in India than in Western countries, but that's not to say that people don't enjoy a drink every now and then. In Pakistan, drinking is much more restricted, and alcohol is usually available only at up-market hotels. Most of the words for different types of alcohol are the same as in English.

a bottle of … wine
… शराब की बोतल … sha·*raab* kee *bo*·tal
… شراب کی بوتل

a glass of … wine
… शराब का गिलास … sha·*raab* kaa glaas
… شراب کا گلاس

red	लाल	لال	laal
white	सफ़ेद	سفید	sa·*fed*

a … of beer
… बियर … bi·*yar*
… بیر

bottle	की बोतल	کی بوتل	kee *bo*·tal
glass	का ग्लास	کا گلاس	kaa glaas

in the bar

बार में • بار میں

Excuse me!
सुनिये। su·ni·*ye*
سنئے۔

I'll have …
मुझे … दीजिये। mu·*je* … *dee*·ji·ye
مجھے … دیجئے۔

Same again, please.
वही फिर से दीजिये। va·*hee* pir se *dee*·ji·ye
وہی پھر سے دیجئے۔

I'll buy you a drink.

मैं ही इस ड्रिंक के पैसे दूँगा/दूँगी। — mayng hee is drink ke *pay*·se *doong*·gaa/*doong*·gee **m/f**

میں ہی اس کے پیسے دوں گا/دوں گی۔

What would you like?

आप क्या लेंगे/लेंगी? — aap kyaa *leng*·ge/*leng*·gee **m/f**

آپ کیا لیں گے/لیں گی؟

It's my round.

मेरी बारी है। — *me*·ree *baa*·ree hay

میری باری ہے۔

How much is it?

यह कितने का है? — yeh *kit*·ne kaa hay

یہ کتنے کا ہے؟

Cheers!

चीयर्स। — *chee*·yars

چئرس۔

culinary etiquette

- If your Indian hosts invite you for a meal, refusing it without a good reason would be an insult to them. It's customary to refuse the first offer, but the second or third should be accepted.
- In rural homes or traditional families the guests will be served first, alone or with the men (as a sign of respect), and the women will eat separately afterwards.
- Most Indians eat with their fingers, but only using the right hand. Never use your left hand to pass or touch food as it's considered unclean – the left hand is reserved for toilet purposes. Try to use just the fingertips of your right hand (not the palm) and always wash your hands before and after the meal.
- Alcohol isn't normally served in Indian homes. If you're drinking from a shared water container, hold it above your mouth and pour avoiding contact with your lips.

self-catering

अपने आप खाना बनाना • اپنے آپ کھانا بنانا

buying food

सामान ख़रीदना • سامان خریدنا

What's the local speciality?
ख़ास लोकल चीज़ क्या है?
خاص لوکل چیز کیا ہے؟
kaas *lo*·kal cheez kyaa hay

What's that?
वह क्या है?
وہ کیا ہے؟
voh kyaa hay

How much is a kilo of …?
एक किलो … कितने
में आता/आती है?
ایک کلو ... کتنے
میں آتا/آتی ہے؟
ek ki·*lo* … *kit*·ne
meng *aa*·taa/*aa*·tee hay **m/f**

Can I taste it?
क्या मैं चख
सकता/सकती हूँ?
کیا میں چکھ سکتا/سکتی ہوں؟
kyaa mayng chak
sak·taa/*sak*·tee hoong **m/f**

Can I have a bag, please?
थैली दीजिये।
تھیلی دیجئے۔
tay·lee *dee*·ji·ye

I'd like …
मुझे … चाहिये।
مجھے ... چاہئے۔
mu·*je* … *chaa*·hi·ye

(200) grams	(दो सौ) ग्राम	(دو سو) گرام	(do sau) graam
(two) kilos	(दो) किलो	(دو) کلو	(do) ki·*lo*
(three) pieces	(तीन) टुकड़े	(تین) ٹکڑے	(teen) *tuk*·re
that one	वह वाला	وہ والا	voh *vaa*·laa

Less.	कम।	کم۔	kam
A bit more.	थोड़ा और।	تھوڑا اور۔	*tho*·raa aur
Enough.	काफ़ी।	کافی۔	*kaa*·fee

self-catering

Where can I find ... ?

... कहाँ मिलेगा/मिलेगी?			... ka·*haang* mi·*le*·gaa/mi·*le*·gee m/f
... کہاں ملیگا/ملیگی؟			
bread	ब्रेड	بریڈ	bred
dairy products	दूध से बनी चीज़ें	دودھ سے بنی چیزیں	dood se ba·*nee* *chee*·zeng
fish	मछली	مچھلی	*mach*·lee
frozen goods	फ्रोज़न फूड्स	فروزن چیزیں	*fro*·zan *chee*·zeng
fruit and vegetables	फल और सब्ज़ी	پھل اور سبزی	pal aur *sab*·zee
meat	गोश्त	گوشت	gosht
poultry	मुर्ग़ी	مرغی	*mur*·gee
seafood	मछली	مچھلی	*mach*·lee
spices	मसाला	مسالہ	ma·*saa*·laa
sweets	मिठाई	مٹھائ	mi·*taa*·ee

cooking utensils

खाना बनाने की चीज़ें • کھانا بنانے کی چیزیں

Could I please borrow a ...?

क्या आप मुझे थोड़ी देर के लिये ... दे सकते/सकती हैं?

کیا آپ مجھے تھوڑی دیر کے لۓ ... دے سکتے/سکتی ہیں؟

kyaa aap mu·*je* *tho*·ree der ke li·*ye* ... de *sak*·te/*sak*·tee hayng m/f

I need a ...

मुझे ... चाहिये।

مجھے ... چاۓ۔

mu·*je* ... *chaa*·hi·ye

chopping board	चॉपिंग बोर्ड	چاپنگ بورڈ	*chaa*·ping bord
frying pan	कड़ाही	کڑاہی	ka·*raa*·hee
saucepan	भगौना	بھگونا	ba·*gau*·naa

Mughlai food

North Indian food is greatly influenced by the Mughals who ruled from the 16th to the 18th century – hence the term 'Mughlai food' (mug·*laa*·ee *kaa*·naa मुग़लाई खाना مغلاۓ کھانا).

vegetarian & special meals

शाकाहारी और विशेष खाना • سبزی خور کا اور خاص کھانا

ordering food

ऑर्डर देना • آرڈر دینا

Is there a … restaurant near here?
क्या यहाँ … रेस्टोरेंट है? — kyaa ya·*haang* … res·*to*·rent hay
کیا یہاں ... ریسٹورینٹ ہے؟

Do you have … food?
क्या आप का खाना … है? — kyaa aap kaa *kaa*·naa … hay
کیا آپ کا کھانا ... ہے؟

halal	हलाल	حلال	ha·*laal*
kosher	कोशर	کوشر	*ko*·shar
vegetarian	शाकाहारी	سبزی خور کا	ⓗ shaa·kaa·*haa*·ree ⓤ sab·*zee* kor kaa

I don't eat …
मैं … नहीं खाता/खाती। — mayng … na·*heeng* *kaa*·taa/*kaa*·tee m/f
میں ... نہیں کھاتا/کھاتی۔

Could you prepare a meal without …?
क्या आप … के बिना खाना तैयार कर सकते/सकती हैं? — kyaa aap … ke bi·*naa* *kaa*·naa *tay*·yaar kar *sak*·te/*sak*·tee hayng m/f
کیا آپ ... کے بغیر کھانا تیار کر سکتے/سکتی ہیں؟

butter	मक्खन	مکھن	*mak*·kan
beef	गाय के गोश्त	گاے کے گوشت	gaai ke gosht
dairy products	दूध से बँनी चीज़ों	دودھ سے بنی چیزوں	dood se ba·*nee* *chee*·zong
eggs	अंडे	انڈے	*an*·de
fish	मछली	مچھلی	*mach*·lee
garlic	लहसुन	لہسن	*lah*·sun
goat	बकरी	بکری	*bak*·re
oil	तेल	تیل	tel
onion	प्याज़	پیاز	pyaaz
pork	सुअर के गोश्त	سؤر کے گوشت	*su*·ar ke gosht
poultry	मुर्गी	مرغی	*mur*·gee

special diets & allergies

विशेष खाना और एलर्जी • خاص کھانا اور الیرجی

I'm (a) ...

मैं ... हूँ। — mayng ... hoong

میں ... ہوں۔

Buddhist	बौद्ध धर्म का/क अनुयायी	بودھ مزہب کا/کی پیرو	ⓗ baud darm kaa/kee a·nu·*yaa*·yee **m/f** ⓤ baud *maz*·hab kaa/kee *pay*·rav **m/f**
Hindu	हिन्दू	ہندو	*hin*·doo
Jewish	यहूदी	یہودی	ya·*hoo*·dee
Muslim	मुसलमान	مسلمان	mu·*sal*·maan
vegan	वीगन	ویگن	*vee*·gan
vegetarian	शाकाहारी	سبزی خور کا	ⓗ shaa·kaa·*haa*·ree ⓤ sab·*zee* kor kaa

I'm allergic to ...

मुझे ... की एलर्जी है। — mu·*je* ... kee e·*lar*·jee hay

مجھے ... کی ایرجی ہے۔

dairy products	दूध से बनी चीज़ों	دودھ سے بنی چیزوں	dood se ba·*nee chee*·zong
eggs	अंडे	انڈے	*an*·de
MSG	एम० एस० जी०	ایم ایس جی	em es jee
nuts	मेवे	میوے	*me*·ve
seafood	मछली	مچھلی	*mach*·lee
shellfish	शेलफ़िश	شیل فش	*shel*·fish

allowed or not?

The term ha·*laal* (हलाल حلال) is used for all permitted foods as dictated by the Qur'an. Its opposite is the word ha·*raam* (हराम حرام) which denotes all foods prohibited by the Muslim holy book.

FOOD

culinary reader

खाना की चीज़ें • کھانے کی چیزیں

This miniguide to Indian and Pakistani cuisine lists dishes and ingredients alphabetically, according to the pronunciation of the Hindi and Urdu words. It's designed to help you get the most out of your gastronomic experience by providing you with food terms that you may see on the menu. For certain dishes we've marked the region or city where they're most popular. Note that nouns have their gender marked as masculine ⓜ or feminine ⓕ.

A

aa·loo ⓜ आलू آلو *potato*

aa·loo bu·*kaa*·raa ⓜ आलू बुख़ारा آلو بوخارا *dried plum*

aa·*loo*·chaa ⓜ आलूचा آلوچا *plum*

aa·loo kaa pa·*raang*·taa ⓜ आलू का पराँठा آلو کا پرنٹھا *fried, triangular bread with potato filling*

aa·loo kee ti·ki·*yaa* ⓕ आलू की टिकिया آلو کی ٹکیا *potato patties*

aam ⓜ आम آم *mango*

aam kaa *paa*·nee ⓜ आम का पानी آم کا پانی *drink made of boiled, unripe mangoes, mint & cumin*

aa·roo ⓜ आड़ू آڑو *peach*

a·*chaar* ⓜ अचार اچار *pickle • marinade*

a·*chaar* kaa pyaaz ⓜ अचार का प्याज़ اچار کا پیاز *pickling onion*

a·chee ta·*rah* pa·*kaa* अच्छी तरह पका اچھّی طرح پکا *well-done*

ad·rak ⓜ अदरक ادرک *ginger*

aj·mod ⓜ अजमोद اخمود *parsley*

aj·*vaa*·in ⓕ अजवाइन اجوائن *thyme*

ak·rot ⓜ अख़रोट اخروٹ *walnut*

am·rood ⓜ अमरूद امرود *guava*

a·*naar* ⓜ अनार انار *pomegranate*

a·*naar* ke *daa*·ne ⓜ अनार के दाने انار کے دانے *pomegranate seeds*

a·*nan*·naas ⓜ अनन्नास انّناس *pineapple*

an·de ⓜ अंडे انڑے *egg*

an·goor ⓜ अंगूर انگور *grape*

an·jeer ⓜ अंजीर انجیر *fig*

ar·har kee daal ⓕ अरहर की दाल ارہر کی دال *large, yellow-brown pulse*

B

baa·daam ⓜ बादाम بادام *almond*

baa·daam kaa kek ⓜ बादाम का केक بادام کا کیک *marzipan*

baa·jee ⓕ भाजी بھاجی *vegetables such as deep-fried eggplant, potato & okra, served with* daal *(West Bengal)*

baaj·raa ⓜ बाजरा باجرا *millet*

baaj·re kee *ro*·tee ⓕ बाजरे की रोटी باجرے کی روڑی *millet bread*

baang ⓜ भांग بھانگ *marijuana leaves (mixed with vegetables & fried into* pa·*kau*·raa*, or drunk in* las·*see* *& other beverages)*

baas·ma·tee ⓕ बासमती باسمتی *basmati rice*

bak·raa ⓜ बकरा بکرا *goat*

band go·*bee* ⓕ बंद गोभी بند گوبھی *red cabbage*

ba·*ree jeeng*·gaa ⓕ बड़ी झींगा بڑی جھینگا *lobster*

barf ⓕ बर्फ़ برف *ice*

bar·fee ⓕ बर्फ़ी برفی *fudge-like sweet, often topped with edible silver foil bar*·taa ⓜ भरता بھرتا *roasted eggplant fried with onions & tomatoes*

ba·*tak* ⓜ बतख़ بتخ *duck*

ba·*tar* do·*saa* ⓜ बटर डोसा بٹر ڈوسا *do·saa smothered in butter*

bayng·gan ⓜ बैंगन بینگن *eggplant*

bayng·gan *baa*·jaa ⓜ बैंगन का भाजा بینگن کا بھاجا *eggplant rings deep-fried in mustard oil & seasoned with salt & chilli powder (Assam, Bengal)*

bayng·gan *bar*·taa ⓜ बैंगन का भरता بینگن کا بھرتا *spicy dish of roasted eggplant, fried with onions & tomatoes (Punjab)*

bel·pu·ree ⓕ भेलपुरी بھیلپوری *crisp-fried thin dough mixed with puffed rice, boiled potatoes, chopped onions, peanuts & spices (Maharashtra)*

ber ⓜ बेर بیر *berry • prune*

ber kaa gosht ⓜ भेड़ का गोश्त بھیڑ کا گوشت *mutton*

be·*san* ⓜ बेसन بیسن *gram or chickpea flour*

bin·dee ⓕ भिंडी بھنڈی *okra*

bir·*yaa*·nee ⓕ बिरयानी بریانی *Mughlai dish of steamed rice, oven-baked with meat, vegetables & spices*

bi·*yar* ⓕ बियर بیر *beer • lager*

boo·*naa aa*·loo ⓜ भूना आलू بھونا آلو *baked potato*

bu·ji·*yaa* ⓜ भुजिया بھجیا *fried lentils with nuts & spices, eaten as a snack*

C

chaach ⓜ छाछ چھاچھ *buttermilk (also known as* ma·*taa)*

chaat ⓕ चाट چھاٹ *snack foods – include* sa·mo·*saa*, *bel*·pu·ree, *fried potato patties & other dishes (Mumbai)*

chaat ma·*saa*·laa ⓜ चाट मसाला چھاٹ مسالا *spice blend of black salt, cumin, sea salt, coriander powder, chilli powder, black pepper & ginger*

chaa·val ⓜ चावल چاول *rice*

chai ⓕ चाय چائے *tea*

cha·*kot*·raa ⓜ चकोतरा چکوترا *grapefruit*

cha·*naa* kee daal ⓕ चनो की दाल چنے کی دال *sweeter version of the yellow split pea*

cha·*paa*·tee ⓕ चपाती چپاتی *unleavened bread cooked on a frying pan, also known as* naan *or ro*·tee

chat·nee ⓕ चटनी چٹنی *chutney*

chee·koo ⓜ चीकू چیکو *sapodilla – fruit that looks like a kiwi fruit on the outside but is brown inside with large black seeds*

chee·nee ⓕ चीनी چینی *sugar*

chee·nee go·*bee* ⓕ चीनी गोभी چینی گوبی *Chinese cabbage*

che·*ree* ⓕ चेरी چیری *cherry*

chi·*raung*·jee ⓕ चिरौंजी چرونجی *Brazil nut*

cho·le ⓜ चोले چھولے *chickpea (Punjab) • spiced chickpea dish served with* poo·ree

chu·*kan*·dar ⓜ चुकंदर چقندر *beetroot*

D

daal ⓕ दाल دال *generic term for cooked & uncooked lentils or pulses*

daal *chee*·nee ⓕ दाल चीनी دال چینی *cinnamon*

daa·roo ⓕ दारू دارو *spirits*

da·*bal* ro·tee ⓕ डबल रोटी ڈبل روٹی *English-style bread*

da·*hee* ⓜ दही دہی *curds*

da·li·*yaa* ⓜ दलिया دلیا *porridge*

dam *aa*·loo ⓜ दम आलू دم آلو *spicy potato curry usually served with* poo·ree

de·*see* देसी دیسی *'local' – foods that are home-grown*

dhok·laa ⓜ धोकला دھوکلا *spongy squares of steamed* be·*san* *topped with fried mustard seeds, coriander leaves & grated coconut (Gujarat)*
dood ⓜ दूध دودھ *milk*
dood kaa *paa*·u·dar ⓜ दूध का पाउडर دودھ کا پاوڈر *powdered milk*
do·*saa* ⓜ डोसा ڈوسا *crepe of fermented rice flour (a breakfast speciality served with* daal *& a bowl of hot* *saam*·baar *or coconut chutney)*

F

fa·*vaa* ⓜ फ़वा فوا *broad bean*
fe·*nee* ⓕ फेनी فینی *sweet rolls made from wheat flour & rice, fried in* gee, *then dipped in sugar syrup (Orissa)*

G

gaai kaa gosht ⓜ गाय का गोश्त گائے کا گوشت *beef*
gaa·jar ⓕ गाजर گاجر *carrot*
gaa·jar kaa *hal*·vaa ⓜ गाजर का हलवा گاجر کا بلوہ *sweet made with carrots, dried fruits, sugar, condensed milk &* gee
gan·naa ⓜ गन्ना گنّا *sugar cane*
gan·ne kaa ras ⓜ गन्ने का रस گنّے کا رس *sugar-cane juice*
garm ma·*saa*·laa ⓜ गर्म मसाला گرم مسالا *an aromatic blend of up to 15 spices – black pepper, cumin, cinnamon, cardamom, cloves, coriander, bay leaves, nutmeg & mace, also known as* *kaa*·laa ma·*saa*·laa *(Maharashtra)*
gee ⓜ घी گھی *clarified butter*
gol *gap*·paa ⓜ गोल गप्पा گول گپّا *deep-fried discs of dough which puff up like* *poo*·ree *(see also* *paa*·nee *poo*·ree*)*
gosht ⓜ गोश्त گوشت *meat*

gu·ji·*yaa* ⓜ गुजिया گجیا *small pastry filled with semolina, condensed milk & sugar fried in* gee
gu·*laab* *jaa*·mun ⓜ गुलाब जामुन گلاب جامن *deep-fried balls of milk dough soaked in rose-flavoured syrup*
gu·*laab* kaa *paa*·nee ⓜ गुलाब का पानी گلاب کا پانی *rose-water extracted from rose petals*
gur ⓜ गुड़ گڑ *sweetening agent with a distinctly musky flavour*

H

ha·*laal* हलाल حلال *halal food – all permitted foods as dictated by the Qur'an*
hal·dee ⓕ हल्दी ہلدی *turmeric*
ha·*leem* हलीम حلیم *tasty wheat porridge cooked with meat & spices*
hal·vaa ⓜ हलवा بلوہ *sweet made with vegetables, cereals, lentils, nuts or fruit*
hans ⓜ हंस ہنس *goose*
ha·*raa* da·ni·*yaa* ⓜ हरा धनिया ہرا دھنیا *coriander leaves*
ha·*raam* हराम حرام *haram food – all prohibited foods as dictated by the Qur'an*
ha·*raa* saag ⓜ हरा साग ہرا ساگ *green leafy vegetable*
ha·*ree* mirch ⓕ हरी मिर्च ہری مرچ *green chilli*

I

i·*laai*·chee ⓕ इलायची الائچی *cardamom*
im·lee ⓕ इमली املی *tamarind*

J

jaa·mun ⓜ जामुन جامن *black plum*
jaa·vi·tree ⓕ जावित्री جاوتری *mace*
ja·*ee* ⓕ जई جئ *rolled oats*

jai·pal ⓜ जयफल جےپھل *nutmeg*
ja·le·bee ⓕ जलेबी جلیبی *orange whorls of fried batter made from milk, semolina & cardamom fried in* gee*, then dipped in syrup*
jam·bu ⓜ जमबु جمبو *chive*
jau ⓜ जौ جو *barley (also called* jo·var*)*
jeeng·gee mach·lee ⓕ झींगी मछली جھینگی مچھلی *prawn*
ji·gar ⓜ जिगर جگر *liver*
jo·var ⓜ जोवर جوار *see* jau
jvaar ⓕ ज्वार جوار *millet*
jvaar kee ro·tee ⓕ ज्वार की रोटी جوار کی روٹی *millet bread*

K

kaa·fee ⓕ कॉफ़ी کافی *coffee*
kaa·joo ⓜ काजू کاجو *cashew nut*
kaa·joo draksh काजू द्रक्श کاجو درکش *cashew & raisin combination used to flavour sweets & ice cream*
kaa·laa ma·saa·laa ⓜ काला मसाला کالا مسالا *see* garm ma·saa·laa
kaa·laa zee·raa ⓜ काला ज़ीरा کالا زیرا *black cumin*
kaa·lee be·ree ⓕ काली बेरी کالی بیری *blackberry*
kaand·vee ⓕ खाण्डवी کھنڈوی *wheat flour mixed with a spoon of oil & water to prepare dough, then rolled flat & cooked on a hotplate (Gujarat)*
ka·baab ⓜ कबाब کباب *term for marinated chunks of ground meat, cooked on a skewer, fried on a hot plate or cooked under a grill*
ka·boo·tar ⓜ कबूतर کبوتر *pigeon*
ka·chau·ree ⓕ कचौरी کچوری *corn & lentil savoury puff, served with a sour tamarind sauce flavoured with fenugreek seeds*
kad·doo ⓜ कद्दू کدّو *pumpkin*
ka·joor ⓜ खजूर کھجور *date*
ka·joor kaa gur ⓜ खजूर का गुड़ کھجور کا گوڑ *date palm jaggery*

kak·ree ⓕ ककड़ी ککڑی *cucumber*
kar·boo·jaa ⓜ करबूजा کربوجہ *cantaloupe*
ka·ree ⓕ कढ़ी کڑھی *sour soup made from powdered barley dissolved in curds • sour* daal*-like dish made of curds &* be·san *(Gujarat, Rajasthan)*
ka·re·laa ⓜ करेला کریلا *bitter gourd*
ka·re ma·saa·le kaa gosht ⓜ खरे मसाले का गोश्त کھرے مسالے کا گوشت *mutton in* garm ma·saa·laa *(Delhi)*
kar·gosh ⓜ खरगोश خرگوش *hare • rabbit*
kat·hal ⓜ कटहल کٹہل *jackfruit*
keer ⓕ खीर کھیر *rich creamy rice pudding made by boiling milk & rice, flavoured with cardamom, saffron, pistachios, flaked almonds, cashews or dried fruit*
ke·laa ⓜ केला کیلا *banana*
ke·sar ⓜ केसर کیسر *saffron*
ke·sar pis·taa ⓜ केसर पिस्ता کیسر پستہ *saffron & pistachio combination used to flavour milk, sweets & ice cream (Gujarat)*
ki·cha·ree ⓕ खिचड़ी کھچڑی *risotto-like dish of rice & lentils cooked with spices*
kish·mish ⓕ किशमिश کشمش *currant • raisin*
kof·taa ⓜ कोफ़्ता کوفتہ *meatballs – often made from goat, beef or lamb*
kor·maa ⓜ कोरमा قورمہ *rich, thickened brown curry of chicken, mutton or vegetables*
ko·shar कोशर کوشر *kosher food*
ku·baa·nee ⓕ खुबानी خبانی *apricot*
kul·chaa ⓜ कुलचा کلچا *a soft, round leavened bread (Andhra Pradesh)*
kul·fee ⓕ कुल्फ़ी قلفی *ice cream made with reduced milk & flavoured with nuts, fruits & berries*
kum·bee ⓕ खुंभी کھمبھی *mushroom*

L

laal *chaa*·val ⓜ लाल चावल لال چاول *brown rice*

laal maangs ⓜ लाल मांस لال منس *red meat (Rajasthan)*

laal *moo*·lee ⓕ लाल मूली لال مولی *red radish*

laal sha·*raab* ⓕ लाल शराब لال شراب *red wine*

laal *shim*·laa mirch ⓕ लाल शिमला मिर्च لال شملا مرچ *red capsicum*

las·see ⓕ लस्सी لسّی *yogurt drink – often flavoured with salt or sugar & rose-water essence*

lau·kee ⓕ लौकी لوکی *green gourd*

laungg ⓕ लौंग لونگ *clove*

lee·chee ⓕ लीची لیچی *lychee, generally eaten fresh*

leh·sun ⓜ लहसुन لہسن *garlic*

lo·bi·*yaa* ⓜ लोबिया لوبیا *black-eyed beans*

M

maah kee daal ⓕ माह की दाल ماہ کی دال *black lentils simmered for hours over a low fire & served with oven-fresh* ro·tee *(Punjab)*

mach·lee ⓕ मछली مچھلی *fish*

ma·dhu ⓜ मधु مدھو *honey*

ma·di·*raa* ⓕ मदिरा مدرا *wine*

maj·jaa ⓜ मज्जा مجّا *bone marrow*

mak·kaa ⓜ मक्का مکّا *corn*

mak·kan ⓜ मक्खन مکّھن *butter*

mak·kee kee *ro*·tee ⓕ मक्की की रोटी مکّی کی روٹی *corn meal* ro·tee *– often accompanied by* sar·song kaa saag *(Punjab)*

ma·*laa*·ee ⓕ मलाई ملائی *cream added for flavour to predominantly vegetarian food*

ma·*saa*·laa ⓜ मसाला مسالا *spice blends*

ma·*saa*·laa baat ⓜ मसाला भाट مسالا بھات *a spicy hot pilau made with vegetables & basmati rice (Maharashtra)*

ma·*saa*·laa do·*saa* ⓜ मसाला डोसा مسالا ڈوسا *large crepe with a filling of potatoes cooked with onions & curry leaves*

ma·*soor* ⓕ मसूर مسور *red lentils*

ma·*taa* ⓜ मठा مٹھا *see* chaach

ma·*tar* ⓜ मटर مٹر *pea*

ma·*tar* kee daal ⓕ मटर की दाल مٹر کی دال *dried split pea*

ma·*tar* pa·*neer* ⓜ मटर पनीर مٹر پنیر *dish of peas & fresh cheese*

may·daa ⓜ मैदा میدا *plain flour*

mee·taa मीठा میٹھا *dessert • sweet* a

mee·taa paan ⓜ मीठा पान میٹھا پان *sweet & spicy* paan

me·*tee* ⓕ मेथी میتھی *fenugreek*

milk *baa*·daam ⓜ मिल्क बादाम ملک بادام *milk flavoured with saffron & almonds*

mirch ⓕ मिर्च مرچ *capsicum • chilli*

mish·taan ⓜ मिष्ठान *any sweet item (Gujarat)*

mis·see *ro*·tee ⓕ मिस्सी रोटी مسّی روٹی *bread made of wheat, gram flour, cooked lentils & water kneaded with spices, rolled flat & cooked on a hotplate*

mi·*taa*·ee ⓕ मिठाई مٹھائی *sweet*

moo·lee ⓕ मूली مولی *white radish*

moong ⓕ मूँग مونگ *mung bean*

moong kee daal ⓕ मूँग की दाल مونگ کی دال *mung bean* daal *– tiny green legumes*

moong·pa·lee ⓕ मूँगफली مونگپھلی *peanut*

moong·pa·lee kaa tel ⓜ मूँगफली का तेल مونگپھلی کا تیل *peanut oil*

mo·*taa* *chaa*·val ⓜ मोटा चावल موٹا چاول *short-grain rice*

mu·*nak*·kaa ⓜ मुनक़्क़ा منقی *see* kish·mish

murg ⓜ मुर्ग़ مرغ *chanterelle, a funnel-shaped mushroom*
mur·gee ⓕ मुर्ग़ी مرغی *chicken • poultry*

N

naan ⓕ नान نان *unleavened bread (also called* cha·*paa*·tee*)*
naa·*ran*·gee ⓕ नारंगी نارنگی *orange*
naa·*ran*·gee kaa *chil*·kaa ⓜ नारंगी का छिलका نارنگی کا چھلکا *zest*
naa·ri·yal ⓜ नारियल ناریل *coconut*
naash·*paa*·tee ⓕ नाशपाती ناشپاتی *pear*
na·*mak* ⓜ नमक نمک *salt*
nam·keen नमकीन نمکین *'salty' – savoury snacks, including anything from* sa·mo·*saa* *&* pa·*kau*·raa *to* bu·ji·*yaa* *& chips*
neem ⓜ नीम نیم *plant whose leaves have a variety of uses, including culinary – used as a vegetable*
nim·boo ⓜ निम्बू نمبو *citrus • lemon • lime*

P

paa·lak ⓜ पालक پالک *spinach*
paa·lak pa·*neer* ⓜ पालक पनीर پالک پنیر *soft cheese in a spicy gravy of puréed spinach, served with fresh, hot* ro·tee *(Delhi)*
paan ⓜ पान پان *mixture of betel nut, lime paste & spices, wrapped up in a betel leaf, eaten as a digestive & mouth freshener (there are two basic types,* *mee*·taa paan *&* *saa*·daa paan*)*
paa·nee *poo*·ree ⓕ पानी पूरी پانی پوری *small crisp puffs of dough filled with spicy tamarind water & sprouted gram, served as a snack (see* gol *gap*·paa*)*
paav *baa*·jee ⓕ पाव भाजी پاؤ بھاجی *spiced vegetables with bread (Mumbai)*
pa·*kau*·raa ⓜ पकौड़ा پکوڑا *fritters of gram flour & spinach*
pal ⓜ फल پھل *fruit*
pal kaa ras ⓜ फल का रस پھل کا رس *fruit juice*
pal me·*ve* ⓜ फल मेवे پھل میوہ *dried fruit*
pa·*neer* ⓜ पनीर پنیر *soft, unfermented cheese made from milk curd*
pa·*par* ⓕ पपड़ پپڑ *pappadams*
pa·*pee*·taa ⓜ पपीता پپیتا *papaya*
pa·*raang*·taa ⓜ पराँठा پرانٹھا *unleavened flaky fried flat bread (sometimes stuffed with* pa·*neer* *or grated vegetables)*
par·val ⓜ परवल پرول *pointed gourd*
pat·taa choor ⓜ पत्ता चूर پتّا چور *borage*
pee·lee *shim*·laa mirch ⓕ पीली शिमला मिर्च پیلی شملا مرچ *yellow capsicum*
pee·lee tez mirch ⓕ पीली तेज़ मिर्च پیلی تیز مرچ *sharp-flavoured, yellow chilli*
pee·ne kee *chee*·zeng ⓕ पीने की चीज़ें پینے کی چیزیں *drinks*
pe·*taa* ⓜ पेठा پیٹھا *crystallised gourd made into a delicious sweet & covered in sugar (Agra)*
pis·taa ⓜ पिस्ता پستہ *pistachio*
pool go·*bee* ⓕ फूल गोभी پھول گوبھی *cauliflower*
poo·ree ⓕ पूड़ी پوڑی *deep-fried bread made from the same dough as* cha·*paa*·tee *• disc of dough that puffs up when deep fried – eaten with various stewed meats & vegetables (Uttar Pradesh)*
pu·*dee*·naa ⓜ पुदीना پدینا *mint*
pu·*laav* ⓜ पुलाव پلاؤ *pilau (rice dish flavoured with spices and cooked in stock – can include meat)*
pul·kaa ⓜ फुलका پھلکا *'puff' – small* ro·tee *baked so that it fills with hot air & puffs up like a balloon (Uttar Pradesh)*
pyaaz ⓜ प्याज़ پیاز *red onion • shallot*

R

raa·ee ⓕ राई رائے *black mustard seeds*
raai·taa ⓜ रायता رائتا *chilled plain curds combined with a number of vegetables or fruit*

raa·jaa mirch ⓕ राजा मिर्च راجہ مرچ *exceptionally hot chilli – makes a fiery pickle when mashed up with burnt dried fish (Nagaland)*

raaj·maa ⓜ राजमा راجمہ *red kidney bean*

rab·ree ⓕ रबड़ी ربڑی *sweet, thickened milk*

ras ⓜ रस رس *gravy • juice*

ra·sam ⓜ रसम رسم *'juice' – tamarind-flavoured vegetable broth, drunk from a glass or added to steamed white rice*

ras·daar chaa·val ⓜ रसदार चावल رسدار چاول *glutinous rice*

ras·gul·laa ⓜ रसगुल्ला رسگلا *'ball of juice' – spongy white balls of* pa·neer *that ooze sugar syrup (West Bengal)*

ro·gan josh ⓜ रोगन जोश روغن جوش *lamb or goat marinated in a rich, spicy sauce, generally flavoured with nutmeg & saffron (Jammu & Kashmir)*

roo·maa·lee ro·tee ⓕ रूमाली रोटी رومالی روٹی *'handkerchief bread' – large wholemeal bread thrown like a pizza base and eaten with kebabs*

ro·tee ⓕ रोटी روٹی *unleavened bread (also called* cha·paa·tee*)*

S

saa·boo daa·naa ⓜ साबूदाना سابو دانہ *sago (a starchy cereal)*

saa·boo daa·naa va·raa ⓜ साबूदाना वड़ा سابو دانہ وڑا *snack made from sago, potato & crushed peanuts, cooked as a patty & eaten with curds & chutney (Maharashtra)*

saa·daa paan ⓜ सादा पान سادا پان paan *with spices (not sweet)*

saag ⓜ साग ساگ *leafy greens*

saam·baar ⓜ साम्बार سامبر *spicy vegetable & lentil stew (South India)*

sab·zee ⓕ सब्ज़ी سبزی *vegetables, generally served with* daal

sa·fed sha·raab ⓕ सफ़ेद शराब سفید شراب *white wine*

sa·mo·saa ⓜ समोसा سموسا *deep-fried pyramid-shaped pastries filled with spiced vegetables & less often meat*

san·desh ⓜ संदेश سندیش *sweets made of* pa·neer *paste & cooked with sugar or jaggery (West Bengal)*

san·ta·raa ⓜ संतरा سنترا *mandarin*

sar·song ⓕ सरसों سرسوں *yellow mustard seed*

sar·song kaa saag ⓜ सरसों का साग سرسوں کا ساگ *spiced purée of mustard greens & spinach*

sar·song kaa tel ⓜ सरसों का तेल سرسوں کا تیل *mustard oil*

saungf ⓕ सौंफ़ سونف *aniseed (seeds are often coated in sugar to make a sweet snack) • fennel*

seb ⓜ सेब سیب *apple*

see·taa·pal ⓜ सीताफल سیتا پھل *pumpkin • squash*

sem ⓜ सेम سیم *haricot bean*

shaak ⓜ शाक شاک *vegetable curry (Gujarat)*

shaa·kaa·haa·ree शाकाहारी شاکاہاری *vegetarian food*

shaa·mee ka·baab ⓜ शामी कबाब شامی کباب *boiled mincemeat, ground with chickpeas & spices & shaped into cutlets (Uttar Pradesh)*

sha·kar·kand ⓜ शकरकंद شکر کند *sweet potatoes*

shal·gam ⓜ शलगम شلغم *parsnip • turnip*

sha·raab ⓕ शराब شراب *wine*

shar·bat ⓕ शरबत شربت *soft drink made with sugar & fruit • milk, almonds & rose petal dish offered by the bride's family to the groom's family (Bangalore)*

sha·ree·faa ⓜ शरीफ़ा شریفہ *custard apple*

sheesh ka·*baab* ⓜ शीश कबाब شیش کباب *shish kebab*
sheh·toot ⓜ शहतूत شہتوت *mulberry*
shim·laa mirch ⓕ शिमला मिर्च شملا مرچ *green capsicum*
shree·kand ⓜ श्रीखंड سریکھنڈ *'ambrosia of the gods' – dessert made from curds, sugar & cardamom garnished with slices of almond & rose petals (Gujarat)*
shree·pal ⓜ श्रीफल سریپھل *quince*
shud gee ⓜ शुद्ध घी شدھ گھی *pure* gee
shyut श्युत *pine nut*
sir·kaa ⓜ सिरका سرکا *vinegar*
si·vay·yaang ⓕ सिवैयाँ سویاں *'little worms' – Italian pasta, made into a milk pudding or fried in* gee *with raisins, flaked almonds & sugar to make a sweet, dry treat*
soo·jee ⓕ सूजी سوجی *semolina*
soo·jee kaa *hal*·vaa ⓜ सूजी का हलवा سوجی کا حلوا *semolina fried in* gee *with mixed dried fruits, icing sugar & milk (Punjab)*
so·yaa ⓜ सोया *dill*
su·*ar* ⓜ सुअर سؤر *wild boar*
su·ar kaa gosht ⓜ सुअर का गोश्त سؤر کا گوشت *bacon • pork*
su·*paa*·ree ⓕ सुपारी سپاری *betel nut*

T

ta·*laa aa*·loo ⓜ तला आलू تلا آلو *fried potato*
tam·*baa*·koo *vaa*·laa ⓜ तंबाकू वाला تمباکو والا paan *with tobacco (also called* zar·daa *vaa*·laa*)*
tan·*doo*·ree chi·*kan* ⓜ तंदूरी चिकन تندوری چکن *chicken marinated in spices & cooked in a clay oven (Punjab)*
tar·booz ⓜ तरबूज़ تربوز *watermelon*
tej *pat*·taa ⓜ तेज पा تیز پتّا *Indian bay leaves*
tel ⓜ तेल تیل *oil*
ti·*fan* ⓜ टिफ़न ٹفن *light meals or snacks eaten throughout the day*
til ⓜ तिल تل *sesame seed*
til kaa tel ⓜ तिल का तेल تل کا تیل *sesame oil*
til·kut ⓜ तिलकुट تلکٹ *thin rectangular wafers of crushed sesame seeds & sugar (Bihar)*
til *lad*·doo ⓜ तिल लड्डू تل لڈو *sesame balls sweetened with jaggery (Bihar)*
to·*foo* ⓜ टोफू ٹوفو *tofu*
tul·see *ban*·du ⓜ तुलसी बन्दू تلسی بندو *sage*
tu·*var* daal ⓕ तुवर दाल تور دال *yellow lentils, boiled with salt & turmeric, then flavoured with* gee *& jaggery – also known as* ar·har kee daal *(Maharashtra)*

U

ul·te ta·*ve* kee *ro*·tee ⓕ उल्टे तवे की रोटी الٹے تاوے کی روٹی *thin bread cooked on an upturned convex griddle (Andhra Pradesh)*
u·*rad* kee daal ⓕ उरद की दाल ارد کی دال *black lentil*

V

va·*nas*·pa·ti tel ⓜ वनस्पति तेल ونسپتی تیل *vegetable oil*
va·*raa* ⓜ वड़ा وڑا *balls of mashed lentils, fried & topped with seasoned curds*
vark ⓜ वर्क़ ورق *flavourless, edible silver foil used to decorate sweets such as* bar·fee

Z

zai·toon kaa tel ⓜ जैतून का तेल زیتون کا تیل *olive oil*
zar·daa *vaa*·laa ⓜ ज़रदा वाला زردہ والا *see* tam·*baa*·koo *vaa*·laa
zee·raa ⓜ ज़ीरा زیرہ *cumin seeds*
zoo·*kee*·nee ⓕ ज़ूकीनी زوکینی *zucchini*

emergencies

आपतकाल • امرجینسی

Help!	मदद कीजिये!	مدد کیجئے!	ma·*dad* *kee*·ji·ye
Stop that!	बस करो!	بس کرو!	bas ka·*ro*
Stop there!	रुको!	رکو!	ru·*ko*
Go away!	जाओ!	جاؤ!	*jaa*·o
Thief!	चोर!	چور!	chor
Fire!	आग!	آگ!	aag
Watch out!	ख़बरदार!	خبردار!	ka·*bar*·daar

signs

आपतकाल विभाग	امرجینسی کا شعبہ	ⓗ *aa*·pat·kaal vi·*baag* ⓤ i·mar·*jen*·see kaa *sho*·baa	**Emergency Department**
अस्पताल	بسپتال	ⓗ *as*·pa·taal ⓗ *has*·pa·taal	**Hospital**
पुलिस	پولیس	pu·*lis*	**Police**
थाना	تھانا	*taa*·naa	**Police Station**

Call the police.
पुलिस को बुलाओ। — pu·*lis* ko bu·*laa*·o
پولیس کو بلاؤ۔

Call a doctor.
डॉक्टर को बुलाओ। — *daak*·tar ko bu·*laa*·o
ڈاکڑر کو بلاؤ۔

Call an ambulance.
एम्बुलेन्स को बुलाओ। — *em*·bu·lens ko bu·*laa*·o
ایمبلینس کو بلاؤ۔

It's an emergency.
इमर्जेन्सी है। — i·mar·*jen*·see hay
امرجینسی ہے۔

There's been an accident.

दुर्घटना हुई है। ⓗ dur·*gat*·naa hu·*ee* hay

حادثہ ہوا ہے۔ ⓤ *haad*·saa hu·*aa* hay

Could you please help?

मदद कीजिये। ma·*dad kee*·ji·ye

مدد کیجئے۔

Can I use your phone?

क्या मैं फ़ोन कर सकता/सकती हूँ? kyaa mayng fon kar *sak*·taa/*sak*·tee hoong m/f

کیا میں فون کر سکتا/سکتی ہوں؟

I'm lost.

मैं रास्ता भूल गया/गयी हूँ। mayng *raas*·taa bool ga·*yaa*/ga·*yee* hoong m/f

میں راستہ بھول گیا/گئی ہوں۔

Where's the toilet?

टॉइलेट कहाँ है? *taa*·i·let ka·*haang* hay

ٹائلیٹ کہاں ہے؟

police

पुलिस • پولیس

Where's the police station?

थाना कहाँ है? *taa*·naa ka·*haang* hay

تھانا کہاں ہے؟

I want to report an offence.

एफ़० आई० आर० दर्ज कराना है। ef *aa*·ee aar darj ka·*raa*·naa hay

ایف-آئی-آر درج کرانا ہے۔

It was him/her.

उसने किया। *us*·ne ki·*yaa*

اسنے کیا۔

I have insurance.

मेरे पास बीमा है। *me*·re paas *bee*·maa hay

میرے پس بیما ہے۔

I've been assaulted.

मुझपर हमला हुआ। — *muj*·par *ham*·laa hu·*aa*

مجھ پر حملہ ہوا۔

I've been raped.

मेरे साथ बलात्कार हुआ। — ⓗ *me*·re saat ba·*laat*·kaar hu·*aa*

میری بیعزّتی ہوی۔ — ⓤ *me*·ree be·*iz*·za·tee hu·*ee*

I've been robbed.

मेरा सामान चोरी हुआ है। — *me*·raa *saa*·man *cho*·ree hu·*aa* hay

میرا سامان چوری ہوا ہے۔

I've been drugged.

मुझे नशीली दवा खिलायी गयी है। — mu·*je* na·*shee*·lee da·*vaa* ki·*laa*·yee ga·*yee* hay

مجھے نشیلی دوا کھلاۓ گئ ہے۔

My … was/were stolen.

… की चोरी हुई है। — … kee *cho*·ree hu·*ee* hay

… کی چوری ہوئ ہے۔

I've lost my …

… खो गया/गयी है। — … ko ga·*yaa*/ga·*yee* hay m/f

… کھو گیا/گئ ہے۔

backpack	बैकपैक	بیکپیک	*bayk*·payk
bags	बैग	بیگ	bayg
credit card	क्रेडिट कार्ड	کریڈٹ کارڈ	*kre*·dit kaard
handbag	झोला	جھولا	*jo*·laa
jewellery	गहने	گہنے	*geh*·ne
money	पैसे	پیسے	*pay*·se
papers	कागज़ात	کاغذات	*kaa*·ga·zaat
passport	पासपोर्ट	پاسپورٹ	*paas*·port
travellers cheques	ट्रेवलर्स चेक्स	ٹریولرس چیکس	*tre*·va·lars cheks
wallet	बटुआ	بٹوا	ba·tu·*aa*

What am I accused of?

मुझ पर क्या आरोप लगाया है? — ⓗ muj par kyaa *aa*·rop la·*gaa*·yaa hay

مجھ پر کیا الزام لگایا ہے؟ — ⓤ muj par kyaa *il*·zaam la·*gaa*·yaa hay

I didn't do it.

मैं ने नहीं किया। — mayng ne na·*heeng* ki·*yaa*

میں نے نہیں کیا۔

I didn't realise I was doing anything wrong.

मुझे मालूम नहीं था कि मैं ग़लत काम कर रहा था/रही थी।

مجھے معلوم نہیں تھا کہ میں غلط کام کر رہا تھا/رہی تھی۔

mu·*je maa*·loom na·*heeng* taa ki mayng ga·*lat* kaam kar ra·*haa* taa/ra·*hee* tee **m/f**

Can I pay an on-the-spot fine?

आपको अभी जुर्माना देकर क्या मामला ख़त्म नहीं कर सकते?

آپ کو ابھی جرمانا دے کر کیا معاملہ ختم نہیں کر سکتے؟

aap ko a·*bee* jur·*maa*·naa de kar kyaa *maam*·laa katm na·*heeng* kar *sak*·te

I want to contact my embassy.

मैं अपने दूतावास को फ़ोन करना चाहता/चाहती हूँ।

میں اپنے سفارتخانہ کو فون کرنا چاہتا/چاہتی ہوں۔

ⓗ mayng *ap*·ne doo·*taa*·vaas ko fon *kar*·naa *chaah*·taa/*chaah*·tee hoong **m/f**

ⓤ mayng *ap*·ne sa·*faa*·rat *kaa*·ne ko fon *kar*·naa *chaah*·taa/*chaah*·tee hoong **m/f**

Can I make a phone call?

क्या मैं फ़ोन कर सकता/सकती हूँ?

کیا میں فون کر سکتا/سکتی ہوں؟

kyaa mayng fon kar *sak*·taa/*sak*·tee hoong **m/f**

Can I have a lawyer (who speaks English)?

मुझे (अंग्रेज़ी बोलनेवाला) वकील चाहिये।

مجھے (انگریزی بولنے والا) وکیل چاہئے۔

mu·*je* (an·*gre*·zee *bol*·ne·*vaa*·laa) va·*keel chaa*·hi·ye

I have a prescription for this drug.

इस दवा के लिये मेरे पास नुसख़ा है।

اس دوا کے لئے میرے پاس نسخہ ہے۔

is da·*vaa* ke li·*ye me*·re paas *nus*·kaa hay

This drug is for personal use.

यह दवा मेरे निजी सेवन करने के लिये ही है।

یہ دوا میری نجی استعمال کے لئے ہی ہے۔

ⓗ yeh da·*vaa me*·re ni·*jee se*·van *kar*·ne ke li·*ye* hee hay

ⓤ yeh da·*vaa me*·re ni·*jee is*·te·maal ke li·*ye* hee hay

doctor

डॉक्टर • ڈاکٹر

Where's the nearest ...?

सब से क़रीब ... कहाँ है? — sab se ka·*reeb* ... ka·*haang* hay

سب سے قریب ... کہاں ہے؟

dentist	डेंटिस्ट	ڈینٹسٹ	*den*·tist
doctor	डॉक्टर	ڈاکٹر	*daak*·tar
emergency department	आपतकाल विभाग	امرجینسی کا شعبہ	ⓗ *aa*·pat·kaal vi·*baag* ⓤ i·mar·*jen*·see kaa *sho*·baa
hospital	अस्पताल	ہسپتال	ⓗ *as*·pa·taal ⓤ *has*·pa·taal
(Western) medical centre	(पाश्चात्य) मेडिकल सेंटर	(مغربی) میدکل سینٹر	ⓗ (*paash*·chaat·ya) *me*·di·kal *sen*·tar ⓤ (*mag*·ri·bee) *me*·di·kal *sen*·tar
optometrist	चश्मे की दुकान	چشمہ کی دکان	*chash*·me kee du·*kaan*
(night) pharmacist	(रात को खुलनेवाला) दवाख़ाना	(رات کو کھلنے والا) دواخانا	(raat ko *kul*·ne·*vaa*·laa) da·vaa·*kaa*·naa

I need a doctor (who speaks English).

मुझे (अंग्रेज़ी बोलनेवाला) डॉक्टर चाहिये। — mu·*je* (an·*gre*·zee *bol*·ne·*vaa*·laa) *daak*·tar *chaa*·hi·ye

مجھے (انگریزی بولنے والا) ڈاکٹر چاہئے۔

Could I see a female doctor?

मुझे लेडी डॉक्टर चाहिये। — mu·*je le*·dee *daak*·tar *chaa*·hi·ye

مجھے لیڈی ڈاکٹر چاہئے۔

Could the doctor come here?

क्या डॉक्टर यहाँ आ सकता है? — kyaa *daak*·tar ya·*haang* aa *sak*·taa hay

کیا ڈاکٹر یہاں آ سکتا ہے؟

I've run out of my medication.

मेरी दवा ख़त्म हुई है। — *me*·ree da·*vaa* katm hu·*ee* hay

میری دوا ختم ہوئ ہے۔

This is my usual medicine.

इस के लिये मैं आम तौर पर यह दवा लेता/लेती हूँ। — is ke li·*ye* mayng aam taur par yeh da·*vaa* *le*·taa/*le*·tee hoong m/f

اس کے لئے میں عام طور پر یہ دوا لیتا/لیتی ہوں۔

My prescription is ...

मेरा नुसख़ा ... है। — *me*·raa *nus*·kaa ... hay

میرا نسخہ ... ہے۔

I've been vaccinated against ...

... का टीका लग चुका है। — ... kaa *tee*·kaa lag *chu*·kaa hay

... کا ٹیکا لگ چکا ہے۔

hepatitis	हेपिटाइटिस	ہیپٹائٹس	he·pi·*taa*·i·tis
tetanus	टिटेनस	ٹٹینس	ti·*te*·nas
typhoid	टाइफ़ोयड्	ٹائفوئڈ	*taa*·i·foyd

Please use a new syringe/needle.

नई सुई इस्तेमाल कीजिए। — *na*·ee *su*·ee is·te·*maal* *kee*·ji·ye

نئ سوئ استعمال کیجئے۔

If you're after a receipt, see **money & banking**, page 71.

symptoms & conditions

लक्षण और बीमारियाँ • نشان اور بیماریاں

I'm sick.

मैं बीमार हूँ। — mayng *bee*·maar hoong

میں بیمار ہوں۔

He/She is having a/an ...

उसे ... हो रहा/रही है। — u·*se* ... ho ra·*haa*/ra·*hee* hay m/f

اسے ... ہو رہا/رہی ہے۔

asthma attack	दमे का दौरा	دمہ کا دورا	da·*me* kaa *dau*·raa
epileptic fit	मिरगी का दौरा	مرگی کا دورا	*mir*·gee kaa *dau*·raa
heart attack	दिल का दौरा	دل کا دورا	dil kaa *dau*·raa

He/She is having an allergic reaction.

उसे एलरजिक प्रतिक्रिया
हो रहा/रही है।
اسے ایلرجک ردّعمل
ہو راہا/رہی ہے۔

ⓗ u·se e·*lar*·jik pra·ti·*kri*·yaa
ho ra·*haa*/ra·*hee* hay **m/f**
ⓤ u·se e·*lar*·jik ra·*de*·a·mal
ho ra·*haa*/ra·*hee* hay **m/f**

I've been injured.

मुझे चोट लगी है।
مجھے چوٹ لگی ہے۔

mu·*je* chot la·*gee* hay

It hurts here.

इधर दर्द हो रहा है।
ادھر درد ہو رہا ہے۔

i·*dar* dard ho ra·*haa* hay

I've been vomiting.

मुझे उल्टी हो रही है।
مجھے الٹی ہو رہی ہے۔

mu·*je* *ul*·tee ho ra·*hee* hay

I feel nauseous.

उल्टी का एहसास हो रहा है।
الٹی کا احساس ہو رہا ہے۔

ul·tee kaa *eh*·saas ho ra·*haa* hay

I feel shivery.

कंपन हो रहा है।
کمپن ہو رہا ہے۔

kam·pan ho ra·*haa* hay

I feel dizzy.

चक्कर आ रहा है।
چکر آ رہا ہے۔

chak·kar aa ra·*haa* hay

I'm dehydrated.

बदन में पानी की कमी है।
بدن میں پانی کی کمی ہے۔

ba·*dan* meng *paa*·nee kee
ka·*mee* hay

I'm on medication for …

… के लिये दवा ले रहा/रही हूँ।
… کے لئے دوا لے رہا/رہی ہوں۔

… ke li·*ye* da·*vaa* le
ra·*haa*/ra·*hee* hoong **m/f**

I have (a/an) …

मुझे … है।
مجھے … ہے۔

mu·*je* … hay

I've recently had (a/an) …

मुझे हाल में … हुआ/हुई है।
مجھے حال میں … ہوا/ہوئی ہے۔

mu·*je* haal meng …
hu·*aa*/hu·*ee* hay **m/f**

AIDS f	एड्स की बीमारी	ایدس کی بیماری	eds kee bee·*maa*·ree
altitude sickness m	ऊँचाई से उल्टी का एहसास	اونچائ سے الٹی کا احساس	oon·*chaa*·ee se *ul*·tee kaa *eh*·saas
asthma m	दमा	دمہ	da·*maa*
bite (sting) m	डंक	ڈنک	dank
cold m	ज़ुकाम	زکام	zu·*kaam*
constipation m	कब्ज़	کبض	kabz
cough f	खाँसी	کھانسی	*kaan*·see
dengue fever m	डेंगू	لال بخار	ⓗ *deng*·goo ⓤ laal bu·*kaar*
diabetes m	मधुमेह	زیابیطس	ⓗ ma·du·*meh* ⓤ zi·*yaa*·bets
diarrhoea m	दस्त	دست	dast
dysentery f	डिसेंट्री	دسینٹری	di·*sen*·tree
fever m	बुख़ार	بخار	bu·*kaar*
headache m	सरदर्द	سر درد	*sar*·dard
lice f	जूँ	جوں	joong
malaria m	मलेरिया	ملیریا	ma·*le*·ri·yaa
nausea m	उल्टी का एहसास	الٹی کا احساس	*ul*·tee kaa *eh*·saas
pain m	दर्द	درد	dard
rash m	रैश	ریش	raysh
sore throat m	गले में दर्द	گلے میں درد	ga·*le* meng dard
sweating m	पसीना	پسینہ	pa·*see*·naa
worms m	पेट में कीड़े	پیٹ میں کیڑے	pet meng *kee*·re

two languages or one?

Although Hindi and Urdu are written in different scripts, they share a common core vocabulary. Therefore, most phrases in this book will be understood by both Hindi and Urdu speakers. Where phrases differ, however, you'll find the following signs before their pronunciation guides: ⓗ for Hindi and ⓤ for Urdu. The difference will generally be the substitution of a word of Sanskrit origin in the case of Hindi with a synonymous word of either Persian or Arabic origin in the case of Urdu.

parts of the body

बदन के अंग • بدن کے حصّے

My … hurts.
… में दर्द है।
… میں درد ہے۔
… meng dard hay

My … is swollen.
… सूज गया/गयी है।
… سوج گیا/گئی ہے۔
… sooj ga·*yaa*/ga·*yee* hay m/f

I can't move my …
मैं … हिला नहीं सकता/सकती।
میں ... ہلا نہیں سکتا/سکتی۔
mayng … hi·*laa* na·*heeng* *sak*·taa/*sak*·tee m/f

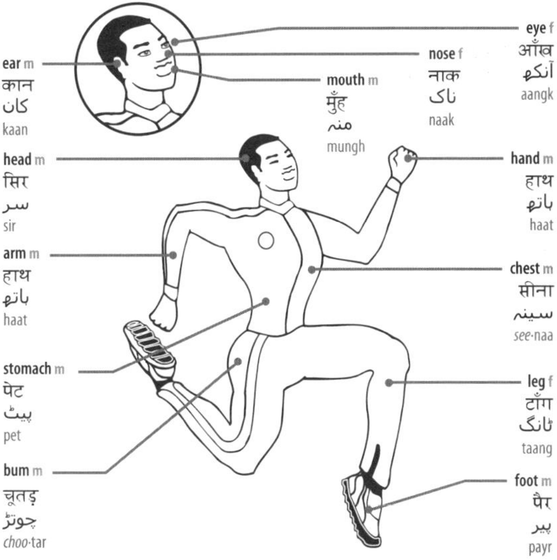

alternative treatments

वैकल्पिक रूपचार • دوسرے علاج

I don't use (Western medicine).

मैं (पाश्चात्य चिकित्सा) का इस्तेमाल नहीं करता/करती।
ⓗ mayng (paash·*chaat*·ya chi·*kit*·saa) kaa *is*·te·maal na·*heeng kar*·taa/*kar*·tee m/f

میں (مغربی علم طب) کا استعمال نہیں کرتا/کرتی۔
ⓤ mayng (*mag*·ri·bee *il*·me tab) kaa *is*·te·maal na·*heeng kar*·taa/*kar*·tee m/f

I prefer …

मैं … पसंद करता/करती हूँ।
میں … پسند کرتا/کرتی ہوں۔
mayng … pa·*sand kar*·taa/*kar*·tee hoong m/f

Can I see someone who practises (acupuncture)?

क्या (एक्यूपंक्चर) करनेवाले को दिखा सकता/सकती हूँ?
کیا (ایکیوپنکچر) کرنے والے کو دکھا سکتا/سکتی ہوں؟
kyaa (ek·yoo·*pank*·char) *kar*·ne·*vaa*·le ko di·*kaa sak*·taa/*sak*·tee hoong m/f

ayurvedic medicine m	आयुर्वेद	آیروید	*aar*·yu·ved
Greco-Islamic medicine f	युनानी चिकित्सा	یونانی علم طب	ⓗ yu·*naa*·nee chi·*kit*·saa ⓤ yu·*naa*·nee *il*·me tab
massage f	मालिश	مالش	*maa*·lish
meditating f	ध्यान लगाने की बात	دھیان لگانے کی بات	dyaan la·*gaa*·ne kee baat
reflexology f	रिफ्लैक्सोलोजी	رفلیکسلوجی	ri·flayk·so·*lo*·jee

allergies

एलरजी • ایلرجی

I have a skin allergy.

मुझे खाल की एलरजी है।
مجھے خال کی ایلرجی ہے۔
mu·*je* kaal kee e·*lar*·jee hay

I'm allergic to …

मुझे … की एलरजी है।
مجھے … کی ایلرجی ہے۔
mu·*je* … kee e·*lar*·jee hay

antibiotics m	एंटीबायोटिकिस	اینٹیبایوٹکس	*en*·tee·baa·*yo*·tiks
anti-inflammatories m	एंटी-इंफ्लैमिटोरीज़	اینٹی انفلیمٹوریز	*en*·tee in·flay·mi·*to*·rees
aspirin m	अस्प्रिन	اسپرن	*as*·prin
bees f	मधुमक्खी	مدھومکّھی	*ma*·du·*mak*·kee
codeine m	कोडीन	کوڈین	*ko*·deen
penicillin m	पैनसिलिन	پینسلن	*pay*·na·si·lin
pollen m	पराग	پراگ	pa·*raag*
sulphur-based drugs f	सल्फ़र से बनी दवा	سلفر سے بنی دوا	*sal*·far se ba·*nee* da·*vaa*

For food-related allergies, see **vegetarian & special meals**, page 119.

pharmacist

दवाख़ाना • دوا خانا

I need something for (a headache).

मुझे (सरदर्द) के लिये कुछ चाहिये।
مجھے (سردرد) کے لئے کچھ چاہئے۔
mu·*je* (*sar*·dard) ke li·*ye* kuch *chaa*·hi·ye

Do I need a prescription for (antihistamines)?

क्या (एंटीहिस्टेमीन्स) के लिये नुसख़ा चाहियें?
کیا (اینٹہسٹیمینس) کے لئے نسخہ چاہئے؟
kyaa (en·tee·his·*to*·meens) ke li·*ye* *nus*·kaa *chaa*·hi·ye

I have a prescription.

मेरे पास नुसख़ा है।
میرے پاس نسخہ ہے۔
me·re paas *nus*·kaa hay

How many times a day?

दिन में कितनी बार लेना है?
دن میں کتنی بار لینا ہے؟
din meng *kit*·nee baar *le*·naa hay

What's the correct dosage?

दिन में कितनी बार दवा लेनी है?
دن میں کتنی بار دوا لینی ہے؟
din meng *kit*·nee baar da·*vaa* *le*·nee hay

antiseptic m	एंटीसेप्टिक	اینٹیسیپٹک	en·tee·*sep*·tik
contraceptives m	कांट्रासेप्टिव्स	کانٹراسیپٹوس	kaan·traa·*sep*·tivs
painkillers f	दर्द दूर करनेवाली दवा	درد دور کرنے والی دوا	dard door *kar*·ne·*vaa*·lee da·*vaa*
rehydration salts m	रेहाइड्रेशन साल्ट्स	ریہائڈرشن سالٹس	re·haa·i·*dra*·shan saalts

dentist

डेंटिस्ट • ڈینٹسٹ

I have a broken tooth.
मेरा एक दांत टूट गया है।
میرا ایک دانت ٹوٹ گیا ہے۔
me·raa ek daant toot ga·*yaa* hay

I have a cavity.
एक दांत में छेद है।
ایک دانت میں چھید ہے۔
ek daant meng ched hay

I have a toothache.
दांत में दर्द है।
دانت میں درد ہے۔
daant men dard hay

I need a filling.
फ़िलिंग चाहिये।
فلنگ چاہئے۔
fi·*ling chaa*·hi·ye

I need an anaesthetic.
एनैस्थेटिक चाहिये।
اینیستھیٹک چاہئے۔
e·nays·*te*·tik *chaa*·hi·ye

My dentures are broken.
मेरे नकली दांत टूट गये हैं।
میرے نکلی دانت ٹوٹ گئے ہیں۔
me·re *nak*·lee daant toot ga·*ye* hayng

My gums hurt.
मसूड़े में दर्द है।
مسوڑے میں درد ہے۔
ma·*soo*·re meng dard hay

I don't want it extracted.
मैं दांत निकलवाना नहीं चाहता/चाहती।
میں دانت نکلوانا نہیں چاہتا/چاہتی۔
mayng daant ni·kal·*vaa*·naa na·*heeng chaah*·taa/*chaah*·tee m/f

DICTIONARY > english–hindi/urdu

Hindi and Urdu nouns and adjectives in this dictionary are in the direct case. Nouns have their gender marked as masculine ⓜ or feminine ⓕ, and the number as sg or pl where necessary. Those adjectives that change form for gender are in the masculine form (for more information on cases and gender, see the **phrasebuilder**). The symbols n, a and v (indicating noun, adjective and verb) have been added for clarity where an English term could be either. The pronunciation of the same Hindi and Urdu word is usually identical, so only one pronunciation guide is given in this dictionary. If a word is pronounced differently in each language, the Hindi pronunciation guide will follow the Devanagari script, and the Urdu pronunciation guide will come after the Arabic script. For food terms, see the **culinary reader**.

A

aboard सवार سوار sa·*vaar*
accident दुर्घटना dur·*gat*·naa ⓕ حادثہ *haad*·sah ⓜ
accommodation रहने की जगह رہنے کی جگہ *reh*·ne kee ja·*gah* ⓕ
across पार پار paar
adaptor अडप्टर اڈپٹر a·*dap*·tar ⓜ
address n पता پتہ pa·*taa* ⓜ
admission (price) प्रवेश शुल्क *pra*·vesh shulk ⓜ اندر جانے کا دام *an*·dar *jaa*·ne kaa daam ⓜ
Africa अफ़्रीका افریکا af·*ree*·kaa ⓜ
after बाद بعد baad
aftershave इत्र عطر i·*tra* ⓜ
again फिर से پھر سے pir se
air conditioner ए० सी० اے-سی e see ⓕ
airline हवाई जहाज़ की कम्पनी ہوائی جہاز کی کمپنی ha·*vaa*·ee ja·*haaz* kee *kam*·pa·nee ⓕ
airplane हवाई जहाज़ ہوائی جہاز ha·*vaa*·ee ja·*haaz* ⓜ
airport हवाई अड्डा ہوائی اڈّا ha·*vaa*·ee *ad*·daa ⓜ
airport tax प्रस्थान कर *pras*·taan kar ⓜ روانگی کا ٹیکس ra·*vaa*·na·gee kaa teks ⓜ
alarm clock अलार्म क्लॉक الارم کلاک a·*laarm* klak ⓜ
alcohol शराब شراب sha·*raab* ⓕ
all सब سب sab
allergy एलरजी ایلرجی e·*lar*·jee ⓕ
alone अकेला اکیلا a·*ke*·laa
ambulance एंबुलेन्स ایمبلینس *em*·bu·lens ⓜ
and और اور aur
ankle टखना ٹکھنا *tak*·naa ⓜ
antibiotics एंटिबायोटिक्स اینٹبایوٹکس en·ti·baa·*yo*·tiks ⓜ pl
antique a पुरातन pu·*raa*·tan قدیم ka·*deem*
antiseptic n एंटिसेप्टिक اینٹسیپٹک en·ti·*sep*·tik ⓜ
appointment अपाइंटमेंट اپائنٹمینٹ a·paa·*int*·ment ⓜ
architect वास्तुकार *vas*·tu·kaar ⓜ&ⓕ ارکیٹیکٹ *ar*·ka·tekt ⓜ&ⓕ
architecture वास्तुकला *vaa*·stu·ka·*laa* ⓕ تعمیرت کا علم taa·*mee*·raat kaa ilm ⓜ
arrivals (airport) आगमन *aa*·ga·man ⓜ sg آمد *aa*·mad ⓜ sg
arm बाज़ू بازو *baa*·zoo ⓜ
art कला ka·*laa* ⓜ فن fan ⓜ
art gallery कला संग्रहालय ka·*laa* san·gra·*haa*·lai ⓜ گیلری *ge*·la·ree ⓕ

A

english–hindi/urdu

artist कलाकार ka·*laa*·kaar ⓜ
فنکار *fan*·kaar ⓜ

ashtray राख़दान راخدان *raak*·daan ⓜ

Asia एशिया ائشیا e·*shi*·yaa ⓜ

aspirin एस्प्रिन ایسپرن *es*·prin ⓕ

assault हमला حملہ *ham*·laa ⓜ

aunt मौसी موسی *mau*·see ⓕ

Australia ऑस्ट्रेलिया آسٹریلیا
aas·*tre*·li·yaa ⓜ

automatic teller machine ए० टी० एम०
آئے-ٹی-ایم e tee em ⓕ

B

B&W (film) ब्लैक एंड व्हाइट
بلیک اینڈ وہائٹ blayk end *vhaa*·it

baby शिशु *shi*·shu ⓜ بچّہ *bach*·chaa ⓜ

baby food शिशु का खाना
shi·shu kaa *kaa*·naa ⓜ
بچّے کا کھانا *bach*·che kaa *kaa*·naa ⓜ

babysitter शिशु की देखभाल करने वाला
shi·shu kee *dek*·baal *kar*·ne *vaa*·laa ⓜ
بچّے کی دیکھبھال کرنے والا
bach·che kee *dek*·baal *kar*·ne *vaa*·laa ⓜ

back (body) पीठ پیٹھ peet ⓕ

backpack बैकपैक بیکپیک *bayk*·payk ⓜ

bad बुरा برا bu·*raa*

bag बैग بیگ bayg ⓜ

baggage सामान سامان *saa*·maan ⓜ

baggage allowance सामान के वज़न की
सीमा *saa*·maan ke va·*zan* kee *see*·maa ⓕ
سامان کے وزن کی حد *saa*·maan ke
va·*zan* kee had ⓕ

baggage claim सामान प्राप्ति *saa*·maan
praap·ti ⓕ بیگیج کلیم *bay*·gayj klaym ⓜ

bakery बेकरी بیکری be·ka·*ree* ⓕ

band बैंड بینڈ baynd ⓜ

bandage पट्टी پٹی *pat*·tee ⓕ

Band-Aid बैंड एड بینڈ آید baynd ayd ⓜ

Bangladesh बंगलादेश بنگلادیش
bang·*laa*·desh ⓜ

bank बैंक بینک baynk ⓜ

bank account बैंक का खाता
بینک کا کھاتا baynk kaa *kaa*·taa ⓜ

banknote बैंकनोट بینکنوٹ *baynk*·not ⓜ

bar बार بار baar ⓜ

bath बाथ باتھ baat ⓜ

bathroom बाथरूम باتھروم *baat*·room ⓜ

battery सेल سیل sel ⓜ

beach समुद्र का तट sa·*mud*·raa kaa tat ⓜ
سمندر کا ساحل
sa·*man*·dar kaa *saa*·hil ⓜ

beautiful सुन्दर *sun*·dar
خوبصورت koob·*soo*·rat

bed पलंग پلنگ pa·*lang* ⓜ

bedding बिस्तर بستر *bis*·tar ⓜ

bedroom सोने का कमरा
سونے کا کمرہ *so*·ne kaa *kam*·raa ⓜ

beer बियर بیر bi·*yar* ⓕ

before पहले پہلے *peh*·le

begin शुरू करना شروع کرنا
shu·*roo* *kar*·naa

behind पीछे پیچھے *pee*·che

Bengali (language) बंगला بنگلا *bang*·laa ⓕ

best सब से अच्छा سب سے اچّھا
sab se *ach*·chaa

better बेहतर بہتر *beh*·tar

bicycle साइकिल سائکل *saa*·i·kil ⓕ

big बड़ा بڑا ba·*raa*

bill n बिल بل bil ⓜ

birthday जन्मदिन *janm*·din ⓜ
سالگرہ *saal*·gi·rah ⓕ

black काला کالا *kaa*·laa

blanket कम्बल کمبل *kam*·bal ⓜ

blister छाला چھالہ *chaa*·laa ⓜ

blocked बंद بند band

blood ख़ून خون koon ⓜ

blood group ब्लडग्रुप بلاڈگرپ
blad·grup ⓜ

blue नीला نیلا *nee*·laa

board (ship etc) सवार करना سوار کرنا
sa·*vaar* *kar*·naa

boarding house गेस्ट हाउस گیسٹ باؤس gest *haa*·us ⓜ
boarding pass टिकट ٹکٹ ti·*kat* ⓜ
book n किताब کتاب ki·*taab* ⓕ
book v बुकिंग कराना بوکنگ کرانا bu·*king* ka·*raa*·naa
booked out (full) फुल فل ful
bookshop किताब की दुकान کتاب کی دکان ki·*taab* kee du·*kaan* ⓕ
boot बूट بوٹ boot ⓜ
border n सीमा سرحد *sar*·had ⓕ
boring बोर بور bor
both दोनों دونوں do·*nong*
bottle बोतल بوتل bo·*tal* ⓕ
bottle opener बोतल खोलने का औज़ार بوتل کھولنے کا اوزار bo·*tal kol*·ne kaa au·*zaar* ⓜ
bowl कटोरी کٹوری ka·*to*·ree ⓕ
box n बक्स بکس baks ⓜ
boy लड़का لڑکا *lar*·kaa ⓜ
boyfriend बॉय फ्रेंड بائ فرینڈ baai frend ⓜ
bra ब्रा برا braa ⓕ
brakes (car) ब्रेक بریک brek ⓜ sg
bread रोटी روٹی *ro*·tee ⓕ
breakfast नाश्ता ناشتہ *naash*·taa ⓜ
bridge पुल پل pul ⓜ
briefcase एटेची ایٹیچی e·*te*·chee ⓕ
broken टूटा ٹوٹا *too*·taa
brother भाई بھائ *baa*·ee ⓜ
brown भूरा بھورا *boo*·raa
building इमारत عمارت i·*maa*·rat ⓕ
burn n जलन جلن ja·*lan* ⓕ
bus बस بس bas ⓕ
business व्यापार *vyaa*·paar ⓜ کاروبار kaa·*ro*·baar ⓜ
business class बिज़नेस क्लास بزنیس کلاس *biz*·nes klaas ⓜ
business person व्यापारी vyaa·*paa*·ree ⓜ کاروباری kaa·ro·*baa*·ree ⓜ
bus station बस स्टेशन بس اسٹیشن bas *ste*·shan ⓜ
bus stop बस स्टॉप بس اسٹاپ bas *is*·taap ⓜ
busy व्यस्त vyast مصروف *mas*·roof
but लेकिन لیکن *le*·kin
butcher's shop कसाई की दुकान کسائ کی دوکان ka·*saa*·ee kee du·*kaan* ⓕ
button बटन بٹن ba·*tan* ⓜ
buy ख़रीदना خریدنا ka·*reed*·naa

C

café कैफ़े کیفے *kay*·fe ⓜ
calculator कैल्क्युलटर کیلکیولٹر kayl·*kyu*·la·tar ⓜ
camera कैमरा کیمرا *kaym*·raa ⓜ
camera shop कैमरा शॉप کیمرا شاپ *kaym*·raa shaap ⓜ
campsite डेरा ڈیرا *de*·raa ⓜ
can n टीन ٹین teen ⓜ
Canada कैनाडा کیناڈا kay·*naa*·daa ⓜ
cancel कैंसल करना کینسل کرنا *kayn*·sal *kar*·naa
can opener टीन खोलने का औज़ार ٹین کھولنے کا اوزار teen *kol*·ne kaa au·*zaar* ⓜ
car गाड़ी گاڑی *gaa*·ree ⓕ
car hire गाड़ी किराये पर लेना گاڑی کرائے پر لینا *gaa*·ree ki·*raa*·ye par *le*·naa ⓜ
car park n गाड़ी पार्क करने की जगह گاڑی پارک کرنے کی جگہ *gaa*·ree paark *kar*·ne kee ja·*gah* ⓕ
car registration कार रेजिस्ट्रेशन کار ریجسٹریشن kaar re·ji·*stre*·shan ⓜ
cash (money) n नक़द نقد na·*kad* ⓜ
cash (a cheque) v कैश करना کیش کرنا kaysh *kar*·naa
cashier कैशियर کیشیر *kay*·shi·yar ⓜ

cassette कैसेट کیسیٹ *kay*·set (m)
castle किला قلعہ ki·*laa* (m)
Catholic कैथोलिक کیتھولک kay·*to*·lik
CD सी० डी० سی-ڈی see dee (f)
cell phone सेल फ़ोन سیل فون sel fon (m)
cemetery क़ब्रिस्तान قبرستان ka·*bri*·staan (m)
centimetre सेंटिमीटर سینٹمیٹر sen·ti·*mee*·tar (m)
centre केंद्र *ken*·dra (m) مرکز *mar*·kaz (m)
chair कुर्सी کرسی *kur*·see (f)
change (money) v भूनाना بھونانا boo·*naa*·naa
change v बदलना بدلنا ba·*dal*·naa
changing room कपड़े बदलने का कमरा کپڑے بدلنے کا کمرہ *kap*·re ba·*dal*·ne kaa *kam*·raa (m)
cheap सस्ता سستہ *sas*·taa
check (bank) n चेक چیک chek (m)
check (bill) n बिल بل bil (m)
check-in n चेक-इन چیک ان chek in (m)
chef ख़ानसामा خانساماں kaan·*saa*·maa (m)
chemist (pharmacy) दवाख़ाना دواخانا da·vaa·*kaa*·naa (m)
chest (body) सीना سینہ *see*·naa (m)
chicken मुर्ग़ी مرغی *mur*·gee (f)
child बच्चा بچّہ *bach*·chaa (m)
children बच्चे بچّہ *bach*·che (m)
child seat बच्चे की कुर्सी بچّوں کی کرسی *bach*·che kee *kur*·see (f)
China चीन چین cheen (m)
church गिरजा گرجا *gir*·jaa (m)
cigarette सिगरेट سگریٹ *sig*·ret (f)
cigarette lighter लाइटर لائٹر *laa*·i·tar (m)
cinema सिनेमा سنیمہ si·*ne*·maa (m)
circus सर्कस سرکس *sar*·kas (m)
citizenship नागरिकता naag·*rik*·taa (f) شہریت *sha*·ha·ri·yat (f)

city शहर شہر sha·*har* (m)
city centre शहर का केंद्र sha·*har* kaa *ken*·dra (m) شہر کا مرکز sha·*har* kaa *mar*·kaz (m)
classical शास्त्रीय shaas·*tree*·ya کلاسکی *klaa*·si·kee
clean a साफ़ صاف saaf
cleaning n सफ़ाई صفائ sa·*faa*·ee (f)
client गाहक گاہک *gaa*·hak (m)
cloakroom क्लोकरूम کلوکروم *klok*·room (m)
close v बंद करना بند کرنا band *kar*·naa
closed बंद بند band
clothing कपड़े کپڑے *kap*·re (m)
clothing store कपड़े की दुकान کپڑے کی دکان *kap*·re kee du·*kaan* (f)
coast समुद्र का तट sa·mu·*dra* kaa tat (m) سمندر کا ساحل sa·*man*·dar kaa *saa*·hil (m)
coffee कॉफ़ी کافی *kaa*·fee (f)
coins (change) सिक्के سکّے *sik*·ke (m) pl
cold (illness) n ज़ुकाम زکام zu·*kaam* (m)
cold (weather) n सर्दी سردی *sar*·dee (f)
colleague सहयोगी seh·*yo*·gee (m)&(f) ہمجولی *ham*·jo·lee (m)&(f)
collect call कलेक्ट कॉल کلیکٹ کال ka·*lekt* kaal (m)
colour रंग رنگ rang (m)
comb n कंघी کنگھی *kan*·gee (f)
come (arrive) आना آنا *aa*·naa
comfortable आरामदायक *aa*·raam·daa·yak آرامدہ *aa*·raam·deh
company (companions) साथ ساتھ saat (m)
complaint n शिकायत شکایت shi·*kaa*·yat (f)
computer कम्प्यूटर کمپیوٹر kam·*pyoo*·tar (m)
concert कॉन्सर्ट کانسرٹ *kaan*·sart (m)
conditioner कंडिशनर کنڈشنر *kan*·di·sha·nar (m)
condom कांडम کنڈم *kaan*·dam (m)
confirm कनफ़र्म करना کنفرم کرنا *kan*·farm *kar*·naa

C

DICTIONARY

connection सम्पर्क *sam*·park ⓜ جوڑ jor ⓜ
constipation कब्ज़ قبض kabz ⓜ
consulate दूतावास doo·*taa*·vaas ⓜ سفارتخانا sa·*faa*·rat *kaa*·naa ⓜ
contact lens कांटेक्ट लेन्स کانٹیکٹ لینس *kaan*·tekt lens ⓜ
convenience store परचून की दुकान پرچوں کی دکان *par*·choon kee du·*kaan* ⓕ
cook v पकाना پکانا pa·*kaa*·naa
corkscrew बोतल खोलने वाला औज़ार بوتل کھولنے والا اوزار bo·*tal kol*·ne *vaa*·laa *au*·zaar ⓜ
cost n दाम daam ⓜ دام *kee*·mat ⓕ
cotton रुई روئی ru·*ee* ⓕ
cotton balls रुई के गोले روئی کا گولے ru·*ee* ke *go*·le ⓜ pl
cough n खाँसी کھانسی *kaan*·see ⓕ
cough medicine खाँसी की दवा کھانسی کی دوا *kaang*·see kee da·*vaa* ⓕ
countryside देहात دیہات de·*haat* ⓜ
cover charge प्रवेश शुल्क *pra*·vesh shulk ⓜ اندر جانے کا قیمت *an*·dar *jaa*·ne kee *kee*·mat ⓕ
crafts (art) हस्तकलाएँ hast·ka·*laa*·eng ⓕ دستکاری das·taa·*kaa*·ree ⓕ
crèche क्रेश کریس kresh ⓜ
credit card क्रेडिट कार्ड کریڈٹ کارڈ *kre*·dit kaard ⓜ
cricket (sport) क्रिकेट کرکیٹ *kri*·ket
cup कप کپ kap ⓜ
currency exchange मुद्रा विनिमय mu·*dra* vi·ni·*mai* ⓜ کرنسی ایکسچینج ka·*ran*·see *eks*·chenj ⓜ
current (electricity) बिजली بجلی *bij*·lee ⓕ
customs (immigration) सीमाधिकार see·*maa*·di·kaar ⓜ کسٹمس *kas*·tams ⓜ
cut v कटना کٹنا *kat*·naa
cutlery काँटा छूरी کانٹا چھوری *kaan*·taa *choo*·ree

D

daily रोज़ روز roz
dance n नाच ناچ naach ⓜ
dance v नाचना ناچنا *naach*·naa
dangerous ख़तरनाक خطرناک ka·*tar*·naak
dark अंधेरा اندھیرا an·*de*·raa ⓜ
date of birth जन्मदिन *janm*·din ⓜ پیدائش کا روز pay·*daa*·ish kaa roz ⓜ
date (time) तारीख़ تاریخ *taa*·reek ⓕ
daughter बेटी بیٹی *be*·tee ⓕ
dawn पौ پو pau ⓜ
day दिन din ⓜ روز roz ⓜ
delay n देर دیر der ⓕ
deliver पहुँचाना پہنچانا pa·hun·*chaa*·naa
dental floss डेंटल फ्लास ڈینٹل فلاس *den*·tal flaas ⓜ
dentist डेंटिस्ट ڈینٹسٹ *den*·tist ⓜ&ⓕ
deodorant डिओडरंट ڈیوڈرنٹ di·*o*·da·rant ⓜ
depart (leave) प्रस्थान करना *pra*·staan *kar*·naa روانہ ہونا ra·*vaa*·nah *ho*·naa
department store डिपार्टमेंट स्टोर ڈپارٹمینٹ سٹور di·*paart*·ment stor ⓜ
departure प्रस्थान *pra*·staan ⓜ روانگی ra·*vaa*·na·gee ⓕ
deposit n डिपोज़िट ڈپوزٹ di·*po*·zit ⓜ
destination मंज़िल منزل *man*·zil ⓕ
Dhaka ढाका ڈھاکا *daa*·kaa ⓜ
diabetes मधुमेह ma·du·*meh* ⓜ ذیابیطس da·yaa·*bee*·tis ⓜ
diaper (nappy) नैपी نیپی *nay*·pee ⓕ
diaphragm डायफ्रैम ڈایفریم *daa*·ya·fraym ⓜ
diarrhoea दस्त دست dast ⓜ
diary डायरी ڈائری *daai*·ree ⓕ
dictionary कोश kosh ⓜ لغت lu·*gat* ⓜ
different अलग a·*lag* مختلف *muk*·ta·lif
dining car डाइनिंग कार ڈائننگ کار *daa*·i·ning kaar ⓕ

dinner रात का खाना رات کا کھانا
raat kaa *kaa*·naa ⓜ
direct a सीधा سیدھا *see*·daa
direct-dial डाइरेक्ट डायल
ڈائریکٹ ڈائل *daa*·i·rekt *daa*·yal
dirty गंदा گندہ *gan*·daa
disabled विकलांग vi·ka·*laang* اپاہج a·*paa*·hij
discount n छूट چھوٹ choot ⓕ
disk (CD/floppy) डिस्क ڈسک disk ⓕ
doctor डॉक्टर ڈاکٹر *daak*·tar ⓜ&ⓕ
dog कुत्ता کتّہ *kut*·taa ⓜ
dollar डॉलर ڈالر *daa*·lar ⓜ
dope (hashish) चरस چرس cha·*ras* ⓜ
double bed डबल बेड ڈبل بیڈ da·*bal* bed ⓜ
double room डबल कमरा ڈبل کمرا
da·*bal kam*·raa ⓜ
down नीचे نیچے *nee*·che
dress n ड्रेस ڈریس dres ⓜ
drink n पीने की चीज़ें
پینے کی چیزیں *pee*·ne kee *chee*·zeng ⓕ
drink v पीना پینا *pee*·naa
drive v चलाना چلانا cha·*laa*·naa
drivers licence गाड़ी चलाने का लाइसेंस
گاڑی چلانے کا لائسینس
gaa·ree cha·*laa*·ne kaa *laa*·i·sens ⓜ
drug (illegal) नशीली दवा نشیلی دوا
na·*shee*·lee da·*vaa* ⓕ
drunk नशे में धुत
نشے میں دھت na·*she* meng dut
dry a सूखा سوکھا *soo*·kaa
dummy (pacifier) डमी ڈمی da·*mee* ⓕ

E

each सब سب sab
ear कान کان kaan ⓜ
early जल्दी جلدی *jal*·dee
earplug इयर-प्लग ائر پلگ i·*yar* plag ⓜ
earrings बालियाँ بالیاں *baa*·li·yaang ⓕ pl
east n पूर्व *poor*·va ⓜ مشرق *mash*·rik ⓜ
eat खाना کھانا *kaa*·naa
economy class इकॉनमी क्लास
اکانمی کلاس i·*kaa*·na·mee klaas ⓜ
electrical store बिजली की दुकान
بجلی کی دکان *bij*·lee kee du·*kaan* ⓕ
electricity बिजली بجلی *bij*·lee ⓕ
elevator लिफ़्ट لفٹ lift ⓜ
email ई मेल ای میل ee mayl ⓕ
embassy दूतावास doo·*taa*·vaas ⓜ
سفارتخانہ sa·*faa*·rat *kaa*·naa ⓜ
emergency आपत *aa*·pat ⓕ
امرجینسی i·mar·*jen*·see ⓕ
empty a ख़ाली خالی *kaa*·lee
end n अन्त ant ⓜ خاتمہ kaa·ta·*mah* ⓜ
engagement मंगनी منگنی *mang*·nee ⓕ
engine इंजन انجن *in*·jan ⓜ
engineer इंजीनियर بنجینیر
in·*jee*·ni·yar ⓜ&ⓕ
England इंग्लैंड انگلینڈ *in*·glaynd ⓜ
English (language) अंग्रेज़ी انگریزی
an·*gre*·zee ⓕ
enough काफ़ी کافی *kaa*·fee
enter अन्दर जाना اندر جانا *an*·dar *jaa*·naa
envelope लिफ़ाफ़ा لفافہ li·*faa*·faa ⓜ
Europe यूरोप یوروپ *yoo*·rop ⓜ
evening शाम شام shaam ⓕ
everything सब कुछ سب کچھ sab kuch
exchange n बदलाव بدلاو *bad*·laav ⓜ
exchange (money) v बदलना بدلنا ba·*dal*·naa
exchange rate विनिमय दर vi·ni·*mai* dar ⓕ
ایکسچینج ریٹ *eks*·chenj ret ⓜ
exhibition प्रदर्शनी pra·*dar*·sha·nee ⓕ
نمائش nu·*maa*·ish ⓕ
exit n निकास نکاس ni·*kaas* ⓜ
expensive महंगा مہنگا ma·*han*·gaa
express mail एक्स्प्रेस मेल
ایکسپریس میل *eks*·pres mel ⓕ
eye आँख آنکھ aangk ⓕ

F

face n मुख muk ⓜ چہرہ *cheh*·raa ⓜ
fall v गिरना گرنا *gir*·naa

family परिवार pa·ri·*vaar* Ⓜ
خاندان *kaan*·daan Ⓜ
fan (machine) पंखा پنکھا *pan*·kaa Ⓜ
far दूर دور door
fast a जल्दी جلدی *jal*·dee
fast v व्रत vrat روزہ رکھنا *ro*·zaa *rak*·naa
fat a मोटा موٹا *mo*·taa
father पिता pi·*taa* Ⓜ والد *vaa*·lid Ⓜ
father-in-law ससुर سسر sa·*sur* Ⓜ
faulty ख़राब خراب ka·*raab*
feel एहसास होना احساس ہونا
eh·saas *ho*·naa
feelings भावनाएँ baav·*naa*·eng Ⓕ pl
جزبات *jaz*·baat Ⓕ pl
festival त्यौहार *tyau*·haar Ⓜ جشن jashn Ⓜ
fever बुख़ार بخار bu·*kaar* Ⓜ
fiancé/fiancée मंगेतर منگیتر
man·*ge*·tar Ⓜ&Ⓕ
film (cinema) फ़िल्म فلم film Ⓕ
film speed फ़िल्म की स्पीड
فلم کی سپیڈ film kee speed Ⓕ
fine a महीन مہین ma·*heen*
finger उँगली انگلی *ung*·lee Ⓕ
first पहला پہلا *peh*·laa
first-aid kit फ़र्स्ट एड किट
فرسٹ ایڈ کٹ farst ed kit Ⓜ
first-class (ticket) प्रथम श्रेणी *pra*·tam *shre*·nee
اوّل درجہ *av*·val *dar*·jaa
first name पहला नाम پہلا نام
peh·laa naam Ⓜ
fish मछली مچھلی *mach*·lee Ⓕ
fish shop मछली की दुकान
مچھلی کی دکان
mach·lee kee du·*kaan* Ⓕ
fishing n मछली पकड़ना مچھلی پکڑنا
mach·lee pa·*kar*·naa Ⓜ
flashlight (torch) टॉर्च ٹارچ taarch Ⓜ
floor फ़र्श فرش farsh Ⓜ
flower फूल پھول pool Ⓜ
fly v उड़ना اڑنا *ur*·naa
food खाना کھانا *kaa*·naa Ⓜ
foot (body) पैर پیر payr Ⓜ
football (soccer) फ़ुटबॉल فٹبال *fut*·baal Ⓜ
footpath पैदलपथ پیدل پتھ *pay*·dal·pat Ⓜ
foreign विदेशी vi·*de*·shee
غیر ملکی gayr *mul*·kee
forest जंगल جنگل *jan*·gal Ⓜ
forever हमेशा के लिये ہمیشہ کے لئے
ha·*me*·shaa ke li·*ye*
fork काँटा کانٹا *kaan*·taa Ⓜ
fortnight पखवाड़ा پکھواڑا pak·*vaa*·raa Ⓜ
fragile नाज़ुक نازک *naa*·zuk
free (available) आज़ाद آزاد *aa*·zaad
free (gratis) मुफ़्त مفت muft
friend दोस्त دوست dost Ⓜ&Ⓕ
fruit फल پھل pal Ⓜ
fry तलना تلنا *tal*·naa
frying pan कड़ाई کڑائی ka·*raa*·ee Ⓕ
full भरा हुआ بھرا ہوا ba·*raa* hu·*aa*
funny मज़ाकिया ma·*jaa*·ki·yaa
مذاقیہ ma·*zaa*·ki·yah
furniture फ़र्निचर فرنچر *far*·ni·char Ⓜ
future n भविष्य ba·*vi*·shya Ⓜ
مستقبل mus·*tak*·bil Ⓜ

G

gas (petrol) पेट्रोल پیٹرول *pet*·rol Ⓜ
gay ख़ुश خوش koosh
Germany जर्मनी جرمنی *jar*·ma·nee Ⓕ
gift तोहफ़ा تہفہ *toh*·faa Ⓜ
girl लड़की لڑکی *lar*·kee Ⓕ
girlfriend गर्लफ़्रेंड گرل فرینڈ *garl*·frend Ⓕ
glass (drinking) गिलास گلاس glaas Ⓜ
glasses चश्मा *chash*·maa Ⓜ عینک *ay*·nak Ⓕ
gloves दस्ताने دستانہ das·*taa*·ne Ⓜ pl
go जाना جانا *jaa*·naa
good a अच्छा اچّھا *ach*·chaa
go out with किसी के साथ जाना
کسی کے ساتھ جانا
ki·*see* ke saat *jaa*·naa

go shopping ख़रीदारी करने जाना خریداری کرنے جانا ka·ree·*daa*·ree *kar*·ne *jaa*·naa
gram ग्राम گرام graam ⓜ
grandchild पोता پوتا *po*·taa ⓜ
grandfather (maternal) नाना نانا *naa*·naa ⓜ
grandfather (paternal) दादा دادا *daa*·daa ⓜ
grandmother (maternal) नानी نانی *naa*·nee ⓕ
grandmother (paternal) दादी دادی *daa*·dee ⓕ
great बढ़िया بڑھیا ba·ri·*yaa*
green हरा ہرا ha·*raa*
grey स्लेटी रंग का سلیٹی رنگ کا *sle*·tee rang kaa
grocery सामान سامان *saa*·maan ⓜ
grow उगना اگنا *ug*·naa
guide (person) गाइड گائڈ *gaa*·id ⓜ&ⓕ
guidebook गाइडबुक گائڈبک *gaa*·id·buk ⓜ
guided tour गाइडेड टूर گائڈیڈ ٹور *gaai*·ded toor ⓜ

H

hairdresser नाई نائی *naa*·ee ⓜ
half आधा آدھا *aa*·daa
hand हाथ ہاتھ haat ⓜ
handbag हैंडबैग ہینڈبیگ *haynd*·bayg ⓜ
handicrafts हस्तकलाएँ hast·ka·*laa*·eng ⓕ pl دستکاری کی چیزیں das·ta·*kaa*·ree kee *chee*·zeng ⓕ pl
handmade हाथ से बना ہاتھ سے بنا haat se ba·*naa*
handsome सुन्दर *sun*·dar خوبصورت koob·*soo*·rat
happy ख़ुश خوش kush
hard (difficult) सख़्त سخت sakt
hat टोपी ٹوپی *to*·pee ⓕ
head सिर سر sir ⓜ
headache सरदर्द سردرد *sar*·dard ⓜ
headlights गाड़ी की बत्ती گاڑی کی بتّی *gaa*·ree kee *bat*·tee ⓕ sg
heart दिल دل dil ⓜ
heart condition दिल की बीमारी دل کی بیماری dil kee bee·*maa*·ree ⓕ
heat n गर्मी گرمی *gar*·mee ⓕ
heater हीटर ہیٹر *hee*·tar ⓜ
heavy भारी بھاری *baa*·ree
help v मदद करना مدد کرنا ma·*dad kar*·naa
here यहाँ یہاں ya·*haang*
high ऊँचा اونچا *oon*·chaa
hike n हाइक ہائک *haa*·ik ⓜ
hiking हाइकिंग ہائکنگ *haai*·king ⓕ
Hindi (language) हिन्दी ہندی *hin*·dee ⓕ
Hindu हिन्दू ہندو *hin*·doo
hire v किराये पर लेना کرائے پر لینا ki·*raa*·ye par *le*·naa
hitchhike हिचहाइक करना ہچہائک کرنا *hich*·haa·ik *kar*·naa
holidays (vacation) छुट्टी چھٹّی *chut*·tee ⓕ
homosexual a समलैंगिक sam·*layn*·gik ہمجنس پرست *ham*·jins pa·*rast*
honeymoon हनीमून ہنیمون ha·*nee*·moon ⓜ
hospital अस्पताल *as*·pa·taal ⓜ ہسپتال *has*·pa·taal ⓜ
hot गर्म گرم garm
hotel होटल ہوٹل *ho*·tal ⓜ
hungry भूखा بھوکا *boo*·kaa
husband पति *pa*·ti ⓜ شوہر *shau*·har ⓜ

I

I मैं میں mayng
ice बर्फ़ برف barf ⓕ
ice cream कुल्फ़ी قلفی *kul*·fee ⓕ
identification परिचय pa·ri·*chai* ⓜ پہچان *peh*·chaan ⓕ
ill बीमार بیمار *bee*·maar
important अहम اہم a·*ham*
included शामिल شامل *shaa*·mil

India इंडिया انڈیا in·*di*·yaa ⓜ
indigestion बदहज़मी بدہضمی bad·ha·za·*mee* ⓕ
influenza फ़्लू فلو floo ⓜ
injection सुई سوئی su·*ee* ⓕ
injury चोट چوٹ chot ⓕ
insurance बीमा بیما *bee*·maa ⓜ
Internet इंटरनेट انٹرنیٹ in·*tar*·net ⓜ
Internet café इंटरनेट कैफ़े انٹرنیٹ کیفے in·*tar*·net *kay*·fe ⓜ
interpreter दुभाषिया du·*baa*·shi·yaa ⓜ&ⓕ ترجمان *tar*·ja·maan ⓜ&ⓕ
Ireland आयरलैंड آئرلینڈ aa·*yar*·laynd ⓜ
iron n लोहा لوہا *lo*·haa ⓜ
Islamabad इस्लामाबाद اسلام آباد is·*laam*·aa·baad
island टापू ٹاپو *taa*·poo ⓜ
itch n खुजली کھوجلی *kuj*·lee ⓕ
itinerary यात्रा का कार्यक्रम *yaa*·traa kaa *kaar*·ya·kram ⓜ سفر نامہ sa·*far* *naa*·mah ⓜ

J

jacket जाकेट جاکیٹ *jaa*·ket ⓜ
Japan जापान جاپان jaa·*paan* ⓜ
jewellery shop ज़ेवरात की दुकान زیورات کی دکان *zev*·raat kee du·*kaan* ⓕ
job नौकरी نوکری *nauk*·ree ⓕ
journalist पत्रकार *pa*·tra·kaar ⓜ&ⓕ اخبار نویس *ak*·baar na·*vees* ⓜ&ⓕ
jumper (sweater) स्वेटर سویٹر *sve*·tar ⓜ

K

key चाबी چابی *chaa*·bee ⓕ
kilogram किलोग्राम کلوگرام ki·*lo*·graam ⓜ
kilometre किलोमीटर کلومیٹر ki·lo·*mee*·tar ⓜ
kitchen रसोई رسوئی ra·*so*·ee ⓕ
knee घुटना گھٹنا *gut*·naa ⓜ
knife चाकू چاقو *chaa*·koo ⓜ

L

lake ताल تال taal ⓜ
language भाषाएँ baa·*shaa*·eng ⓕ pl زبانیں za·*baa*·neng ⓕ pl
laptop लैपटॉप لیپ ٹاپ *layp*·taap ⓜ
late (not early) देर دیر der
laundry (clothes) धुलाई دھلائی du·*laa*·ee ⓕ
law क़ानून قانون *kaa*·noon ⓜ
lawyer वकील وکیل va·*keel* ⓜ&ⓕ
leather चमड़ा چمڑا *cham*·raa ⓜ
left luggage (office) सामान रखने की जगह سامان رکھنے کی جگہ *saa*·maan *rak*·ne kee ja·*gah* ⓕ
leg भ५ ٹانگ taangg ⓕ
lens लेन्स لینس lens ⓜ
lesbian लेज़्बियन لیزبین *lez*·bi·yan ⓕ
less कम کم kam
letter (mail) पत्र pa·*tra* ⓜ خط kat ⓜ
library पुस्तकालय pus·ta·*kaa*·lai ⓜ کتب خانہ ka·*tab* *kaa*·nah ⓜ
life jacket लाइफ़जॉकेट لائفجاکیٹ *laa*·if·*jaa*·ket ⓜ
lift (elevator) लिफ़्ट لفٹ lift ⓜ
light n रोशनी روشنی *rosh*·nee ⓕ
light (weight) a हल्का ہلکا *hal*·kaa
lighter (cigarette) लाइटर لائٹر *laa*·i·tar ⓜ
line लकीर لکیر la·*keer* ⓕ
lipstick लिपस्टिक لپسٹک *lip*·stik ⓕ
liquor store शराब की दुकान شراب کی دکان sha·*raab* kee du·*kaan* ⓕ
listen सुनना سننا *sun*·naa
local a लोकल لوکل *lo*·kal
lock n ताला تالا *taa*·laa ⓜ
locked बन्द بند band
long लम्बा لمبا *lam*·baa
lost खोया हुआ کھویا ہوا *ko*·yaa hu·*aa*
lost property office लावारिस सामान का दफ़्तर لاوارث سامان کا دفتر laa·*vaa*·ris *saa*·maan kaa *daf*·tar ⓜ

love n प्यार pyaar ⓜ محبّت mu·*hob*·bat ⓕ
lubricant तेल تیل tel ⓜ
luggage सामान سامان *saa*·maan ⓜ
lunch दिन का खाना دن کا کھانا din kaa *kaa*·naa ⓜ
luxury n ऐश्वर्य aysh·*var*·ya ⓜ عیاشی ay·*yaa*·shee ⓕ

M

mail (post) n डाक ڈاک daak ⓕ
mailbox मेलबक्स میلبکس *mayl*·baks ⓜ
make-up n मेक अप میک اپ mayk ap ⓜ
man आदमी آدمی *aad*·mee ⓜ
manager प्रबंधक pra·*ban*·dak ⓜ منیجر ma·*ne*·jar ⓜ
map नक्शा نقشہ *nak*·shaa ⓜ
market बाज़ार بازار *baa*·zaar ⓜ
marry शादी करना شادی کرنا *shaa*·dee *kar*·naa
massage v मालिश करना مالش کرنا *maa*·lish *kar*·naa
masseur/masseuse मालिश करनेवाला مالش کرنےوالا *maa*·lish *kar*·ne·*vaa*·laa ⓜ&ⓕ
match (sports) खेल کھیل kel ⓜ
matches (cigarette) माचिस ماچس *maa*·chis ⓜ
mattress बिस्तर بستر *bis*·tar ⓜ
measles छोटी माता چھوٹی ماتا *cho*·tee *maa*·taa ⓕ
meat गोश्त گوشت gosht ⓜ
medicine (medication) दवा دوا da·*vaa* ⓕ
menu मेन्यू مینیو *men*·yoo ⓜ
message संदेश *san*·desh ⓜ پیغام *pay*·gaam ⓜ
metre मीटर میٹر *mee*·tar ⓜ
midnight रात के बारह बजे رات کے بارہ بجے raat ke *baa*·rah ba·*je* ⓕ
milk दूध دودھ dood ⓜ
millimetre मिलिमीटर ملیمیٹر mi·li·*mee*·tar ⓜ
mineral water मिनरल वाटर منرل واٹر *min*·ral *vaa*·tar ⓜ
minute मिनट منٹ mi·*nat* ⓜ
mirror आइना آئینہ *aa*·i·naa ⓜ
mobile phone सेल फ़ोन سیل فون sel fon ⓜ
money पैसे پیسے *pay*·se ⓜ
month महीना مہینہ ma·*hee*·naa ⓜ
morning (6am–1pm) सवेरा سویرا sa·*ve*·raa ⓜ
mother माँ maang ⓕ امّیجان *am*·mee·jaan ⓕ
mother-in-law सास ساس saas ⓕ
motorcycle मोटरसाइकिल موٹرسائکل *mo*·tar·*saa*·i·kil ⓕ
motorway मोटरवे موٹروے mo·*tar*·ve ⓜ
mountain पर्वत *par*·vat ⓜ پہاڑ pa·*haar* ⓜ
mouth मुँह منہ mungh ⓜ
movie (cinema) फ़िल्म فلم film ⓕ
museum संग्रहालय san·gra·*haa*·lai ⓜ عجائبگھر a·jaa·*yab*·gaar ⓜ
music संगीत *san*·geet ⓜ موسیقی moo·*see*·kee ⓕ
musician संगीतकार *san*·geet·kaar ⓜ&ⓕ موسیقار moo·*see*·kaar ⓜ&ⓕ
Muslim मुसलमान مسلمان mu·*sal*·maan
my मेरा میرا *me*·raa

N

nail clippers नेल कटर نیل کٹر nel ka·*tar* ⓜ
name नाम نام naam ⓜ
napkin नैपकिन نیپکن *nayp*·kin ⓜ
nappy नैपी نیپی *nay*·pee ⓕ
nausea उल्टी का एहसास الٹی کا احساس *ul*·tee kaa *eh*·saas ⓜ
near(by) पास پاس paas
nearest सब से पास سب سے پاس sab se paas
necklace हार ہار haar ⓜ
needle (sewing) सुई سوئی su·*ee* ⓕ

Netherlands नैदरलैंड्स نیدرلینڈس nay·*dar*·lands ⓜ
new नया نیا na·*yaa*
New Delhi नई दिल्ली نئ دلّی na·*ee* *dil*·lee ⓕ
news ख़बर خبر ka·*bar* ⓕ
newsagency अख़बारवाला اخباروالا *ak*·baar·*vaa*·laa ⓜ
newspaper अख़बार اخبار *ak*·baar ⓜ
New Year नया साल نیا سال na·*yaa* saal ⓜ
New Zealand न्यू ज़ीलैंड نیو زیلینڈ nyoo *zee*·land ⓜ
next (month) अगला اگلا *ag*·laa
night रात رات raat ⓕ
no नहीं نہیں na·*heeng*
noise शोर-गुल شورغل *shor*·gul ⓜ
nonsmoking नॉन स्मोकिंग نان سموکنگ naan *smo*·king
north n उत्तर *ut*·tar ⓜ شمال shu·*maal* ⓜ
nose नाक ناک naak ⓕ
notebook कापी کاپی *kaa*·pee ⓕ
nothing कुछ नहीं کچھ نہیں kuch na·*heeng*
now अब اب ab
number नम्बर نمبر *nam*·bar ⓜ
nurse नर्स نارس nars ⓕ

O

off (food) बासी باسی *baa*·see
oil तेल تیل tel ⓜ
old पुराना پرانا pu·*raa*·naa
on पर پر par
once एक बार ایک بار ek baar
one-way ticket एक तरफ़ा टिकट ایک طرفہ ٹکٹ ek ta·ra·*faa* ti·*kat* ⓜ
open a खुला کھلا ku·*laa*
opening hours खुलने का समय *kul*·ne kaa sa·*mai* ⓜ کھلنے کا وقت *kul*·ne kaa vakt ⓜ
orange (colour) नारंगी نارنگی naa·*ran*·gee
other दूसरा دوسرا *doos*·raa
our हमारा ہمارا ha·*maa*·raa
outside बाहर باہر *baa*·har

P

pacifier (dummy) पैसिफ़ायर پیسفایر pay·si·*faa*·yar ⓜ
package (packet) पैकेट پیکیٹ *pay*·ket ⓜ
padlock ताला تالا *taa*·laa ⓜ
pain दर्द درد dard ⓜ
painful दर्दनाक دردناک *dard*·naak
painkillers दर्द दूर करने की दवा درد دور کرنے کی دوا dard door *kar*·ne kee da·*vaa* ⓕ
painter तस्वीर बनाने वाला تصویر بنانے والا *tas*·veer ba·*naa*·ne *vaa*·laa ⓜ
painting (artwork) तस्वीर تصویر *tas*·veer ⓕ
Pakistan पाकिस्तान پاکستان paa·ki·*staan*
palace महल محل ma·*hal* ⓜ
pants (trousers) पैंट پینٹ paynt ⓕ sg
paper काग़ज़ کاغز *kaa*·gaz ⓜ
paperwork काग़ज़ का काम کاغز کا کام *kaa*·gaz kaa kaam ⓜ
parents माँ बाप maang baap ⓜ والدین *vaa*·li·den ⓜ
park n पार्क پارک paark ⓜ
party (entertainment/politics) पार्टी پارٹی *paar*·tee ⓕ
passenger सवारी سواری sa·*vaa*·ree ⓕ
passport पासपोर्ट پاسپورٹ *paas*·port ⓜ
passport number पासपोर्ट का नम्बर پاسپورٹ کا نمبر *paas*·port kaa *nam*·bar ⓜ
past a अतीत a·*teet* گذشتہ gu·*zash*·tah
path रास्ता راستہ *raas*·taa ⓜ
pay v पैसे देना پیسے دینا *pay*·se *de*·naa
payment भुगतान *bug*·taan ⓜ پیمینٹ *pay*·ment ⓜ

pen पेन پین pen ⓕ
penis लंड لنڈ land ⓜ
penknife पैन नाइफ़ پین نائف payn *naa*·if ⓜ
pensioner पैंशनर پینشنر *payn*·sha·nar ⓜ
perfume इत्र عطر i·*tra* ⓜ
petrol पेट्रोल پیٹرول *pet*·rol ⓜ
pharmacy दवाख़ाना دواخانا da·vaa·*kaa*·naa ⓜ
phone book फ़ोन डायरेक्ट्री فون ڈائریکٹری fon daai·*rek*·tree ⓕ
phone box पी० सी० ओ० پی-سی-او pee see o ⓜ
phone card फ़ोन कार्ड فون کارڈ fon kaard ⓜ
photograph फ़ोटो فوٹو *fo*·to ⓜ
photographer फ़ोटोग्राफ़र فوٹوگرافر fo·to·*graa*·far ⓜ
phrasebook फ़्रेसबुक فریس بک *fres*·buk ⓕ
picnic पिकनिक پکنک *pik*·nik ⓜ
pill गोली گولی *go*·lee ⓕ
pillow तकिया تکیہ ta·ki·*yaa* ⓜ
pillowcase तकिये का खोल ta·ki·*ye* kaa kol ⓜ تکیہ کا غلاف ta·ki·*ye* kaa gi·*laaf* ⓜ
pink गुलाबी گلابی gu·*laa*·bee
plane हवाई जहाज़ ہوائ جہاز ha·*vaa*·ee ja·*haaz* ⓜ
plate प्लेट پلیٹ plet ⓜ
platform (train) प्लैटफोर्म پلیٹفورم *playt*·form ⓜ
play n नाटक *naa*·tak ⓜ ڈراما *draa*·mah ⓜ
plug n प्लग پلاگ plag ⓜ
point (dot) n बिन्दु بندو *bin*·du ⓜ
police पुलिस پولیس pu·*lis* ⓕ
police station थाना تھانہ *taa*·naa ⓜ
postage टिकट का दाम ti·*kat* kaa daam ⓜ ٹکٹ کا دام ti·*kat* kee *kee*·mat ⓕ
postcard पोस्टकार्ड پوسٹکارڈ *post*·kaard ⓜ
post code पिन कोड پن کوڈ pin kod ⓜ
poster पोस्टर پوسٹر *pos*·tar ⓜ
post office डाक ख़ाना ڈاک خانہ daak *kaa*·naa ⓜ
pregnant गर्भवती *garb*·va·tee حاملہ *haa*·mi·lah
premenstrual tension मासिक धर्म का तनाव *maa*·sik daarm kaa ta·*naav* ⓜ ماہواری کا تناو maah·*vaa*·ree kaa ta·*naav* ⓜ
price दाम daam ⓜ دام *kee*·mat ⓕ
private निजी ni·*jee* ذاتی *zaa*·tee
public telephone सार्वजनिक फ़ोन *saar*·va·ja·nik fon ⓜ پی-سی-او pee see o ⓜ
public toilet जन सुविधा jan su·vi·*daa* ⓕ عام ٹائلیٹ aam *taa*·i·let ⓜ
pull खींचना کھینچنا *keench*·naa
purple बैंगनी بینگنی *bayng*·nee

Q

quiet शान्त shaant خاموش *kaa*·mosh

R

railway station रेलवे स्टेशन ریلوے سٹیشن *rel*·ve *ste*·shan ⓜ
rain बारिश بارش *baa*·rish ⓕ
raincoat बरसाती برساتی bar·*saa*·tee ⓕ
rare (not common) दुर्लभ *dur*·lab غیر معمولی gayr maa·*moo*·lee
razor उस्तरा استرا *us*·ta·raa ⓜ
razor blade रेज़र ब्लेड ریزر بلیڈ re·*zar* bled ⓜ
receipt रसीद رسید ra·*seed* ⓕ
recommend सिफ़ारिश करना سفارش کرنا si·*faa*·rish *kar*·naa
red लाल لال laal
refrigerator रेफ़्रिजिरेटर ریفرجریٹر re·fri·ji·*re*·tar ⓜ
refund n रिफ़ंड رفنڈ ri·*fand* ⓜ
registered mail रेजिस्टड मेल ریجسٹڈ میل re·*jis*·tad mayl ⓕ
rent n किराया کرایا ki·*raa*·yaa ⓜ

repair v मरम्मत करना مرمّت کرنا ma·*ram*·mat *kar*·naa
reservation बुकिंग بکنگ bu·*king* ⓕ
restaurant रेस्टोरेंट ریسٹورینٹ res·*to*·rent ⓜ
return v वापस आना واپس آنا *vaa*·pas *aa*·naa
return ticket वापसी टिकट واپسی ٹکٹ *vaa*·pa·see ti·*kat* ⓕ
right (correct) ठीक ٹھیک teek
right (not left) दाहिना داہنہ *daa*·hi·naa
ring (jewellery) अंगूठी انگوٹھی an·*goo*·tee ⓕ
road सड़क سڑک sa·*rak* ⓕ
romantic रोमानी رومانی ro·*maa*·nee
room कमरा کمرہ *kam*·raa ⓜ
room number कमरे का नम्बर کمرے کا نمبر *kam*·re kaa *nam*·bar ⓜ
ruins खंडहर کھنڈہر *kan*·da·har ⓜ sg
rupee रुपया روپیہ ru·pa·*yaa* ⓜ

S

safe a तिजोरी تجوری ti·*jo*·ree ⓕ
safe sex सेफ़ सैक्स سیف سیکس sef sayks ⓜ
sanitary napkins सैनिट्री नैपकिन्स़ سنیٹری نیپکنس say·*nit*·ree *nayp*·kins ⓜ
scarf स्कॉर्फ़ سکارف skaarf ⓜ
school स्कूल اسکول skool ⓜ
science विज्ञान *vig*·yaan ⓜ سائنس *saa*·ins ⓜ
scientist वैज्ञानिक vayg·*yaa*·nik ⓜ&ⓕ سائنسدان saa·*ins*·daan ⓜ&ⓕ
scissors कैंची قینچی *kayn*·chee ⓕ
Scotland स्कॉटलैंड سکاٹلینڈ *skaat*·laynd ⓜ
sculpture मूर्ति *moor*·tee ⓕ بت but ⓜ
sea समुद्र sa·*mud*·raa ⓜ سمندر sa·*man*·dar ⓜ
season मौसम موسم *mau*·sam ⓜ
seat कुरसी کرسی *kur*·see ⓕ
seatbelt पेट्टी پیٹی *pe*·tee ⓕ
second (after first) a दूसरा دوسرا *doos*·raa
second-hand पुराना پورانا pu·*raa*·naa
send भेजना بھیجنا *bej*·naa
service charge सर्विस चार्ज سروس چارج *sar*·vis chaarj ⓜ
service station पेट्रोल पम्प پیٹرول پمپ *pet*·rol pamp ⓜ
sex संभोग *sam*·bog ⓜ جنس jins ⓜ
share (a dorm) एक साथ रहना ایک ساتھ رہنا ek saat *reh*·naa
share (with) बाँटना بانٹنا *baangt*·naa
shave v दाढ़ी बनाना *daa*·ree ba·*naa*·naa حجامت بنانا ha·*jaa*·mat ba·*naa*·naa
shaving cream शेविंग क्रेम شیونگ کریم she·*ving* kreem ⓜ
sheet (bed) चादर چادر *chaa*·dar ⓕ
shirt कुरता کرتہ *kur*·taa ⓜ
shoes जूते جوتے *joo*·te ⓜ pl
shoe shop जूते की दुकान جوتے کی دکان *joo*·te kee du·*kaan* ⓕ
shop n दुकान دکان du·*kaan* ⓕ
shopping centre बाज़ार بازار *baa*·zaar ⓜ
short (height/length) छोटा چھوٹا *cho*·taa
shorts कच्छा کچّھا *kach*·chaa ⓜ sg
shoulders कंधे کندھے *kan*·de ⓜ pl
shout चिल्लाना چلّانا chil·*laa*·naa
show v दिखाना دکھانا di·*kaa*·naa
shower n शॉवर شاور *shaa*·var ⓜ
shut v बंद करना بند کرنا band *kar*·naa
sick उल्टी الٹی *ul*·tee
silk रेशम ریشم *re*·sham ⓜ
silver चांदी چاندی *chaan*·dee ⓕ
single सिंगल سنگل *sin*·gal
single room सिंगल कमरा سنگل کمرہ *sin*·gal *kam*·raa ⓜ
sister बहन بہن be·*han* ⓕ
size (clothes) नाप ناپ naap ⓕ
skirt लहंगा لہنگا la·*han*·gaa ⓜ
sleep n नींद نیند neend ⓕ
sleeping bag स्लीपिंग बैग سلیپنگ بیگ *slee*·ping bayg ⓜ

sleeping car शयनकार شین گار sha·*yan*·kaar ⓜ
slowly धीरे धीरे *dee*·re *dee*·re آہستہ aa·*his*·taa
small छोटा چھوٹا *cho*·taa
smell n बू بو boo ⓕ
smile n मुस्कान مسکان *mus*·kaan ⓕ
smoke n धुआँ دھواں du·*aang* ⓜ
snack n नाश्ता ناشتہ *naash*·taa ⓜ
snow n बर्फ़ برف barf ⓕ
soap साबुन صابن *saa*·bun ⓜ
socks मोज़े موزے *mo*·ze ⓜ pl
some कुछ کچھ kuch
son बेटा بیٹا *be*·taa ⓜ
soon जल्दी جلدی *jal*·dee
south n दक्षिण *dak*·shin ⓜ جنوب ja·*noob* ⓜ
souvenir निशानी نشانی ni·*shaa*·nee ⓕ
souvenir shop निशानियों की दुकान نشانیوں کی دکان ni·*shaa*·ni·yong kee du·*kaan* ⓕ
Spain स्पेन سپین spen ⓜ
speak बोलना بولنا *bol*·naa
spoon चम्मच چمّچ *cham*·mach ⓜ
sports store खेल की दुकान کھیل کی دکان kel kee du·*kaan* ⓕ
sprain v मोच आना موچ آنا moch *aa*·naa
spring (season) बहार بہار ba·*haar* ⓕ
stairway सीढ़ी *see*·ree ⓕ زینہ *zee*·nah ⓜ
stamp n टिकट ٹکٹ ti·*kat* ⓜ
stand-by ticket स्टैंड-बाई टिकट سٹینڈ بائ ٹکٹ staynd *baa*·ee ti·*kat* ⓜ
station स्टेशन سٹیشن *ste*·shan ⓜ
stockings मोज़े موزے *mo*·ze ⓜ pl
stomach पेट پیٹ pet ⓜ
stomachache पेट में दर्द پیٹ میں درد pet meng dard ⓜ
stop v ठहरना ٹھہرنا *tehr*·naa
street सड़क سڑک sa·*rak* ⓕ
string डोरी ڈوری *do*·ree ⓕ
student छात्र *chaa*·tra ⓜ طالب علم *taa*·li·be ilm ⓜ
subtitles सबटायटल्स سبٹائٹلس sab·*taai*·tals ⓜ
suitcase सूटकेस سوٹکیس *soot*·kes ⓜ
summer गर्मी के दिन گرمی کے دن *gar*·mee ke din ⓜ
sun सूरज سورج *soo*·raj ⓜ
sunblock सनब्लॉक سنبلاک *san*·blaak ⓜ
sunburn सनबर्न سنبرن *san*·barn ⓜ
sunglasses धूप का चश्मा دھوپ کا چشمہ doop kaa *chash*·maa ⓜ
sunrise सूर्योदय soor·*yo*·dai ⓜ طلوع آفتاب tu·*loo* *aaf*·taab ⓜ
sunset सूर्यास्त *soor*·yaast ⓜ غروب آفتاب gu·*roob* *aaf*·taab ⓜ
supermarket सुपरमार्केट سپرمارکیٹ su·par·*maar*·ket ⓜ
surface mail आम डाक عام ڈاک aam daak ⓕ
surname परिवार का नाम pa·ri·*vaar* kaa naam ⓜ خاندان کا نام *kaan*·daan kaa naam ⓜ
sweater स्वेटर سویٹر *sve*·tar ⓜ
sweet a मीठा میٹھا *mee*·taa
swim v तैरना تیرنا *tayr*·naa
swimming pool स्विमिंग पूल سومنگ پول *svi*·ming pool ⓜ
swimsuit तैरने का कपड़ा تیرنے کے کپڑا *tayr*·ne kaa *kap*·raa ⓜ

T

tailor दर्ज़ी درزی *dar*·zee ⓜ
take photographs फ़ोटो खींचना فوٹو لینا *fo*·to *keench*·naa
tampon टैम्पाईन ٹیمپان *taym*·paan ⓜ
tap नल نل nal ⓜ
tasty लज़ीज़ لذیذ la·*zeez*
taxi टैक्सी ٹیکسی *tayk*·see ⓕ
taxi stand टैक्सी स्टैंड ٹیکسی سٹینڈ *tayk*·see staynd ⓜ
teacher टीचर ٹیچر *tee*·char ⓜ&ⓕ

teaspoon छोटा चम्मच چھوٹا چمچ *cho*·taa *cham*·mach ⓜ
telegram तार تار taar ⓜ
telephone n टेलीफ़ोन ٹیلیفون *te*·lee·fon ⓜ
telephone centre पी० सी० ओ० پی-سی-او pee see o ⓜ
television टेलीविज़न ٹیلیوزن te·*lee*·vi·zan ⓜ
temperature तापमान تاپمان *taap*·maan ⓜ
tennis टेनिस ٹینس *te*·nis ⓜ
tennis court टेनिस कार्ट ٹینس کورٹ *te*·nis kaart ⓜ
that वह وہ voh
theatre थिएटर تھیٹر ti·ya·*tar* ⓜ
thermometer थेममीटर تھیممیٹر te·ma·*mee*·tar ⓜ
thirst प्यास پیاس pyaas ⓕ
this यह یہ yeh
throat गला گلا ga·*laa* ⓜ
ticket टिकट ٹکٹ ti·*kat* ⓜ
ticket collector टी० टी० ٹی ٹی tee tee ⓜ
ticket office टिकटघर ٹکٹگھر ti·*kat*·gar ⓜ
time समय sa·*mai* ⓜ وقت vakt ⓜ
time difference समय में अन्तर sa·*mai* meng *an*·tar ⓜ وقت میں فرق vakt meng fark ⓜ
timetable समय सारणी sa·*mai saa*·ra·nee ⓕ ٹائم ٹیبل *taa*·im *te*·bal ⓜ
tin (can) टीन ٹین teen ⓜ
tin opener टीन खोलने का औज़ार ٹین کھولنے کا اوزار teen *kol*·ne kaa *au*·zaar ⓜ
tip n नोक نوک nok ⓕ
tired थका हुआ تھکا ہوا ta·*kaa* hu·*aa*
tissue टिश्यू ٹشیو tish·*yoo* ⓜ
today आज آج aaj
together एक साथ ایک ساتھ ek saat
toilet टॉइलेट ٹئلیٹ *taa*·i·let ⓜ
toilet paper टाइलेट पेपर ٹیلیٹ پیپر *taa*·i·let *pe*·par ⓜ
tomorrow कल کل kal
tone (voice) लहजा لہجہ *leh*·jaa ⓜ
tonight आज रात آج رات aaj raat
too (expensive) बहुत بہت ba·*hut*
toothache दाँत में दर्द دانت میں درد daant meng dard ⓜ
toothbrush ब्रुश برش brush ⓜ
toothpaste दाँतमंजन daant·*man*·jan ⓜ دانت منجن toot pest ⓜ
toothpick टूथपिक توتھپک *toot*·pik ⓜ
torch टॉर्च ٹارچ taarch ⓜ
tour n दौरा دورا *dau*·raa ⓜ
tourist n पर्यटक *par*·ya·tak ⓜ&ⓕ سیّاح *sai*·yaah ⓜ&ⓕ
tourist office पर्यटन ऑफ़िस *par*·ya·tan *aa*·fis ⓜ سیاحوں کا آفس *sai*·yaa·hong kaa *aa*·fis ⓜ
towel तौलिया تولیہ *tau*·li·yaa ⓜ
tower मीनार مینار *mee*·naar ⓕ
traffic यातायात yaa·*taa*·yaat ⓜ ٹریفک *tre*·fik ⓜ
traffic lights बी بتّی *bat*·tee ⓕ
train ट्रेन ٹرین tren ⓕ
train station स्टेशन سٹیشن *ste*·shan ⓜ
tram ट्राम ٹرام traam ⓕ
transit lounge ट्रेंज़िट लाउंज ٹرینزٹ لاونج *tren*·zit *laa*·unj ⓜ
translate अनुवाद करना a·nu·*vaad kar*·naa ترجمہ کرنا *tar*·ju·mah *kar*·naa
travel agency ट्रेवल एजेंट ٹریول ایجینٹ *tre*·val e·jent ⓜ
travellers cheque ट्रेवलर्स चेक ٹریولرس چیک *tre*·va·lars chek ⓜ
trousers पैंट پینٹ paynt ⓕ sg
try (attempt) v कोशिश करना کوشش کرنا *ko*·shish *kar*·naa
tube (tyre) ट्यूब ٹیوب tyoob ⓜ
TV टी० वी० ٹی-وی tee vee ⓕ
tweezers ट्वीज़र्स ٹویزرس *tvee*·zars ⓜ
twin beds ट्विन बेड्ज़ ٹون بیڈز tvin bedz ⓜ
tyre टायर ٹایر *taa*·yar ⓜ

U

umbrella छाता چھاتا *chaa*·taa ⓜ
uncomfortable असुविधाजनक a·su·vi·*daa*·ja·*nak* غیر آرامدہ gayr *aa*·raam·deh
underwear कच्छा کچھا *kach*·chaa ⓜ
university विश्वविद्यालय vish·va·vid·*yaa*·lai ⓜ یونیورسٹی yoo·ni·*var*·si·tee ⓕ
until (time) तक تک tak
up ऊपर اوپر *oo*·par
urgent ज़रूरी ضروری za·*roo*·ree
Urdu (language) उर्दू اردو *ur*·doo ⓕ
USA अमरीका امریکا am·*ree*·kaa ⓜ

V

vacant ख़ाली خالی *kaa*·lee
vacation छुट्टी چھٹّی *chut*·tee ⓕ
vaccination टीका ٹیکا *tee*·kaa ⓜ
validate वेलिडेट करना ویلڈیٹ کرنا *ve*·li·det *kar*·naa
vegetable n सब्ज़ी سبزی *sab*·zee ⓕ
vegetarian a शाकाहारी shaa·kaa·*haa*·ree سبزیخور *sab*·zee·kor
view n दृश्य *dri*·shya ⓜ منظر *man*·zar ⓜ
village गाँव گاؤں gaa·on ⓜ
visa वीसा ویسا *vee*·saa ⓜ

W

wait v इंतज़ार करना انتظار کرنا *in*·ta·zaar *kar*·naa
waiter बेरा بیرا *be*·raa ⓜ&ⓕ
waiting room प्रतीक्षाकक्ष pra·*teek*·shaa·kaksh ⓜ انتظار کرنے کاکمرہ *in*·ta·zaar *kar*·ne kaa *kam*·raa ⓜ
walk v पैदल जाना پیدل جانا *pay*·dal *jaa*·naa
wallet बटुआ بٹوا ba·tu·*aa* ⓜ
warm a गर्म گرم garm
wash (something) धोना دھونا *do*·naa
watch n घड़ी گھڑی ga·*ree* ⓕ
water पानी پانی *paa*·nee ⓜ
wedding शादी شادی *shaa*·dee ⓕ
weekend वीक एंड ویک اینڈ veek end ⓜ
west n पश्चिम *pash*·chim ⓜ مغرب *mag*·rib ⓜ
wheelchair व्हील चैयर ویل چئر vheel *chay*·yar ⓜ
when कब کب kab
where कहाँ کہاں ka·*haang*
white सफ़ेद سفید sa·*fed*
who कौन کون kaun
why क्यों کیوں kyong
wife पत्नी *pat*·nee ⓕ بیوی *bee*·vee ⓕ
window खिड़की کھڑکی *kir*·kee ⓕ
wine शराब شراب sha·*raab* ⓕ
with के साथ کے ساتھ ke saat
without के बिना ke bi·*naa* کے بغیر ke ba·*gayr*
woman स्त्री stree ⓕ خاتون *kaa*·toon ⓕ
wood लकड़ी لکڑی *lak*·ree ⓕ
wool ऊन اون oon ⓜ
world दुनिया دنیا du·ni·*yaa* ⓕ
write लिखना لکھنا *likh*·naa

Y

yellow पीला پیلا *pee*·laa
yes जी हाँ جی ہاں jee haang
yesterday कल کل kal
you sg pol&pl आप آپ aap
youth hostel यूथ हॉस्टल یوتھ ہاسٹل yoot *haas*·tal ⓜ

Z

zip/zipper ज़िप زپ zip ⓜ
zodiac राशि راشی *raa*·shi ⓕ
zoo चिड़ियाघर چڑیاگھر chi·ri·*yaa*·gar ⓜ

The words in this Hindi–English dictionary are ordered according to the Hindi alphabet (presented in the table below). Note that some Hindi characters change their primary forms when combined with each other – that's why some of the words grouped under a particular character may seem to start with a different character (for more information, see **pronunciation**, page 13). Hindi nouns and adjectives are in the direct case. Nouns have their gender marked as masculine ⓜ or feminine ⓕ. Those adjectives that change form for gender are in the masculine form (for more information on cases and gender, see the **phrasebuilder**, page 17). The symbols n, a and v (indicating noun, adjective and verb) have been added for clarity where an English term could be either. If you're having trouble understanding Hindi, hand over this dictionary to a Hindi-speaking person, so they can look up the word they need and show you the English translation.

hindi vowels										
अ	आ	इ	ई	उ	ऊ	ऋ	ए	ऐ	ओ	औ
hindi consonants										
क	ख	ग	घ	ङ	च	छ	ज	झ	ञ	ट
ठ	ड	ढ	ण	ड़	ढ़	त	थ	द	ध	न
प	फ	ब	भ	म	य	र	ल	व	श	ष
स	ह									

अ

अंग्रेज़ी an·*gre*·zee ⓕ **English (language)**
अन्दर जाना *an*·dar *jaa*·naa **enter**
अख़बार *ak*·baar ⓜ **newspaper**
अगला *ag*·laa **next (month)**
अच्छा *ach*·chaa **good** a
अनुवाद करना a·nu·*vaad kar*·naa **translate**
अब ab **now**
अस्पताल *as*·pa·taal ⓜ **hospital**
अहम a·*ham* **important**
आज aaj **today**
आज रात aaj raat **tonight**
आदमी *aad*·mee ⓜ **man**
आधा *aa*·daa **half**
आना *aa*·naa **arrive • come**
आप aap **you** sg pol&pl
आपत *aa*·pat ⓕ **emergency**

इ

इंटरनेट in·*tar*·net ⓜ **Internet**
इंडिया *in*·di·yaa ⓜ **India**

उ

उड़ना *ur*·naa **fly** v
उत्तर *ut*·tar ⓜ **north**
उर्दू *ur*·doo ⓕ **Urdu (language)**
उल्टी का एहसास *ul*·tee kaa *eh*·saas ⓜ **nausea**
उस्तरा *us*·ta·raa ⓜ **razor**

ए

ए० टी० एम० e tee em ⓕ **ATM**
ए० सी० e see ⓕ **air conditioner**
एंटिबायोटिक्स en·ti·baa·*yo*·tiks ⓜ **antibiotics**
एंटिसेप्टिक en·ti·*sep*·tik ⓜ **antiseptic** n
एंबुलेन्स *em*·bu·lens ⓜ **ambulance**
एक तरफ़ा टिकट ek ta·ra·*faa* ti·*kat* ⓜ **one-way ticket**
एक साथ रहना ek saat *reh*·naa **share (a dorm)**
एक्स्प्रेस मेल *eks*·pres mayl ⓕ **express mail**
एलरजी e·*lar*·jee ⓕ **allergy**
एशिया e·*shi*·yaa ⓜ **Asia**
एस्प्रिन *es*·prin ⓕ **aspirin**
एहसास होना *eh*·saas *ho*·naa **feel**

क

कम्बल *kam*·bal ⓜ **blanket**
कच्छा *kach*·chaa ⓜ **underwear**
कटना *kat*·naa **cut** v
कटोरी ka·*to*·ree ⓕ **bowl**
कब kab **when**
कम kam **less**
कमरा *kam*·raa ⓜ **room**
कल kal **tomorrow • yesterday**
कहाँ ka·*haang* **where**
काँटा *kaan*·taa ⓜ **fork**
कांडम *kaan*·dam ⓜ **condom**
काग़ज़ *kaa*·gaz ⓜ **paper**
काफ़ी *kaa*·fee **enough**
काला *kaa*·laa **black**
किराया ki·*raa*·yaa ⓜ **rent** n
किराये पर लेना ki·*raa*·ye par *le*·naa **hire** v
कुछ kuch **some**
कुछ नहीं kuch na·*heeng* **nothing**
कुरता *kur*·taa ⓜ **shirt**
कुरसी *kur*·see ⓕ **seat**
के बिना ke bi·*naa* **without**
के साथ ke saat **with**
केंद्र *ken*·dra ⓜ **centre**
कैंसल करना *kayn*·sal *kar*·naa **cancel**
कैमरा *kaym*·raa ⓜ **camera**
कैश करना kaysh *kar*·naa **cash (a cheque)** v
कोश kosh ⓜ **dictionary**
कोशिश करना *ko*·shish *kar*·naa **try** v
कौन kaun **who**
क्यों kyong **why**

ख

ख़तरनाक ka·*tar*·naak **dangerous**
ख़बर ka·*bar* ⓕ **news**
ख़राब ka·*raab* **faulty**
ख़रीदना ka·*reed*·naa **buy**
खाँसी *kaan*·see ⓕ **cough** n
खाना *kaa*·naa **eat**
खाना *kaa*·naa ⓜ **food**
ख़ाली *kaa*·lee **empty • vacant**
खिड़की *kir*·kee ⓕ **window**
खुला ku·*laa* **open** a
ख़ुश kush **happy**
खोया हुआ *ko*·yaa hu·*aa* **lost**

ग

गंदा *gan*·daa **dirty**
गर्भवती *garb*·va·tee **pregnant**
गर्म garm **hot • warm**
गाड़ी *gaa*·ree ⓕ **car**
गाड़ी चलाने का लाइसेंस *gaa*·ree cha·*laa*·ne kaa *laa*·i·sens ⓜ **drivers licence**
गिलास glaas ⓜ **glass (drinking)**
गोश्त gosht ⓜ **meat**

च

चम्मच *cham*·mach ⓜ **spoon**
चलाना cha·*laa*·naa **drive** v
चश्मा *chash*·maa ⓜ **glasses**
चाक़ू *chaa*·koo ⓜ **knife**
चादर *chaa*·dar ⓕ **sheet (bed)**

चाबी *chaa*·bee (f) **key**
चेक chek (m) **cheque (bank)**
चोट chot (f) **injury**

छ

छात्र *chaa*·tra (m) **student**
छुट्टी *chut*·tee (f) **holidays • vacation**
छूट choot (f) **discount**
छोटा *cho*·taa **short (height/length) • small**

ज

ज़रूरी za·*roo*·ree **urgent**
जल्दी *jal*·dee **early • fast • quickly • soon**
जाना *jaa*·naa **go**
जी हाँ jee haang **yes**
ज़ुकाम zu·*kaam* (m) **cold (illness)**
जूते *joo*·te (m) **shoes**

ट

टखना *tak*·naa (m) **ankle**
टॉइलेट *taa*·i·let (m) **toilet**
टायर *taa*·yar (m) **tyre**
टॉर्च taarch (m) **flashlight (torch)**
टिकट ti·*kat* (m) **stamp • ticket**
टीन खोलने का औज़ार
teen *kol*·ne kaa *au*·zaar (m) **can opener**
टूटा *too*·taa **broken**
टेलीफ़ोन *te*·lee·fon (m) **telephone**
टेलीविज़न te·*lee*·vi·zan (m) **television**
ट्रेन tren (f) **train**

ड

डबल कमरा da·*bal kam*·raa (m) **double room**
डाक daak (f) **mail • post**
डॉक्टर *daak*·tar (m)&(f) **doctor**
डेंटिस्ट *den*·tist (m)&(f) **dentist**
डेरा *de*·raa (m) **campsite**
डोरी *do*·ree (f) **string** n

त

तक tak **until**
तापमान *taap*·maan (m) **temperature**
तार taar (m) **telegram**
तारीख़ *taa*·reek (f) **date (time)**
ताला *taa*·laa (m) **lock** n
तिजोरी ti·*jo*·ree **safe** a
तेल tel (m) **oil**
तैरना *tayr*·naa **swim** v
तोहफ़ा *toh*·faa (m) **gift**
तौलिया *tau*·li·yaa (m) **towel**

द

दक्षिण *dak*·shin (m) **south**
दर्द dard (m) **pain**
दर्द दूर करने की दवा
dard door *kar*·ne kee da·*vaa* (f) **painkillers**
दवा da·*vaa* (f) **medicine (medication)**
दवाख़ाना da·vaa·*kaa*·naa (m) **pharmacy**
दस्त dast (m) **diarrhoea**
दाँत में दर्द daant meng dard (m) **toothache**
दाँतमंजन daant·*man*·jan (m) **toothpaste**
दाम daam (m) **cost • price**
दाहिना *daa*·hi·naa **right (direction)**
दिखाना di·*kaa*·naa **show** v
दिन din (m) **day**
दिन का खाना din kaa *kaa*·naa (m) **lunch**
दिल की बीमारी dil kee bee·*maa*·ree (f)
heart condition
दुकान du·*kaan* (f) **shop** n
दुर्घटना dur·*gat*·naa (f) **accident**
दूतावास doo·*taa*·vaas (m) **embassy**
दूध dood (m) **milk**
दुभाषिया du·*baa*·shi·yaa (m)&(f) **interpreter**
दूर door **far**
दूसरा *doos*·raa **other • second (after first)**
देर der (f) **delay** n
देर der **late (not early)**
दोनों do·*nong* **both**
दोस्त dost (m)&(f) **friend**
दौरा *dau*·raa (m) **tour** n

ध

धीरे धीरे *dee*·re *dee*·re **slowly**
धुआँ du·*aang* ⓜ **smoke** n
धुलाई du·*laa*·ee ⓕ **laundry (clothes)**
धोना *do*·naa **wash (something)**

न

नई दिल्ली na·*ee dil*·lee ⓕ **New Delhi**
नक़द na·*kad* ⓜ **cash • money**
नक्शा *nak*·shaa ⓜ **map**
नया na·*yaa* **new**
नशीली दवा na·*shee*·lee da·*vaa* ⓕ **drug (illegal)**
नहीं na·*heeng* **no**
नाक naak ⓕ **nose**
नाप naap ⓕ **size (clothes)**
नाम naam ⓜ **name**
नाश्ता *naash*·taa ⓜ **breakfast**
निकास ni·*kaas* ⓜ **exit** n
निशानियों की दुकान ni·*shaa*·ni·yong kee du·*kaan* ⓕ **souvenir shop**
नींद neend ⓕ **sleep** n
नीचे *nee*·che **down**
नौकरी *nauk*·ree ⓕ **job**

प

पकाना pa·*kaa*·naa **cook** v
पता pa·*taa* ⓜ **address** n
पति *pa*·ti ⓜ **husband**
पट्टी *pat*·tee ⓕ **bandage**
पत्नी *pat*·nee ⓕ **wife**
पत्र pa·*tra* ⓜ **letter (mail)**
पर par **on**
परिचय pa·ri·*chai* ⓜ **identification**
परिवार का नाम pa·ri·*vaar* kaa naam ⓜ **surname**
पर्यटक *par*·ya·tak ⓜ&ⓕ **tourist**
पर्यटन ऑफ़िस *par*·ya·tan *aa*·fis ⓜ **tourist office**
पर्वत *par*·vat ⓜ **mountain**
पलंग pa·*lang* ⓜ **bed**
पश्चिम *pash*·chim ⓜ **west**
पहला *peh*·laa **first**
पहले *peh*·le **before**
पानी *paa*·nee ⓜ **water**
पास paas **near(by)**
पिता pi·*taa* ⓜ **father**
पीछे *pee*·che **behind**
पीना *pee*·naa **drink** v
पीला *pee*·laa **yellow**
पुराना pu·*raa*·naa **old**
पुलिस pu·*lis* ⓕ **police**
पूर्व *poor*·va **east**
पेट में दर्द pet meng dard ⓜ **stomachache**
पेन pen ⓕ **pen**
पैंट paynt ⓕ **pants (trousers)**
पैकेट *pay*·ket ⓜ **package • packet**
पैदल जाना *pay*·dal *jaa*·naa **walk** v
पैसे *pay*·se ⓜ **money**
पैसे देना *pay*·se *de*·naa **pay** v
पोस्ट ऑफ़िस post *aa*·fis ⓜ **post office**
पोस्टकार्ड *post*·kaard ⓜ **postcard**
प्यार pyaar ⓜ **love** n
प्यास pyaas ⓕ **thirst**
प्रथम श्रेणी *pra*·tam *shre*·nee ⓕ **first-class ticket**
प्रस्थान करना *pra*·staan *kar*·naa **depart • leave**
प्लेट plet ⓜ **plate**

फ

फल pal ⓜ **fruit**
फ़िल्म film ⓕ **cinema • movie**
फ़ोटो *fo*·to ⓜ **photograph**
फ़ोन कार्ड fon kaard ⓜ **phone card**

ब

बंगला *bang*·laa ⓕ **Bengali (language)**
बंगलादेश bang·*laa*·desh ⓜ **Bangladesh**

बंद band **closed**
बच्चा *bach*·chaa ⓜ **baby • child**
बटुआ ba·tu·*aa* ⓜ **wallet**
बड़ा ba·*raa* **big**
बदलना ba·*dal*·naa **exchange (money)** v
बस bas ⓕ **bus**
बहुत ba·*hut* **too (expensive)**
बाज़ार *baa*·zaar ⓜ **market**
बाद baad **after**
बारिश *baa*·rish ⓕ **rain** n
बाहर *baa*·har **outside**
बिजली *bij*·lee ⓕ **electricity**
बिल bil ⓜ **bill** n
बीमा *bee*·maa ⓜ **insurance**
बीमार *bee*·maar **ill**
बुकिंग bu·*king* ⓕ **reservation**
बुकिंग कराना bu·*king* ka·*raa*·naa **book** v
बुख़ार bu·*kaar* ⓜ **fever**
बुरा bu·*raa* **bad**
बेरा *be*·raa ⓜ&ⓕ **waiter**
बैंक का खाता baynk kaa *kaa*·taa ⓜ **bank account**
बोतल bo·*tal* ⓕ **bottle**
बोलना *bol*·naa **speak**
ब्रुश brush ⓜ **toothbrush**
ब्रेक brek ⓜ **brake (car)** n

भ

भरा हुआ ba·*raa* hu·*aa* **full**
भारी *baa*·ree **heavy**
भूखा *boo*·kaa **hungry**
भूनाना boo·*naa*·naa **change (money)** v
भेजना *bej*·naa **send**

म

मछली *mach*·lee ⓕ **fish** n
मज़ाकिया ma·*jaa*·ki·yaa **funny**
मदद करना ma·*dad* *kar*·naa **help** v
मरम्मत करना ma·*ram*·mat *kar*·naa **repair** v
महंगा ma·*han*·gaa **expensive**
महीना ma·*hee*·naa ⓜ **month**
माँ maang ⓕ **mother**
माचिस *maa*·chis ⓜ **matches (cigarette)**
मिनट mi·*nat* ⓜ **minute**
मीठा *mee*·taa **sweet** a
मुद्रा विनिमय mu·*dra* vi·ni·*mai* ⓜ **currency exchange**
मुफ़्त muft **free (gratis)**
मुसलमान mu·*sal*·maan **Muslim**
मेन्यू *men*·yoo ⓜ **menu**
मेरा *me*·raa **my**
मैं mayng **I**
मोटरवे mo·*tar*·ve ⓜ **motorway**
मोटरसाइकिल *mo*·tar·*saa*·i·kil ⓕ **motorcycle**

य

यह yeh **he • it • she • this**
यहाँ ya·*haang* **here**
यातायात yaa·*taa*·yaat ⓜ **traffic**

र

रसीद ra·*seed* ⓕ **receipt**
रसोई ra·*so*·ee ⓕ **kitchen**
रहने की जगह *reh*·ne kee ja·*gah* ⓕ **accommodation**
रात raat ⓕ **night**
रात का खाना raat kaa *kaa*·naa ⓜ **dinner**
रिफ़ंड ri·*fand* ⓜ **refund** n
रुपया ru·pa·*yaa* ⓜ **rupee**
रेस्टोरेंट res·*to*·rent ⓜ **restaurant**
रोशनी *rosh*·nee ⓕ **light** n

ल

लम्बा *lam*·baa **long**
लड़का *lar*·kaa ⓜ **boy**
लड़की *lar*·kee ⓕ **girl**
लहंगा la·*han*·gaa ⓜ **skirt**
लाल laal **red**

लावारिस सामान का दफ़्तर laa·*vaa*·ris *saa*·maan kaa *daf*·tar ⓜ **lost property office**
लिखना *likh*·naa **write**
लिफ़्ट lift ⓜ **elevator**
लेकिन *le*·kin **but**

व

वकील va·*keel* ⓜ&ⓕ **lawyer**
वापस आना *vaa*·pas *kar*·naa **return** v
वापसी टिकट *vaa*·pa·see ti·*kat* ⓕ **return ticket**
विकलांग vi·ka·*laang* **disabled**
विनिमय दर vi·ni·*mai* dar ⓕ **exchange rate**
वीसा *vee*·saa ⓜ **visa**
व्यापार *vyaa*·paar ⓜ **business**

श

शराब sha·*raab* ⓕ **alcohol • wine**
शहर sha·*har* ⓜ **city**
शान्त shaant **quiet**
शाकाहारी shaa·kaa·*haa*·ree **vegetarian**
शाम shaam ⓕ **evening**
शामिल *shaa*·mil **included**
शॉवर *shaa*·var ⓜ **shower** n
शिशु *shi*·shu ⓜ **baby**
शोर-गुल *shor*·gul ⓜ **noise**

स

संगीत *san*·geet ⓜ **music**
संदेश *san*·desh ⓜ **message**
संभोग *sam*·bog ⓜ **sex**
सख़्त sakt **difficult • hard**
सड़क sa·*rak* ⓕ **road • street**
सफ़ेद sa·*fed* **white**
सब sab **all • each**
सब्ज़ी *sab*·zee ⓕ **vegetable** n
समय sa·*mai* ⓜ **time**
समलैंगिक sam·*layn*·gik **homosexual** a
समुद्र sa·*mud*·raa ⓜ **sea**
समुद्र का तट sa·*mud*·raa kaa tat ⓜ **beach**
सरदर्द *sar*·dard ⓜ **headache**
सर्दी *sar*·dee ⓕ **cold (weather)**
सवेरा sa·*ve*·raa ⓜ **morning (6am–1pm)**
सस्ता *sas*·taa **cheap**
साइकिल *saa*·i·kil ⓕ **bicycle**
साफ़ saaf **clean** a
साबुन *saa*·bun ⓜ **soap**
सामान *saa*·maan ⓜ **baggage (luggage)**
सामान प्राप्ति *saa*·maan *praap*·ti ⓕ **baggage claim**
सामान रखने की जगह *saa*·maan *rak*·ne kee ja·*gah* ⓕ **left luggage (office)**
सिंगल कमरा *sin*·gal *kam*·raa ⓜ **single room**
सिक्के *sik*·ke ⓜ **coins**
सिगरेट *sig*·ret ⓕ **cigarette**
सिफ़ारिश करना si·*faa*·rish *kar*·naa **recommend**
सीधा *see*·daa **direct** a
सीमाधिकार see·*maa*·di·kaar ⓜ **customs (immigration)**
सुन्दर *sun*·dar **beautiful**
सूरज *soo*·raj ⓜ **sun**
सेल sel ⓜ **battery**
स्टेशन *ste*·shan ⓜ **station**
स्त्री stree ⓕ **woman**
स्लेटी रंग का *sle*·tee rang kaa **grey**

ह

हरा ha·*raa* **green**
हवाई अड्डा ha·*vaa*·ee *ad*·daa ⓜ **airport**
हवाई जहाज़ ha·*vaa*·ee ja·*haaz* ⓜ **airplane**
हाइक *haa*·ik ⓜ **hike** n
हिन्दी *hin*·dee ⓕ **Hindi (language)**
हिन्दू *hin*·doo **Hindu**
होटल *ho*·tal ⓜ **hotel**

The words in this Urdu–English dictionary are ordered according to the Urdu alphabet (presented in the table below). Note that some Urdu characters change their primary forms when combined with each other – that's why some of the words grouped under a particular character may seem to start with a different character (for more information, see **pronunciation**, page 13). Urdu nouns and adjectives in this dictionary are in the direct case. Nouns have their gender marked as masculine ⓜ or feminine ⓕ. Those adjectives that change form for gender are in the masculine form (for more information on cases and gender, see the **phrasebuilder**, page 17). The symbols n, a and v (indicating noun, adjective and verb) have been added for clarity where an English term could be either. If you're having trouble understanding Urdu, hand over this dictionary to an Urdu-speaking person, so they can look up the word they need and show you the English translation.

urdu alphabet								
ا	ب	پ	ت	ٹ	ث	ج	چ	ح
خ	د	ڈ	ذ	ر	ڑ	ز	ژ	س
ش	ص	ض	ط	ظ	ع	غ	ف	ق
ک	گ	ل	م	ن	و	ہ	ی	

آ

آپ aap **you** sg pol&pl
آج aaj **today**
آج رات aaj raat **tonight**
آدمی *aad*·mee ⓜ **man**
آدھا *aa*·daa **half**
آنا *aa*·naa **arrive • come**

ا

اب ab **now**
اپاہج a·*paa*·hij **disabled**
اچّھا *ach*·chaa **good** a
احساس ہونا *eh*·saas *ho*·naa **feel**
اخبار *ak*·baar ⓜ **newspaper**
اردو *ur*·doo ⓕ **Urdu (language)**
اڑنا *ur*·naa **fly** v
استرا *us*·ta·raa ⓜ **razor**
اگلا *ag*·laa **next (month)**
الٹی کا احساس *ul*·tee kaa *eh*·saas ⓜ **nausea**
امرجینسی i·mar·*jen*·see ⓕ **emergency**
امّیجان *am*·mee·jaan ⓕ **mother**
انٹرنیٹ in·*tar*·net ⓜ **Internet**
اندر جانا *an*·dar *jaa*·naa **enter**
انڈیا *in*·di·yaa ⓜ **India**
انگریزی an·*gre*·zee ⓕ **English (language)**
اور aur **and**
اوّل درجہ *av*·val *dar*·jaa ⓜ **first-class ticket**
اونچا *oon*·chaa **high**
اہم a·*ham* **important**

اے-ٹی-ایم e tee em (f) **ATM**
ائے-سی e see (f) **air conditioner**
ای میل ee mayl (f) **email**
ایسپرن *es*·prin (f) **aspirin**
ایک ساتھ رہنا ek saat *reh*·naa **share (a dorm)**
ایک طرفہ ٹکٹ ek ta·ra·*faa* ti·*kat* (m) **one-way ticket**
ایکسپریس میل *eks*·pres mayl (f) **express mail**
ایلرجی e·*lar*·jee (f) **allergy**
ایمبلینس *em*·bu·lens (m) **ambulance**
اینٹیبایوٹکس en·ti·baa·*yo*·tiks (m) **antibiotics**
اینٹسیپٹک en·ti·*sep*·tik (m) **antiseptic** n

ب

باتھروم *baat*·room (m) **bathroom**
بارش *baa*·rish (f) **rain** n
بازار *baa*·zaar (m) **market**
باہر *baa*·har **outside**
بٹوا ba·tu·*aa* (m) **wallet**
بجلی *bij*·lee (f) **electricity**
بچّہ *bach*·chaa (m) **baby • child**
بخار bu·*kaar* (m) **fever**
بدلنا ba·*dal*·naa **exchange (money)** v
برا bu·*raa* **bad**
برش brush (m) **toothbrush**
بریک brek (m) **brake (car)**
بڑا ba·*raa* **big**
بس bas (f) **bus**
بعد baad **after**
بکنگ bu·*king* (f) **reservation**
بل bil (m) **bill** n
بند band **closed**
بنگلا *bang*·laa (f) **Bengali (language)**
بوتل bo·*tal* (f) **bottle**
بوکنگ کرانا bu·*king* ka·*raa*·naa **book** v
بولنا *bol*·naa **speak**
بھاری *baa*·ree **heavy**
بہت ba·*hut* **too (expensive)**
بھرا ہوا ba·*raa* hu·*aa* **full**
بھورا *boo*·raa **brown**
بھوکا *boo*·kaa **hungry**
بھیجنا *bej*·naa **send**
بیرا *be*·raa (m)&(f) **waiter**
بیما *bee*·maa (m) **insurance**
بیمار *bee*·maar **ill**
بینک کا کھاتا baynk kaa *kaa*·taa (m) **bank account**
بیوی *bee*·vee (f) **wife**

پ

پاس paas **near(by)**
پانی *paa*·nee (m) **water**
پتہ pa·*taa* (m) **address**
پٹّی *pat*·tee (f) **bandage**
پر par **on**
پرانا pu·*raa*·naa **old**
پکانا pa·*kaa*·naa **cook** v
پلنگ pa·*lang* (m) **bed**
پلیٹ plet (m) **plate**
پوسٹ آفس post *aa*·fis (m) **post office**
پوسٹکارڈ *post*·kaard (m) **postcard**
پولیس pu·*lis* (f) **police**
پہاڑ pa·*haar* (m) **mountain**
پہچان *peh*·chaan (f) **identification**
پھل pal (m) **fruit**
پہلا *peh*·laa **first**
پہلے *peh*·le **before**
پیاس pyaas (f) **thirst**
پیٹ میں درد pet meng dard (m) **stomachache**
پیچھے *pee*·che **behind**
پیدل جانا *pay*·dal *jaa*·naa **walk** v
پیسے *pay*·se (m) **money**
پیسے دینا *pay*·se *de*·naa **pay** v
پیغام *pay*·gaam (m) **message**
پیکیٹ *pay*·ket (m) **package • packet**
پیلا *pee*·laa **yellow**
پین pen (f) **pen**

پینا *pee*·naa **drink** v
پینٹ paynt (f) **trousers**

ت

تاپمان *taap*·maan (m) **temperature**
تار taar (m) **telegram**
تاریخ *taa*·reek (f) **date (time)**
تالا *taa*·laa (m) **lock** n
تجوری ti·*jo*·ree **safe** a
ترجمان *tar*·ja·maan (m)&(f) **interpreter**
ترجمہ کرنا *tar*·ju·mah *kar*·naa **translate**
تک tak **until**
تولیہ *tau*·li·yaa (m) **towel**
تہفہ *toh*·faa (m) **gift**
تھکا ہوا ta·*kaa* hu·*aa* **tired**
تیرنا *tayr*·naa **swim** v
تیل tel (m) **oil**

ٹ

ٹارچ taarch (m) **flashlight (torch)**
ٹایر *taa*·yar (m) **tyre**
ٹرین tren (f) **train**
ٹکٹ ti·*kat* (m) **stamp • ticket**
ٹوٹا *too*·taa **broken**
ٹھہرنا *tehr*·naa **stop** v
ٹئلیٹ *taa*·i·let (m) **toilet**
ٹیکسی *tayk*·see (f) **taxi**
ٹیلیفون *te*·lee·fon (m) **telephone** n
ٹیلیوزن te·*lee*·vi·zan (m) **television**
ٹین کھولنے کا اوزار
teen *kol*·ne kaa *au*·zaar (m) **tin opener**

ج

جانا *jaa*·naa **go**
جلدی *jal*·dee **early • fast • quickly • soon**
جنس jins (m) **sex**
جنوب ja·*noob* (m) **south**
جوتے *joo*·te (m) **shoes**
جی ہاں jee haang **yes**

چ

چابی *chaa*·bee (f) **key**
چادر *chaa*·dar (f) **sheet (bed)**
چاقو *chaa*·koo (m) **knife**
چلانا cha·*laa*·naa **drive** v
چمّچ *cham*·mach (m) **spoon**
چوٹ chot (f) **injury**
چھٹّی *chut*·tee (f) **holidays • vacation**
چھوٹ choot (f) **discount**
چھوٹا *cho*·taa **short (height/length) • small**
چیک chek (m) **cheque (bank)**

ح

حادثہ *haad*·sah (m) **accident**
حاملہ *haa*·mi·lah **pregnant**

خ

خاتون *kaa*·toon (f) **woman**
خالی *kaa*·lee **empty • vacant**
خاموش *kaa*·mosh **quiet**
خاندان کا نام *kaan*·daan kaa naam (m)
surname
خبر ka·*bar* (f) **news**
خراب ka·*raab* **faulty**
خریدنا ka·*reed*·naa **buy**
خط kat (m) **letter (mail)**
خطرناک ka·*tar*·naak **dangerous**
خوبصورت koob·*soo*·rat **beautiful**
خوش kush **happy**

د

دانت منجن daant·*man*·jan (m) **toothpaste**
دانت میں درد daant meng dard (m)
toothache
داہنہ *daa*·hi·naa **right (direction)**
درد dard (m) **pain**
درد دور کرنے کی دوا
dard door *kar*·ne kee da·*vaa* (f) **painkillers**

دست dast (m) **diarrhoea**
دکان du·*kaan* (f) **shop** n
دکھانا di·*kaa*·naa **show** v
دل کی بیماری dil kee bee·*maa*·ree (f) **heart condition**
دن کا کھانا din kaa *kaa*·naa (m) **lunch**
دوا da·*vaa* (f) **medicine (medication)**
دواخانا da·vaa·*kaa*·naa (m) **pharmacy**
دودھ dood (m) **milk**
دور door **far**
دورا *dau*·raa (m) **tour** n
دوست dost (m)&(f) **friend**
دوسرا *doos*·raa **other • second (after first)**
دونوں do·*nong* **both**
دھلائ du·*laa*·ee (f) **laundry (clothes)**
دھواں du·*aang* (m) **smoke** n
دھونا *do*·naa **wash (something)**
دھیرے دھیرے *dee*·re *dee*·re **slowly**
دیر der (f) **delay** n
دیر der **late (not early)**

ڈ

ڈاک daak (f) **mail • post**
ڈاکٹر *daak*·tar (m)&(f) **doctor**
ڈبل کمرا da·*bal kam*·raa (m) **double room**
ڈوری *do*·ree (f) **string** n
ڈیرا *de*·raa (m) **campsite**
ڈینٹسٹ *den*·tist (m)&(f) **dentist**

ر

رات raat (f) **night**
رات کا کھانا raat kaa *kaa*·naa (m) **dinner**
رسوئ ra·*so*·ee (f) **kitchen**
رسید ra·*seed* (f) **receipt**
رفنڈ ri·*fand* (m) **refund** n
روانہ ہونا ra·*vaa*·nah *ho*·naa **depart • leave**
روپیہ ru·pa·*yaa* (m) **rupee**
روز roz (m) **day**
روشنی *rosh*·nee (f) **light** n
رہنے کی جگہ *reh*·ne kee ja·*gah* (f) **accommodation**
ریسٹورینٹ res·*to*·rent (m) **restaurant**

س

سامان *saa*·maan (m) **baggage (luggage)**
سامان رکھنے کی جگہ *saa*·maan *rak*·ne kee ja·*gah* (f) **left luggage (office)**
سائکل *saa*·i·kil (f) **bicycle**
سب sab **all**
سبزی *sab*·zee (f) **vegetable** n
سٹیشن *ste*·shan (m) **station**
سردرد *sar*·dard (m) **headache**
سردی *sar*·dee (f) **cold (weather)**
سڑک sa·*rak* (f) **road • street**
سستہ *sas*·taa **cheap**
سفارتخانہ sa·*faa*·rat *kaa*·naa (m) **embassy**
سفارش کرنا si·*faa*·rish *kar*·naa **recommend**
سفید sa·*fed* **white**
سکّے *sik*·ke (m) **coins**
سگریٹ *sig*·ret (f) **cigarette**
سلیٹی رنگ کا *sle*·tee rang kaa **grey**
سمندر sa·*man*·dar (m) **sea**
سمندر کا ساحل sa·*man*·dar kaa *saa*·hil (m) **beach**
سنگل کمرا *sin*·gal *kam*·raa (m) **single room**
سورج *soo*·raj (m) **sun**
سویرا sa·*ve*·raa (m) **morning (6am–1pm)**
سیاحوں کا آفس *sai*·yaa·hong kaa *aa*·fis (m) **tourist office**
سیدھا *see*·daa **direct** a
سیل sel (m) **battery**
سیّاح *sai*·yaah (m)&(f) **tourist** n

ش

شام shaam (f) **evening**
شامل *shaa*·mil **included**
سبزیخور *sab*·zee·kor **vegetarian**
شاور *shaa*·var (m) **shower** n

شراب sha·*raab* (f) **alcohol • wine**
شمال shu·*maal* (m) **north**
شورغل *shor*·gul (m) **noise**
شوہر *shau*·har (m) **husband**
شہر sha·*har* (m) **city**

ص

صابن *saa*·bun (m) **soap**
صاف saaf **clean** a

ض

ضروری za·*roo*·ree **urgent**

ط

طالب علم *taa*·li·be ilm (m) **student**

ع

عینک *ay*·nak (f) **glasses**

ف

فلم film (f) **cinema • movie**
فوٹو *fo*·to (m) **photograph**
فون کارڈ fon kaard (m) **phone card**

ق

قیمت *kee*·mat (f) **cost • price**

ک

کاروبار kaa·*ro*·baar (m) **business**
کاغذ *kaa*·gaz (m) **paper**
کافی *kaa*·fee **enough**
کالا *kaa*·laa **black**
کانٹا *kaan*·taa (m) **fork**
کب kab **when**
کٹنا *kat*·naa **cut** v
کٹوری ka·*to*·ree (f) **bowl**
کچھ kuch **some**
کچھ نہیں kuch na·*heeng* **nothing**
کچھا *kach*·chaa (m) **underwear**
کرایا ki·*raa*·yaa (m) **rent** n
کرائے پر لینا ki·*raa*·ye par *le*·naa **hire** v
کرتہ *kur*·taa (m) **shirt**
کرسی *kur*·see (m) **seat**
کوشش کرنا *ko*·shish *kar*·naa **try** v
کل kal **tomorrow • yesterday**
کم kam **less**
کمبل *kam*·bal (m) **blanket**
کمرا *kam*·raa (m) **room**
کنڈم *kaan*·dam (m) **condom**
کون kaun **who**
کہاں ka·*haang* **where**
کھانا *kaa*·naa **eat**
کھانا *kaa*·naa (m) **food**
کھانسی *kaan*·see (f) **cough** n
کھڑکی *kir*·kee (f) **window**
کھلا ku·*laa* **open** a
کھویا ہوا *ko*·yaa hu·*aa* **lost**
کے بغیر ke ba·*gayr* **without**
کے ساتھ ke saat **with**
کیش کرنا kaysh *kar*·naa **cash (a cheque)** v
کینسل کرنا *kayn*·sal *kar*·naa **cancel**
کیوں kyong **why**

گ

گاڑی *gaa*·ree (f) **car**
گاڑی پارک کرنے کی جگہ
gaa·ree paark *kar*·ne kee ja·*gah* (f) **car park**
گاڑی چلانے کا لائسینس *gaa*·ree
cha·*laa*·ne kaa *laa*·i·sens (m) **drivers licence**
گرم garm **hot • warm**
گرمی *gar*·mee (f) **heat**
گلاس glaas (m) **glass (drinking)**
گندہ *gan*·daa **dirty**
گوشت gosht (m) **meat**
گھڑی ga·*ree* (f) **watch** n

ل

لال laal **red**
لاوارث سامان کا دفتر laa·*vaa*·ris *saa*·maan kaa *daf*·tar ⓜ **lost property office**
لڑکا *lar*·kaa ⓜ **boy**
لڑکی *lar*·kee ⓕ **girl**
لغت lu·*gat* ⓜ **dictionary**
لفٹ lift ⓜ **elevator**
لکھنا *likh*·naa **write**
لمبا *lam*·baa **long**
لہنگا la·*han*·gaa ⓜ **skirt**
لیکن *le*·kin **but**

م

مچھلی *mach*·lee ⓕ **fish**
محبّت mu·*hob*·bat ⓕ **love** n
مدد کرنا ma·*dad kar*·naa **help** v
مذاقیہ ma·*zaa*·ki·yah **funny**
مرکز *mar*·kaz ⓜ **centre**
مرمّت کرنا ma·*ram*·mat *kar*·naa **repair** v
مسلمان mu·*sal*·maan **Muslim**
مشرق *mash*·rik ⓜ **east**
مغرب *mag*·rib ⓜ **west**
مفت muft **free (gratis)**
موسیقی moo·*see*·kee ⓕ **music**
مہنگا ma·*han*·gaa **expensive**
مہینہ ma·*hee*·naa ⓜ **month**
میٹھا *mee*·taa **sweet** a
میرا *me*·raa **my**
میں mayng **I**
مینیو *men*·yoo ⓜ **menu**

ن

ناپ naap ⓕ **size (clothes)**
ناشتہ *naash*·taa ⓜ **breakfast**
ناک naak ⓕ **nose**
نام naam ⓜ **name**
نشانیوں کی دکان ni·*shaa*·ni·yong kee du·*kaan* ⓕ **souvenir shop**
نشیلی دوا na·*shee*·lee da·*vaa* ⓕ **drug (illegal)**
نقد na·*kad* ⓜ **cash • money**
نقشہ *nak*·shaa ⓜ **map**
نکاس ni·*kaas* ⓜ **exit** n
نمبر *nam*·bar ⓜ **number**
نوکری *nauk*·ree ⓕ **job**
نہیں na·*heeng* **no**
نیا na·*yaa* **new**
نیچے *nee*·che **down**
نیلا *nee*·laa **blue**
نیند neend ⓕ **sleep** n

و

واپس آنا *vaa*·pas *kar*·naa **return** v
واپسی ٹکٹ *vaa*·pa·see ti·*kat* ⓕ **return ticket**
والد *vaa*·lid ⓜ **father**
وقت vakt ⓜ **time**
وکیل va·*keel* ⓜ&ⓕ **lawyer**
ویسا *vee*·saa ⓜ **visa**

ہ

ہائک *haa*·ik ⓜ **hike** n
ہرا ha·*raa* **green**
ہسپتال *has*·pa·taal ⓜ **hospital**
ہمارا ha·*maa*·raa **our**
ہمجنس پرست *ham*·jins pa·*rast* **homosexual** a
ہندو *hin*·doo **Hindu**
ہندي *hin*·dee ⓕ **Hindi (language)**
ہوائ اڈّا ha·*vaa*·ee *ad*·daa ⓜ **airport**
ہوائ جہاز ha·*vaa*·ee ja·*haaz* ⓜ **airplane**
ہوٹل *ho*·tal ⓜ **hotel**

ي

یہ yeh **he • it • she • this**
یہاں ya·*haang* **here**

Bengali

bengali

- national language
- official state language
- widely understood

For more details, see the **introduction**, page 171.

INTRODUCTION

সূচনা

Bengali is spoken by approximately 220 million people, ranking it as the fourth most spoken language in the world. As well as being the official language of Bangladesh and the Indian states of Tripura and West Bengal, it's also spoken by large communities in North America and parts of Europe and the Middle East.

Bengali was derived from Magadhi Prakrit, the official language during the reign of the great Indian emperor Asoka (272-231 BC). The tongue now recognisable as Old Bengali had developed by about 1000AD, complete with its distinctive Brahmi script. At that time, Bengali was strongly flavoured with *ţaţ*·b'a·va তাতভাবা (Prakrit words) and *ţaţ*·sa·ma তাতসামা (Sanskrit words). This linguistic concoction was spiced up with Persian, Arabic and Turkish vocabulary when Bengal was conquered by Muslims in the 12th century AD. Europeans started to colonise Asia 400 years later, and Bengali acquired a certain tang of Portuguese, Dutch, French and English. The current script and alphabet were standardised in 1778 to facilitate printing, then fine-tuned in the mid-19th century.

The Bengali language has a rich literary tradition which dates back to 1000AD with the *Caryapada*, a unique manuscript of Buddhist songs discovered in the collection of Nepal's royal family and published in 1916. Until the 19th century, all Bengali works were written in rhymed verse, and prose became widely used only under the influence of Sanskrit texts and European colonists. Today's Bengali has two literary forms – *sha*·d'u·b'a·sha সাধুভাষা (lit: elegant language), the traditional literary style of 16th century Middle Bengali, and *chohl*·ţi·b'a·sha চলতি ভাষা (lit: running language), a more colloquial form based on the Bengali spoken in Kolkata.

at a glance …

language name: Bengali

name in language: বাংলা *bang*·la

language family: the Indic group of the Indo-Aryan family of Indo-European languages

approximate number of speakers: 220 million

close relatives: Assamese, Hindi, Oriya, Sanskrit

donations to English: chaulmoogra, jute

Rabindranath Tagore is the best-known Bengali author, a strong Indian patriot and prodigious writer in both traditional and contemporary styles. His vast oeuvre, including novels, essays, plays and poetry, was to make him the first Asian winner of the Nobel Prize for Literature in 1913. Tagore's religio-philosophical writing elevated him to the status of a poet-sage on the subcontinent, and the national anthems of both India and Bangladesh are his compositions.

The 1947 Partition of India and Pakistan may not have had an impact on how the Bengali tongue was structured, but it certainly had a huge impact on who was able to speak the language. In the original division of land, the territory of Bengal was separated into the Indian state of West Bengal and the Pakistani state of East Pakistan (today's Bangladesh). There was great internal strife over which official language Pakistan would choose – in the end, only Urdu was granted official status, despite the high percentage of Bengali speakers in East Pakistan. A strong pro-Bengali language reform movement was formed to redress this imbalance. Tensions reached their peak on 21 February 1952, when students from Dhaka University were shot dead by police as they protested in support of the Bengali language. Two years later, Bengali was made an official language of Pakistan. The date of 21 February was subsequently commemorated as Language Martyrs' Day within Bangladesh and West Bengal, and the UNESCO declared it the International Mother Language Day. In 1971, following the resolution of the Liberation War between the state of Pakistan and Bengali citizens, Bangladesh became an independent nation with Bengali as its national language.

This book gives you the practical phrases you need to get by in Bengali, as well as all the fun, spontaneous phrases that can lead to a better understanding of Bengali speakers. Once you've got the hang of how to pronounce Bengali words, the rest is just a matter of confidence. Local knowledge, new relationships and a sense of satisfaction are on the tip of your tongue. So don't just stand there, say something!

abbreviations used in the Bengali section

a	adjective
acc	accusative
adv	adverb
dat	dative
f	feminine
gen	genitive
inf	informal
int	intimate
lit	literal translation
loc	locative
m	masculine
n	noun
nom	nominative
pl	plural
pol	polite
sg	singular
v	verb

Bengali, like many of the languages of South Asia, is rich in sounds. Quite a few of the sounds in Bengali aren't used in English and can be a little confronting at first. Don't worry though – just use the coloured pronunciation guides provided next to the Bengali script throughout this phrasebook, practise a little bit, and you'll soon be able to communicate with the locals.

vowel sounds

Most Bengali vowel sounds are very similar to English ones. The most important thing to focus on is the length of the vowels (like the difference between the sounds a and aa).

vowel sounds

symbol	english equivalent	bengali example
a	run	*bang*·la
ą	tap	ąk
aa	rather	*aa*·mar
ai	aisle	*koh*·ţ'ai
ay	mail	*ee*·mayl
e	red	e·ta
ee	bee	beesh
i	bit	*ing*·re·ji
o	shot	dosh
oh	both	*oh*·shud'
oy	boy	*moy*·la
u	put	dud'
ui	quick	dui

consonant sounds		
symbol	english equivalent	bengali example
b	**big**	boy
b'	**blight** (aspirated **b**)	*b'a*·loh
ch	**cheat**	*cha*·bi
ch'	**cheese** (aspirated **ch**)	*ch'e*·le
d	**doubt**	dosh
d'	**din** (aspirated **d**)	*bud'*·baar
đ	retroflex **d**	*ţ'an*·đa
đ'	aspirated retroflex **d**	*đ'a*·ka
f	**frog**	*foh*·kir
g	**go**	*ga*·ŗi
g'	**language** (aspirated **g**)	g'um
h	**hit**	haaţ
j	**juggle**	*ja*·na·la
j'	**jam** (aspirated **j**)	*j'or*·na
k	**skin**	kaj
k'	**kick** (aspirated **k**)	*k'o*·bohr
l	**loud**	lal
m	**man**	*mo*·ja
n	**no**	nam
ng	**king** (nasal sound)	*bang*·la
p	**spit**	*pa*·ni
p'	**pit** (aspirated **p**)	p'ol
r	**run** (but slightly trilled)	raaţ
ŗ	retroflex **r**	*ga*·ŗi
s	**so**	*raa*·sţa
t	**talk**	*ta*·ka
t'	**tin** (aspirated **t**)	*t'an*·da
ţ	retroflex **t**	*ţu*·mi
ţ'	aspirated retroflex **t**	*ţ'a*·mun
y	**yes**	*bi*·ye

consonant sounds

Bengali consonants are mostly pronounced the same as English ones, but there are some significant differences. In Bengali there's an important distinction between 'aspirated' and 'unaspirated' consonants – you'll get the idea if you hold your hand in front of your mouth to feel your breath, and say 'pit' (where the 'p' is aspirated) and 'spit' (where it's unaspirated). In our pronunciation guides we've used the apostrophe (as in b') to show when you need to make an aspirated sound – you need to say this as a strong 'h' sound after the consonant.

You'll also see that some consonant sounds in our pronounciation guides have a cedilla underneath them, like ţ. These are 'retroflex' sounds, which means you bend your tongue backwards to make the sound. The closest you can get to this in English is to say 'art' but as one flap on the roof of the mouth for the 'r' sound.

The sounds v, w and z are only found in words taken from English, and are pronounced the same as in English.

syllables & word stress

In our coloured pronunciation guides, words are divided into syllables with dots (eg *bo*·ch'ohr 'year') to help you pronounce them. Word stress in Bengali is very subtle, and varies in different regions of the Indian subcontinent. Stress normally falls on the first syllable (eg *b'a*·loh 'good'). Just follow our pronunciation guides – the stressed syllable is always in italics.

reading & writing

Bengali is written in the Brahmi script, which is also used to write Assamese, Garo, Manipuri and Mundari. It's written from left to right, and there are 43 characters in the primary forms (ie characters not combined with each other) – 32 for consonants and 11 for vowels. For the most part, Brahmi is a phonetic system, which means that one symbol is always pronounced the same way.

Vowels are traditionally listed first in Brahmi. Vowels can be written as independent letters (see the first table on page 176). However, when added to consonants they're written using a variety of diacritical marks, which are placed above, below, before or after the consonant they belong to, as shown in the second table.

Consonants (see the primary forms in the third table) are arranged according to where the sound comes from in your mouth (from the throat to the lips). Each one includes an o, as they're represented as syllabic units and always have that sound in their basic form. When consonants follow directly after each other, they're written with special conjunct letters. Note that some characters are pronounced the same way – eg শ, ষ and স are all pronounced as sho.

Most punctuation marks in Bengali look the same as in English, except the full stop – a short vertical line (।) is used instead of a dot at the end of a sentence.

vowels										
অ o	আ a	ই i	ঈ i	উ u	ঊ u	ঋ ri	এ e	ঐ i	ও oh	ঔ *oh*·u

vowels with vowel diacritics										
ক ko	কা ka	কি ki	কী ki	কু ku	কূ ku	কৃ kri	কে ke	কৈ *ko*·i	কো koh	কৌ *koh*·u

consonants								
ক ko	খ k'o	গ go	ঘ g'o	ঙ *u*·mon	চ cho	ছ ch'o	জ jo	ঝ j'o
ঞ *ee*·o	ট to	ঠ t'o	ড đo	ঢ đ'o	ণ no	ত ţo	থ ţ'o	দ do
ধ d'o	ন no	প po	ফ fo	ব bo	ভ b'o	ম mo	য jo	র ro
ল lo	শ sho	ষ sho	স sho	হ ho				

a–z phrasebuilder

কথা বলা

contents

The list below shows which grammatical structures you can use to say what you want. Look under each function – in alphabetical order – for information on how to build your own phrases. For example, to tell the taxi driver where your hotel is, look for **giving directions/orders** and you'll be directed to information on **demonstratives, postpositions,** etc. A glossary of grammatical terms is included at the end of this book (see page 297). Abbreviations like nom and acc in the literal translations for each example refer to the case of the noun – this is explained in the **glossary** and in **case**. Bengali script is not included in this chapter.

affixes

giving directions/orders • indicating location

Bengali uses both prefixes (syllables joined to the beginning of words) and suffixes (syllables joined to the end of words) to show various bits of grammatical information, such as articles, noun cases, plurals, postpositions, verb tenses etc. Prefixes and suffixes are also known as affixes.

station	*ste*·shohn	(lit: station-nom)
go	*ja*·wa	(lit: go)
We'll go to the station.	*aam*·ra *ste*·shoh·ne *ja*·boh	(lit: we station-loc will-go)

See **articles, case, plurals, postpositions** and **verbs** for more information.

adjectives & adverbs

describing people/things • doing things

Adjectives precede the nouns they describe, and adverbs precede the verbs they go with. They have only one form, which is often used as both the adjective and the adverb.

a good hotel
ąk·ta *b'a*·loh *hoh*·tel (lit: one good hotel)

You speak English well.
ţu·mi *b'a*·loh *ing*·re·ji *ko*·ţ'a *bo*·len (lit: you good English-acc talk do)

articles

describing people/things • naming people/things

The Bengali equivalents of 'a/an' and 'the' are only used for emphasis. To say 'the', add ·ta to the end of the noun. To say 'a/an', add *ąk*·ta (lit: one) before the noun.

daughter	*me*·e	(lit: daughter)
the daughter	*me*·e·ta	(lit: daughter-the)
a daughter	*ąk*·ta *me*·e	(lit: one daughter)

See also **case**.

be

doing things • indicating location

The verb 'be' is not used in Bengali as it is in English. To describe something or to say where something is, you don't need to use a verb at all.

This meal is delicious.	ay *k'a*·bar·ta *mo*·ja	(lit: this meal-nom delicious)
Your torch is here.	*ţoh*·mar torch *e*·k'a·ne	(lit: your torch-nom here)

See also **case, have, possession** and **there is/are**.

case

describing people/things • giving directions/orders • indicating location • naming people/things • possessing

Bengali is a 'case' language, which means that endings are added to nouns and pronouns to show their role and relationship to other elements in the sentence. There are four cases in Bengali, as shown in the table below:

noun cases	
nominative nom – shows the subject of the sentence	
This bag is very heavy. ay bąg k'ub *b'a*·ri	(lit: this bag-nom very heavy)
accusative acc – shows the object of the sentence	
Did you see that bag? oy *bąg*·ta *de*·k'e·ch'oh	(lit: that bag-acc you-see)
genitive gen – shows possession ('of')	
The colour of this bag is very nice. ay *bąg*·tar rong k'ub *shun*·dohr	(lit: this bag-gen colour-nom very nice)
locative loc – shows location ('in', 'on', 'at', 'with' etc)	
It's in her bag. *e*·ta ohr *bą*·ge *aa*·ch'e	(lit: it her bag-loc have)

In this chapter, the case of each noun has been given in the literal translations to show you how the system works. Bengali nouns in lists in the rest of this book, in the **culinary reader** and in the **dictionary**, are in the nominative case. You can use the nominative case in any phrase and be understood just fine, although this won't always be completely correct within a sentence.

demonstratives

describing people/things • giving directions/orders • naming people/things • pointing things out

Bengali has one word for 'this' and 'these' (ay) and a second word for 'that' and 'those' (oy). These words are placed before the noun they refer to.

These bags belong to that man.
ay *bąg*·gu·loh oy *lohk*·tar (lit: these bags-nom that man-gen)

have

doing things • possessing

The verb *aa*·ch'e (lit: have) can be used to translate both 'be' and 'have'. The same form of the verb is used for all persons. When expressing possession, it's accompanied by a possessive pronoun (her, your), not by a personal pronoun (she, you).

Do you have a torch?
ţoh·mar torch *aa*·ch'e (lit: your torch-nom have)

She has a pocket knife.
ohr *ąk*·ta *po*·ket *ch'u*·ri *aa*·ch'e (lit: her one pocket knife-nom have)

It's in her bag.
e·ta ohr *bą*·ge *aa*·ch'e (lit: it her bag-loc have)

See also **be** and **possession**.

negatives

negating

For the present tense, use nai (not) to make your sentence negative. For the future or the past, use na (not). Both words are placed at the end of a sentence.

He's at the hotel now.
u·ni *q*·k'ohn *hoh*·te·le (lit: he now hotel-loc)

He's not at the hotel now.
u·ni *q*·k'ohn *hoh*·te·le nai (lit: he now hotel-loc not)

He will stay at the hotel tomorrow.
u·ni *aa*·ga·mi·kaal *hoh*·te·le *ţ'ak*·ben (lit: he tomorrow hotel-loc stay)

He won't stay at the hotel tomorrow.
u·ni *aa*·ga·mi·kaal *hoh*·te·le *ţ'ak*·ben na (lit: he tomorrow hotel-loc stay not)

personal pronouns

naming people/things • possessing

Bengali distinguishes three 'levels' of formality – there are three different forms for 'you': intimate (*ţu*·i), used with very close friends and kids, informal (*ţu*·mi), for friends and younger people, and polite (*aap*·ni), used with older people and strangers. We've used the terms appropriate for the context throughout this phrasebook. Also note that Bengali has only one word for 'he' and 'she'.

	polite	informal	intimate
I		*aa*·mi	
you sg	*aap*·ni	*ţu*·mi	*ţu*·i
he/she	*u*·ni	oh	
it		*e*·ta	
we		*aam*·ra	
you pl	*aap*·na·ra	*ţohm*·ra	*ţoh*·ra
they	*u*·na·ra	*oh*·ra	

plurals

describing people/things • naming people/things

Plurals are formed by adding the suffix ·ra to nouns representing people and ·gu·loh to objects and animals.

singular		plural	
student	*ch'aţ*·roh	students	*ch'aţ*·roh·ra
book	*boh*·i	books	*boh*·i·gu·loh

possession

describing people/things • naming people/things • possessing

To show possession in Bengali, use one of the possessive pronouns in the table below before the thing which is owned. Bengali has three different forms for 'your': intimate (ţohr), used with very close friends and kids, informal (*ţoh*·mar), for friends and younger people, and polite (*aap*·nar), used with older people and strangers. Also note that Bengali has only one word for 'his' and 'her'. For more information, see **be**, **case**, **have**, **personal pronouns** and **postpositions.**

This is her bag. ay ohr bąg (lit: this her bag-nom)

	polite	informal	intimate
my		*aa*·mar	
your sg	*aap*·nar	*ţoh*·mar	ţohr
his/her	*u*·nar	ohr	
its		e·tar	
our		*aa*·ma·der	
your pl	*aap*·nar	*ţoh*·mar	ţohr
their	*u*·na·der	*oh*·der	

postpositions

giving directions/orders • indicating location • pointing things out

Where English has prepositions, Bengali has postpositions – eg the words *oh*·pa·re (across) and *ka*·ch'e (near) come after the noun, which is usually in the genitive case.

across the street	*ras*·ţar *oh*·pa·re	(lit: street-gen across)
near the post office	post *o*·fi·sher *ka*·ch'e	(lit: post office-gen near)

Here are some more common suffixes – the equivalents of English prepositions:

postpositions					
at	·te	for	·john·noh	from	·ţ'he·ke
in	·e	on	·e	to	·e

See also **affixes**, **case** and **possession**.

questions

asking questions • making requests

To turn a statement into a question, raise your tone towards the end of the sentence. You can also add ki (lit: what) after the subject of the sentence or at the very end.

This room is free.	ay rum *k'a*·li *aa*·ch'e	(lit: this room-nom free have)
Is this room free?	ay rum ki *k'a*·li *aa*·ch'e	(lit: this room-nom what free have)

The question words (listed below) are generally placed at the end of the sentence.

question words			
how	*kq*·mohn	where	*koh*·ţ'ai
how much	*ko*·toh *k'a*·nik	which	*kohn*·ta
how many	*koy*·ta	who sg	ke
what	ki	who pl	*ka*·ra
when	*ko*·k'ohn	why	*kq*·noh

What's the address? *ţ'i*·ka·na ki (lit: address-**nom** what)

To make a polite request, use the word *ek*·tu (a little) plus the dictionary form of the verb followed by *koh*·ren (do) in the appropriate form (see **verbs** for information on how to change the verb 'do').

Could you please help me?
aa·ma·ke *ek*·tu *sha*·haj·joh *kohr*·ţe *paa*·ren (lit: me a-little help do can)

See also **word order**.

there is/are

negating • pointing things out

To say 'there is/are' use *aa*·ch'e (lit: have), and for 'there isn't/aren't' use nai (lit: no).

There's a fan in my room.
aa·mar *ru*·me fan *aa*·ch'e (lit: my room-**loc** fan-**nom** have)

There isn't a fan in my room.
aa·mar *ru*·me fan nai (lit: my room-**loc** fan-**nom** no)

See also **be** and **negatives**.

verbs

asking questions • doing things • giving directions/orders • making requests • negating

To form different verb tenses in Bengali, use the dictionary form of a verb plus the appropriate form of the verb *koh*·ren (do), which changes according to tense and person. The endings for present, past and future tenses are shown in the tables below.

We travel by train.
aam·ra *tre*·ne *ja*·ţaaţ *koh*·ri (lit: we train-**loc** travel do)

We travelled by train.
aam·ra *tre*·ne *ja*·ţaaţ *koh*·re·ch'i·lam (lit: we train-**loc** travel did)

We'll travel by train.
aam·ra *tre*·ne *ja*·ţaaţ *kohr*·boh (lit: we train-**loc** travel will-do)

present tense		
I/we	·i	*koh*·ri
you sg&pl	·oh	*koh*·roh
he/she/it/they inf	·e	*koh*·re
he/she/they pol	·en	*koh*·ren
past tense		
I/we	·i·lam	*koh*·re·ch'i·lam
you sg&pl	·i·le	*koh*·re·ch'i·le
he/she/it/they inf	·i·loh	*koh*·re·ch'i·loh
he/she/they pol	·i·len	*koh*·re·ch'i·len
future tense		
I/we	·boh	*kohr*·boh
you sg&pl	·be	*kohr*·be
he/she/it/they inf	·be	*kohr*·be
he/she/they pol	·ben	*kohr*·ben

See also **negatives**.

word order

asking questions • doing things • giving directions/ orders • making requests • negating

Basic Bengali word order is subject-object-verb.

I speak Bengali.
aa·mi *bang*·la *bohl*·ţe *paa*·ri (lit: I Bengali-acc speak can)

I don't speak Bengali.
aa·mi *bang*·la *bohl*·ţe *paa*·ri nai (lit: I Bengali-acc speak can not)

Do you speak Bengali?
aap·ni *bang*·la *bohl*·ţe *paa*·ren (lit: you Bengali-acc speak can)

See also **negatives** and **questions**.

language difficulties

ভাষার সমস্যা

Do you speak (English)?
আপনি কি (ইংরেজি) বলতে পারেন? — *aap*·ni ki (ing·*re*·ji) *bohl*·ţe *paa*·ren

Does anyone speak (English)?
কেউ কি (ইংরেজি) বলতে পারেন? — *ke*·u ki (ing·*re*·ji) *bohl*·ţe *paa*·ren

Do you understand?
আপনি কি বুঝতে পারছেন? — *aap*·ni ki *buj'*·ţe *paar*·ch'en

Yes, I understand.
হ্যা, আমি বুঝতে পারছি। — hąng *aa*·mi *buj'*·ţe *paar*·ch'i

No, I don't understand.
না, আমি বুঝতে পারছি না। — na *aa*·mi *buj'*·ţe *paar*·ch'i na

I speak (English).
আমি (ইংরেজি) বলতে পারি। — *aa*·mi (ing·*re*·ji) *bohl*·ţe *paa*·ri

I don't speak (Bengali).
আমি (বাংলা) বলতে পারি না। — *aa*·mi (*bang*·la) *bohl*·ţe *paa*·ri na

I speak a little.
আমি অল্প বলতে পারি। — *aa*·mi *ol*·poh *bohl*·ţe *paa*·ri

I know a few words of Bengali.
আমি অল্প বাংলা বলতে পারি। — *aa*·mi *ol*·poh *bang*·la *bohl*·ţe *paa*·ri

I'm studying Bengali.
আমি বাংলা পড়ছি। — *aa*·mi *bang*·la *pohŗ*·ch'i

I can't read Bengali characters.
আমি বাংলা অক্ষর পড়তে পারি না। — *aa*·mi *bang*·la *ok*·k'ohr *pohŗ*·ţe *paa*·ri na

at a loss for words?

For many 'modern' words – related to accommodation, business, technology, transport, etc – the English term is used alongside the Bengali one (slightly adapted to Bengali pronunciation, of course). When you do get by with English, you can thank the British Raj and the prevalence of 'international' English.

What does *'ach'*·ch'a' mean?	
'আচ্ছা' মানে কি?	*ach'*·ch'a *maa*·ne ki
Can you write it in English?	
ইংরেজিতে লিখেন?	*ing*·re·ji·ţe *li*·k'en

How do you ...?	কি ভাবে ...?	ki *b'a*·be ...
pronounce this	এটা উচ্চারন করেন	*e*·ta uch·*cha*·rohn *koh*·ren
write 'b'ai'	'ভাই' লিখেন	b'ai *li*·k'en

Could you please ...?	... প্লিজ?	... pleez
repeat that	আবার বলেন	*aa*·bar *boh*·len
speak more slowly	আরো ধিরে বলেন	*aa*·roh *d'i*·re *boh*·len
write it down	লিখে দেন	*li*·k'e den

it's all about you, you, you

In Bengali, there are three forms of 'you' which differ in their level of formality. Always use the formal form of 'you' (*aap*·ni) with older people (even if the age difference is very small), in professional relationships and with strangers.

Use the informal form of 'you' (*ţu*·mi) with friends, younger people or close colleagues. Only address someone in the *ţu*·mi form if you're invited to do so. It's an honour to be addressed informally and the switch will happen only when the time's right. Tricky!

The intimate form of 'you' (ţui) is only used with extremely close friends, younger siblings and kids. This form is sometimes used in a derogatory way and to insult people, no matter how formal the relationship is.

In this book all phrases have the form of 'you' appropriate for the situation (ie generally the formal *aap*·ni except in **love**, page 250, and **kids' talk**, page 234, where the informal *ţu*·mi is used).

numbers & amounts

সংখ্যা এবং পরিমান

cardinal numbers

সংখ্যা

1	এক	ąk
2	দুই	dui
3	তিন	ţeen
4	চার	chaar
5	পাচ	paach
6	ছয়	ch'oy
7	সাত	shaaţ
8	আট	aat
9	নয়	noy
10	দশ	dosh
11	এগারো	*ą*·gaa·roh
12	বারো	*baa*·roh
13	তেরো	*ţą*·roh
14	চৌদ্দ	*chohd*·doh
15	পনের	*poh*·ne·roh
16	ষোল	*shoh*·loh
17	সতেরো	*sho*·te·roh
18	আঠারো	*aat'*·aa·roh
19	উনিশ	*u*·nish
20	বিশ	beesh
30	তিরিশ	*ţi*·rish
40	চল্লিশ	*chohl*·lish
50	পঞ্চাশ	*pon*·chaash
60	ষাট	shaat
70	সত্তুর	*shohţ*·ţur
80	আশি	*aa*·shi
90	নব্বই	*nohb*·bo·hi
100	এক শ	ąk shoh
200	দুই শ	dui shoh
1,000	এক হাজার	ąk *haa*·jaar
100,000	এক লাখ	ąk laak'
1,000,000	দশ লাখ	dosh laak'

ordinal numbers

তুলনামূলক সংখ্যা

1st	প্রথম	*proh*·ţ'ohm
2nd	দ্বিতীয়	dee·*ţi*·oh
3rd	তৃতীয়	ţree·*ţi*·oh
4th	চতুর্থ	*choh*·ţur·ţ'oh
5th	পঞ্চম	*pon*·chohm

fractions

ভগ্নাংশ

a quarter	সোয়া	*shoh*·a
a third	তিন ভাগের এক ভাগ	ţin *b'a*·ger ąk b'ag
a half	আর্ধেক	*or*·d'ek
three-quarters	পৌনে	*poh*·ne

useful amounts

প্রয়জনীয় সংখ্যা

How many?	কয়টা?	*koy*·ta
How much?	কত?	*ko*·ţoh
How much? (uncountable things eg flour)	কতখানিক?	*ko*·ţoh·k'a·nik
How much? (small quantities eg salt, medicine)	কতটুকু?	*ko*·ţoh·tu·ku

Please give me ...	আমাকে ... দেন, প্লিজ।	*aa*·ma·ke ... dąn pleez
a few	কয়েকটা	*ko*·ek·ta
less	আরো কম	*a*·roh kom
a little	একটু	*ek*·tu
many	অনেক	*o*·nek
more	আরো	*a*·roh
some	কিছু	*ki*·chu

telling the time

সময় বলা

Bengalis use the 12-hour clock. There's no such concept as 'am' or 'pm' – the time of the day is indicated by adding *sho*·kaal সকাল (morning), *du*·pur দুপুর (afternoon), or raaţ রাত (night) before the time. To tell the time, add the suffix ·ta to the ordinal number which indicates the hour.

What time is it?	কয়টা বাজে?	*koy*·ta *baa*·je
It's (ten) o'clock.	(দশটা) বাজে।	(*dosh*·ta) *baa*·je
Five past (ten).	(দশটা) বেজে পাঁচ।	(*dosh*·ta) *be*·je pach
Quarter past (ten).	সোয়া (দশটা)।	*shoh*·aa (*dosh*·ta)
Half past (ten).	সাড়ে (দশটা)।	*shaa*·ŗe (*dosh*·ta)
Quarter to (ten).	পৌনে (দশটা)।	*poh*·ne (*dosh*·ta)
Twenty to (ten).	(দশটা) বাজতে বিশ।	(*dosh*·ta) *baaj*·te beesh

At what time ...?	কটার সময় ...?	*ko*·tar *sho*·moy ...
At (seven) am.	সকাল (সাতটায়)।	*sho*·kaal (*shaţ*·ta)
At (two) pm.	দুপুর (দইটায়)।	*du*·pur (*dui*·ta)
At (seven) pm.	রাত (সাতটায়)।	raaţ (*shaţ*·ta)

the calendar

ক্যালেন্ডার

days

Monday	সোমবার	*shohm*·baar
Tuesday	মঙ্গলবার	*mohng*·gohl·baar
Wednesday	বুধবার	*bud'*·baar
Thursday	বৃহস্পতিবার	*bri*·hohsh·poh·ţi·baar
Friday	শুক্রবার	*shuk*·roh·baar
Saturday	শনিবার	*shoh*·ni·baar
Sunday	রবিবার	*roh*·bi·baar

months

January	জানুয়ারি	*jaa*·nu·aa·ri
February	ফেব্রুয়ারি	*feb*·ru·aa·ri
March	মার্চ	maarch
April	এপ্রিল	*ep*·reel
May	মে	me
June	জুন	jun
July	জুলাই	*ju*·laai
August	আগস্ট	*aa*·gohst
September	সেপ্টেমবার	*sep*·tem·baar
October	অক্টোবার	*ok*·toh·baar
November	নভেম্বার	*no*·b'em·baar
December	ডিসেম্বার	*di*·sem·baar

dates

What date is it today?
আজ কত তারিখ? — aaj *ko*·toh *taa*·rik

It's (18 October).
আজ (আঠারই অক্টোবার)। — aaj (*aa*·t'aa·roh·i *ok*·toh·baar)

seasons

spring	বশন্ত	*bo*·shohn·ţoh
summer	গ্রিষ্ম	*grish*·shoh
rainy season	বর্ষা	*bor*·sha
autumn	শরৎ	*sho*·roth
harvesting season	হেমন্ত	*he*·mon·toh
winter	শীত	sheeţ

bengali seasons

In Bangladesh and West Bengal there are six seasons in the calendar year. Three of them are quite distinguishable: summer (February–May), the rainy season (June–October) and winter (November–February). Less distinctive seasons are: spring (February–March), or the transition from cooler to warmer weather, autumn (September–October), when the heat isn't so severe, and the harvesting season (November–December), which signalls winter approaching.

present

বর্তমান

this …		
morning	আজ সকাল	aaj *sho*·kaal
afternoon	আজ দুপুর	aaj *du*·pur
week	এই সপ্তাহ	ay *shop*·ţaa
month	এই মাস	ay maash
year	এই বছর	ay *bo*·ch'ohr
today	আজকে	*aaj*·ke
tonight	আজ রাতে	aaj *ra*·ţe

past

অতীত

yesterday …	গতকাল …	*go*·ţoh·kaal …
morning	সকাল	*sho*·kaal
afternoon	দুপুর	*du*·pur
evening	বিকাল	*bee*·kaal
last …	গত …	*go*·ţoh …
night	রাত	raaţ
week	সপ্তাহ	*shop*·ţaa
month	মাস	maash
year	বছর	*bo*·ch'ohr
since (May)	(মে) থেকে	(me) *ţ'e*·ke
(three days) ago	(তিন দিন) আগে	(ţin din) *aa*·ge

future

ভবিষ্যৎ

tomorrow …	আগামিকাল …	*aa*·ga·mi·kaal …
morning	সকাল	*sho*·kaal
afternoon	দুপুর	*du*·pur
evening	বিকাল	*bee*·kaal

next …	আগামি …	*aa*·ga·mi …
week	সপ্তাহ	*shop*·ţaa
month	মাস	maash
year	বছর	*bo*·ch'ohr
until (June)	(জুন) পর্যন্ত	(joon) *pohr*·john·ţoh
in (six) days	(ছয়) দিনে	(ch'oy) *di*·ne

during the day

দিনের বেলায়

afternoon	দুপুর	*du*·pur
day	দন	din
evening	বিকাল	*bee*·kaal
midday	দুপুর	*du*·pur
midnight	মধ্যরাত	*mohd*·d'oh·raaţ
morning	সকাল	*sho*·kaal
night	রাত	raaţ
sunrise	সুর্য্যউদয়	*shur*·jo·u·day
sunset	সুর্য্যাস্ত	*shur*·ja·sţoh

bengali calendar

The Bengali calendar is 594 years behind the Gregorian calendar – 2005 AD is actually the year 1411 in the Bengali calendar. The Bengali year starts around mid-April on the English calendar.

বৈশাখ	*boy*·shak'	**mid-April to mid-May**
জৈ্যষ্ঠ	*joh*·ish·t'oh	**mid-May to mid-June**
আষাঢ়	*a*·shaŗ	**mid-June to mid-July**
শ্রাবন	*sra*·bohn	**mid-July to mid-August**
ভাদ্র	*b'ad*·roh	**mid-August to mid-September**
আশ্বিন	*ash*·shin	**mid-September to mid-October**
কার্তিক	*kar*·ţik	**mid-October to mid-November**
অগ্রায়হন	*og*·rai·hon	**mid-November to mid-December**
পৌষ	*poh*·ush	**mid-December to mid-January**
মাঘ	mag'	**mid-January to mid-February**
ফালগুন	*fal*·gun	**mid-February to mid-March**
চৈত্র	*choy*·ţroh	**mid-March to mid-April**

getting around

চলাফেরা

Which … goes to (Comilla)?	কোন … (কুমিল্লা) যায়?	kohn … (ku·*mil*·laa) jay
bus	বাস	bas
train	ট্রেন	tren
tram	ট্র্যাম	tram
Is this the … to (Chittagong)?	এই … কি (চিটাগাঙের)?	ay … ki (*chi*·ta·gang·er)
boat	নৌকা	*noh*·u·ka
ferry	ফেরি	*fe*·ri
plane	প্লেন	plen
When's the … (bus)?	… (বাস) কখন?	… (bas) *ko*·k'ohn
first	প্রথম	*proh*·t'ohm
next	পরের	*po*·rer
last	শেষ	shesh

What time does it leave?
কখন ছাড়বে? — *ko*·k'ohn *ch'aaṛ*·be

How long will it be delayed?
কত দেরি হবে? — *ko*·toh *de*·ri *ho*·be

Is this seat available?
এই সিট কি খালি? — ay seet ki *k'aa*·lee

That's my seat.
ওটা আমার সিট। — *oh*·taa *aa*·mar seet

Please tell me when we get to (Sylhet).
(সিলেট) আসলে আমাকে বলবেন, প্লিজ। — (*si*·let) *aash*·le *aa*·maa·ke *bohl*·ben pleez

tickets

টিকেট

Where do I buy a ticket?
কোথায় টিকেট কিনবো? — *koh*·ţ'ai *ti*·ket *kin*·boh

Where's the booking office for foreigners?
বিদেশিদের জন্য বুকিং অফিস কোথায়? — bi·de·*shi*·der *john*·noh *bu*·king o·feesh *koh*·ţ'ai

Do I need to book well in advance?
এ্যাডভান্স বুকিং লাগবে কি? — *ąđ*·vaans *bu*·king *laag*·be ki

Is there a waiting list?
ওয়েটিং লিস্ট আছে কি? — *we*·ting leest *aa*·ch'e ki

Is it a direct route?
এটা কি ডাইরেক্ট রাস্তা? — e·ta ki *đai*·rekt *raa*·sţa

A … ticket (to Dhaka).	(ঢাকার) জন্য একটা … টিকেট।	(*đ'aa*·kaar) *john*·noh *ąk*·ta … *ti*·ket
1st-class	ফার্স্ট ক্লাস	farst klaas
2nd-class	সেকেন্ড ক্লাস	*se*·kend klaas
child's	বাচ্চার	*baach*·char
one-way	ওয়ানওয়ে	*wan*·way
return	রিটার্ন	*ri*·tarn
student	ছাত্র	*ch'aţ*·roh

I'd like a/an … seat.	আমাকে একটা … সিট দেন।	*aa*·ma·ke *ąk*·ta … seet den
aisle	মাঝের	*ma*·j'er
nonsmoking	ধুমপান নিষেধ এলাকায়	*d'um*·paan *ni*·shed' e·la·ka·e
smoking	ধুমপান এলাকায়	*d'um*·paan e·la·ka·e
window	জানালার ধারে	*ja*·na·lar *d'a*·re

Is there (a) …?	… আছে কি?	… *aa*·ch'e ki
air conditioning	এয়ারকন্ডিশনার	e·aar·kon·di·shoh·nar
blanket	কম্বল	*kom*·bohl
sick bag	বমির ব্যাগ	*boh*·mir bąg
toilet	টয়লেট	*toy*·let

How long does the trip take?
যেতে কতক্ষন লাগবে? *je*·ţe *ko*·tohk·k'ohn *laa*·ge

What time should I check in?
কটার সময় চেক ইন করব? *ko*·tar *sho*·moy chek in *kohr*·boh

I'd like to ... my ticket, please.	আমার টিকেট ... করতে চাই।	*aa*·mar *ti*·ket ... *kohr*·ţe chai
cancel	ক্যান্সেল	*kqn*·sel
change	বদলাতে	*bod*·la·ţe
confirm	কনফার্ম	*kon*·farm

luggage

মালাপত্র

Where can I find a/the ...?	কোথায় ...?	*koh*·ţ'ai ...
baggage claim	ব্যাগেজ ক্লেম	*bq*·gej klem
luggage locker	লাগেজ লকার	*laa*·gej *lo*·kar

My luggage has been ...	আমার মাল ...	*aa*·mar *laa*·gej ...
damaged	ড্যামেজ হয়েছে	*đq*·mej *hoh*·e·ch'e
lost	হারিয়ে গেছে	*haa*·ri·ye *gq*·ch'e
stolen	চুরি হয়েছে	*chu*·ri *hoh*·e·ch'e

Can I have some coins?
আমাকে কিছু কয়েন দেন? *aa*·maa·ke *ki*·ch'u *ko*·en dąn

plane

প্লেন

Where's the ...?	কোথায় ...?	*koh*·ţ'ai ...
airport shuttle	এয়ারপোর্ট বাস	*e*·aar·poht baas
arrivals hall	এ্যারাইভাল	*q*·rai·vaal
departures hall	ডিপার্চার	*đi*·par·char
duty-free shop	ডিউটি ফ্রি	*đi*·u·ti free
gate (8)	গেইট (৮)	gayt (ayt)

Where does flight (BG007) arrive?

ফ্লাইট (বিজি ০০৭) কোন গেটে আসবে? | flait (*bi*·ji *shun*·noh *shun*·noh shaaţ) kohn *ge*·te *aash*·be

Where does flight (BG007) depart?

ফ্লাইট (বিজি ০০৭) কোন গেটে থেকে যাবে? | flait (*bi*·ji *shun*·noh *shun*·noh shaaţ) kohn *ge*·te *the*·ke *jaa*·be

ride the rocket

The highlight of travel in Bangladesh is the 'rocket' (*ro*·ket রকেট), but it's not the latest thing in air-travel technology, as the name might suggest. The 'rocket' is actually a small paddle-wheel passenger steamer that runs daily between Dhaka and Khulna. It's a semi-luxurious boat by Bangladeshi standards and allows travellers to cruise the mighty rivers experiencing the breathtaking panorama of the lush green countryside.

bus & coach

বাস এবং কোচ

How often do buses come?

কতক্ষন পর পর বাস আসে? | *ko*·ţohk·k'ohn por por bas *aa*·she

What's the next stop?

পরের স্টপ কি? | *po*·rer stop ki

I'd like to get off at (Mongla).

আমি (মঙ্গলাতে) নামতে চাই। | *aa*·mi (*mong*·laa·te) *naam*·ţe chai

Where's the queue for female passengers?

মহিলা প্যাসেঞ্জারদের লাইন কোথায়? | *moh*·hi·la *pq*·sen·jar·der *la*·in *koh*·ţ'ai

Where are the seats for female passengers?

মহিলা প্যাসেঞ্জারদের সিট কোথায়? | *moh*·hi·la *pq*·sen·jar·der seet *koh*·ţ'ai

... bus	... বাস	... bas
city	শহর	*sho*·hohr
express	এক্সপ্রেস	*eks*·pres
intercity	ইন্টারসিটি	*in*·tar·see·ti
local	লোকাল	*loh*·kaal
ordinary	অর্ডিনারি	*o*·đi·naa·ri

train

ট্রেন

What station is this?
এটা কোন স্টেশন? — *e*·taa kohn *ste*·shohn

What's the next station?
পরের স্টেশন কি? — *po*·rer *ste*·shohn ki

Does it stop at (Bagerhat)?
এটা কি (বাগেরহাট) থামে? — *e*·ta ki (*baa*·ger·hat) *ţ'a*·me

Do I need to change?
আমাকে কি চেঞ্জ করতে হবে? — *aa*·maa·ke ki chenj *kohr*·ţe *ho*·be

Is it ...?	এটা কি ...?	*e*·taa ki ...
air-conditioned	এয়ারকন	*e*·aar·kon
direct	ডাইরেক্ট	*dai*·rekt
express	এক্সপ্রেস	*eks*·pres
a sleeper	স্লিপার	*slee*·paar

Which carriage is (for) ...?	... কমপার্টমেন্ট কোনটা?	... *kom*·part·ment *kohn*·taa
(Hobiganj)	(হবিগঞ্জ)-এর	(*hoh*·bi·gonj)·er
1st class	ফার্স্ট ক্লাস	farst klaas
dining	খাওয়ার	*k'ha*·war

boat

নৌকা

What's the river/sea like today?
আজকে নদী/সমুদ্র কেমন থাকবে? — *aaj*·ke *noh*·di/*shoh*·mud·roh *kq*·mohn *t'aak*·be

What's the weather forecast?
ওয়েদার ফোরকাস্ট কি? — *we*·daar *fohr*·kaast ki

Are there life jackets?
লাইফ জ্যাকেট আছে? — laif *jq*·ket *aa*·ch'e

I feel seasick.
আমার বমি আসছে। — *aa*·maar *boh*·mi *aash*·che

cabin	কেবিন	*kq*·bin
captain	ক্যাপ্টেন	*kqp*·ten
deck	ডেক	dek
lifeboat	লাইফবোট	*laif*·boht

taxi

ট্যাক্সি

I'd like a taxi ...	আমার ... ট্যাক্সি লাগবে।	*aa*·mar ... *tak*·si *laag*·be
at (9am)	সকাল (নটায়)	*sho*·kal (*noy*·ta)
now	এখন	*q*·k'ohn
tomorrow	আগামিকাল	*aa*·gaa·mi·kaal

Where's the taxi rank?
ট্যাক্সি স্ট্যান্ড কোথায়? — *tqk*·si stąnđ *koh*·ţ'ai

Is this taxi available?
এই ট্যাক্সি খালি? — ay *tqk*·si *k'aa*·li

Please put the meter on.
প্লিজ মিটার লাগান। — pleez *mee*·tar *laa*·gan

How much is it to ...?
... যেতে কত লাগবে? — ... *je*·ţe *ko*·toh *laag*·be

Please take me to this address.
আমাকে এই ঠিকানায় নিয়ে যান। — *aa*·ma·ke ay *t'i*·kaa·nai *ni*·ye jaan

We need (three) seats.
আমাদের (তিন) সিট লাগবে। — *aa*·maa·der (ţeen) seet *laag*·be

Slow down.	আস্তে করেন।	*aas*·ţe *koh*·ren
Stop here.	এখানে থামেন।	e·k'aa·ne *ţ'aa*·men
Wait here.	এখানে অপেক্ষা করেন।	e·k'aa·ne o·*pek'*·ka *koh*·ren

car & motorbike

গাড়ি এবং মটরসাইকেল

hire

I'd like to hire a/an ...	আমি একটা ... ভাড়া করতে চাই।	*aa*·mi *ąk*·ta ... *b'a*·ŗa *kohr*·te chai
4WD	ফোর হুয়িল ড্রাইভ	fohr weel draiv
automatic	অটোম্যাটিক	o·*toh*·mą·tik
car	গাড়ি	*gaa*·ŗi
manual	ম্যানুয়েল	*mą*·nu·al
motorbike	মটরসাইকেল	*mo*·tohr·sai·kel

with (a) ...	... সহ	... *sho*·hoh
air conditioning	এয়ারকন্ডিশনার	*e*·aar·kon·di·shoh·nar
driver	ড্রাইভার	*drai*·var

How much for ... hire?	... ভাড়া করতে কত লাগবে?	... *b'a*·ŗa *kohr*·ţe *ko*·ţoh *laag*·be
daily	দৈনিক	*do*·hi·nik
weekly	সাপ্তাহিক	*shap*·ţa·hik

Does that include insurance/mileage?
এটা কি ইন্সুরেন্স/পেট্রোল সহ? — *e*·ta ki *in*·shu·rens/*pet*·rohl *sho*·hoh

Do you have a road map?
রাস্তার ম্যাপ আছে কি? — *raa*·sţar mąp *aa*·ch'e ki

on the road

What's the speed limit?
স্পিড লিমিট কি? — speed *lee*·mit ki

Is this the road to (Rangamati)?
এটা কি (রাঙ্গামাটির) রাস্তা? — *e*·ta ki (*raang*·a·maa·tir) *raa*·sţa

Where's a petrol station?
পেট্রোল স্টেশন কোথায়? — *pet*·rohl *ste*·shohn *koh*·ţ'ai

Please fill it up.
ভর্তি করে দেন, প্লিজ। — *b'ohr*·ţi *koh*·re dąn pleez

I'd like (20) litres.
আমার (বিশ) লিটার লাগবে। — *aa*·mar (beesh) *li*·tar *laag*·be

road signs

It's very unlikely you'll find any road signs in Bengali, but to be on the safe side ...

প্রবেশ নিষেধ	*proh*·besh *ni*·shed'	**No Entry**
থামুন	*t'a*·mun	**Stop**

diesel	ডিজেল	*di*·zel
unleaded (octane)	অকটেন	*ok*·ten
regular	পেট্রোল	*pet*·rohl

Can you check the ...?	আপনি কি ... চেক করতে পারেন?	*aap*·ni ki ... chek *kohr*·ţe *paa*·ren
oil	তেল	ţel
tyre pressure	চাকার প্রেসার	*chaa*·kar *pre*·shar
water	পানি	*paa*·ni

(How long) Can I park here?
আমি এখানে (কতক্ষন) গাড়ি রাখতে পারবো?
aa·mi *e*·k'a·ne (*ko*·tohk·k'ohn) *gaa*·ŗi *raak'*·ţe *paar*·boh

Do I have to pay?
আমাকে কি দাম দিতে হবে?
aa·ma·ke ki dam *di*·ţe *ho*·be

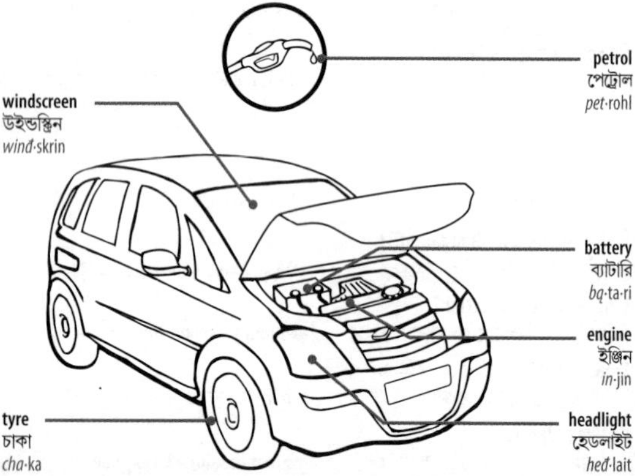

problems

I need a mechanic.
আমার একজন মেকানিক লাগবে। *aa*·mar *ąk*·john *me*·kaa·nik *laag*·be

I've had an accident.
আমার একটা এ্যাকসিডেন্ট হয়েছে। *aa*·mar *ąk*·ta *ąk*·si·dent *hoh*·e·ch'e

The car/motorbike has broken down (at Manikganj).
গাড়ি/মটরসাইকেল (মানিকগঞ্জে) নষ্ট হয়ে গেছে। *gaa*·ŗi/*mo*·tohr·sai·kel (*ma*·nik·gon·je) *nosh*·toh *hoh*·e *gą*·ch'e

I have a flat tyre.
আমার গাড়ির একটা চাকা পাঙ্কচার হয়ে গেছে। *aa*·mar *gaa*·ŗir *ąk*·ta *chaa*·ka *pank*·char *hoh*·e *gą*·ch'e

I've lost my car keys.
আমার গাড়ির চাবি হারিয়ে গেছে। *aa*·mar *gaa*·ŗir *chaa*·bi *haa*·ri·ye *gą*·ch'e

I've run out of petrol.
আমার পেট্রোল শেষ হয়ে গেছে। *aa*·mar *pet*·rohl shesh *hoh*·e *gą*·ch'e

Can you fix it (today)?
(আজকে) ঠিক করতে পারবেন? (*aaj*·ke) t'ik *kohr*·ţe *par*·ben

How long will it take?
কতক্ষন লাগবে? *ko*·ţohk·k'ohn *laag*·be

bicycle

সাইকেল

I'd like …	আমি … চাই।	*aa*·mi … chai
my bicycle repaired	আমার সাইকেল মেরামত করাতে	*aa*·mar *sai*·kel *mą*·ra·moţ *ko*·ra·ţe
to buy a bicycle	একটা সাইকেল কিনতে	*ąk*·ta *sai*·kel *kin*·ţe
to hire a bicycle	একটা সাইকেল ভাড়া করতে	*ąk*·ta *sai*·kel *b'a*·ŗa *kohr*·ţe

I'd like a ... bike.	আমি একটা ... বাইক চাই।	*aa*·mi *qk*·ta ... baik chai
mountain	মাউনটেন	*maa*·un·ten
racing	রেসিং	*re*·sing
second-hand	সেকেন্ড হ্যান্ড	*se*·kend hạnd

Do I need a helmet?
আমার কি হেলমেট লাগবে? — *aa*·mar ki *hel*·met *laag*·be

I have a puncture.
আমার একটা পান্কচার আছে। — *aa*·mar *qk*·ta *pank*·char *aa*·ch'e

local transport

স্থানীয় যানবাহন

I need a rickshaw.
আমার একটা রিকশা চাই। — *aa*·mar *qk*·ta *rik*·sha chai

I need an autorickshaw.
আমার একটা স্কুটার চাই। — *aa*·mar *qk*·ta *sku*·tar chai

Are there any shared jeeps?
এখানে কি শেয়ার জিপ পাওয়া যায়? — e·k'a·ne ki *she*·ar jeep *pa*·wa jai

Can we agree on a fare?
ভাড়া ঠিক করেন? — *b'a*·ṛa t'ik *koh*·ren

Can we share a ride?
শেয়ারে ভাড়া করবেন? — *she*·a·re *b'a*·ṛa *kohr*·ben

Are you waiting for more people?
আরো লোকের জন্য অপেক্ষা করছেন? — *aa*·roh *loh*·ker *john*·noh o·pek·k'a *kohr*·ch'en

How many people can ride on this?
এটাতে কতজন লোক উঠতে পারবে? — e·taa·ţe *ko*·ţoh·john lohk uţ'·ţe *paar*·be

Can you take us around the city, please?
আমাদের শহরে ঘুরাতে পারেন, প্লিজ? — *aa*·ma·der *sho*·hoh·re *g'u*·raa·ţe *paa*·ren pleez

border crossing

সিমান্ত পারাপার

I'm ...	আমি ...	*aa*·mi ...
in transit	ট্রান্জিটে আছি	*traan*·zee·te *aa*·ch'i
on business	ব্যবসার কাজে এসেছি	*bqb*·shaar *kaa*·je *e*·she·ch'i
on holiday	ছুটিতে আছি	*ch'u*·ti·ţe *aa*·ch'i

I'm here for (two) ...	আমি এখানে (দুই) ... আছি।	*aa*·mi *e*·k'a·ne (dui) ... *aa*·ch'i
days	দিন	din
months	মাস	maash
weeks	সপ্তাহ	*shop*·taa·hoh

I'm going to (Tangail).
আমি (টাঙ্গাইল) যাচ্ছি। — *aa*·mi (*taang*·ail) *jaach*·ch'i

I'm staying at (the Parjatan Motel).
আমি (পর্যটন মোটেলে) আছি। — *aa*·mi (*por*·joh·ton *moh*·te·le) *aa*·ch'i

Do I need a special permit?
আমার কি বিশেষ পারমিট লাগবে? — *aa*·mar ki *bi*·shesh *par*·mit *laag*·be

Is it a restricted area?
এটা কি নিষিদ্ধ এলাকা? — *e*·ta ki *ni*·shid'·d'oh *e*·laa·ka

listen for ...

একা	*q*·ka	**alone**
দল	dol	**group**
পরিবার	*poh*·ri·bar	**family**
পরিচয়	*poh*·ri·choy	**identification**
ভিসা	*vi*·sa	**visa**

at customs

কাস্টমস-এ

I have nothing to declare.
আমার ডিকলিয়ার করার কিছু নাই। *aa*·mar *đik*·li·aar *koh*·rar *ki*·ch'u nai

I have something to declare.
আমার কিছু ডিকলিয়ার করতে হবে। *aa*·mar *ki*·ch'u *đik*·li·aar *kohr*·ţe *ho*·be

Do I have to declare this?
আমার কি এটা ডিকলিয়ার করতে হবে? *aa*·mar ki *e*·ta *đik*·li·aar *kohr*·ţe *ho*·be

I didn't know I had to declare it.
আমি জানতাম না এটা ডিকলিয়ার করতে হবে। *aa*·mi *jaan*·ţaam naa *e*·ta *đik*·li·aar *kohr*·ţe *ho*·be

That's (not) mine.
ওটা আমার (না)। *oh*·ta *aa*·mar (na)

signs

ইমিগ্রেশন	i·mi·*gre*·shohn	**Immigration**
কাস্টমস	*kas*·tohms	**Customs**
কোয়ারান্টিন	*kwa*·ran·tin	**Quarantine**
ডিউটি ফ্রি	*đi*·u·ti fri	**Duty-Free**
পাসপোর্ট কন্ট্রোল	*pas*·pohrt kon·*trohl*	**Passport Control**

Where's a/the ...?	... কোথায়?	... *koh*·ţ'ai
bank	ব্যাংক	bąnk
market	বাজার	*baa*·jar
tourist office	পর্যটন কেন্দ্র	*pohr*·joh·tohn *ken*·droh

It's ...	এটা ...	*e*·ta ...
behind ...	...-এর পিছনে	...·er *pi*·ch'oh·ne
close	কাছাকাছি	*ka*·ch'a·ka·ch'i
here	এখানে	*e*·k'a·ne
in front of ...	...-এর সামনে	...·er *shaam*·ne
near ...	...-এর কাছে	...·er *ka*·ch'e
next to ...	...-এর পাসে	...·er *pa*·she
on the corner	কর্নারে	*koŗ*·na·re
opposite ...	...-এর উল্টো দিকে	...·er *ul*·toh *di*·ke
straight ahead	সোজা	*shoh*·ja
there	ঐ যে	oy je

Turn ...	... টার্ন করবেন	... taarn *kohr*·ben
at the corner	কর্নারে	*koŗ*·na·re
at the traffic lights	ট্র্যাফিক লাইটে	*trą*·fik *lai*·te
left	বামে	*baa*·me
right	ডানে	*daa*·ne

by ...	... করে	... *koh*·re
bus	বাসে	*ba*·se
rickshaw	রিকশা	*rik*·sha
taxi	ট্যাক্সিতে	*tak*·si
train	ট্রেনে	*tre*·ne

on foot	পায়ে হেটে	*paa*·e *he*·te

What's the address?
ঠিকানা কি? — *ţ'i*·kaa·na ki

How far is it?
এটা কত দুর? — e·ta *ko*·ţoh dur

How do I get there?
ওখানে কি ভাবে যাব? — *oh*·k'a·ne ki *b'a*·be *ja*·boh

Can you show me (on the map)?
আমাকে (ম্যাপে) দেখাতে পারেন? — *aa*·ma·ke (*mq*·pe) *dq*·k'a·ţe *paa*·ren

north	উত্তর	*uţ*·ţohr
east	পূর্ব	*pur*·boh
south	দক্ষিন	*dohk'*·k'in
west	পশ্চিম	*pohsh*·chim

city	শহর	*sho*·hohr
street	রাস্তা	*raas*·ţa
suburb	এলাকা	*e*·la·ka
village	গ্রাম	gram

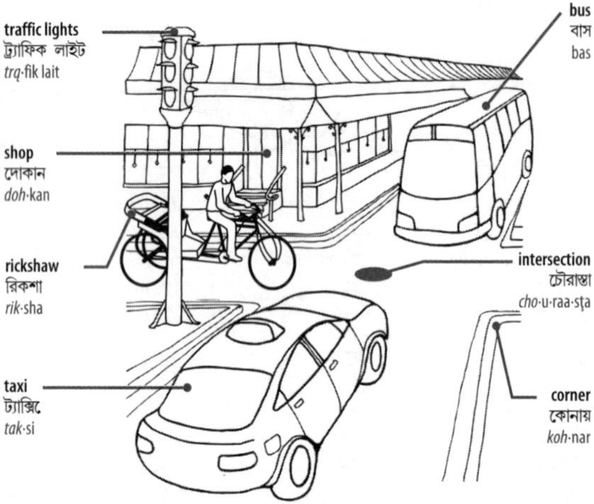

accommodation

আবাস

finding accommodation

আবাসের খোঁজ

Where's a ...?	... কোথায়?	... *koh*·ţ'ai
guesthouse	গেস্ট হাউস	gest *ha*·us
hotel	হোটেল	*hoh*·tel
resthouse (government-run guesthouse)	রেস্ট হাউস	rest *ha*·us
tourist bungalow	ট্যুরিস্ট বাংলো	*tu*·rist *baang*·loh
youth hostel	ইউথ হস্টেল	*ee*·uţ' *hos*·tel
Can you recommend somewhere ...?	বলতে পারেন কোনো ... যায়গা কোথায়?	*bohl*·ţe *paa*·ren *koh*·noh ... *ja*·e·gaa *koh*·ţ'ai
cheap	সস্তা	*sho*·sţa
good	ভাল	*b'a*·loh
luxurious	লাক্সারি	*lak*·sha·ri
nearby	কাছাকাছি	*ka*·ch'a·ka·ch'i
romantic	রোমান্টিক	*roh*·man·tik
What's the address?	ঠিকানাটা কি?	*ţ'i*·ka·na·ta ki

For responses, see **directions**, page 207.

booking ahead & checking in

বুকিং ও চেক-ইন

I'd like to book a room, please.
আমি একটা রুম বুক করতে চাই, প্লিজ।
aa·mi *qk*·ta rum buk *kohr*·ţe chai pleez

I have a reservation.
আমার একটা বুকিং আছে।
aa·mar *qk*·ta *bu*·king *aa*·ch'e

My name's ...
আমার নাম ...
aa·mar naam ...

Do you have a	আপনার কি …	*aap*·nar ki …
… room?	রুম আছে?	rum *aa*·ch'e
double	ডবল	*do*·bohl
single	সিঙ্গেল	*sin*·gel

How much is it per …?	প্রতি … কত?	*proh*·ţi … *ko*·ţoh
person	জনে	*jo*·ne
night	রাতে	*raa*·ţe
week	সপ্তাহে	*shop*·ţa·he

For (three) nights/weeks.
(তিন) রাতের/সপ্তাহের জন্য। — (ţeen) *raa*·ţer/*shop*·ţa·her *john*·noh

From (2 July) to (6 July).
(জুলাই দুই) থেকে (জুলাই ছয়) পর্যন্ত। — (*ju*·lai dui) *ţ'e*·ke (*ju*·lai ch'oy) *pohr*·john·ţo

Can I see it?
আমি কি এটা দেখতে পারি? — *aa*·mi ki *e*·ta *dek'*·ţe *paa*·ri

I'll take it.
আমি এটা নিব। — *aa*·mi *e*·ta *ni*·boh

Do I need to pay upfront?
আমার কি অগ্রিম দিতে হবে? — *aa*·mar ki *oh*·grim *di*·ţe *ho*·be

Can I pay by …?	আমি কি …-এ পে করতে পারি?	*aa*·mi ki …·e pe *kohr*·ţe *paa*·ri
credit card	ক্রেডিট কার্ড	*kre*·đit kaarđ
travellers cheque	ট্র্যাভেলার্স চেক	*trą*·ve·lars chek

For other methods of payment, see **shopping**, page 216.

requests & queries

অনুরোধ এবং প্রশ্ন

When/Where is breakfast served?
কোথায়/কখন ব্রেকফাস্ট হবে? — *koh*·ţ'ai/*ko*·k'on *brek*·fast *ho*·be

Please wake me at (seven).
আমাকে (সাতটায়) তুলে দেবেন, প্লিজ। — *aa*·ma·ke (*shaţ*·ta) *ţu*·le *de*·ben pleez

Is there ...?	এখানে কি ... আছে?	*e*·k'a·ne ki ... *aa*·ch'e
air conditioning	এয়ারকন্ডিশনার	*e*·aar·kon·đi·shoh·nar
heating	হিটার	*hi*·tar
hot water	গরম পানি	*go*·rohm *pa*·ni
running water	কলের পানি	*ko*·ler *pa*·ni
Is the bathroom ...?	গোসল খানা কি ...?	*goh*·sohl *k'a*·na ki ...
communal	কমন	*ko*·mohn
private	প্রাইভেট	*prai*·vet
Are the toilets ...?	টয়লেট কি ...?	*toy*·let ki ...
Indian-style	প্যান	paņ
Western-style	কমোড	*ko*·mohd

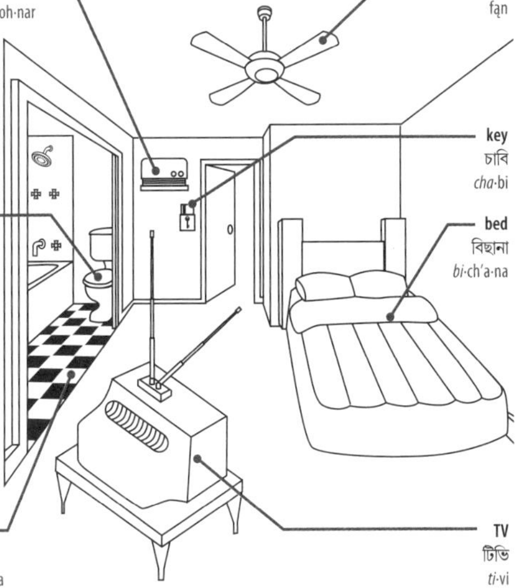

Do you … here?	আপনি কি এখানে … পারেন?	*aap*·ni ki *ek*·k'a·ne … *paa*·ren
arrange tours	ট্যুর এ্যারেঞ্জ করতে	tur ą·*renj kohr*·te
change money	টাকা ভাঙ্গাতে	*ta*·ka *b'ang*·ga·te

Do you have a/an …?	আপনার কি … আছে?	*aap*·nar ki … *aa*·che
elevator	লিফ্‌ট	lift
safe	লকার	*lo*·kar
washerman	ধোপা	*d'o*·pa

Can I use the …?	আমি কি … ব্যাবহার করতে পারি?	*aa*·mi ki … *bą*·boh·har *kohr*·ţe *paa*·ri
kitchen	রান্না ঘর	*ran*·na ghor
telephone	টেলিফোন	*te*·li·fohn

Could I have …, please?	আমাকে … দিতে পারেন, প্লিজ?	*aa*·ma·ke … *di*·ţe *paa*·ren pleez
an extra blanket	একটা এক্স্‌ট্রা কম্বল	*ąk*·ta *ek*·stra *kom*·bohl
a mosquito net	একটা মশারি	*ąk*·ta *mo*·sha·ri
my key	আমার চাবি	*aa*·mar *cha*·bi
a receipt	একটা রিসিট	*ąk*·ta ri·*seet*

Is there a message for me?
আমার জন্য কি কোন ম্যাসেজ আছে?
aa·mar *john*·noh ki *koh*·noh *mą*·sej *aa*·ch'e

Can I leave a message for someone?
আমি কি কারো জন্য ম্যাসেজ রাখতে পারি?
aa·mi ki *ka*·roh *john*·noh *mą*·sej *rak'*·ţe *paa*·ri

complaints

কমপ্লেন

It's too …	এখানে বেশি …	*e*·k'a·ne *be*·shi …
bright	আলো	*aa*·loh
cold	ঠান্ডা	*ţ'aan*·đa
dark	অন্ধকার	*on*·d'oh·kar
expensive	দাম	daam
noisy	শব্দ	*shob*·doh
small	ছোট	*choh*·toh

PRACTICAL

The … doesn't work.	… কাজ করে না।	… kaaj *koh*·re na
air conditioner	এয়ারকন্ডিশনার	*e*·aar·kon·đi·shoh·nar
fan	ফ্যান	fąn
toilet	টয়লেট	*toy*·let

This (pillow) isn't clean.
এই (বালিশটা) পরিষ্কার না। — ay (*ba*·lish·ta) *poh*·rish·kar na

I'm locked out of my room.
আমি রুমের বাইরে আটকে গেছি। — *aa*·mi *ru*·mer *bai*·re *at*·ke *gą*·ch'i

checking out

চেক আউট

What time is checkout?
চেক আউট ক'টার সময়? — chek *aa*·ut *ko*·tar *sho*·moy

Can I have a late checkout?
আমি কি দেরিতে চেক আউট করতে পারি? — *aa*·mi ki *de*·ri·ţe chek *aa*·ut *kohr*·ţe *paa*·ri

Can you call a taxi for me?
আমার জন্য একটা ট্যাক্সি ডাকতে পারেন? — *aa*·mar *john*·noh *ąk*·ta *tąk*·si *đak*·ţe *paa*·ren

I'd like a taxi at (11) o'clock.
আমার (এগারোটার) সময় ট্যাক্সি লাগবে। — *aa*·mar (*ą*·ga·roh·tar) *sho*·moy *tąk*·si *laag*·be

Can I leave my bags here?
আমার ব্যাগ কি এখানে রেখে যেতে পারি? — *aa*·mar bąg ki *e*·k'a·ne *re*·k'e *je*·te *paa*·ri

Could I have my …, please?	আমার … দেবেন, প্লিজ?	*aa*·mar … *de*·ben pleez
deposit	ডিপোজিট	*đi*·poh·zit
passport	পাসপোর্ট	*paa*·spohrt
valuables	জিনিসগুলো	*ji*·nish *gu*·loh

I'll be back …	আমি … ফিরবো।	*aa*·mi … *p'ir*·boh
in (three) days	(তিন) দিন পরে	(ţeen) din *po*·re
on (Tuesday)	(মঙ্গলবার)-এ	(*mohng*·gohl baar)·e

I'm leaving now.
আমি এখন যাচ্ছি।
aa·mi *q*·k'ohn *jach*·ch'i

I had a great stay, thank you.
আমার খুব ভাল লেগেছে, ধন্যবাদ।
aa·mar k'ub *b'a*·loh *le*·ge·ch'e *d'ohn*·noh·bad

renting

ভাড়া

Do you have a/an ... for rent?	একটা ... ভাড়া পাওয়া যাবে?	*qk*·ta ... *b'a*·ŗa *pa*·wa *ja*·be
apartment	এ্যাপার্টমেন্ট	*q*·part·ment
house	বাড়ী	*ba*·ŗi
room	রুম	rum

staying with locals

স্থানীয় লোকের সঙ্গে থাকা

Can I stay at your place?
আপনার এখানে কি আমি থাকতে পারি?
aap·nar *e*·k'a·ne ki *aa*·mi *ţ'ak*·ţe *paa*·ri

Is there anything I can do to help?
আপনার উপকারে আমি কি কিছু করতে পারি?
aap·nar *u*·poh·ka·re *aa*·mi ki *ki*·ch'u *kohr*·ţe *paa*·ri

Can I ...?	আমি ... পারি?	*aa*·mi ... *paa*·ri
do the dishes	প্লেট ধুতে	plet *d'u*·ţe
set the table	টেবিল লাগাতে	*te*·bil *la*·ga·ţe
take out the rubbish	ময়লা ফেলতে	*moy*·la *fel*·ţe

Thanks for your hospitality.
আপনার আতিথিয়তার জন্য ধন্যবাদ।
aap·nar *a*·ţi·ţ'i·o·ţar *john*·noh *d'ohn*·noh·bad

shopping
কেনাকাটা

looking for …

গু খোঁজে

Where's a/the …?	… কোথায়?	… *koh*·ţ'ai
department store	ডিপার্টমেন্ট স্টোর	đi·*part*·ment stohr
khadi shop	খাদির দোকান	*k'a*·dir *doh*·kan
market	বাজার	*ba*·jar
station	ষ্টেশন	*ste*·shohn
supermarket	সুপার মার্কেট	*su*·par *mar*·ket

Where can I buy (a padlock)?
(একটা তালা) কোথায় কিনতে পাওয়া যাবে?
(*ąk*·ta *ţa*·la) *koh*·ţ'ai *kin*·ţe *pa*·wa *ja*·be

For responses, see **directions**, page 207.

making a purchase

কেনা

I'm just looking.
আমি দেখছি।
aa·mi *dek*·ch'i

I'd like to buy (an adaptor plug).
একটা (এড্যাপ্টার প্লাগ) কিনতে চাই।
ąk·ta (ą·*đąp*·tar plag) *kin*·ţe chai

How much is it?
এটার দাম কত?
e·tar dam *ko*·ţoh

Can you write down the price?
দামটা কি লিখে দিতে পারেন?
dam·ta ki *li*·k'e *di*·ţe *paa*·ren

Do you have any others?
আর কি আছে?
ar ki *aa*·ch'e

Can I look at it?
এটা দেখতে পারি?
e·ta *dek'*·ţe *paa*·ri

Do you accept …?	আপনি কি … নেন?	*aap*·ni ki … nen
credit cards	ক্রেডিট কার্ড	*kre*·đit karđ
debit cards	ডেবিট কার্ড	*đe*·bit karđ
travellers cheques	ট্র্যাভেলার্স চেক	*trą*·ve·lars chek

Could I have a …, please?	একটা … দিতে পারেন, প্লিজ?	*ąk*·ta … *di*·ţe *paa*·ren pleez
bag	ব্যাগ	bąg
receipt	রিসিট	ri·*seet*

I'd like …, please.	আমি … চাই, প্লিজ।	*aa*·mi … chai pleez
my change	আমার ভাঙ্গতি	*aa*·mar *b'ang*·ţi
a refund	পয়সা ফেরত	*poy*·sha *fe*·rohţ
to return this	এটা ফেরত দিতে	e·ta *fe*·rohţ *di*·ţe

Can you order it for me?
আমার জন্য অর্ডার দিতে পারেন? — *aa*·mar *john*·noh *o*·đar *di*·ţe *paa*·ren

Could I have it wrapped?
এটা কি রাপ করে দিতে পারেন? — e·ta ki rąp *koh*·re *di*·ţe *paa*·ren

Does it have a guarantee?
এটার কি গ্যারান্টি আছে? — e·tar ki *gą*·ran·ti *aa*·ch'e

Can I have it sent overseas?
এটা কি বিদেশে পাঠাতে পারি? — e·ta ki *bi*·de·she *pa*·ţ'a·ţe *paa*·ri

Can I pick it up later?
এটা কি পরে এসে নিতে পারি? — e·ta ki *po*·re *e*·she *ni*·ţe *paa*·ri

It's faulty.
এটা নষ্ট। — e·ta *nosh*·toh

local talk

baksheesh	বকসিশ	*bohk*·shish
bargain	দরাদরি	*doh*·ra·doh·ri
fixed-price shop	ফিক্সড প্রাইস দোকান	fik·sed praiz *doh*·kan
good deal	ভাল দাম	*b'a*·loh dam
rip-off	ছিল	ch'il
sale	রিডাকশন	*ri*·đak·shohn
specials	স্পেশাল	*spe*·shal

bargaining

দরাদরি

That's too expensive.
বেশী দাম। — *be*·shi dam

Can you lower the price?
দাম কমান। — dam *ko*·man

Do you have something cheaper?
আরো কম দামি কিছু আছে? — *a*·roh kom *da*·mi *ki*·ch'u *aa*·ch'e

I'll give you (30 taka).
আমি (তিরিশ টাকা) দিব। — *aa*·mi (*ţi*·rish *ta*·ka) *di*·boh

I don't have much money.
আর পয়সা নাই। — aar *poy*·sha nai

I'll think about it.
চিন্তা করে নেই। — *chin*·ţa *koh*·re nay

books & reading

বই পত্র

Is there an English-language ...?	এখানে কি ইংরেজি ... আছে?	*e*·k'a·ne ki *ing*·re·ji ... *aa*·ch'e
bookshop	বইয়ের দোকান	*boh*·i·er *doh*·kan
section	সেক্সন	*sek*·shohn
Do you have a/an ...?	আপনার কাছে কি কোন ... আছে?	*aap*·nar *ka*·ch'e ki *koh*·noh ... *aa*·ch'e
book by Rabindranath Tagore	রবিন্দ্রনাথ ঠাকুরের বই	roh·*bin*·droh·naţ' *t'a*·ku·rer *boh*·i
entertainment guide	বিনোদন গাইড	*bi*·noh·dohn gaiđ
I'd like a ...	আমি একটা ... চাই।	*aa*·mi *qk*·ta ... chai
dictionary	ডিকশনারি	*dik*·shoh·na·ri
newspaper (in English)	(ইংরেজি) খবরের কাগজ	(*ing*·re·ji) *k'o*·boh·rer *ka*·gohj

clothes

কাপড়-চোপড়

My size is …	আমার সাইজ …	*aa*·mar saiz …
(40)	(চল্লিশ)	(*chohl*·lish)
small	স্মল	smol
medium	মিডিয়াম	*mi*·đi·am
large	লার্জ	larj

Can I try it on?
একটু পোরে দেখতে পারি? — *ek*·tu *poh*·re *dek'*·ţe *paa*·ri

It doesn't fit.
এটা ফিট করে না। — *e*·ta fit *koh*·re na

For clothing items and colours, see the **dictionary**.

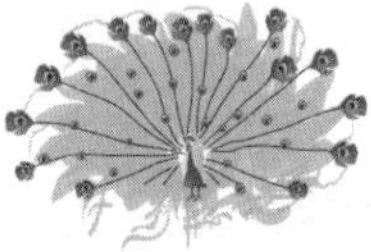

hairdressing

চুলের পরিচর্যা

I'd like a …	আমি … চাই।	*aa*·mi … chai
colour	চুলে রং করতে	*chu*·le rong *kohr*·ţe
haircut	চুল কাটতে	chul *kat*·ţe
shave	সেভ করতে	shev *kohr*·ţe
trim	চুল ছাটতে	chul *ch'at*·ţe

Don't cut it too short.
বেশি ছোট করবেন না। — *be*·shi *choh*·toh *kohr*·ben na

Please use a new blade.
নতুন ব্লেড ব্যবহার করেন, প্লিজ। — *noh*·ţun bled *bą*·boh·har *koh*·ren pleez

Shave it all off.
সবটা সেভ করে ফেলে দেন। — *shob*·ta shev *koh*·re *fe*·le dąn

music

সংগীত

I'd like a …	আমি একটা … চাই।	*aa*·mi *ąk*·ta … chai
blank tape	ব্ল্যাঙ্ক টেপ	bląnk tep
CD	সিডি	*si*·đi
DVD	ডিভিডি	*đi*·vi·đi
video	ভিডিও	*vi*·đi·o

I'm looking for something by a local singer/band.
আমি দেশি শিল্পীর/ব্যান্ডের কিছু খুজছি। — *aa*·mi *de*·shi *shil*·pir/*bąn*·đer *ki*·ch'u *k'uj*·ch'i

What's their best recording?
ওদের বেস্ট রেকর্ডিং কি? — *oh*·der best re·*kor*·đing ki

Can I listen to this?
আমি এটা শুনতে পারি? — *aa*·mi *e*·ta *shun*·ţe *paa*·ri

photography

আলোকচিত্র

I need a/an … film for this camera.	এই ক্যামেরার জন্য আমার … ফিল্ম লাগবে।	ay *ką*·me·rar *john*·noh *aa*·mar … film *laag*·be
APS	এপিএস	*e*·pi·es
B&W	ব্ল্যাক এন্ড ওয়াইট	bląk ąnd wait
colour	কালার	*ka*·lar
slide	স্লাইড	slaiđ
(200) speed	(দুই শ) স্পিড	(dui shoh) speeđ
Do you have … for this camera?	আপনার কাছে এই ক্যামেরার … আছে?	*aap*·nar *ka*·ch'e ay *ką*·me·rar … *aa*·che
batteries	ব্যাটারি	*bą*·ta·ri
memory cards	মেমোরি কার্ড	*me*·moh·ri karđ

Can you develop this film?
এই ফিল্মটা ডেভেলাপ করতে পারেন? — ay *film*·ta *de*·ve·lap *kohr*·ţe *paa*·ren

Can you recharge the battery for my digital camera?

আমার ডিজিটাল ক্যামেরার ব্যাটারিটা রিচার্জ করতে পারেন?	*aa*·mar *đi*·ji·tal *ką*·me·rar *bą*·tạ·ri·ta *ri*·charj *kohr*·ţe *paa*·ren

Can you transfer photos from my camera to CD?

আমার ক্যামেরা থেকে ছবি সি-ডিতে তুলতে পারেন?	*aa*·mar *ka*·me·ra *ţ'e*·ke *ch'oh*·bi *si*·đi·ţe *ţul*·ţe *paa*·ren

When will it be ready?

এটা কখন রেডি হবে?	e·ta *ko*·k'ohn *re*·di *ho*·be

How much is it?

এটা কত?	e·ta *ko*·ţoh

repairs

মেরামত

Can I have my ... repaired here?	আমার ... কি মেরামত করাতে পারি?	*aa*·mar ... ki *me*·ra·moţ *ko*·ra·ţe *paa*·ri
When will my ... be ready?	আমার ... কখন রেডি হবে?	*aa*·mar ... *ko*·k'ohn *re*·đi *ho*·be
backpack	ব্যাগপ্যাক	*bąg*·pąk
camera	ক্যামেরা	*ką*·me·ra
glasses	চশমা	*chosh*·ma
shoes	জুতা	*ju*·ţa

souvenirs

bangles	চুড়ি	*chu*·ṛi
batik	বাটিক	*ba*·tik
drum	তবলা	*ţob*·la
incense	ধুপ	d'up
pottery	মাটির জিনিস	*ma*·tir *ji*·nish
rug	ছোট কার্পেট	*choh*·toh *kar*·pet
sandals	স্যান্ডেল	*sąn*·đel
sari	শাড়ি	*sha*·ṛi
scarf	স্কার্ফ	skarf
shawl	শাল	shal
sitar	সিতার	*si*·ţar
statue	মূর্তি	*mur*·ţi

the internet

ইন্টারনেট

Where's the local Internet café?
কাছাকাছি ইন্টারনেট ক্যাফে কোথায়? *ka*·ch'a·ka·ch'i *in*·tar·net *ką*·fe *koh*·ţ'ai

I'd like to ...	আমি ... চাই।	*aa*·mi ... chai
check my email	আমার ই-মেল চেক করতে	*aa*·mar *ee*·mayl chek *kohr*·ţe
get Internet access	ইন্টারনেট এ্যাকসেস	*in*·tar·net *ąk*·ses
use a printer	প্রিন্টার ব্যবহার করতে	*prin*·tar *bą*·boh·har *kohr*·ţe
use a scanner	স্ক্যানার ব্যবহার করতে	*ską*·nar *bą*·boh·har *kohr*·ţe
Do you have (a) ...?	আপনার কি ... আছে?	*aap*·nar ki ... *aa*·ch'e
Macs	ম্যাক	mak
PCs	পি-সি	*pi*·si
Zip drive	জিপ ড্রাইভ	zip draiv
How much per ...?	প্রতি ...-য় কত?	*proh*·ţi ...·e *ko*·ţoh
hour	ঘন্টা	*g'on*·ta
(five) minutes	(পাচ) মিনিট	(pach) *mi*·nit
page	পাতা	*pa*·ţa

How do I log on?
কি ভাবে লগ অন করবো? ki *b'a*·be log on *kohr*·boh

Please change it to the English-language setting.
প্লিজ, ইংরেজি সেটিং দেন। pleez *ing*·re·ji *se*·ting dąn

It's crashed.
ক্র্যাস করেছে। krąsh *koh*·re·ch'e

I've finished.
আমার শেষ। *aa*·mar shesh

mobile/cell phone

মোবাইল ফোন

I'd like a …	… চাই।	… chai
charger for my phone	আমার ফোনের জন্য একটা চার্জার	*aa*·mar *foh*·ner *john*·noh *ąk*·ta *char*·jar
mobile/cell phone for hire	একটা মোবাইল ফোন ভাড়া করতে	*ąk*·ta *moh*·bail fohn *b'a*·ṛa *kohr*·ţe
prepaid mobile/cell phone	প্রিপেড মোবাইল ফোন	*pri*·payd *moh*·bail fohn
SIM card for your network	আপনার নেটওয়ার্কের জন্য সিম কার্ড	*aap*·nar *net*·war·ker *john*·noh sim karđ

What are the rates?
রেট কি? — rayt ki

(30 taka) per minute.
মিনিটে (তিরিশ টাকা)। — *mi*·ni·te (*ţi*·rish *ta*·ka)

Is roaming available?
রোমিং আছে কি? — *roh*·ming *aa*·ch'e ki

phone

ফোন

What's your phone number?
আপনার ফোন নম্বর কি? — *aap*·nar fohn *nom*·bohr ki

Where's the nearest public phone?
কাছাকাছি পাবলিক ফোন কোথায়? — *ka*·ch'a·ka·ch'i *pab*·lik fohn *ko*·ţ'ai

Can I look at a phone book?
টেলিফোন ডিরেক্টরি চেক করতে পারি? — *te*·li·fohn *di*·rek·tri chek *kohr*·ţe *paa*·ri

What's the country code for (New Zealand)?
(নিউজিল্যান্ডের) কোড কি? — (*nyu*·zi·ląn·đer) kohđ ki

I want to ...	আমি ... চাই।	*aa*·mi ... chai
buy a phonecard	একটা ফোনকার্ড কিনতে	*ąk*·ta *fohn*·karđ *kin*·ţe
call (Singapore)	(সিঙ্গাপুরে) কল করতে	(*sin*·ga·pu·re) kol *kohr*·ţe
make a (local) call	একটা (লোকাল) কল করতে	*ąk*·ta (*loh*·kal) kol *kohr*·ţe
reverse the charges	চার্জটা রিভার্স করতে	*charj*·ta *ri*·vars *kohr*·ţe
speak for (three) minutes	(তিন) মিনিট কথা বলতে	(ţeen) *mi*·nit *ko*·ţ'a *bohl*·ţe
How much does ... cost?	... কত লাগবে?	... *ko*·ţoh *laag*·be
a (three)-minute call	একটা (তিন) মিনিটের কলে	*ąk*·ta (ţeen) *mi*·ni·ter *ko*·le
each extra minute	প্রতি এক্সট্রা মিনিটে	*proh*·ţi *ek*·stra *mi*·ni·te

The number is ...
নম্বরটা হচ্চে ... — *nom*·bohr·ta *hohch'*·ch'e ...

It's engaged.
এঙ্গেজ। — *en*·gej

The connection's bad.
কানেকশনটা খারাপ। — *ka*·nek·shohn·ta *k'a*·rap

I've been cut off.
লাইন কেটে গেছে। — lain *ke*·te *gą*·ch'e

civilities

Bengalis believe that actions speak louder than words – gratitude is expressed through tone of voice and attitude instead of phrases like 'thank you'. The absence of these civilities, so common among English speakers, shouldn't be interpreted as rudeness. If you want to thank someone, you can use the phrase *o*·nek *d'oh*·noh·baad অনেক ধন্যবাদ (thank you very much). To make a polite request or apologise, an English 'please' or 'sorry' will do.

post office

পোস্ট অফিস

I want to send a/an ...	আমি একটা ... পাঠাতে চাই।	*aa*·mi *qk*·ta ... *pa*·ţ'a·ţe chai
fax	ফ্যাক্স	faks
letter	চিঠি	*chi*·ţ'i
parcel	পার্সেল	*par*·sel
postcard	পোস্ট কার্ড	pohst karđ

I want to buy a/an ...	আমি একটা ... কিনতে চাই।	*aa*·mi *qk*·ta ... *kin*·ţe chai
aerogram	এ্যারোগ্রাম	*q*·roh·gram
envelope	এনভেলাপ	*en*·ve·lap
stamp	স্ট্যাম্প	stąmp

snail mail

airmail	এয়ার মেলে	*e*·ar mayl
express mail	এক্সপ্রেস মেলে	*ek*·spres mayl
registered mail	রেজিস্ট্রি মেলে	*re*·ji·stri mayl
sea mail	সি মেলে	si mayl
surface mail	সারফেস মেলে	*sar*·fes mayl

Please send it by air/surface mail to (Australia).
এটা প্লিজ বাই এয়ার/সারফেস মেলে (অস্ট্রেলিয়া) পাঠান। — *e*·ta pleez bai *e*·ar/*sar*·fes mayl (*o*·stre·li·a) *pa*·ţ'an

It contains (souvenirs).
এটাতে (সুভেনিয়ার) আছে। — *e*·ta·ţe *su*·ve·ni·ar *aa*·ch'e

Is there any mail for me?
আমার কোন চিঠি আছে? — *aa*·mar *koh*·noh *chi*·t'i *aa*·ch'e

customs declaration	কাষ্টমস ডিকলিয়ারেশন	*ka*·stohms *di*·kli·a·re·shohn
domestic	ডামেস্টিক	doh·*me*·stik
international	আন্তর্জাতিক	*an*·ţohr·ja·ţik
mailbox	পোস্ট বক্স	pohst boks
postcode	পোস্ট কোড	pohst kohđ

money & banking

টাকা-পয়সা ও ব্যাংক

What time does the bank open?
কয়টার সময় ব্যাংক খোলে? — *ko*·tar *sho*·moy bąnk *k'oh*·le

Where's a/an ...?	... কোথায়?	... *koh*·ţ'ai
automated teller machine	এ-টি-এম	*e*·ti·em
foreign exchange office	ফরেন এক্সচেঞ্জ অফিস	*fo*·ren eks·*chenj* *o*·fish

I'd like to ...	আমি ... চাই।	*aa*·mi ... chai
cash a cheque	চেক ভাঙ্গাতে	chek *b'ang*·ga·ţe
change money	টাকা ভাঙ্গাতে	*ta*·ka *b'ang*·ga·ţe
change a travellers cheque	একটা ট্র্যাভেলার্স চেক ভাঙ্গাতে	*ąk*·ta *trą*·ve·lars chek *b'ang*·ga·ţe
get a cash advance	ক্যাশ এ্যাডভান্স	kąsh ąd·*vans*
withdraw money	টাকা তুলতে	*ta*·ka *ţul*·ţe

What's the ...?	... কি?	... ki
exchange rate	এক্সচেঞ্জ রেট	eks·*chenj* ret
charge for that	ওটার জন্য চার্জ	*oh*·tar *john*·noh charj

Do you accept ...?	আপনি কি ... নেন?	*aap*·ni ki ... nen
credit cards	ক্রেডিট কার্ড	*kre*·đit karđ
debit cards	ডেবিট কার্ড	*đe*·bit karđ
travellers cheques	ট্র্যাভেলার্স চেক	*trą*·ve·lars chek

I'd like ..., please.	আমি ... চাই, প্লিজ।	*aa*·mi ... chai pleez
my change	আমার ভাঙ্গতি	*a*·mar *b'ang*·ţi
a receipt	একটা রিসিট	*ąk*·ta ri·*seet*
a refund	পয়সা ফেরত	*poy*·sha *fe*·rohţ
to return this	এটা ফেরত দিতে	*e*·ta *fe*·rohţ *di*·ţe

How much is it?
এটা কত? — *e*·ta *ko*·ţoh

It's free.
এটা ফ্রী। — *e*·ta free

It's (300) taka.
এটা (তিন শ) টাকা। — *e*·ta (*ţin*·shoh) *ta*·ka

It's (100) rupees.
এটা (এক শ) রুপি। — *e*·ta (ąk shoh) *ru*·pi

Can you write down the price?
দামটা লিখে দিতে পারেন? — *dam*·ta *li*·k'e *di*·ţe *paa*·ren

Can you give me some change?
আমাকে ভাঙ্গতি দিতে পারেন? — *aa*·ma·ke *b'ang*·ţi *di*·ţe *paa*·ren

Can you give me some smaller notes?
আমাকে ছোট নোট দিতে পারেন? — *aa*·ma·ke *ch'o*·toh noht *di*·ţe *paa*·ren

Do you change money here?
এখানে কি টাকা ভাঙ্গানো যাবে? — *e*·k'a·ne ki *ta*·ka *b'ang*·ga·noh *ja*·be

There's a mistake in the bill.
বিলে ভুল আছে। — *bi*·le b'ul *aa*·ch'e

count the money

The currency of Bangladesh is the taka (*ta*·ka টাকা), which is made up of 100 poishas (*poy*·sha পয়সা). There are notes for 2, 5, 10, 20, 50, 100, 500 and 1000 taka, and coins for 5, 10, 25 and 50 poishas, and for 1, 2 and 5 taka. In West Bengal, the currency is the rupee (*ru*·pi রুপি).

1	১	ąk
2	২	dui
3	৩	ţeen
4	৪	chaar
5	৫	paach
6	৬	ch'oy
7	৭	shaaţ
8	৮	aat
9	৯	noy
10	১০	dosh

sightseeing

প্রাকৃতিক দৃশ্য

I'd like a/an ...	আমি একটা ... চাই।	*aa*·mi *qk*·ta ... chai
audio set	অডিও সেট	*o*·đi·o set
catalogue	ক্যাটালগ	*kq*·ta·log
guide	গাইড	gaiđ
guidebook in English	ইংরেজি গাইড বই	*ing*·re·ji gaiđ *boh*·i
(local) map	(এই এলাকার) ম্যাপ	(ay *e*·la·kar) mąp

Do you have information on ... sights?	আপনার কাছে কি ... সাইটের কোন তথ্য আছে?	*aap*·nar *ka*·ch'e ki ... *sai*·ter *koh*·noh *ţohţ*·ţ'oh *aa*·ch'e
cultural	সাংস্কৃতিক	*shank*·skri·ţik
historical	ঐতিহাসিক	*oy*·ţi·ha·shik
religious	ধর্মীয়	*d'ohr*·mi·o

I'd like to see ...	আমি ... দেখতে চাই।	*aa*·mi ... *dek'*·ţe chai
forts	কেল্লা	*kel*·la
mosques	মসজিদ	*mos*·jid
temples	মন্দির	*mon*·dir
tombs	মাজার	*ma*·jar

What's that?
ওটা কি? — *oh*·ta ki

Who made it?
এটা কে তৈরী করেছে? — *e*·ta ke *ţoy*·ri *koh*·re·ch'e

How old is it?
এটা কত পুরানো? — *e*·ta *ko*·ţoh *pu*·ra·noh

Could you take a photo of me?
আমার একটা ছবি তুলে দেবেন? — *aa*·mar *qk*·ta *ch'oh*·bi *ţu*·le *de*·ben

Can I take a photo (of you)?
আমি (আপনার) একটা ছবি নিতে পারি? — *aa*·mi (*aap*·nar) *qk*·ta *ch'o*·bi *ni*·ţe *paa*·ri

getting in

প্রবেশ

What time does it open?
এটা কখন খুলে? — *e*·ta *ko*·k'ohn *k'u*·le

What's the admission charge?
টিকেট কত? — *ti*·ket *ko*·ţoh

Is there a discount for ...?	... জন্য কোন কনসেশন আছে?	... *john*·noh *koh*·noh *kon*·se·shohn *aa*·ch'e
children	বাচ্চাদের	*baach*·cha·der
families	ফ্যামিলির	*fą*·mi·lir
groups	গ্রুপের	*gru*·per
older people	বয়স্কদের	*boy*·oh·skoh·der
students	ছাত্রদের	*ch'aţ*·ţroh·der

tours

পর্যটন

When's the next ...?	এর পরের ... কখন?	er *poh*·rer ... *ko*·k'ohn
boat trip	নৌকা ভ্রমন	*no*·hu·ka *b'roh*·mohn
day trip	ডে ট্রিপ	đay trip
tour	ট্যুর	tur

Is ... included?	এটা কি ... সহ?	*e*·ta ki ... *sho*·hoh
accommodation	থাকার ব্যবস্থা	*ţ'a*·kar *bą*·boh·sţ'a
food	খাবার	*k'a*·bar
transport	যানবাহন	*jan*·ba·hohn

How long is the tour?
ট্যুরটা কতক্ষন? — *tur*·ta *ko*·tohk·k'ohn

What time should we be back?
আমাদের কখন ফিরতে হবে? — *aa*·ma·der *ko*·k'ohn *fir*·ţe *ho*·be

I'm with them.
আমি ওদের সাথে। — *aa*·mi *oh*·der *sha*·ţ'e

I've lost my group.
আমার গ্রুপ হারিয়ে ফেলেছি। — *aa*·mar grup *ha*·ri·ye *fe*·le·ch'i

business

ব্যাবসা

Where's the …?	… কোথায়?	… *koh*·ţ'ai
business centre	বিজনেস সেন্টার	*biz*·nes *sen*·tar
conference	সম্মেলন	*shom*·me·lon
meeting	মিটিং	*mee*·ting

I'm attending a …	আমি একটা …-এ এসেছি।	*aa*·mi *ąk*·ta …·e e·she·chi
conference	সম্মেলন	*shom*·me·lon
course	কোর্স	kohrs
meeting	মিটিং	*mee*·ting
trade fair	ট্রেড ফেয়ার	tređ *fe*·ar

I'm with …	আমি … সাথে আছি।	*aa*·mi … *sha*·ţ'e *aa*·ch'i
my colleague	আমার কলিগের	*aa*·mar *ko*·li·ger
my colleagues	আমার কলিগদের	*aa*·mar *ko*·lig·der
(two) others	আরো (দু)জনের	*aa*·roh (*dui*·)jo·ner

I'm alone.
আমি একা। — *aa*·mi *ą*·ka

I have an appointment with …
আমার …-এর সাথে এ্যাপয়েন্টমেন্ট আছে। — *aa*·mar …·er *sha*·ţ'e *ą*·po·ent·ment *aa*·ch'e

I'm staying at …, room …
আমি …-এ, রুম …-এ আছি। — *aa*·mi …·e rum …·e *aa*·ch'i

I'm here for (two) days/weeks.
আমি এখানে (দুই) দিন/সপ্তাহ আছি। — *aa*·mi e·k'a·ne (dui) din/*shop*·ţa *aa*·ch'i

Here's my business card.
এই যে আমার বিজনেস কার্ড। — ay je *aa*·mar *biz*·nes karđ

What's your …?	আপনার … কি?	*aap*·nar … ki
address	ঠিকানা	*ţ'i*·ka·na
email address	ইমেইল এ্যাড্রেস	*ee*·mayl *ąđ*·res
fax number	ফ্যাক্স নম্বর	fąks *nom*·bohr

I need ...	আমার ... লাগবে।	*aa*·mar ... *laag*·be
a computer	একটা কম্পিউটার	*ąk*·ta *kom*·pyu·tar
an Internet connection	একটা ইন্টারনেট কানেকশন	*ąk*·ta *in*·tar·net *ka*·nek·shohn
an interpreter	একজন দোভাষী	*ąk*·john *doh*·b'a·shi
to send a fax	একটা ফ্যাক্স পাঠাতে	*ąk*·ta fąks *pa*·ţ'a·ţe

That went very well.
ওটা খুব ভাল হয়েছে। — *oh*·ta k'ub *b'a*·loh *hoh*·e·ch'e

Thank you for your time.
আপনার সময়ের জন্য ধন্যবাদ। — *aap*·nar *shoh*·moy·er *john*·noh *d'ohn*·noh·bad

Shall we go for a drink?
আমরা কি ড্রিন্ক করতে যাব? — *aam*·ra ki đrink *kohr*·ţe *ja*·boh

Shall we go for a meal?
আমরা কি খেতে যাব? — *aam*·ra ki *k'e*·ţe *ja*·boh

It's on me.
এটা আমি খাওয়াব। — *e*·ta *aa*·mi *k'a*·wa·boh

etiquette tips

- Physical contact between men and women in public is frowned upon, whether it's between foreigners or locals.
- Modesty is expected on all social occasions. In conversation with Bengalis, avoid any mention of sex or sexuality. As for clothing, women should steer clear of sleeveless shirts, shorts and short skirts.

specific needs

বিশেষ প্রয়োজন

senior & disabled travellers

বয়স্ক ও পঙ্গু পর্যটক

There aren't many facilities for disabled travellers available in India and Bangladesh, but you'll find that people are generally very helpful and forthcoming.

I have a disability.
আমি পঙ্গু। — *aa*·mi *pohn*·gu

I'm blind.
আমি অন্ধ। — *aa*·mi *on*·d'oh

I'm deaf.
আমি কানে শুনি না। — *aa*·mi *ka*·ne *shu*·ni na

I need assistance.
আমার সাহায্য লাগবে। — *aa*·mar *sha*·haj·joh *laag*·be

Is there wheelchair access?
হুইলচেয়ার নিয়ে ঢুকার ব্যাবস্থা আছে কি? — *weel*·che·ar *ni*·ye *d'u*·kar *bą*·boh·sţ'a *aa*·ch'e ki

Is there a lift?
এখানে কি লিফ্‌ট আছে? — e·k'a·ne ki lift *aa*·ch'e

Are there disabled toilets?
এখানে কি ডিজএবেল টয়লেট আছে? — e·k'a·ne ki *di*·zą·bel *toy*·let *aa*·ch'e

Are there rails in the bathroom?
বাথরুমে কি রেল আছে? — *baţ*·ru·me ki rel *aa*·ch'e

Could you help me cross the street safely?
আমাকে রাস্তা পার হতে সাহায্য করবেন? — *aa*·ma·ke *raa*·sţa par *hoh*·ţe *sha*·haj·joh *kohr*·ben

Is there somewhere I can sit down?
কোথাও বসতে পারি? — *koh*·ţ'a·o *bohsh*·ţe *paa*·ri

women travellers

মহিলা পর্যটক

Bangladesh and West Bengal are usually very safe, and the general attitude towards women is one of respect. It's up to you, to a great extent, to keep yourself safe. As the local women are naturally careful and reserved, any different behaviour from a foreigner could send the wrong message to local men.

Unwanted attention or hassle from men towards foreign and local women alike can be limited by dressing modestly, not returning stares and not engaging in inane conversations with men, which can all be seen as a bit of a turn on. Don't worry too much about the local language – in these situations, your body language is more important than verbal. In fact, speaking English can act as a deterrent.

I'm here with my girlfriend/boyfriend.
আমি এখানে আমার বান্ধবির/ বন্ধুর সাথে এসেছি। — *aa*·mi *e*·k'a·ne *aa*·mar *ban*·đ'o·bir/ *bohn*·đ'ur *sha*·ţ'e *e*·she·chi

Excuse me, I have to go now.
এক্সকিউজ মি, আমি এখন আসি। — *ek*·ski·uz mi *aa*·mi *q*·k'ohn *aa*·shi

Leave me alone!
আমাকে ছেড়ে দেন! — *aa*·ma·ke *ch'e*·ŗe den

local talk

Get lost!	আপনি এখন যান!	*aap*·ni *q*·k'on jan
Piss off!	গেলি!	*ge*·li

travelling with children

শিশুদের নিয়ে ভ্রমন

Is there a ...?	... আছে?	... *aa*·ch'e
discount for children	বাচ্চাদের জন্য কনসেশন	*baach*·cha·der *john*·noh *kon*·se·shohn
family room	ফ্যামিলি রুম	*fq*·mi·li rum
family ticket	ফ্যামিলি টিকেট	*fq*·mi·li *ti*·ket

I need a/an ...	আমার একটা ... লাগবে।	*aa*·mar *ąk*·ta ... *laag*·be
(English-speaking) babysitter	(ইংরেজি বলতে পারা) আয়া	(*ing*·re·ji *bohl*·ţe *pa*·ra) *aay*·aa
highchair	হাই চেয়ার	hai *che*·ar
potty	পটি	*po*·ti
pram	প্র্যাম	prąm
sick bag	বমির ব্যাগ	*boh*·mir bąg

Do you sell ...?	আপনি কি ... বিক্রি করেন?	*aap*·ni ki ... *bi*·kri *koh*·ren
baby wipes	বেবি ওয়াইপ	*be*·bi waip
disposable nappies	ডাইপার	*dai*·par
painkillers for infants	ছোট বাচ্চাদের পেইনকিলার	*ch'oh*·toh *baach*·cha·der *payn*·ki·lar

Where's the nearest ...?	কাছাকাছি ... কোথায়?	*ka*·ch'a·ka·ch'i ... *koh*·ţ'ai
playground	খেলার মাঠ	*k'ą*·lar maţ'
theme park	থিম পার্ক	ţ'eem park
toy shop	খেলনার দোকান	*k'ąl*·nar *doh*·kan

Are there any good places to take children around here?
বাচ্চাদের নেওয়ার মত কাছাকাছি কোন ভাল জায়গা আছে?
baach·cha·der *ną*·war *mo*·toh *ka*·ch'a·ka·ch'i *koh*·noh *b'a*·loh *jay*·ga *aa*·ch'e

Are children allowed?
বাচ্চাদের নেওয়া যাবে?
baach·cha·der *ną*·wa *ja*·be

Is there space for a pram?
প্র্যামটা রাখার জায়গা হবে?
prąm·ta *ra*·k'ar *jay*·ga *ho*·be

Where can I change a nappy?
কোথায় ন্যাপি বদলাতে পারি?
koh·ţ'ai *ną*·pi *bod*·la·ţe *paa*·ri

Is this suitable for (four)-year-old children?
এটা (চার) বছরের বাচ্চাদের জন্য কি ঠিক?
e·ta (char) *bo*·ch'oh·rer *baach*·cha·der *john*·noh ki ţ'ik

Do you know a dentist/doctor who is good with children?
বাচ্চাদের জন্য ভাল ডেন্টিষ্ট/ডাক্তার চিনেন?
baach·cha·der *john*·noh *b'a*·loh *đen*·tist/*đak*·ţar *chi*·nen

If your child is sick, see **health**, page 273.

kids' talk

The family is the cornerstone of Bengali society, both economically and socially. Asking about family and children is generally a good way to start a conversation.

How many children do you have?		
আপনার কয় ছেলে-মেয়ে?		*aap*·nar koy *ch'e*·le·me·e
Is this your first child?		
এটা কি আপনার প্রথম বাচ্চা?		e·ta ki *aap*·nar *proh*·ţ'ohm *baach*·cha
Is it a boy or a girl?		
এটা ছেলে না মেয়ে?		e·ta *ch'e*·le na *me*·e
What's his/her name?		
ওর নাম কি?		ohr naam ki
How old is he/she?		
ওর বয়স কত?		ohr *boy*·osh *ko*·ţoh
Does he/she go to school?		
ও কি স্কুলে যায়?		oh ki *sku*·le jay
Is he/she well-behaved?		
ও কি লক্ষি?		oh ki *lohk*·k'i

Everywhere you go in Bangladesh and India you'll be greeted by children keen to strike up a conversation with you. Here are a few questions they'll be happy to answer.

When's your birthday?		
আপনার জন্মদিন কবে?		*aap*·nar *jon*·moh·din *ko*·be
Do you go to school?		
তুমি কি স্কুলে যাও?		*ţu*·mi ki *sku*·le *ja*·o
What grade are you in?		
তুমি কোন গ্রেডে পড়?		*ţu*·mi kohn *gre*·đe *po*·ŗoh
Do you learn English?		
তুমি কি ইংরেজি শেখ?		*ţu*·mi ki *ing*·re·ji *she*·k'oh
Do you like ...?	তামার কি ... ভাল লাগে?	*ţoh*·mar ki ... *b'a*·loh *la*·ge
school	স্কুল	skul
sport	খেলাধুলা	*k'q*·la·d'u·la
your teacher	তোমার টিচারকে	*ţoh*·mar *ti*·char·ke

basics

মুল কথা

Yes.	হ্যাঁ।	hạng
No.	না।	naa
Please.	প্লিজ।	pleez
Thank you (very much).	(অনেক) ধন্যবাদ।	(*o*·nek) *d'oh*·noh·baad
Excuse me. (to get attention)	শুনুন।	*shu*·nun
Excuse me. (to get past)	একটু দেখি।	*ek*·tu *de*·k'i
Sorry.	সরি।	*so*·ri
Forgive me.	মাফ করবেন।	maf *kohr*·ben

greetings & goodbyes

অভিনন্দন ও বিদায়

Western-style greetings like 'good morning' and 'hello' aren't normally used in Bengali. While English speakers in big cities will appreciate hearing English greetings – you might even hear young city dwellers greeting each other casually with a hai হায় (hi) or bai বায় (bye) – you should generally use the terms below.

Muslim men usually shake hands when greeting, but women generally just accompany their greeting with a smile. Hindu men and women greet others by joining the palms of their hands together and holding them close to the chest as they slightly bow the head and say their greeting.

Hello. (Muslim greeting)
আস্সালাম ওয়ালাইকুম। as·*sa*·lam wa·*lai*·kum

Hello. (Muslim response)
ওয়ালাইকুম আস্সালাম। wa·*lai*·kum as·*sa*·lam

Hello. (Hindu greeting and response)
নমস্কার। *no*·mohsh·kar

How are you?
কেমন আছেন? *kq*·mohn *aa*·ch'en

Fine, and you?
ভাল, আপনি? *b'a*·loh *aap*·ni

What's your name?
আপনার নাম কি? *aap*·nar naam ki

My name is ...
আমার নাম ... *aa*·mar naam ...

I'd like to introduce you to ...
...-এর সাথে আপনার পরিচয় করিয়ে দেই। ...·er *sha*·ţ'e *aap*·nar *poh*·ri·choy *koh*·ri·ye day

This is my ...	এটা আমার ...	e·ta *aa*·mar ...
colleague	কলিগ	*ko*·lig
daughter	মেয়ে	*me*·e
friend	বন্ধু	*bohn*·d'u
husband	স্বামী	*sha*·mi
son	ছেলে	*ch'e*·le
wife	স্ত্রী	ştree

For other family members, see the **dictionary**.

I'm pleased to meet you.
আপনার সাথে পরিচিত হয়ে খুশি হয়েছি। *aap*·nar *sha*·ţ'e *poh*·ri·chi·toh *hoh*·e *k'u*·shi *hoh*·e·ch'i

A pleasure to meet you, too.
আমিও। *aa*·mi·o

See you later.
পরে দেখা হবে। *po*·re *dq*·k'a *ho*·be

Goodbye/Good night. (Muslim)
আল্লাহ হাফেজ। *al*·laa *ha*·fez

Goodbye/Good night. (Hindu)
নমস্কার। *no*·mosh·kar

Bon voyage! (Muslim)
আল্লাহ হাফেজ। *al*·laa *ha*·fez

Bon voyage! (Hindu)
নমস্কার। *no*·mosh·kar

addressing people

সম্বধন

Mr/Sir	মিস্টার/স্যার	*mis*·tar/sar
Ms/Miss	মিজ/মিস	miz/mis
Mrs/Madam	মিসেস/ম্যাডাম	*mi*·ses/*mą*·dam
Sahib m	সাহেব	*sha*·heb
Begum (Sahib) f	বেগম (সাহেব)	*be*·gohm (*sha*·heb)

title holders

Never address anyone by their name unless you know the person quite well. In formal situations, always add 'Mr' (in English) before the name of a man or *sha*·heb after it. The equivalent for women is 'Mrs/Miss' and *be*·gohm or *be*·gohm *sha*·heb respectively. You can use the Bengali terms for everyone, but you'll notice that the English ones are common in a professional environment.

Even in more casual situations, you shouldn't address an older person only by their first name. Add the word b'ai (brother) or *a*·pa (older sister) after the first name when addressing people who are slightly older or deserve respect. A Muslim man who has done the pilgrimage to Mecca is usually called *ha*·ji *sha*·heb. The word dohşţ (friend) is the equivalent of the Australian 'mate' or US 'buddy' and is used casually between men.

making conversation

আলাপ

What's the news?
কি খবর? — ki *k'o*·bohr

Are you here on holiday?
আপনি কি ছুটিতে আছেন? — *aap*·ni ki *ch'u*·ti·ţe *aa*·ch'en

I'm here ...	আমি এখানে ... এসেছি।	*aa*·mi *e*·k'a·ne ... *e*·she·chi
for a holiday	ছুটিতে	*ch'u*·ti·ţe
on business	ব্যাবসার কাজে	*bąb*·shar *ka*·je
to study	পড়তে এসেছি	*pohŗ*·ţe *e*·she·chi

How long are you here for?
আপনি এখানে কতদিন আছেন? *aap*·ni e·k'a·ne *ko*·ţoh·din *aa*·ch'en

I'm here for (four) weeks/days.
আমি এখানে (চার) সপ্তাহ/দিন আছি। *aa*·mi e·k'a·ne (char) *shop*·ta·ho/din *aa*·ch'i

nationalities

জাতীয়তা

Where are you from?
আপনি কোথা থেকে এসেছেন? *aap*·ni *koh*·ţai *ţ'e*·ke *e*·she·chen

I'm from ...	আমি ... থেকে এসেছি।	*aa*·mi ... *ţ'e*·ke *esh*·chi
Australia	অস্ট্রেলিয়া	*o*·stre·li·a
Canada	ক্যানাডা	*ką*·na·da
England	ইংল্যান্ড	*ing*·ląnd
New Zealand	নিউ জিল্যান্ড	nyu *zi*·ląnd
Singapore	সিঙ্গাপুর	*sing*·a·pur
the USA	আমেরিকা	*ą*·me·ri·ka

age

বয়স

How old are you?
আপনার বয়স কত? *aap*·nar *boy*·ohsh *ko*·toh

How old is your daughter/son?
আপনার মেয়ের/ছেলের বয়স কত? *aap*·nar *me*·er/*ch'e*·ler *boy*·ohsh *ko*·toh

I'm ... years old.
আমার বয়স ... *aa*·mar *boy*·ohsh ...

He/She is ... years old.
ওর বয়স ... ohr *boy*·ohsh ...

For your age, see **numbers & amounts**, page 189.

family

পরিবার

I'm ...	আমি ...	*aa*·mi ...
married	বিবাহিত	*bi*·ba·hi·ţoh
single	অবিবাহিত	*o*·bi·ba·hi·ţoh

Are you married?
আপনি কি বিবাহিত? — *aap*·ni ki *bi*·ba·hi·ţoh

Do you have any children?
আপনার ছেলে মেয়ে আছে? — *aap*·nar *ch'e*·le me *aa*·ch'e

occupations & studies

চাকরি ও লেখাপড়া

What's your occupation?
আপনি কি করেন? — *aap*·ni ki *koh*·ren

I'm self-employed.
আমার নিজের ব্যবসা আছে। — *aa*·mar *ni*·jer *bqb*·sha *aa*·ch'e

I'm a ...	আমি ...	*aa*·mi ...
businessperson	ব্যাবসায়ি m&f	*bqb*·shai
cook	বাবুর্চি m&f	*ba*·bur·chi
doctor	ডাক্তার m&f	*đak*·ţar
journalist	সাংবাদিক m&f	*shang*·ba·dik
salesperson	দোকানদার m&f	*doh*·kan·dar
servant	কাজের লোক m&f	*ka*·jer lohk
tailor/seamstress	দরজি m&f	*dohr*·ji
teacher	শিক্ষক/শিক্ষীকা m/f	*shik*·k'ohk/*shik*·k'i·ka

I work in ...	আমি ...-এ কাজ করি।	*aa*·mi ...·e kaaj *koh*·ri
administration	প্রসাশন	*proh*·sha·shohn
health	হেল্থ	helţ'
sales & marketing	মার্কেটিং	*mar*·ke·ting

I'm ...	আমি ...	*aa*·mi ...
retired	রিটায়ার্ড	ri·*tai*·erd
unemployed	বেকার	*be*·kar

What are you studying?
আপনি কি পড়ছেন? — *aap*·ni ki *pohr̥*·ch'en

I'm studying …	আমি … পড়ছি।	*aa*·mi … *pohr̥*·ch'i
Bengali	বাংলা	*bang*·la
Hindi	হিন্দি	*hin*·di
humanities	হিউম্যানিটিজ	*hyu*·mą·ni·tiz
science	বিজ্ঞান	*big*·gan
Urdu	উর্দু	*ur̥*·du

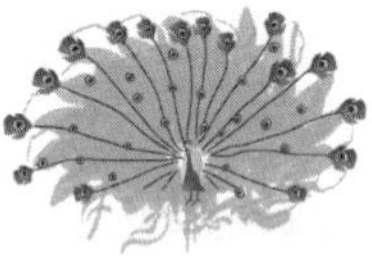

farewells

বিদায়

Here's my …	এই যে আমার …	ay je *aa*·mar …
What's your …?	আপনার … কি?	*aap*·nar … ra
address	ঠিকানা	*ţ'i*·ka·na
email address	ইমেইল এ্যাড্রেস	*ee*·mayl *ąđ*·res
phone number	ফোন নম্বর	fohn *nohm*·bohr

I'll …	আমি …	*aa*·mi …
keep in touch	যোগাযোগ রাখবো	*johg*·ga·johg *rak'*·boh
miss you	তোমাকে মিস করব	*ţoh*·ma·ke mis *kohr*·boh
visit you	তোমার সাথে দেখা করতে আসবো	*ţoh*·mar *sha*·ţ'e *dą*·k'a *kohr*·ţe *aash*·boh

I have to leave (tomorrow).
আমাকে (আগামিকাল) যেতে হবে। — *aa*·ma·ke (*aa*·ga·mi·kaal) *je*·ţe *ho*·be

It's been great meeting you.
তোমার সাথে দেখা হয়ে খুব ভাল লাগল। — *ţo*·mar *sha*·ţ'e *dą*·k'ą *hoh*·e k'ub *b'a*·loh *lag*·loh

Keep in touch.
যোগাযোগ রেখ। — *johg*·ga·johg *re*·k'oh

common interests

সাধারন রুচি

What do you do in your spare time?
অবসর সময় কি করেন? *ob*·shor *sho*·moy ki *koh*·ren

Do you like ...?	আপনি কি ... পছন্দ করেন?	*aap*·ni ki ... *po*·ch'ohn·doh *koh*·ren
I (don't) like ...	আমি ... পছন্দ করি (না)।	*aa*·mi ... *po*·ch'ohn·doh *koh*·ri (na)
art	শিল্পকলা	*shil*·poh·ko·la
chess	দাবা	*da*·ba
dancing	নাচছ	*naach*·ch'e
films	ছবি দেখতে	*ch'o*·bi *dek'*·ţe
music	মিউজিক	mi·*u*·zik
painting	পেইন্টিং	*payn*·ting
politics	রাজনীতি	*raj*·nee·ţi
reading	বই পড়তে	*boh*·i *pohr*·ţe
sport	খেলাধুলা	*k'q*·la·d'u·la
theatre	থিয়েটার	*ţ'i*·e·tar
TV	টিভি দেখতে	*ti*·vi *dek'*·te
yoga	যোগ ব্যায়াম	johg *be*·am

For sporting activities, see **sport**, page 244.

music

সংগীত

Which ... do you like?	আপনি কোন ... পছন্দ করেন?	*aap*·ni kohn ... *po*·ch'on·doh *koh*·ren
band	ব্যান্ড	bạnđ
music	মিউজিক	mi·*u*·zik
singers	গায়ক	*gai*·ohk

Do you ...?	আপনি কি ...?	*aap*·ni ki ...
go to concerts	কন্সার্টে যান	*kon*·sar·te jaan
listen to music	মিউজিক শুনেন	mi·*u*·zik *shuh*·nen
play an instrument	কোন যন্ত্র বাজাতে পারেন	*koh*·noh *jon*·ţroh *baa*·ja·ţe *paa*·ren
sing	গান গাইতে পারেন	gaan *gai*·ţe *paa*·ren

Planning to go to a concert? See **tickets**, page 196, and **going out**, page 247.

cinema & theatre

সিনেমা ও থিয়েটার

What's showing at the cinema/theatre tonight?
আজ রাতে সিনেমায়/থিয়েটারে কি চলছে? — aaj *raa*·ţe *si*·ne·ma·e/*ţ'i*·e·ta·re ki *chohl*·ch'e

Is it in English?
এটা কি ইংরেজিতে? — *e*·ta ki *ing*·re·ji·ţe

Does it have (English) subtitles?
(ইংরেজিতে) সাবটাইটেল আছে কি? — (*ing*·re·ji) *sab*·tai·tel *a*·ch'e ki

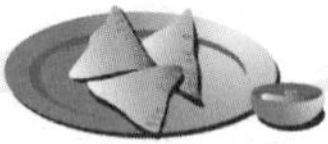

I feel like going to a ...	আমার ... দেখতে ইচ্ছা হচ্ছে।	*aa*·mar ... *dek'*·te *ich*·ch'a *hoh*·ch'e
Did you like the ...?	আপনার কি ...-টা ভাল লেগেছে?	*aap*·nar ki ...·ta *b'a*·loh *le*·ge·ch'e
film	ছবি	*ch'oh*·bi
play	নাটক	*naa*·tohk

I (don't) like ...	আমি ... পছন্দ করি (না)।	*aa*·mi ... *po*·ch'ohn·doh *koh*·ri (na)
action movies	মারামারির ছবি	*maa*·ra·maa·rir *ch'oh*·bi
Bengali cinema	বাংলা ছবি	*bang*·la *ch'oh*·bi
comedies	হাসির ছবি	*ha*·shir *ch'oh*·bi
drama	নাটক	*naa*·tohk
Hindi movies	হিন্দি ছবি	*hin*·di *ch'o*·bi

art

চিত্রকলা

When's the gallery/museum open?
গ্যালারি/যাদুঘর কখন খোলে? — *ga*·la·ri/*mi*·u·zi·am *ko*·k'ohn *k'oh*·le

What kind of art are you interested in?
আপনি কি ধরনের ছবি পছন্দ করেন? — *aap*·ni ki *d'o*·roh·ner *ch'o*·bi *po*·ch'on·doh *koh*·ren

What's in the collection?
কালেকশনে কি আছে? — *ka*·lek·shoh·ne ki *a*·ch'e

What do you think of ...?
আপনি ...-এর সমন্ধে কি মনে করেন? — *aap*·ni ...·er *shom*·mohn·d'e ki *moh*·ne *koh*·ren

It's an exhibition of ...
এটা ...-এর প্রদর্শনী। — e·ta ...·er *pro*·dohr·shoh·ni

I'm interested in ...
আমি ...-এ ইন্টারেসটেড। — *aa*·mi ...·e *in*·te·re·sted

I like the works of ...
আমার ...-এর কাজ ভাল লাগে। — *aa*·mar ...·er kaj *b'a*·loh *la*·ge

It reminds me of ...
এটা ...-এর কথা মনে করিয়ে দেয়। — e·ta ...·er *ko*·t'a *moh*·ne *koh*·ri·ye day

architecture	স্থাপত্য	*st'a*·pot·toh
art	শিল্পকলা	*shil*·poh·ko·la
batik	বাটিক	*ba*·tik
carpet weaving	কার্পেট বুনন	*kar*·pet *bu*·non
ceramics	সিরামিক	*si*·ra·mik
embroidery	এমব্রোয়ডারি	*em*·broy·da·ri
metal craft	মেটালের কাজ	*me*·ta·ler kaj
painting (the art)	পেন্টিং	*payn*·ting
painting (canvas)	চিত্রকলা	*chit*·roh·ko·la
period	কাল	kaal
sculpture	স্কাল্পচার	*skalp*·char
statue	মূর্তি	*mur*·ti
style	স্টাইল	stail
technique	কায়দা	*ka*·e·da
woodwork	কাঠের কাজ	*ka*·t'er kaaj

sport

খেলাধুলা

What sport do you …?	আপনি কি স্পোর্ট …?	*aap*·ni kohn spohrt …
follow	ফলো করেন	*fo*·loh *koh*·ren
play	খেলেন	*k'ą*·len
I play/do …	আমি … খেলি।	*aa*·mi … *k'e*·li
I follow …	আমি … ফলো করি।	*aa*·mi … *fo*·loh *koh*·ri
athletics	এ্যাথলেটিকস	*ąţ'*·le·tiks
basketball	বাস্কেট বল	*baa*·sket bol
chess	দাবা	*da*·ba
cricket	ক্রিকেট	*kri*·ket
football (soccer)	ফুটবল	fut·bol
golf	গল্ফ	golf
hockey	হকি	*ho*·ki
karate	ক্যারাটি	*ka*·ra·ti
polo	হর্স পোলো	hors *poh*·loh
tennis	টেনিস	*te*·nis
volleyball	ভলিবল	*vo*·li·bol
wrestling	রেসলিং	*re*·sling

hold your breath

A folk game called *ha*·đu·đu কাবাডি or *ka*·ba·đi হাডুডু is now the national game of Bangladesh. It's played by two teams of 12 players, and each team has a home court to control. To play, a member of team A visits the court of team B, holding his breath and chanting *ha*·đu·đu *ha*·đu·đu … or *ka*·ba·đi *ka*·ba·đi … His aim is to tag as many team B players as possible and get back to his own court without losing his breath. Team B have to protect themselves from getting tagged, while trying to force the team A player to lose his breath before he goes 'home'. If a team B player has been tagged and the team A member has returned to his home court with breath intact, the tagged player is out for the duration of the game. Each team takes turns to visit the other court, and the team which loses all its players first loses the game.

feelings & opinions

অনুভুতি এবং মতামত

feelings

অনুভুতি

Are you ...?	আপনার কি ...?	*aap*·nar ki ...
I'm (not) ...	আমার ... (না)।	*aa*·mar ... (nai)
cold	ঠান্ডা লাগছে	*ţ'an*·đa *laag*·ch'e
happy	খুশি লাগছে	*k'u*·shi *laag*·ch'e
hot	গরম লাগছে	*go*·rohm *laag*·ch'e
hungry	ক্ষিদা পেয়েছে	*k'i*·da *pe*·e·ch'e
sad	দুঃখ লাগছে	*duk*·k'oh *laag*·ch'e
thirsty	তেষ্টা পেয়েছে	*ţesh*·ta *pe*·e·ch'e
Are you ...?	আপনি কি ...?	*aap*·ni ki ...
I'm (not) ...	আমি ... (না)।	*aa*·mi ... (na)
tired	টায়ার্ড	*tai*·ard
well	ভাল	*b'a*·loh

If you're not feeling well, see **health**, page 273.

politics & social issues

রাজনৈতিক এবং সামাজিক ব্যাপার

Bengalis enjoy discussions on any global issues and will happily link them to the situation in their own country. When it comes to local issues, although they may criticise their own socio-political situation, they won't easily accept this from foreigners. Exercise a little caution when voicing your opinion – some people are very passionate about politics and the parties they support.

Did you hear about ...?
আপনি কি ...-এর ব্যাপারে শুনেছেন? *aap*·ni ki ...·er *bą*·pa·re *shu*·ne·ch'en

How do people feel about ...?
...-এর ব্যাপারে লোকে
কি মনে করে?
... ·er *bą*·pa·re *loh*·ke
ki *moh*·ne *koh*·re

the caste system	জাত	jaţ
child labour	শিশুস্রম	*shi*·shu·srohm
the dispute over Kashmir	কাশমির বিবাদ	*kash*·mir *bi*·bad
indigenous issues	অধিবাসিদের বিষয়াদি	*oh*·d'i·ba·shi·der *bi*·shoy·a·di
traditional Indian clothing	ভারতীয় দেশজ পোষাক	*b'a*·roh·ţi·o *de*·shoj *poh*·shak
pilgrimage (Hindu)	তীর্থ	*ţir*·ţ'o
pilgrimage (Muslim)	হজ্ব	hoj
poverty	দারিদ্র	*da*·ri·dro
racism	বর্নবাদ	*bor*·noh·bad
religious extremism	ধর্মীয় মৌলবাদ	*d'ar*·mi·yo *mo*·u·loh·bad
terrorism	সন্ত্রাশ	*shon*·ţrash
unemployment	বেকারত্ব	*be*·ka·roţ·ţoh
the war in …	…-এ যুদ্ধ	…·e *jud*·d'oh

the environment

পরিবেশ

Is there a … problem here?
এখানে কি কোন …-এর সমস্যা আছে?
e·k'a·ne ki *koh*·noh …·er *sho*·mohsh·sha *aa*·ch'e

What should be done about …?
…-এর ব্যাপারে কি করা উচিত?
…·er *bq*·pa·re ki *koh*·ra *u*·chiţ

deforestation	বন উজাড়িকরন	bon *u*·ja·ŗi·ko·rohn
drought	খরা	*k'o*·ra
endangered species	বিপন্নায়া প্রানী	*bi*·pon·na·ya *pra*·ni
flood	বন্যা	*bon*·na
hunting	শিকার	*shi*·kar
hydroelectricity	জলবিদ্যুৎ	*jol*·bid·duţ
ozone layer	ওজোন স্তর	*oh*·zohn sţor
pesticides	কীটনাশক	*keet*·na·shohk
pollution	দূষন	*du*·shohn
recycling programme	পূনর্ব্যাবহার কর্মসূচি	*pu*·nohr·bạ·boh·har *kor*·moh·shu·chi
toxic waste	বিষক্তিয়া আবর্জনা	*bi*·shok·ti·ya *aa*·bohr·joh·na
water supply	পানির সাপলাই	*pa*·nir *sap*·lai

SOCIAL

where to go

কোথায় যাওয়া যায়

The most popular forms of entertainment for Bengalis are eating out, theatre and concerts. In villages you may also come across *ja*·tra যাত্রা (folk theatre performances, sometimes with music), which happen only a few times a year, beginning just after dark and running until the very early morning.

What's there to do in the evenings?
বিকালে কি করা যায়? — *bi*·ka·le ki *koh*·ra jay

Do you know a good restaurant?
আপনার কি একটা ভাল রেস্তোরা জানা আছে? — *aap*·nar ki *ąk*·ta *b'a*·loh *res*·ţoh·ra *ja*·na *aa*·ch'e

What's on ...?	... কি চলছে?	... ki *chohl*·ch'e
locally	এখানে	e·k'aa·ne
this weekend	এই ছুটিতে	ay *ch'u*·ti·ţe
today	আজকে	*aaj*·ke
tonight	আজ রাতে	aaj *raa*·ţe

I feel like going to a ...	আমার ... যেতে ইচ্ছা হচ্ছে।	*aa*·mar ... *je*·ţe *ich*·ch'a *hohch*·ch'e
bar	বারে	*ba*·re
café	ক্যাফেটেরিয়ায়	*ką*·fe·te·ri·a·e
concert	কনসার্টে	*kon*·sar·te
folk theatre performance	যাত্রায়	*ja*·tra·e
nightclub	নাইট ক্লাবে	nait *klaa*·be
party	পার্টিতে	*par*·ti·ţe
regional music performance	পল্লী গীতির আসরে	*pohl*·li *gi*·ţir *aa*·shoh·re
restaurant	রেস্তোরায়	*res*·toh·ra·e
traditional dance performance	দেশি নাচ দেখতে	*de*·shi naach *dek'*·ţe

Is there a local … guide?	… গাইড আছে কি?	… gaiđ *aa*·ch'e ki
entertainment	বিনোদন	*bi*·noh·dohn
film	সিনেমা	*ch'oh*·bi

Where can I find …?	… কোথায়?	… *koh*·ţ'ai
clubs	ক্লাব	klaab
places to eat	খাওয়ার জায়গা	*k'aa*·war *jai*·ga

For more on bars and drinks, see **eating out**, page 255.

social no-nos

- Gays and lesbians aren't accepted, recognised or even mentioned in Bengali-speaking areas, so be discreet if you're travelling with your partner.
- Drinking alcohol is a no-no from a social and religious point of view.

invitations

আমন্ত্রন

Where would you like to go (tonight)?
(আজ রাতে) কোথায় যাবেন? — (aaj *raa*·ţe) *koh*·ţ'ai *jaa*·ben

Would you like to do something (tomorrow)?
(আগামিকাল) কি কিছু করতে চান? — (*aa*·ga·mi·kaal) ki *ki*·ch'u *kohr*·ţe chan

We're having a party.
আমরা একটা পার্টি করছি। — *aam*·ra *qk*·ta *par*·ti *kohr*·ch'i

You should come.
আপনাকে আসতে হবে। — *ţoh*·ma·ke *aash*·ţe *ho*·be

Do you want to come to the (concert) with me?
আমার সাথে (কনসার্টে) যাবেন? — *aa*·mar *sha*·ţ'e (*kon*·sar·te) *jaa*·ben

Would you like to go for (a) …?	আপনি কি … যাবেন?	*aap*·ni ki … *jaa*·ben
coffee	কফি খেতে	*ko*·fi *k'e*·ţe
meal	খেতে	*k'e*·te
tea	চা খেতে	cha *k'e*·ţe
walk	হাটতে	*haat*·ţe

responding to invitations

আমন্ত্রনের উত্তরে

Yes, I'd love to.
হ্যাঁ, নিশ্চয়। — hąng *nish*·cho·hi

No, I'm afraid I can't.
না দুক্ষিত, আমি পারবো না। — naa *duk*·k'i·ţoh *aa*·mi *par*·boh naa

What about tomorrow?
আগামিকাল? — *aa*·ga·mi·kal

No, thank you.
না, ধন্যবাদ। — naa *đ'ohn*·no·bad

For other responses, see **women travellers**, page 232.

arranging to meet

সাক্ষাতের ব্যাবস্থা

What time will we meet?
কয়টার সময় আমরা দেখা করব? — *ko*·tar *sho*·moy *aam*·ra *dą*·k'a *kohr*·boh

Where will we meet?
আমরা কোথায় দেখা করব? — *aam*·ra *koh*·ţ'ai *dą*·k'a *kohr*·boh

Let's meet at …	চলেন … দেখা করি।	*cho*·len … *dą*·k'a *koh*·ri
(eight) o'clock	(আট্টার) সময়	(*aat*·tar) *sho*·moy
the entrance	গেটে	*ge*·te

Where shall we go?
আমরা কোথায় যেতে পারি? — *aam*·ra *koh*·ţai *je*·ţe *paa*·ri

I'll pick you up.
আমি আপনাকে তুলবো। — *aa*·mi *aap*·na·ke *ţul*·boh

See you later.
পরে দেখা হবে। — *po*·re *dą*·k'a *ho*·be

love

ভালবাসা

Will you ...?	তুমি কি ...?	*ţu*·mi ki ...
go out with me	আমার সাথে বেড়াতে যাবে	*aa*·mar *sha*·ţ'e *be*·ŗa·ţe *ja*·be
meet my parents	আমার বাবা মার সাথে দেখা করবে	*aa*·mar *ba*·ba mar *sha*·ţ'e *dą*·k'a *kohr*·be
marry me	তুমি আমাকে বিয়ে করবে	*ţu*·mi *aa*·ma·ke *bi*·ye *kohr*·be

I love you.
আমি তোমাকে ভালবাসি। — *aa*·mi *ţoh*·ma·ke *b'a*·loh·ba·shi

I think we're good together.
আমরা একসাথে খুব ভাল যাই। — *aam*·ra *ąk*·sha·ţ'e k'ub *b'a*·loh jai

I don't think it's working out.
আমার মনে হয় না এটা কাজ করছে। — *aa*·mar *moh*·ne *ho*·e na e·ta kaj *kohr*·ch'e

I never want to see you again.
আমি তোমার সাথে আর দেখা করতে চাই না। — *aa*·mi *ţo*·mar *sha*·ţ'e aar *dą*·k'a *kohr*·ţe chai na

drugs

I don't take drugs.
আমি ড্রাগ নেই না। — *aa*·mi draag nay na

I take ... occasionally.
আমি মাঝেমাঝে ... নেই। — *aa*·mi *ma*·j'e·ma·j'e ... nay

Do you want to have a smoke?
আপনি কি এক টান দিবেন? — *aap*·ni ki ąk taan *di*·ben

Do you have a light?
আপনার কি লাইটার আছে? — *aap*·nar ki *lai*·tar *aa*·ch'e

I'm high.
আমি এখন হাই। — *aa*·mi *ą*·k'ohn hai

If the police are talking to you about drugs, see **police**, page 272.

religion

ধর্ম

What's your religion?
আপনার ধর্ম কি? — *aap*·nar *d'or*·moh ki

I'm not religious.
আমি ধার্মিক না। — *aa*·mi *d'ar*·mik na

I'm agnostic.
আমি আল্লাহকে বিশ্বাষ করি না। — *aa*·mi *al*·la·ke *bish*·shash *koh*·ri na

I'm ...	আমি ...	*aa*·mi ...
Buddhist	বৌদ্ধ	*bohd*·đ'oh
Catholic	ক্যাথলিক	ka̦·*ţ'oh*·lik
Christian	খৃষ্টান	*k'rish*·taan
Hindu	হিন্দু	*hin*·du
Jain	জৈন	joyn
Jewish	জুয়িশ	*ju*·ish
Muslim	মসলমান	mu·*sohl*·man
Sikh	সিখ	sheek'
Zoroastrian	জোরাসট্রিয়ান	*zo*·ra·stri·an

I (don't) believe in ...	আমি ... বিশ্বাস করি (না)।	*aa*·mi ... *bish*·shash *koh*·ri (na)
fate	ভাগ্যে	*b'ag*·ge
future telling	ভবিষ্যৎ বানিতে	*b'oh*·bish·shoţ *ba*·ni·ţe

Where can I ...?	আমি কোথায় ... পারি?	*aa*·mi *koh*·ţ'ai ... *paa*·ri
pray (Muslim)	নামাজ পড়তে	*na*·maj *pohŗ*·ţe
worship (Hindu)	পূজা করতে	*pu*·ja *kohr*·ţe

food for gods

Hindus have a tradition of offering *proh*·shad প্রসাদ (blessed food) to the gods for spiritual nourishment before sharing it among devotees.

cultural differences

সামাজিক ব্যাবধান

Is this a local or national custom?

এই চর্চা কি আ’লিক না জাতীয়? — ay *chor*·cha ki *aan*·choh·lik na *ja*·ţi·o

I didn't mean to do/say anything wrong.

আমি খারাপ কিছু করতে/বলতে চাই নাই। — *aa*·mi *k'a*·rap *ki*·ch'u *kohr*·ţe/*bohl*·ţe chai nai

I don't want to offend you.

আমি আপনাকে অপমান করতে চাই না। — *aa*·mi *aap*·na·ke *o*·poh·man *kohr*·ţe chai na

I'm not used to this.

আমি এটাতে অভ্যাস্ত না। — *aa*·mi *e*·ta·ţe *ob*·b'ạ·sţoh na

This is different.

এটা ভিন্ন ধরনের। — e·ta *b'in*·noh *d'o*·roh·ner

This is interesting.

এটা ইন্টারেস্টিং। — e·ta *in*·te·re·sting

I'm sorry, it's against my ...	আমি দঃখিত, এটা আমার ... বিরুদ্ধে।	*aa*·mi *duk'*·ki·ţoh *e*·ta *aa*·mar ... *bi*·rud·d'e
beliefs	বিশ্বাষের	*bish*·shash
religion	ধর্মের	*đ'or*·mer

body language

- Feet are considered unclean, so take your shoes off before entering a mosque, a Hindu temple or someone's home. Don't sit with the soles of your feet pointing towards another person or a Buddha statue.
- The thumbs-up sign and winking (particularly towards women) are both considered rude. Staring, on the other hand, is very common among Bengalis, who don't have the same concept of privacy as Western visitors – they don't mean any harm by this.
- When hailing a rickshaw, stick your arm straight out and wave your hand downwards – the Western way of waving your arm upwards will be understood as 'Go away!'

outdoors

ঘরের বাইরে

hiking

পায়ে হেটে

Where can I …?	কোথায় …?	*koh*·ţ'ai …
buy supplies	কেনাকাটা করব	*ke*·na·ka·ta *kohr*·boh
find someone who knows this area	লোক পাবো যে এই এলাকা চেনে	lohk *pa*·boh je ay *e*·la·ka *che*·ne
get a map	ম্যাপ পাব	mąp *pa*·boh

How …?	কত …?	*ko*·ţoh …
high is the climb	উচা এই পাহাড়	*u*·cha ay *pa*·haŗ
long is the trail	লম্বা এই রাস্তা	*lom*·ba ay *raa*·sţa

Which is the … route?	কোন রাস্তা সবচেয়ে …?	kohn *raa*·sţa *shob*·che …
easiest	সোজা	*shoh*·ja
shortest	অল্প	*ol*·poh

Where can I find the …?	… কোথায়?	… *koh*·ţ'ai
nearest village	নিকটতম গ্রাম	*ni*·kot graam
toilets (city/country)	টয়লেট/পায়খানা	*toy*·let/*pai*·k'a·na

Does this path go to …?
এই রাস্তা কি …-য় যায়? — ay *raa*·sţa ki …·e jay

Do we need a guide?
আমাদের কি গাইড লাগবে? — *aa*·ma·der ki gaiđ *laag*·be

weather

আবহাওয়া

What's the weather like?
আজকের আবহাওয়া কেমন? — *aaj*·ker *a*·boh·ha·wa *ką*·mohn

What will the weather be like tomorrow?
আগামিকালের আবহাওয়া কেমন? — *aa*·ga·mi·ka·ler *a*·boh·ha·wa *ką*·mohn

It's …		
cold	ঠান্ডা	*ţan*·đa
dry	শুকনা	*shuk*·na
hot	গরম	*go*·rohm
humid	ভেজা	*b'e*·ja
raining	বৃষ্টি	*brish*·ti
sunny	রোদ	rohd

drought	খরা	*k'o*·ra
flood	বন্যা	*bon*·na
monsoon	বর্ষা	*bor*·sha

… season	… কাল	… kaal
harvesting	হেমন্ত	*he*·mon·toh
rainy	বর্ষা	*bor*·sha

flora & fauna

গাছ-পালা ও জীব

What … is that?	এইটা কি …?	*ay*·ta ki …
animal	জন্তু	*john*·ţu
plant	গাছ	gaach'

local plants & animals

banyan tree	বট গাছ	bot gaach'
teak forest	শাল বাগান	shaal *ba*·gan
water lily	শাপলা	*shap*·la
camel	উট	ut
cow	গরু	*goh*·ru
crocodile	কুমির	*ku*·mir
monkey	বানর	*ba*·nohr
elephant	হাতী	*haa*·ţi
rhinoceros	রাইনো	*rai*·no
snake	সাপ	shap
tiger	বাঘ	baag'

basics

মূল শব্দ

breakfast	নাস্তা	*naash*·ţa
lunch	দুপুরের খাওয়া	*du*·pu·rer k'a·wa
dinner	রাতের খাওয়া	*raa*·ţer k'a·wa
snack	নাস্তা	*naash*·ţa
to eat/drink	খান	k'an

finding a place to eat

খাওয়ার জায়গার খোজ

Where would you go for (a) …?	… জন্য কোথায় যাবো?	… *john*·no *koh*·ţ'ai *ja*·boh
celebration	একটা উৎসবের	*ąk*·ta *uţ*·sho·ber
cheap meal	সস্তা খাবারের	*shos*·ţa·e *k'a*·ba·rer
local specialities	এখানকার বিশেষ খাবারের	*e*·k'an·kar *bi*·shesh *k'a*·ba·rer
Can you recommend a …?	একটা ভাল … কোথায় হবে বলেন তো?	*ąk*·ta *b'a*·lo … *koh*·ţ'ai *ho*·be *boh*·len *ţoh*
café	ক্যাফেটেরিয়া	*ką*·fe·te·ri·a
restaurant	রেস্তোরা	*res*·ţoh·ra
I'd like to reserve a table for …	আমি … একটা টেবিল রিজার্ভ করতে চাই।	*aa*·mi … *ąk*·ta *te*·bil *ri*·zarv *kohr*·ţe chai
(two) people	(দুই) জনের জন্য	(dui) *jo*·ner *john*·no
(eight) o'clock	(আট্টার) সময়	(*aat*·tar) *sho*·moy
I'd like the …, please.	আমি … চাই, প্লিজ।	*aa*·mi … chai pleez
drink list	ড্রিঙ্কের লিস্টটা	*đrin*·ker *list*·ta
menu	ম্যেনুটা	*me*·nu·ta
nonsmoking section	নন স্মোকিং সেকশন	non *smoh*·king *sek*·shohn

listen for ...

বন্ধ।	*bon*·d'oh	**We're closed.**
খালি নাই।	*k'a*·li nai	**We're full.**
মেনু নাই।	*me*·nu nai	**There's no menu.**
কি খাবেন বলেন।	ki *k'a*·ben *boh*·len	**Tell us what you'd like.**

restaurant

রেস্তোরা

What would you recommend?
আপনি কি খেতে বলেন? — *aap*·ni ki *k'e*·ţe *boh*·len

What's in that dish?
এই খাবারে কি কি আছে? — ay *k'a*·ba·re ki ki *aa*·ch'e

What's that called?
ওটাকে কি বলে? — *oh*·ta·ke ki *boh*·le

I'll have that.
আমি ওটা নিব। — *aa*·mi *oh*·ta *ni*·boh

I'd like it with/ without ...	আমাকে ... সহ/ ছাড়া দেন।	*aa*·ma·ke ... *sho*·hoh/ *ch'a*·ŗa dąn
chilli	মরিচ	*moh*·rich
garlic	রসুন	*roh*·shun
oil	তেল	ţel
pepper	গোল মরিচ	gohl *moh*·rich
salt	নুন	nun
spices	মসলা	*mosh*·la

I'd like it ...	আমি ... চাই।	*aa*·mi ... chai
I don't want it ...	আমি ... চাই না।	*aa*·mi ... chai na
boiled	সিদ্ধ	*shid*·d'oh
fried	ভাজা	*b'a*·ja
medium	মাঝারি	*ma*·j'a·ri
steamed	ভাপানো	*b'a*·pa·noh

For other specific meal requests, see **vegetarian & special meals**, page 263.

at the table

টেবিলে বসে

Please bring …	… আনেন প্লিজ।	… *aa*·nen pleez
an ashtray	একটা এ্যাসট্রে	*qk*·ta *qsh*·tre
the bill	বিলটা	*bil*·ta
a fork	একটা কাটা	*qk*·ta *ka*·ta
a glass	একটা গ্লাস	*qk*·ta glash
a knife	একটা ছুরি	*qk*·ta *ch'u*·ri
a serviette	একটা ন্যাপকিন	*qk*·ta *nqp*·kin
a spoon	একটা চামুচ	*qk*·ta *cha*·much

I didn't order this.
আমি এটা অর্ডার দেই নাই। — *aa*·mi e·ta *o*·dar dai nai

There's a mistake in the bill.
বিলে ভুল আছে। — *bi*·le b'ul *aa*·ch'e

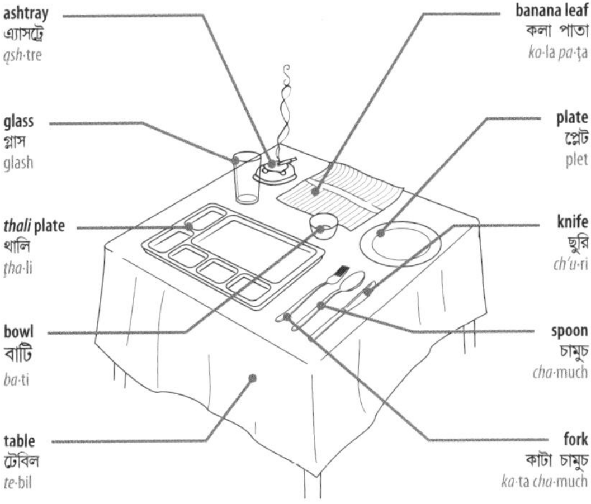

look for ...

এ্যাপেটাইজার	*a*·*pe*·tai·zar	**Appetisers**
রুটি	*ru*·ti	**Breads**
সুপ	sup	**Soups**
সালাদ	*sa*·laad	**Salads**
মেইন কোর্স	mayn kohrs	**Main Courses**
ডাল	đaal	**Lentils**
ভাত	b'aaţ	**Rice Dishes**
মাংসো	*mang*·shoh	**Meat Dishes**
মাছ	maach	**Fish & Seafood**
সবজি	*shohb*·ji	**Vegetables**
আচার চাটনি	*aa*·char *chat*·ni	**Chutneys & Relishes**
মিষ্টি	*mish*·ti	**Desserts**
পানীয়	*pa*·ni·o	**Drinks**

For more words you might find on a menu, see the **culinary reader**, page 265.

talking food

খাবারের কথাবার্তা

This is ...	এটা ...	*e*·ta ...
oily	তেল বেশি	ţel *be*·shi
spicy	মসলা বেশি	*mosh*·la *be*·shi
superb	দারুন	*da*·run
sweet	মিষ্টি	*mish*·ti
(too) cold	(বেশি) ঠান্ডা	(*be*·shi) *ţ'an*·đa

That was delicious.
খুব মজা ছিল। — k'ub *mo*·ja *ch'i*·loh

I love the local cuisine.
আমার এখানকার খাবার খুব ভাল লাগে। — *aa*·mar *e*·k'an·kar *k'a*·bar k'ub *b'a*·loh *la*·ge

nonalcoholic drinks

পানীয়

(boiled) water	(সিদ্ধ) পানি	(*shid*·d'oh) *pa*·ni
orange juice	অরেঞ্জ জুস	orenj jus
soft drink	কোল্ড ড্রিঙ্ক	kold dreenk
(sparkling) mineral water	(স্পার্কলিং) মিনেরাল ওয়াটার	(*spark*·ling) mi·*ne*·ral *wa*·tar
a glass of (cold) water ...	এক গ্লাস (ঠান্ডা) পানি ...	ąk glash (*ţ'an*·đa) *pa*·ni ...
with ice	বরফ সহ	*bo*·rof *sho*·hoh
without ice	বরফ ছাড়া	*bo*·rof *ch'a*·ŗa
(cup of) coffee ...	(কাপ) কফি ...	(kap) *ko*·fi ...
(cup of) tea ...	(কাপ) চা ...	(kap) cha ...
with (milk)	(দুধ) সহ	(dud') *sho*·hoh
without (sugar)	(চিনি) ছাড়া	(*chi*·ni) *ch'a*·ŗa

local drinks

ফালুদা	*fa*·lu·da	**ice cream on jelly flavoured with rose-water**
ডাবের পানি	*đa*·ber *pa*·ni	**green coconut water**
বাদামের সরবত	*baa*·da·mer *shor*·bohţ	**milk flavoured with almonds**
আখের রস	*aa*·k'er rosh	**sugar-cane juice**
সরবত	*shor*·bohţ	**sherbet**
তাড়ি	*ţa*·ŗi	**fermented date juice**
লাচ্ছি	*las*·si	**yogurt drink**

alcoholic drinks

মাদকীয় পানীয়

Drinking alcohol and going to bars isn't part of Bengali culture. Since the few bars that can be found are associated with hotels, embassies and clubs mostly visited by Westerners, the use of English terms is actually the norm.

a bottle/glass of	এক বোতল/গ্লাস	ąk *bo*·tohl/glash
… wine	… ওয়াইন	… wain
dessert	ডেজার্ট	*de*·zart
red	রেড	red
sparkling	স্পার্কলিং	*spark*·ling
white	ওয়াইট	wait

a … of beer	এক … বিয়ার	ąk … *bi*·ar
bottle	বোতল	*boh*·ţohl
glass	গ্লাস	glash
jug	জগ	jog
pint	পাইন্ট	paint

in the bar

বার

As drinking alcohol isn't accepted from a social and religious point of view, bars are hard to come by and asking about them may offend some people.

I'll have …
আমি … চাই। — *aa*·mi … chai

Same again, please.
আগেরটাই, প্লিজ। — *a*·ger·tai pleez

I'll buy you a drink.
আপনাকে আমি ড্রিংক খাওয়াবো। — *aap*·na·ke *aa*·mi dreenk *k'a*·wa·boh

What would you like?
আপনাকে কি দিতে পারি? — *aap*·na·ke ki *di*·ţe *pa*·ri

It's my round.
এবার আমার পালা। — *e*·bar *aa*·mar *pa*·la

How much is that?
এটা কত? — *e*·ta *ko*·ţoh

buying food

খাদ্য দ্রব্য কেনা কাটা

What's the local speciality?
এখানকার বিশেষ খাবার কি? — *e*·k'an·kar *bi*·shesh *k'a*·bar ki

What's that?
ওটা কি? — *oh*·ta ki

How much is (a kilo of cheese)?
(এক কিলো পনির) কত? — (ąk *ki*·loh *poh*·nir) *ko*·ţoh

How much is it?
এটা কত? — *e*·ta *ko*·ţoh

Can I have a bag, please?
একটা ব্যাগ দিতে পারেন, প্লিজ? — *ąk*·ta bąg *di*·ţe *paa*·ren pleez

I don't need a bag, thanks.
আমার ব্যাগ লাগবে না। — *aa*·mar bąg *laag*·be na

I'd like ...	আমি ... চাই।	*aa*·mi ... chai
(200) grams	(দুই শ) গ্রাম	(dui shoh) gram
(two) kilos	(দুই) কিলো	(dui) *ki*·loh
(six) slices/pieces	(ছয়) টুকরা	(ch'oy) *tuk*·ra
that one	ঐটা	*oh*·i·ta
Do you have ...?	আপনার কাছে ... কিছু আছে কি?	*aap*·nar *ka*·ch'e ... *ki*·ch'u *aa*·ch'e ki
anything cheaper	আরো অল্প দামী	*aa*·roh *ol*·poh *da*·mi
other kinds	অন্য ধরনের	*on*·noh *d'o*·roh·ner
Less.	কম।	kom
A bit more.	আরেকটু।	*a*·rek·tu
Enough.	যথেষ্ঠ।	jo·*ţ'esh*·toh

Where can I find the ... section?	... সেকশন কোথায়?	... *sek*·shohn *koh*·ţ'ai
bread	রুটির	*ru*·tir
dairy	দুধের	*du*·d'er
fish	মাছের	*maa*·ch'er
frozen goods	ফ্রোজেন জিনিসের	*froh*·zen *ji*·ni·sher
fruit and vegetable	শাক সবজির	shak *shohb*·jir
meat	মাংসের	*mang*·sher
poultry	হাস মুরগীর	hash *mur*·gir
seafood	মাছ-টাছের	*maach'*·taa·ch'er
spices	মসলার	*mosh*·lar
sweets	মিষ্টির	*mish*·tir

listen for ...

আপনাকে কি সাহায্য করতে পারি? *aap*·na·ke ki *sha*·haj·joh *kohr*·ţe *paa*·ri	**Can I help you?**
আপনি কি চান? *aap*·ni ki chan	**What would you like?**
আর কিছু? aar *ki*·ch'u	**Anything else?**
ওটা (১০০ টাকা)। *oh*·ta (*ąk*·shoh *ta*·ka)	**That's (100 taka).**

cooking utensils

রান্নার সরঞ্জাম

Could I please borrow a ...?	আমি কি একটা ... ধার করতে পারি, প্লিজ?	*aa*·mi ki *ąk*·ta ... d'ar *kohr*·ţe *paa*·ri pleez
I need a ...	আমার একটা ... লাগবে।	*aa*·mar *ąk*·ta ... *laag*·be
bowl	বাটি	*ba*·ti
chopping board	চপিং বোর্ড	*cho*·ping bohrd
frying pan	তাওয়া	*ta*·wa
knife	ছুরি	*ch'u*·ri
saucepan	হাড়ি	*ha*·ŗi
spoon	চামুচ	*cha*·much

vegetarian & special meals

ভেজিটেরিয়ান ও বিশেষ খাদ্য

ordering food

খাদ্য অর্ডার করা

Is there a vegetarian restaurant near here?

কাছাকাছি কি কোন ভেজিটেরিয়ান রেস্তোরা আছে? — *ka*·ch'a·ka·ch'i ki *koh*·noh *ve*·ji·te·ri·an *res*·ţoh·ra *aa*·ch'e

Do you have halal food?

আপনার কাছে কি হালাল খাবার আছে? — *aap*·nar *ka*·ch'e ki *ha*·lal *k'a*·bar *aa*·ch'e

I don't eat ...	আমি ... খাই না।	*aa*·mi ... k'ai na
Could you prepare a meal without ...?	আপনি কি ... ছাড়া খাবার তৈরী করতে পারেন?	*aap*·ni ki ... *ch'a*·ŗa *k'a*·bar ţoh·i·ri *kohr*·ţe *paa*·ren
beef	গরুর মাংস	*goh*·rur *mang*·shoh
butter	মাখন	*ma*·k'ohn
eggs	ডিম	ḍim
fish	মাছ	maach
garlic	রসুন	*roh*·shun
meat	মাংস	*maang*·shoh
milk	দুধ	dud'
oil	তেল	ţel
onion	পিয়াজ	*pi*·aaj
pork	শুয়রের মাংস	*shu*·oh·rer *mang*·shoh
poultry	হাস-মুরগী	hash *mur*·gi

to eat or not to eat

Be careful with the words *ha*·ram হারাম (haram food) and *ha*·lal হালাল (halal food) – the first term is used for all prohibited foods as dictated by the Qur'an, and the second one covers all foods which the Qur'an permits.

special diets & allergies

বিশেষ খাদ্য এবং এ্যালার্জি

I'm on a special diet.
আমি বিশেষ ডায়েটে আছি। — *aa*·mi *bi*·shesh *day*·te *aa*·ch'i

I'm vegan.
আমি মাছ মাংস ডিম দুধ খাই না। — *aa*·mi maach *mang*·shoh dim dud' k'ai na

I'm vegetarian.
আমি ভেজিটেরিয়ান। — *aa*·mi *ve*·ji·te·ri·an

I'm (a) ...	আমি ...	*aa*·mi ...
Buddhist	বৌদ্ধ	*bo*·ud'·d'oh
Hindu	হিন্দু	*hin*·du
Jewish	জু	ju
Muslim	মুসলমান	*mu*·sohl·man

I'm allergic to ...	আমার ...-এ এ্যালার্জি আছে।	*aa*·mar ...·e *q*·lar·ji *aa*·ch'e
dairy produce	দুধ জাতিয় খাবার	dud' *ja*·ţi·o *k'a*·bar
eggs	ডিম	đim
MSG	টেস্টিং সল্ট	*tes*·ting solt
nuts	বাদাম	*baa*·dam
shellfish	চিংড়ি মাছ	*ching*·ṛi maach'

street food

চটপটি	*chot*·poh·ti	**boiled dried green peas blended with spices, chilli, black salt & tamarind water & served hot**
ঝালমুড়ি	*j'al*·mu·ṛi	**popped rice mixed with spices**
ফুচকা	*fuch*·ka	**small crisp puffs of dough filled with spicy tamarind water**
হালিম	*ha*·lim	**tasty wheat & lentil porridge cooked with meat & spices**

These Bengali dishes and ingredients are listed according to the way they're pronounced, in English alphabetical order, so you can easily understand what's on offer and ask for what takes your fancy. For certain dishes we've marked the region or city where they're most popular.

A

aa·chaar আচার *pickles*
aa·da আদা *ginger*
aak' আখ *sugar cane*
aa·k'er rosh আখের রস *sugar-cane juice*
aak'·roht আখরোট *walnut*
aa·lu আলু *potato*
aa·lu·bu·k'a·ra আলুবুখারা *dried plum*
aa·lu pa·*ra*·ta আলু পারাটা *fried bread with potato filling*
aa·lur chop আলুর চপ *potato patties*
aa·lur dom আলুর দম *spicy potato curry, usually served with* pu·ri
aam আম *mango*
aa·na·rosh আনারস *pineapple*
aa·pel আপেল *apple*
aa·ta আটা *wholemeal flour*
aa·ṭa p'ol আতা ফল *custard apple*
ang·ur আঙ্গুর *grapes*
an·jir আনজির *fig*
a̧·*pe*·tai·zar এ্যাপেটাইজার *appetisers*

B

baa·dam বাদাম *almond*
baa·da·mer *shor*·bohṭ বাদামের সরবত *milk flavoured with almonds*
baang·i বাংগী *cantaloupe*
b'aaṭ ভাত *cooked white rice*
ba·d'a·koh·pi বাধাকপি *cabbage*
ba·d'a·koh·pir *đaal*·na বাধাকপির ডালনা *finely shredded & fried cabbage, potato, tomato & green peas*
b'a·ji ভাজি *lightly spiced vegetables*
bash·mo·ṭi chaal বাসমতি চাল *basmati rice*
beet·rut বিটরুট *beetroot*
be·gun বেগুন *eggplant*
be·gun *b'a*·ji বেগুন ভাজি *eggplant rings fried in vegetable oil & seasoned with salt & red chilli powder*
be·gun *b'or*·ṭa বেগুন ভরতা *mashed roasted eggplant with chopped onions & green coriander leaf*
be·shohn বেশন *gram or chickpea flour*
bi·ri·*a*·ni বিরিয়ানি *steamed rice oven-baked with meat, potato & spices*
bohr·fi বরফি *fudge-like sweet, often topped with edible silver foil*
boh·ṛi বড়ী *dried lentil balls*
boh·roh·i বরই *berry • prune*
bo·ṛa বড়া *fried balls of mashed lentils*
bo·ṛoh *ching*·ṛi বড় চিংড়ি *lobster*
bo·rohf বরফ *ice*
b'or·ṭa ভরতা *generic name for mashed, roasted or steamed vegetables mixed with chopped onions & green coriander*
b'ut·ta ভুট্টা *corn*

C

cha চা *tea*

chaal চাল *rice*

ch'a·na ছানা *milk soured by using lemon or vinegar*

cha·na·chur চানাচুর *savoury snack of fried lentils & nuts with dry roasted spices*

cha·nar dal·na চানার ডালনা *thicker, spicier version of* j'ohl *or curry, with home-made cottage cheese, peas & potatoes*

cha·pa·ti চাপাতি *unleavened bread cooked on a frying pan – the most common variety of bread (also called* ru·ti *and* naan*)*

chat·ni চাটনি *chutney*

chi·na·baa·dam চিনাবাদাম *peanut*

chi·na ba·d'a·koh·pi চিনা বাধাকপি *Chinese cabbage*

ching·ṛi maach' চিংড়ি মাছ *prawn*

chi·ni চিনি *sugar*

ch'o·la ছোলা *chickpea • spiced chickpea dish*

ch'oh·lar đaal ছোলার ডাল *slightly sweeter version of the yellow split pea*

chom·chom চমচম *dessert made with* ch'a·na *& cooked in sugar syrup*

chot·poh·ti চটপটি *street snack served hot & made of boiled dried green peas blended with spices, chilli, black salt & tamarind water*

D

đaal ডাল *generic term for cooked & uncooked lentils or pulses*

đaal ar b'a·ja ডাল আর ভাজা *deep-fried eggplant, potato & okra*

đa·ber pa·ni ডাবের পানি *green coconut water*

đa·lim ডালিম *pomegranate*

dar·chi·ni দারচিনি *cinnamon*

d'e·ṛohsh ঢেড়শ *okra*

đim ডিম *egg*

đi·mer đaal·na ডিমের ডালনা *curried eggs & rice*

đi·mer đe·vil ডিমের ডেভিল *devilled eggs*

d'oh·ne pa·ṭa ধনে পাতা *coriander leaves*

do·pi·a·ja দোপিয়াজা *'double onion' – stewed meat or fish with lots of onion*

doy দই *curd, similar to yogurt – the natural version is a base for milder curry dishes such as* kohr·ma *&* re·za·la*, the sweeter version is a popular dessert*

doy maach' দই মাছ *fish cooked in a curd sauce with onion, ginger, garlic & chilli*

dud' দুধ *milk*

dud' she·mai দুধ সেমাই *dessert made with roasted vermicelli, milk, sugar, cardamom powder & raisins*

E

ee·lish maach' ইলিশ মাছ *hilsa fish*

e·lach এলাচ *cardamom*

F

fa·lu·da ফালুদা *ice cream on jelly flavoured with rose-water*

fuch·ka ফুচকা *small crisp puffs of dough filled with spicy tamarind water & sprouted gram, served as fast food or snacks*

G

ga·johr গাজর *carrot*

ga·joh·rer ha·lu·a গাজরের হালুয়া *sweet made with carrots, dried fruits, sugar, condensed milk &* g'i

g'i ঘি *clarified butter*

gi·la গিলা *giblets*

goh·lap jam গোলাপ জাম *deep-fried balls of milk-powder dough soaked in rose-flavoured syrup*

goh·lap pa·ni গোলাপ পানি *rose-water extracted from rose petals*

gohl moh·rich গোল মরিচ *pepper*

goh·rur mang·shoh গরুর মাংস *beef*

go·rohm mosh·la গরম মসলা *spices that add aroma rather than spicyness – bay leaves, black pepper, cinnamon, cardamom, cloves, nutmeg & mace*
guṛ গুড় *jaggery – sweetening agent made at the first stage of sugar production*
gur·da গুর্দা *kidney*

H

ha·lal হালাল *halal food – all permitted foods as dictated by the Qur'an*
ha·lim হালিম *tasty wheat & lentil porridge cooked with meat & spices*
ha·lu·a হালুয়া *sweet made with vegetables, cereals, lentils, nuts or fruit*
ha·ram হারাম *haram food – all prohibited foods as dictated by the Qur'an*
hash হাস *duck*
hash mur·gi হাস-মুরগী *poultry*
hoh·lud হলুদ *turmeric*

J

j'aal ঝাল *hot (spicy) • spicy dish that includes ground mustard seeds & chilli • chilli*
jaf·ran জাফরান *saffron*
j'al·mu·ṛi ঝালমুড়ি *popped rice mixed with spices*
jam·bu·ra জাম্বুরা *grapefruit*
ja·u জাউ *barley*
jee·ra জিরা *cumin seeds*
ji·la·pi জিলাপি *orange whorls of fried batter made from curd &* be·shohn *fried in vegetable oil, then dipped in syrup*
joh·in জৈন *thyme*
j'ohl ঝোল *gravy in a curry*
jor·da sho·hoh paan জরদা সহ পান paan *with tobacco*
joy·fol জয়ফল *nutmeg*
joy·oh·tri জয়ত্রী *mace*
jus জুস *fruit juice (also called* p'o·ler rosh*)*

K

ka·bab কাবাব *marinated chunks of ground meat, cooked on a skewer in a clay oven, fried on a hot plate or cooked under a grill*
ka·chaa na কাচা না *well-done*
ka·cha moh·rich কাচা মরিচ *green chilli*
ka·ju baa·dam কাজু বাদাম *cashew nut*
ka·loh jee·ra কালো জিরা *'black cumin' – dull black seeds with a more refined flavour than cumin*
kap·si·kam ক্যাপসিকাম *paprika*
k'a·shir mang·shoh খাসির মাংস *goat meat • mutton*
ka·ṭ'al কাঠাল *jackfruit*
k'a·ti g'i খাটি ঘি *pure* g'i
kee·ma pa·ra·ta কিমা পারাটা *fried, circular bread with mincemeat filling*
k'eer খীর *rich creamy rice pudding*
k'ee·ra ক্ষিরা *gherkin*
k'e·jur খেজুর *date*
k'e·ju·rer guṛ খেজুরের গুড় *date palm jaggery*
k'i·chu·ṛi খিচুড়ি *risotto-like dish of rice & lentils cooked with spices*
kish·mish কিসমিস *currant • raisin*
k'ish·sha খিস্সা *sweet dish of milk reduced by simmering, often flavoured with saffron & almonds*
ko·fi কফি *coffee*
koh·bu·ṭor কবুতর *pigeon*
koh·du কদু *green gourd • pumpkin*
kohf·ṭa কোফতা *meatballs – often made from goat, beef or lamb*
koh·li·ja কলিজা *liver (Bangladesh)*
kohl·ji কলজি *liver (West Bengal)*
kohr·ma কোরমা *rich but mildly spiced curry of chicken, mutton or vegetables, thickened with yogurt or coconut milk*
ko·la কলা *banana*
kom·la কমলা *mandarin*

k'or·gohsh খরগোস *hare • rabbit*
ko·roh·la করলা *bitter gourd*
k'u·ba·ni খুবানি *apricot*
kul·fi কুলফি *ice-cream made with reduced milk & flavoured with a variety of nuts, like green pistachios or almonds*

L

lach·ch'i লাচ্ছি *curd drink – often flavoured with salt or sugar & rose-water essence*
lad·du লাড্ডু *'sweet meats' – usually balls made with* *be*·shohn
lal chal লাল চাল *brown rice*
lạng·ṛa aam ল্যাংড়া আম *mango variety*
las·si লাচ্ছি *yogurt drink*
la·u লাউ *green gourd*
le·bu লেবু *citrus • lemon • lime*
le·mohn gras লেমন গ্রাস *lemon grass*
li·chu লিচু *lychee*
lo·bohn লবন *salt (also called* nun*)*
long লঙ্গ *clove*
lu·chi লুচি *fried flour puffs*

M

maach' মাছ *fish*
maach' *b'a*·ja মাছ ভাজা *lightly spiced shallow-fried fish*
maa·ch'er chop মাছের চপ *crumbed, deep-fried fish cakes made with mashed potato, chilli, onion, ginger, garlic & fish*
maa·ch'er *choṛ*·choh·ṛi মাছের চড়চড়ি *fish curry made of very small fish cooked with onion, garlic & mustard*
maa·ch'er *koh*·chu·ṛi মাছের কচুড়ি *fish fritters*
maa·k'ohn মাখন *butter*
maa·lai মালাই *cream*
mang·shoh মাংস *meat*
mash·rum মাশরুম *mushroom*
me·ṭ'i মেথি *fenugreek*
mish·ti মিষ্টি *dessert • a sweet*
mish·ti *a*·lu মিষ্টি আলু *sweet potato*
mish·ti paan মিষ্টি পান *betel leaf with sweet spices*
mod মদ *wine • spirits*
moh·d'u মধু *honey*
mohg·lai *pa*·ra·ta মগলাই পারাটা *fried, square bread filled with egg & mincemeat*
moh·rich মরিচ *chilli*
moh·ta chaal মোটা চাল *short-grain rice*
moj·ja মজ্জা *bone marrow*
mosh·la মসলা *spice*
mo·tohr মটর *pea*
mo·tohr *poh*·nir মটর পনির *dish of peas & fresh cheese*
mo·tohr *shu*·ti মটর শুটি *green split pea*
mo·tohr *shu*·tir *koh*·chu·ṛi মটর শুটির কচুরি *deep-fried bread with a filling of ground green-pea paste*
mo·u·ri মৌরি *aniseed • fennel (also available coated in sugar to make a sweet snack)*
moy·da ময়দা *plain flour*
mug đaal মুগ ডাল *mung bean* đaal *– tiny yellow oval lentils*
mu·la মূলা *radish*
mu·rab·ba মুরাব্বা *conserves with sugar*
mur·gi মুরগী *chicken • poultry*
mur·gir *tor*·ka·ri মুরগীর তরকারি *chicken curry*
mu·ṛoh *g'on*·toh মুড়ো ঘন্টো *head of fish cooked with lentils*
mu·shu·ṛer đaal মুশুরের ডাল *red lentils*

N

naan নান *see* *cha*·pa·ti
nar·kel নারকেল *coconut*
na·ṛu নাড়ু *grated coconut cooked in sugar & cardamom & formed into small balls*
nash·pa·ṭi নাশপাতি *pears*

neem নীম *plant whose bitter tasting leaves have a variety of uses including medicinal, cosmetic, environmental & culinary – used as a vegetable*

nohn·ţa নোনতা *'salty' – savoury snacks, including anything from* sa·mu·sa *&* pa·pohŗ *to chips &* cha·na·chur

nun নুন *salt*

P

paa·lohng shaak পালং শাক *spinach*

paan পান *betel leaf (eaten with a mixture of betel nut, lime paste & spices, used as a digestive & mouth freshener) – can be* mish·ti *(sweet) or* shaa·da *(plain)*

pa·esh পায়েস *rice pudding cooked for birthdays & weddings (see also* k'eer*)*

pa·ni·o পানীয় *drinks*

pan·ţu·a পানতুয়া *like* goh·lap jam *but made of* ch'a·na *& thickened milk instead of milk powder*

pa·pohŗ পাপোড় *pappadams*

pa·ra·ta পারাটা *unleavened flaky fried flat bread – more substantial versions are stuffed with* poh·nir*, grated vegetables or mincemeat*

pa·u·dar dud' পাউডার দুধ *powdered milk*

pa·u·ru·ti পাউরুটি *Western-style bread*

pe·a·ra পেয়ারা *guava*

pe·pe পেপে *papaya*

pe·sţa পেস্তা *pistachio*

phul·koh·pi ফুলকপি *cauliflower*

pi·aaj পিয়াজ *onion • shallot*

pi·ţ'a পিঠা *generic name for traditional desserts made with rice flour & jaggery*

poh·nir পনির *soft, unfermented cheese made from milk curd*

poh·sţer·da·na পাস্তেরদানা *poppy seeds*

p'ol ফল *fruit*

p'o·ler rosh ফলের রস *fruit juice*

pu·di·na পুদিনা *mint*

pu·ri পুরি *dish of dough filled with mashed potato or* đaal *that puffs up when deep-fried*

R

ra·bŗi রাবড়ি *sweet, thickened milk*

rai রাই *black mustard seeds*

rai·ţa রাইতা *plain curd combined with vegetables or fruit, served chilled*

raj ha·sher mang·shoh রাজ হাসের মাংস *goose meat*

re·za·la রেজালা *rich but mild meat or chicken curry, cooked with selected spices & yogurt*

ro·shoh·gul·la রসগোল্লা *'ball of juice' – spongy white balls of* ch'a·na *that ooze the sugar syrup they've been boiled in*

roh·shun রসুন *garlic*

ru·ti রুটি *see* cha·pa·ti

S

sa·laad সালাদ *salad*

sa·mu·sa সামুসা *deep-fried pyramid-shaped pastries filled with spiced vegetables & sometimes meat*

shaa·da paan সাদা পান *betel leaf with basic accompaniments such as limestone (not sweet)*

shaak শাক *leafy greens*

sha·gu শাগু *sago*

shal·gom শালগম *parsnip • turnip*

she·mai সেমাই *fine roasted pasta fried in* g'i *with raisins, flaked almonds & sugar to make a sweet, dryish treat*

shik ka·bab শিক কাবাব *marinated mincemeat wrapped around iron spikes, cooked in a* ţohn·dur

shing·ga·ŗa সিঙ্গারা *version of* sa·mu·sa *– the filling is often made with cauliflower, green peas & peanuts*

shohb·ji সবজি *vegetables*

shohr·she সরষে *yellow mustard seed*

shohr·she ee·lish সরষে ইলিশ *hilsa fish cooked in a very hot mustard sauce*
shohr·sher ţel সরষের তেল *mustard oil*
shon·desh সন্দেশ *sweets made of ch'a·na paste, lightly cooked with sugar or jaggery*
shor·bohţ সরবত *generic name for non-fizzy soft drinks, usually made of light syrup & flavoured with fruit*
sho·sha শশা *cucumber*
shu·ji সুজি *semolina*
shu·ohr শুয়র *wild boar • pig*
shu·oh·rer mang·shoh শুয়রের মাংস *bacon • pork*
shu·pa·ri সুপারি *betel nut, basic accompaniment with paan*
sir·ka সিরকা *vinegar*
soh·fe·da সফেদা *sapodilla – brown fruit that looks like a kiwi fruit on the outside but is brown inside with large black seeds*
sup সুপ *soup*

T

ţa·ŗi তাড়ি *fermented date juice*
ţeel তিল *sesame seed*
ţee·ler lad·du তিলের লাড্ডু *sesame balls sweetened with jaggery*
ţee·ler ţel তিলের তেল *sesame oil*
tej·pa·ţa তেজপাতা *Indian bay leaves*
ţel তেল *oil*
ţe·ţul তেতুল *tamarind*
ţohn·dur তন্দুর *clay oven fired with charcoal*
ţohn·du·ri chi·ken তন্দুরি চিকেন *chicken cooked in a ţohn·dur after being marinated in spices*
ţohr·muj তরমুজ *watermelon*
tor·ka·ri তরকারি *curry*

V

ve·ji·te·bil o·el ভেজিটেবিল ওয়েল *vegetable oil*
vi·ne·gar ভিনেগার *vinegar (see also sir·ka)*

table manners

It's normal to use your fingers to eat, but only with the right hand – the left hand is considered unclean (as it's used for toilet purposes). Keep this in mind when you're giving or receiving gifts, but especially when you're eating. A container (like a plate or a glass of water) can be taken with the left hand, but the food itself can't be touched, so only put bread into your mouth with the right hand. Likewise, when drinking from a shared bottle hold it above the mouth and pour to avoid contact with your lips. Always wash your hands before and after the meal.

emergencies

এমার্জেন্সি

Help!	বাচান!	*ba*·cha·o
Stop!	থামুন!	*ţ'a*·mun
Go away!	চলে যান!	*choh*·le jan
Thief!	চোর!	chohr
Fire!	আগুন!	*aa*·gun
Watch out!	দেখুন!	*de*·k'un

signs

এমারজেন্সি ডিপার্টমেন্ট	e·*mar*·jen·si đi·*part*·ment	**Emergency Department**
পুলিশ স্টেশন	*pu*·lish *ste*·shohn	**Police Station**
হাসপাতাল	*hash*·pa·ţal	**Hospital**

Call the police.
পুলিশ ডাকেন। *pu*·lish *da*·ken

Call a doctor.
ডাক্তার ডাকেন। *đak*·ţar *da*·ken

Call an ambulance.
এ্যাম্বুলেন্স ডাকেন। *ąm*·bu·lens *da*·ken

It's an emergency.
এটা একটা এমারজেন্সি। e·ta *ąk*·ta e·*mar*·jen·si

Could you please help?
একটু সাহায্য করতে পারেন? *ek*·tu *sha*·haj·joh *kohr*·ţe *paa*·ren

Can I use your phone?
আপনার ফোন ব্যাবহার করতে পারি কি? *aap*·nar fohn *bą*·boh·har *kohr*·ţe *pa*·ri ki

Where are the toilets?
টয়লেট কোথায়? *toy*·let *koh*·ţ'ai

I'm lost.
আমি হারিয়ে গেছি। *aa*·mi *ha*·ri·ye *gą*·ch'i

police

পুলিশ

Where's the police station?
পুলিশ স্টেশন কোথায়? — *pu*·lish *ste*·shohn *koh*·ţai

I've been ...	আমাকে ...	*aa*·ma·ke ...
He/She has been ...	ওকে ...	*oh*·ke ...
assaulted	মারধোর করেছে	*mar*·d'ohr *koh*·re·ch'e
drugged	ড্রাগ দিয়েছে	drag *di*·ye·ch'e
raped	ধর্শন করেছে	*d'or*·shon *koh*·re·ch'e
robbed	ছিনতাই করেছে	*ch'in*·ţai *koh*·re·ch'e

My ... was/were stolen.	আমার ... চুরি হয়েছে।	*aa*·mar ... *chu*·ri *hoh*·e·ch'e
I've lost my ...	আমার ... হারিয়ে গেছে।	*aa*·mar ... *ha*·ri·ye *gą*·ch'e
bags	ব্যাগ	bąg
jewellery	গহনা	*go*·hoh·na
money	টাকা	*ta*·ka
papers	কাগজ পত্র	*ka*·gohj *poţ*·roh
passport	পাসপোর্ট	*pas*·pohrt
wallet	ওয়ালেট	*wa*·let

What am I accused of?
আমার অপরাধ কি? — *aa*·mar *o*·poh·rad' ki

I want to contact my embassy/consulate.
আমি আমার এ্যাম্বাসির/কনসুলেটের সাথে যোগাযোগ করতে চাই। — *aa*·mi *aa*·mar *em*·bą·sir/*kon*·su·le·ter *sha*·ţ'e *johg*·a·johg *kohr*·ţe chai

Can I make a phone call?
আমি কি একটা ফোন করতে পারি? — *aa*·mi ki *ąk*·ta fohn *kohr*·ţe *paa*·ri

Can I have a lawyer (who speaks English)?
আমি কি একজন উকিল পেতে পারি (যে ইংরেজিতে কথা বলতে পারে)? — *aa*·mi ki *ąk*·john *u*·kil *pe*·ţe *paa*·ri (je *ing*·re·ji·ţe *ko*·ţ'a *bohl*·ţe *paa*·re)

This drug is for personal use.
এই ঔষধ আমার নিজের ব্যাবহারের জন্য। — ay *oh*·shud' *aa*·mar *ni*·jer *bą*·boh·har·er *john*·noh

I have a prescription for this drug.
আমার এই ঔষধের জন্য প্রেসক্রিপশন আছে। — *aa*·mar ay *oh*·shud'·er *john*·noh *pres*·krip·shohn *aa*·ch'e

doctor

ডাক্তার

Where's the nearest ...?	কাছাকাছি ... কোথায়?	*ka*·ch'a·ka·ch'i ... *koh*·ţai
dentist	ডেন্টিষ্ট	*đen*·tist
doctor	ডাক্তার	*đak*·ţar
emergency department	এমারজেন্সি ডিপার্টমেন্ট	e·*mar*·jen·si đi·*part*·ment
hospital	হাসপাতাল	*hash*·pa·ţal
optometrist	চশমার দোকান	*chosh*·mar *doh*·kan
(night) pharmacist	(রাতে খোলা) ঔষধের দোকান	(*raa*·ţe *k'oh*·la) *oh*·shud'·er *doh*·kan

I need a doctor (who speaks English).
আমার একজন ডাক্তার লাগবে (যিনি ইংরেজিতে কথা বলতে পারেন)।
aa·mar *qk*·john *đak*·ţar *laag*·be (*ji*·ni *ing*·re·ji·ţe *ko*·ţ'a *bohl*·ţe *paa*·re)

Could I see a female doctor?
আমি কি মহিলা ডাক্তার দেখাতে পারি?
aa·mi ki *moh*·hi·la *đak*·ţar *dq*·k'a·ţe *paa*·ri

Could the doctor come here?
ডাক্তার কি এখানে আসতে পারেন?
đak·ţar ki *e*·k'a·ne *aash*·ţe *paa*·ren

I've run out of my medication.
আমার ঔষুধ শেষ হয়ে গেছে।
aa·mar *oh*·shud shesh *hoh*·e *gq*·ch'e

My prescription is ...
আমার প্রেসক্রিপশন ...
aa·mar *pres*·krip·shohn ...

Please use a new syringe/needle.
নতুন সিরিঞ্জ/শুই ব্যবহার করেন।
no·tun *si*·rinj/shui *bq*·boh·har *koh*·ren

I've been vaccinated against ...	আমার ...-এর ইনজেকশন দেয়া আছে।	*aa*·mar ...·er *in*·jek·shohn *de*·a *aa*·ch'e
hepatitis A/B/C	হেপাটাইটিস এ/বি/সি	he·*pa*·tai·tis e/bi/si
tetanus	টিটেনাস	*ti*·te·nas
typhoid	টাইফয়েড	*tai*·foyđ

symptoms & conditions

উপসর্গ এবং অবস্থা

I'm sick.	আমি অসুস্থ।	*aa*·mi *o*·shush·ţ'oh
I've been injured.	আমি আহত হয়েছি।	*aa*·mi *aa*·ho·ţoh *ho*·he·ch'i
It hurts here.	এখানে ব্যাথা করছে।	e·k'a·ne *bq*·ţ'a *kohr*·ch'e
He/She is having a/an ...	ওর ... হচ্ছে।	ohr ... *hohch'*·ch'e
allergic reaction	এলার্জিক রিয়াকশন	*q*·lar·jik *ri*·ąk·shohn
asthma attack	এ্যাজমার এ্যাটাক	*qz*·mar ą·*tqk*
epileptic fit	এপিলেপ্টিক ফিট	*e*·pi·lep·tik fit
heart attack	হার্ট এ্যাটাক	hart ą·*tqk*
I feel ...	আমার ... লাগছে।	*aa*·mar ... *lag*·ch'e
better	আগে থেকে ভাল	*aa*·ge *ţ'e*·ke *b'a*·loh
worse	আগে থেকে খারাপ	*aa*·ge *ţ'e*·ke *k'a*·rap

I feel nauseous.
আমার বমি ভাব লাগছে। — *aa*·mar *boh*·mi b'ab *lag*·ch'e

I've been vomiting.
আমার বমি হচ্ছিল। — *aa*·mar *boh*·mi *hoh*·ch'i·loh

I feel dizzy.
আমার মাথা ঘুরছে। — *aa*·mar *ma*·ţ'a *g'ur*·ch'e

I feel shivery.
আমার কাপুনি হচ্ছে। — *aa*·mar *ka*·pu·ni *hohch'*·ch'e

I'm dehydrated.
আমার ডিহাইড্রেশন হয়েছে। — *aa*·mar *đi*·hai·đre·shohn *hoh*·e·ch'e

I'm on medication for ...
আমার ...-এর ঔষধ চলছে। — *aa*·mar ...·er *oh*·shud' *chohl*·ch'e

I have (a/an) ...
আমার (একটা) ... আছে। — *aa*·mar (*qk*·ta) ... *aa*·che

I've recently had (a/an) ...
আমার ইদানিং (একটা) ... হয়েছে। — *aa*·mar *i*·da·ning (*qk*·ta) ... *hoh*·e·ch'e

AIDS	এইডস	ayds
asthma	এ্যাজমা	*qz*·ma
bite/sting	পোকার কামড়	*poh*·kar *ka*·mohr̩
cold n	ঠান্ডা	*t̯'an*·đa
constipation	কন্সটিপেশন	*kons*·ti·pe·shohn
cough n	কাশি	*ka*·shi
dengue fever	ডেঙ্গু জ্বর	*đeng*·u jor
diabetes	ডাইবেটিস	*đai*·be·tis
diarrhoea	ডাইরিয়া	*đai*·ri·a
dysentery	ডিসেন্ট্রি	*đi*·sen·tri
fever	জ্বর	jor
headache	মাথা ব্যাথা	*ma*·t̯'a *bq*·t̯'a
lice	উকুন	*u*·kun
lump	গোটা	*goh*·ta
malaria	ম্যালেরিয়া	*mq*·le·ri·a
nausea	বমি ভাব	*boh*·mi b'ab
pain	ব্যাথা	*bq*·t̯'a
period	মেন্স	mens
pregnant	গর্ভবতি	*gor*·b'oh·boh·t̯i
rash	র‍্যাশ	rqsh
sore throat	গলা ব্যাথা	*go*·la *bq*·t̯'a
sweating	ঘাম হচ্ছে	g'am *hohch'*·ch'e
worms	কৃমি	*kri*·mi

allergies

এল্যার্জি

I'm allergic to ...	আমার ...-এ এল্যার্জি আছে।	*aa*·mar ... ·e *q*·lar·ji *aa*·ch'e
He/She is allergic to ...	ওর ...-এ এল্যার্জি আছে।	ohr ... ·e *q*·lar·ji *aa*·ch'e
antibiotics	এ্যান্টিবায়োটিক	*qn*·ti·bai·o·tik
anti-inflammatories	ব্যাথার ঔষুধ	*bq*·t̯'ar *oh*·shud'
aspirin	এ্যাসপিরিন	*qs*·pi·rin
bees	মৌমাছির কামোড়	*mo*·u·ma·ch'ir *ka*·mohr̩
codeine	কোডিন	*koh*·đin
penicillin	পেনিসিলিন	*pe*·ni·si·lin
sulphur-based drugs	সালফার ড্রাগ	*sal*·far drag

I have a skin allergy.

আমার স্কিন এল্যার্জি আছে। *aa*·mar skin *q*·lar·ji *aa*·ch'e

For food-related allergies, see **vegetarian & special meals**, page 263.

parts of the body

শরির

My … hurts.

আমার … ব্যথা করছে। *aa*·mar … *bq*·t̥'a *kohr*·ch'e

My … is swollen.

আমার … ফুলে গেছে। *aa*·mar … *fu*·le *gq*·ch'e

I can't move my …

আমার … নাড়াতে পারছি না। *aa*·mar … *na*·ṛa·t̥e *par*·ch'i na

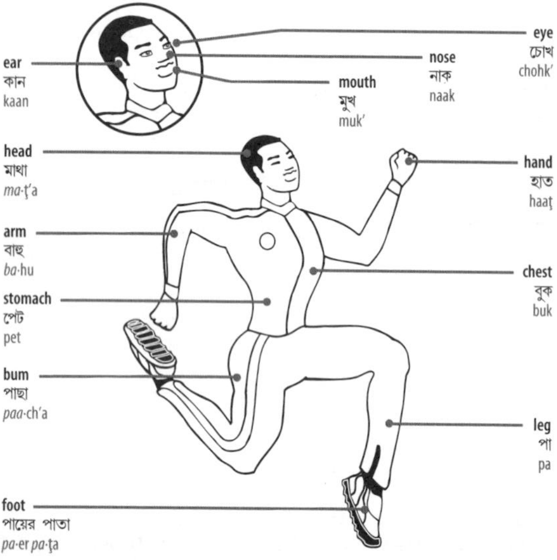

alternative treatments

ব্যাতিক্রম চিকিৎসা

I don't use (Western medicine).

আমি (বিদেশি ঔষধ ব্যাবহার) করি না। — *aa*·mi (*bi*·de·shi *oh*·shud' *bą*·bo·har) *koh*·ri na

I prefer …

আমি … পছন্দ করি। — *aa*·mi … *po*·ch'ohn·doh *koh*·ri

Can I see someone who practises (acupuncture)?

(আকুপান্কচার) প্র্যাকটিস করেন এমন লোকের সাথে দেখা করতে পারি? — (*a*·ku·pank·char) *prąk*·tis *koh*·ren *ą*·mohn *loh*·k'er *sha*·ţ'e *dą*·k'a *kohr*·ţe *paa*·ri

ayurvedic medicine	আয়ুরবেদিক	*a*·yur·be·dik
faith healer	পির	pir
homeopathic medicine	হোমিওপ্যাথি	*hoh*·mi·o·pą·ţ'i
massage	ম্যাসাজ	*mą*·saj
yoga	যোগ ব্যায়াম	johg *bą*·am

pharmacist

ঔষধের দোকান

I need something for (a headache).

আমার (মাথা ব্যাথার) জন্য কিছু লাগবে। — *aa*·mar (*ma*·ţ'a *bą*·ţ'ar) *john*·noh *ki*·ch'u *laag*·be

Do I need a prescription for (antihistamines)?

আমার কি (এ্যান্টিহিস্টামিনের) জন্য প্রেসক্রিপশন লাগবে? — *aa*·mar ki (*ąn*·ti·his·ta·mi·ner) *john*·noh *pres*·krip·shohn *laag*·be

I have a prescription.

আমার প্রেসক্রিপশন আছে। — *aa*·mar *pres*·krip·shohn *aa*·ch'e

How many times a day?

দিনে কয়বার? — *di*·ne *koy*·bar

antiseptic n&a	এ্যান্টিসেপটিক	*qn*·ti·sep·tik
Band-Aid	ব্যান্ডএইড	*bqnđ*·ayđ
condoms	কন্ডম	*kon*·dohm
contraceptives	কন্ট্রাসেপটিভ	*kon*·tra·sep·tiv
insect repellent	ইনসেক্ট রিপেলেন্ট	*in*·sekt *ri*·pe·lent
painkillers	ব্যাথার ঔষুধ	*bq*·ţ'ar *o*·shud'
thermometer	থারমোমিটার	*ţ'ar*·moh·mi·tar
rehydration salts	স্যালাইন	*sq*·lain

holy basil

Among Hindus, *ţul*·shi তুলসি (lit: holy basil) is considered too sacred to be used in cooking. However, it's made into a herbal tea that's good for relieving colds and flu.

dentist

ডেন্টিষ্ট

I have a …	আমার … আছে।	*aa*·mar … *aa*·ch'e
broken tooth	একটা ভাঙ্গা দাত	*qk*·ta *b'an*·ga daaţ
cavity	একটা ক্যাভিটি	*qk*·ta *kq*·vi·ti
toothache	দাতে ব্যাথা	*daa*·ţe *bq*·ţ'a

I've lost a filling.
আমার একটা ফিলিং পড়ে গেছে। — *aa*·mar *qk*·ta *fi*·ling *poh*·ŗe *gq*·ch'e

My dentures are broken.
আমার ডেনচার ভেঙ্গে গেছে। — *aa*·mar *đen*·char *b'eng*·ge *gq*·ch'e

My gums hurt.
আমার মাড়িতে ব্যাথা। — *aa*·mar *ma*·ŗi·ţe *bq*·ţ'a

I don't want it extracted.
আমি এটা ফেলতে চাই না। — *aa*·mi *e*·ta *fel*·ţe chai na

I need an anaesthetic.
আমার এ্যানেসথেসিয়া লাগবে। — *aa*·mar *q*·nes·ţ'e·shi·a *laag*·be

I need a filling.
আমার একটা ফিলিং লাগবে। — *aa*·mar *qk*·ta *fi*·ling *laag*·be

Bengali nouns in this dictionary are in the nominative case (for more information on cases, see the **phrasebuilder**, page 180). The symbols n, a and v (indicating noun, adjective and verb) have been added for clarity where an English term could be either.

A

accident দুর্ঘটনা *dur*·g'o·toh·na
accommodation থাকার ব্যবস্থা *ţ'a*·kar *bq*·bohs·ţa
across ও পার oh par
adaptor এ্যাডাপ্টার *q*·đap·tar
address n ঠিকানা *t'i*·ka·na
admission (price) ভর্তি ফি *b'ohr*·ţi fee
Africa আফরিকা *aaf*·ri·ka
after পরে *po*·re
aftershave আফটার-সেভ *af*·tar·shev
again আবার *aa*·bar
air conditioner এয়ারকন্ডিশনার *e*·ar·kon·đi·shoh·nar
airline এয়ারলাইন *e*·ar·lain
airmail এয়ার মেলে *e*·ar·mayl
airplane প্লেন plen
airport এয়ারপোর্ট *e*·ar·pohrt
airport tax এয়ারপোর্ট ট্যাক্স *e*·ar·pohrt taks
alarm clock এ্যালার্ম ঘড়ি *q*·larm *g'oh*·ŗi
alcohol মদ mod
all সব shob
allergy এ্যালার্জি *q*·lar·ji
alone একা *q*·ka
ambulance এ্যামবুলেন্স *qm*·bu·lens
and এবং *e*·bohng
ankle গোড়ালি *goh*·ŗa·li
antibiotics এ্যান্টিবায়োটিক *qn*·ti·bai·o·tik
antique n এ্যান্টিক *qn*·tik
antiseptic n&a এ্যান্টিসেপটিক *qn*·ti·sep·tik
appointment এ্যাপয়ন্টমেন্ট *q*·poynt·ment
architect স্থপতি *sţ'o*·poh·ţi
architecture স্থাপত্য *sţ'a*·pohţ'·ţoh
arm বাহু *ba*·hu'
arrivals (airport) আগমন *aa*·goh·mohn
arrive আগমন *aa*·goh·mohn
art চিত্রকলা *chiţ*·roh·ko·la
art gallery আর্ট গ্যালারি art *gq*·la·ri
artist শিল্পী *shil*·pi
ashtray এ্যাসট্রে *qsh*·tre
Asia এশিয়া *e*·shi·a
aspirin এ্যাসপিরিন *q*·spi·rin
assault n&v মারধর *mar*·d'or
aunt খালা *k'a*·la
Australia অস্ট্রেলিয়া *o*·stre·li·a
automatic teller machine এটিএম *e*·ti·em

B

B&W (film) ব্ল্যাক এন্ড ওয়াইট bląk ąnd wait
baby বাচ্চা *baach*·cha
baby food বেবি ফুড *be*·bi fuđ
babysitter আয়া *aay*·aa
back (body) পিঠ peeţ'
backpack ব্যাক প্যাক bąk pąk
bad খারাপ *k'a*·rap
bag ব্যাগ bąg
baggage ব্যাগেজ *bq*·gej
baggage allowance ব্যাগেজ এলাউয়েন্স *bq*·gej *q*·la·u·ens
baggage claim ব্যাগেজ ক্লেইম *bq*·gej klaym
bakery বেকারি *be*·ka·ri
band ব্যান্ড bąnđ
bandage ব্যান্ডেজ *bqn*·đej
Band-Aid ব্যান্ডএইড *bqnđ*·ayđ
Bangladesh বাংলাদেশ *bang*·la·desh
bank n ব্যাংক bąnk
bank account ব্যাংক এ্যাকাউন্ট bąnk *q*·ka·unt
banknote ব্যাংকনোট *bqnk*·noht

bar বার baar
bath গোসল *goh*·sohl
bathroom গোসল খানা *goh*·sohl *k'a*·na
battery ব্যাটারি *bą*·ta·ri
beach বীচ beech
beautiful সুন্দর *shun*·dohr
beauty salon বিউটি পারলার *bi*·u·ti *paŗ*·lar
bed বিছানা *bi*·ch'a·na
bedding বিছানাপত্র *bi*·ch'a·na·poţ·roh
bedroom বেডরুম *bеđ*·rum
beer বিয়ার *bi*·ar
before আগে *aa*·ge
begin শুরু *shu*·ru
behind পিছন *pi*·ch'ohn
Bengali (language) বাংলা *bang*·la
best সবচেয়ে ভাল *shob*·che *b'a*·loh
better আরো ভালো *aa*·roh *b'a*·loh
bicycle সাইকেল *sai*·kel
big বড় *bo*·ŗoh
bill বিল beel
birthday জন্মদিন *jon*·moh·din
black কালো *ka*·loh
blanket কম্বল *kom*·bohl
blister ফোসকা *fohsh*·ka
blocked আটকে গেছে *aat*·ke *gą*·ch'e
blood রক্ত *rok*·ţoh
blood group ব্লাড গ্রুপ blad grup
blue নিল neel
boarding house হস্টেল *ho*·stel
boarding pass বোর্ডিং পাস *boh*·ding pas
book n বই *boh*·i
book (make a reservation) v বুকিং *bu*·king
booked out (full) ফুল ful
bookshop বইয়ের দোকান *boh*·i·er *doh*·kan
boots বুট but
border n বর্ডার *bo*·đar
boring বোরিং *boh*·ring
both দুটোই *du*·toy
bottle বোতল *boh*·ţohl
bottle opener বোতল ওপেনার *boh*·ţohl *oh*·pe·nar
bowl বাটি *ba*·ti
box n বাক্স *bak*·shoh
boy ছেলে *ch'e*·le
boyfriend বন্ধু *bohn*·d'u
bra ব্রা bra
brakes ব্রেক brek
bread রুটি *ru*·ti
breakfast নাস্তা *nash*·ţa
bridge ব্রিজ brij
briefcase ব্রিফকেস *brif*·kes
brochure ব্রোসের *bro*·sher
broken ভাঙ্গা *b'ang*·a
brother ভাই b'ai
brown খয়রি *k'oy*·ri
buffet বুফে *bu*·fe
building বিলডিং *bil*·ding
burn n পোড়া *poh*·ŗa
bus বাস bas
business ব্যবসা *bąb*·sha
business class বিজনেস ক্লাস *biz*·nes klas
businessperson ব্যবসাই *bąb*·shai
busker ফকির *foh*·kir
bus station বাস স্টেশন bas *ste*·shohn
bus stop বাস স্টপ bas stop
busy ব্যাস্ত *bą*·sţoh
but কিন্তু *kin*·ţu
butcher's shop মাংসের দোকান *mang*·sher *doh*·kan
button বোতাম *boh*·ţam
buy কেনা *ke*·na

C

café ক্যাফেটেরিয়া *ką*·fe·te·ri·a
cake shop কেকের দোকান *ke*·ker *doh*·kan
calculator ক্যালকুলেটার *kąl*·ku·le·tar
camera ক্যামেরা *ką*·me·ra
camera shop ক্যামেরার দোকান *ką*·me·rar *doh*·kan
can (tin) ক্যান ką n
Canada ক্যানাডা *ką*·na·đa
cancel ক্যান্সেল *kąn*·sel
can opener ক্যান ওপেনার kąn *oh*·pe·nar
car গাড়ি *ga*·ŗi
car hire গাড়ি ভাড়া *ga*·ŗi *b'a*·ŗa
car owner's title গাড়ির মালিকের নাম *ga*·ŗir *ma*·li·ker naam

carpark কারপার্ক *kar*·park
car registration গাড়ির রেজিসট্রেশন *ga*·ŗir *re*·jis·tre·shohn
cash n&v ক্যাশ kąsh
cash (a cheque) v চেক ভাঙ্গানো chek *b'ang*·ga·noh
cashier ক্যাশিয়ার *ką*·shi·ar
cash register ক্যাশ কাউন্টার *ką*sh *ka*·un·tar
cassette ক্যাসেট *ką*·set
castle রাজ প্রাসাদ raj *pra*·shad
cathedral চার্চ charch
Catholic n ক্যাথলিক *ką*·ţ'oh·lik
CD সিডি *see*·dee
cell phone মোবাইল ফোন *moh*·bail fohn
cemetery কবরস্তান *ko*·bohr·sţan
centimetre সেন্টিমিটার *sen*·ti·mi·tar
centre মাঝখানে *maj'*·k'a·ne
chair চেয়ার *che*·ar
champagne স্যামপেইন *shąm*·payn
change (coins) n ভাংতি *b'ang*·ţi
change v বদল *bo*·dohl
change (money) v ভাঙ্গানো *b'ang*·ga·noh
changing room চেন্জিং রুম *chen*·jing rum
cheap সস্তা *sho*·sţa
check-in v চেক-ইন *chek*·in
cheese পনির *poh*·nir
chef বাবুর্চি *ba*·bur·chi
chest বুক buk
cheque (bank) চেক chek
cheque (bill) বিল beel
chicken মুরগী *mur*·gi
child বাচ্চা *baach*·cha
children বাচ্চারা *baach*·cha·ra
child seat বাচ্চার সিট *baach*·char seet
chilli মরিচ *moh*·rich
China চায়না *chai*·na
chocolate চকলেট *chok*·let
Christmas খৃষ্টমাস *kris*·mas
church চার্চ charch
cigar সিগার *si*·gar
cigarette সিগারেট *si*·ga·ret
cigarette lighter সিগারেট লাইটার *si*·ga·ret *lai*·tar
cinema সিনেমা *si*·ne·ma
circus সারকাস *sar*·kas
citizenship সিটিজেনসিপ *si*·ti·zen·ship
city শহর *sho*·hohr
city centre সিটি সেন্টার *si*·ti *sen*·tar
classical ক্লাসিকাল *kla*·si·kal
clean a পরিষ্কার *poh*·rish·kar
cleaning পরিষ্কার করা *poh*·rish·kar *ko*·ra
client ক্লাইয়েন্ট *klai*·ent
close v বন্ধ *bon*·d'oh
closed বন্ধ *bon*·d'oh
clothing কাপড় চোপড় *ka*·pohŗ *choh*·pohŗ
clothing store কাপড়-চোপড়ের দোকান *ka*·pohŗ·choh·poh·rer *doh*·kan
coast সমুদ্রের ধার *shoh*·mud·rer d'ar
coffee কফি *ko*·fi
coins খুচরা *k'uch*·ra
cold (illness) n ঠান্ডা *t'an*·đa
cold a ঠান্ডা *t'an*·đa
colleague কলিগ *ko*·lig
collect call কালেক্ট কল *ka*·lekt kol
colour রঙ্গ rong
comb n চিরুনি *chi*·ru·ni
come আসুন *aa*·shun
comfortable আরাম *aa*·ram
companion সাথী *sha*·ţ'i
company (friends) সঙ্গ *shon*·goh
complain নালিশ *na*·lish
computer কম্পিউটার *kom*·pyu·tar
concert কনসার্ট *kon*·sart
conditioner কন্ডিশনার *kon*·di·shoh·nar
condom কন্ডম *kon*·dohm
confession দোষ স্বিকার dohsh *shi*·kar
confirm কনফার্ম *kon*·farm
connection যোগাযোগ *joh*·ga·johg
constipation কন্সটিপেশন *kon*·sti·pe·shohn
consulate কনসুলেট *kon*·su·let
contact lens কন্টাক্ট লেন্স *kon*·takt lens
convenience store জেনারেল স্টোর *je*·na·ral stohr
cook n বাবুর্চি *ba*·bur·chi
corkscrew কর্ক স্ক্রু kork skru
cost n খরচ *k'o*·rohch
cotton সূতি *shu*·ţi
cotton balls তুলা *ţu*·la

C

english–bengali

cough n&v কাশি *ka*·shi
cough medicine কাশির ঔষধ *ka*·shir *oh*·shud'
countryside পল্লী গ্রাম *pohl*·li graam
crafts (art) হস্তশিল্প *ho*·stoh·shil·poh
credit card ক্রেডিট কার্ড *kre*·đit karđ
cup কাপ kap
currency exchange টাকা ভাঙ্গানো *ta*·ka *b'ang*·ga·noh
current (electricity) কারেন্ট *ka*·rent
customs (immigration) কাস্টম্‌স *ka*·stohms
cut v কাটা *ka*·ta
cutlery কাটা-চামুচ *ka*·ta·*cha*·much

D

daily প্রতিদিন *proh*·ţi·din
dance n নাচ naach
dancing নাচছে *naach*·ch'e
dangerous বিপদজনক *bi*·pod·jo·nohk
dark অন্ধকার *on*·d'oh·kar
date (appointment) ডেট đet
date (time) তারিখ *ţa*·rik'
date of birth জন্মতারিখ *jon*·moh·ţa·rik'
daughter মেয়ে *me*·e
dawn ভোর b'ohr
day দিন din
day after tomorrow আগামি পরশু *a*·ga·mi *pohr*·shu
day before yesterday গত পরশু *go*·toh *pohr*·shu
delay n&v দেরি *de*·ri
deliver ডেলিভারি *đe*·li·va·ri
dental floss ডেন্টাল ফ্লস *đen*·tal flos
dentist ডেন্টিষ্ট *đen*·tist
deodorant ডিওডারেন্ট *đi*·o·đa·rent
depart গমন *go*·mohn
department store ডিপার্টমেন্ট স্টোর *đi*·part·ment stohr
departure বহির্গমন *boh*·hir·go·mohn
deposit n ডিপোজিট đi·*poh*·zit
destination গন্তব্য *gon*·tob·boh
Dhaka ঢাকা *đ'a*·ka
diabetes ডায়বেটিজ *đai*·be·tiz
diaper ডাইপার *đai*·par
diaphragm ডায়াফ্রাম *đai*·a·fram
diarrhoea ডায়েরিয়া *đai*·ri·a
diary ডাইরি *đai*·ri
dictionary ডিকশনারি *đik*·shoh·na·ri
different ভিন্ন *b'in*·noh
dining car খাবার কমপার্টমেন্ট *k'a*·bar *kom*·part·ment
dinner রাতের খাবার *ra*·ţer *k'a*·bar
direct a ডাইরেক্ট *đai*·rekt
direct-dial ডাইরেক্ট ডায়েল *đai*·rekt *da*·el
dirty ময়লা *moy*·la
disabled পঙ্গু *pohng*·gu
discount ডিসকাউন্ট *đis*·ka·unt
disk (CD/floppy) ডিস্ক đisk
doctor ডাক্তার *đak*·ţar
documentary ডকুমেন্টারি *đo*·ku·men·ta·ri
dog কুকুর *ku*·kur
dollar ডলার *đo*·lar
dope গাজা *ga*·ja
double bed ডবল বেড *đo*·bohl beđ
double room ডবল রুম *đo*·bohl rum
down নিচে *ni*·che
dress n জামা *ja*·ma
drink n পানিয় *pa*·ni·o
drive v ড্রাইভ đraiv
drivers licence ড্রাইভারস লাইসেন্স *đrai*·vars *lai*·sens
drug (illegal) ড্রাগ đrag
drunk মাতাল *ma*·ţal
dry a শুকনা *shuk*·na
duck হাস hash
dummy (pacifier) চুশনি *chush*·ni

E

each প্রত্যেক *prohţ*·ţek
ear কান kaan
early আগে আগে *aa*·ge *aa*·ge
earplugs ইয়ার প্লাগ *i*·ar plag
earrings কানের দুল *kaa*·ner dul
east পূর্ব *pur*·boh
Easter ইস্টার *is*·tar
eat খাওয়া *k'a*·wa
economy class ইকোনমি ক্লাস *ee*·ko·no·mi klas

electrical store ইলেকট্রিকাল জিনিষের দোকান
ee·lek·tri·kal ji·ni·sher doh·kan
electricity ইলেকট্রিসিটি ee·lek·tri·si·ti
elevator লিফট্ lift
email ইমেইল ee·mayl
embassy দূতাবাস du·ţa·bash
emergency এমার্জেন্সি e·mar·jen·si
empty a খালি k'a·li
end n&v শেষ shesh
engagement ইংগেজমেন্ট eeng·gej·ment
engine ইঞ্জিন in·jin
engineer প্রকৌশলী pro·ko·u·shoh·li
engineering প্রকৌশল pro·ko·u·shohl
England ইংল্যান্ড ing·ląnd
English (language) ইংরেজি ing·re·ji
enough যথেষ্ট jo·ţ'esh·toh
enter প্রবেশ pro·besh
entertainment guide বিনোদন গাইড
bi·noh·dohn gaiđ
envelope এনভেলাপ en·ve·lap
euro ইউরো ee·o·roh
Europe ইউরোপ ee·o·rohp
evening সন্ধ্যা shohn·d'a
everything সবকিছু shob·ki·ch'u
exchange (give gifts) v উপহার দেওয়া
u·po·har dą·wa
exchange (money) v ভাঙ্গানো b'ang·ga·noh
exchange rate এক্সচেঞ্জ রেট eks·chenj ret
exhibition প্রদর্শনী pro·dor·shoh·ni
exit v বাহির ba·hir
expensive দামি da·mi
express mail এক্সপ্রেস মেল ek·spres mayl
eye চোখ chohk'

F

face মুখ muk'
fall v পড়ে যাওয়া poh·ŗe ja·wa
family পরিবার poh·ri·bar
family name (surname) সারনেম sar·nem
fan (electric) ফ্যান fąn
far দূর dur
fast a জোরে joh·re
fat a মোটা moh·ta
father বাবা ba·ba
father-in-law শশুর shoh·shur
faulty নষ্ট nosh·toh
feel অনুভব oh·nu·b'ob
feelings অনুভূতি oh·nu·b'u·ţi
festival উৎসব uţ·shob
fever জ্বর jor
fiancé হবু বর hoh·bu bor
fiancée হবু স্ত্রী hoh·bu sţree
film (camera) ফিল্ম film
film (cinema) ছবি ch'o·bi
film speed ফিল্ম স্পিড film speeđ
fine a ভাল b'a·loh
finger আঙ্গুল ang·gul
first প্রথম proh·ţ'ohm
first-aid kit ফার্স্ট এইড বক্স farst ayđ boks
first-class (ticket) ফার্স্ট ক্লাস farst klas
first name ভাল নাম b'a·loh naam
fish মাছ maach'
fish shop মাছের দোকান maa·ch'er doh·kan
fishing মাছ ধরা maach' d'o·ra
flashlight (torch) টর্চ torch
floor মেঝে me·j'e
flower ফুল p'ul
fly v প্লেনে ভ্রমন ple·ne b'roh·mohn
food খাবার k'a·bar
foodstuffs খাদ্য দ্রব্য k'ad·doh drohb·boh
foot (body) পায়ের পাতা pa·yer pa·ţa
football (soccer) ফুটবল fut·bol
footpath ফুটপাত fut·paţ
foreign বিদেশ bi·desh
forest বন bon
forever চিরতরে chi·roh ţo·re
fork কাটা ka·ta
fortnight দুই সপ্তাহ dui shop·ţa
fragile নরম no·rohm
free (gratis) নির্দোষ nir·dohsh
free (not bound) মুক্ত muk·ţoh
friend বন্ধু bohn·d'u
frozen food ফ্রোজেন খাবার froh·zen k'a·bar
fruit ফল p'ol
fry ভাজা b'a·ja
frying pan তাওয়া ţa·wa

full ভরা *b'o*·ra
funny হাসির *ha*·shir
furniture আসবাবপত্র *ash*·bab·po·ţroh
future n ভবিষ্যত *b'oh*·bish·shoţ

G

Germany জার্মানি *jar*·ma·ni
gift উপহার *u*·poh·har
gig চান্স chans
girl মেয়ে *me*·e
girlfriend বান্ধবি *ban*·d'oh·bi
glass (drinking) গ্লাস glas
glasses চশমা *chosh*·ma
go যান jan
good a ভাল *b'a*·loh
go out with সাথে যান *sha*·ţ'e jan
go shopping বাজার করা *ba*·jar *ko*·ra
grandchild নাতি *na*·ţi
grandfather (maternal) নানা *na*·na
grandfather (paternal) দাদা *da*·da
grandmother (maternal) নানি *na*·ni
grandmother (paternal) দাদি *da*·di
gray ছাই রং ch'ai rong
great মহৎ *mo*·hohţ
green সবুজ *shoh*·buj
grey ছাই রং ch'ai rong
grocery (goods) নিত্য প্রয়োজনীয় জিনিষ *niţ*·ţoh *proh*·yo·joh·ni·o *ji*·nish
grocery (shop) নিত্য প্রয়োজনীয় জিনিষের দোকান *niţ*·ţoh *proh*·yo·joh·ni·o *ji*·ni·sher *doh*·kan
grow বড় হওয়া *bo*·ŗoh *ho*·a
guide (person) গাইড gaiđ
guidebook গাইড বই gaiđ *boh*·i
guided tour গাইডেড টুর *gai*·đeđ tur

H

hairdresser নাপিত *na*·piţ
half অর্ধেক *or*·d'ek
hand হাত haaţ'
handbag হ্যান্ডব্যাগ hạnđ bạg
handicrafts হস্তশিল্প *ho*·sţoh·shil·poh
handmade হাতে তৈরি *haa*·ţe ţo·hi·ri
handsome সুদর্শন *shu*·dor·shohn
happy সুখী *shu*·k'i
hard কঠিণ *koh*·t'in
hat টুপি *tu*·pi
have আছে *aa*·ch'e
hay fever এ্যালার্জি *ą*·lar·ji
head মাথা *ma*·ţ'a
headache মাথাব্যাথা *ma*·ţ'a·bą·ţ'a
headlights হেডলাইট *heđ*·lait
heart হার্ট hart
heart condition হার্ট কন্ডিশন hart *kon*·đi·shohn
heat n গরম *go*·rohm
heater হিটার *hi*·tar
heavy ভারি *b'a*·ri
help n&v সাহায্য *sha*·haj·joh
her (possessive) ওর ohr
here এখানে *e*·k'a·ne
high উচা *u*·cha
highway মহাসড়ক *mo*·ha·sho·ŗok
hike v পায়ে হাটা *pa*·e *ha*·ta
Hindi (language) হিন্দি *hin*·di
Hindu (person) হিন্দু *hin*·du
hire n&v ভাড়া *b'a*·ŗa
his ওর ohr
holidays (vacation) ছুটি *ch'u*·ti
honeymoon হানিমুন *ha*·ni·mun
hospital হাসপাতাল *hash*·pa·ţal
hot গরম *go*·rohm
hotel হোটেল *hoh*·tel
hungry ক্ষুধার্ত *k'u*·d'ar·ţoh
husband স্বামি *shaa*·mi

I

ice বরফ *bo*·rohf
ice cream আইস্ক্রিম *ais*·krim
identification পরিচয় *poh*·ri·choy
identification card আইডেন্টিটি কার্ড *ai*·đen·ti·ti kard
ill অসুস্থ *o*·shu·sţ'oh
important গুরুত্বপূর্ন *gu*·ruţ·ţoh·pur·noh
included সহ *sho*·hoh
India ভারত *b'a*·rohţ

indigestion **বদহজম** *bod*·ho·johm
influenza ইনফ্লুয়েন্জা *in*·flu·en·za
injection ইনজেকশন *in*·jek·shohn
injury হত *ho*·ţoh
insurance ইন্সুরেন্স *in*·shu·rens
intermission বিরতি *in*·tar·mi·shohn
Internet ইন্টারনেট *in*·tar·net
Internet café ইন্টারনেট ক্যাফে *in*·tar·net *kq*·fe
interpreter দোভাষী *doh*·b'a·shi
Ireland আইয়ারল্যান্ড *ai*·ar·lạnđ
iron n ইসতিরি *i*·sţri
Islamabad ইসলামাবাদ is·la·ma·*bad*
island দ্বীপ deep
itch v চুলকানো *chul*·ka·noh
itinerary প্রোগ্রাম *pro*·gram

J

jacket জ্যাকেট *jq*·ket
Japan জাপান ja·*paan*
jeans জিন্স jeens
jet lag জেট ল্যাগ jet lạg
jewellery shop গহনার দোকান *go*·hoh·nar *doh*·kan
job কাজ kaj
journalist সাংবাদিক *shang*·ba·dik
jumper (sweater) সয়েটার *swe*·tar

K

key চাবি *cha*·bi
kilogram কিলো *ki*·loh
kilometre কিলোমিটার *ki*·loh·mi·tar
kind a দয়ালু *do*·ya·lu
kitchen রান্না ঘর *ran*·na g'or
knee হাটু *ha*·tu
knife ছুরি *ch'u*·ri

L

lake লেক lek
language ভাষা *b'a*·sha
laptop ল্যাপটপ *lqp*·top
late (not early) দেরি *de*·ri
laundry (place) লন্ড্রি *lon*·đri
law আইন ain
lawyer উকিল *u*·kil
leather চামড়া *cham*·ŗa
left luggage (office) লেফট্ লাগেজ left *la*·gej
leg পা pa
lens (eye/camera) লেন্স lens
less কম kom
letter চিঠি *chi*·ţ'i
library লাইব্রেরি *lai*·bre·ri
life jacket লাইফ জ্যাকেট laif *jq*·ket
lift (elevator) লিফ্ট lift
light n বাতি *ba*·ţi
light (weight) a হালকা *hal*·ka
lighter (cigarette) লাইটার *lai*·tar
like v পছন্দ *po*·ch'ohn·doh
like (similar to) মতন *mo*·tohn
lipstick লিপস্টিক *lip*·stik
liquor store মদের দোকান *mo*·der *doh*·kan
listen শুনুন *shu*·nun
local n স্থানীয় এলাকা *sţ'a*·ni·o *e*·la·ka
lock n&v তালা *ţa*·la
locked তালা বন্দ্ধ *ţa*·la *bon*·d'oh
long লম্বা *lom*·ba
lost হারিয়ে গেছে *ha*·ri·ye *gq*·ch'e
lost property office লস্ট প্রপার্টি অফিস lost *pro*·par·ti *o*·fish
love n ভালবাসা *b'a*·loh·ba·sha
lubricant (cream) ক্রিম krim
lubricant (oil) তেল ţel
luggage মালপত্র *mal*·poţ·roh
lunch দুপুরের খাওয়া *du*·pu·rer *k'a*·wa
luxury লাক্সারি *lak*·sha·ri

M

mailbox পোস্ট বক্স pohst boks
mail (post) পোস্ট pohst
make-up মেক আপ mek ap
man পুরুষ লোক *pu*·rush lohk
manager ম্যানেজার *mq*·ne·jar
map ম্যাপ mạp
market বাজার *ba*·jar
marry বিয়ে *bi*·ye

massage মালিশ *ma*·lish
match (sports) ম্যাচ mạch
matches দেশলাই *desh*·lai
mattress গদি *goh*·di
measles হাম ham
meat মাংস *mang*·shoh
medicine (medication) ঔষধ *oh*·shud'
menu ম্যেনু *me*·nu
message সংবাদ *shong*·bad
metre মিটার *mi*·tar
midnight মধ্যরাত *mohd*·d'oh·raaţ
milk দুধ dud'
millimetre মিলিমিটার *mi*·li·mi·tar
mineral water মিনেরাল ওয়াটার *mi*·ne·ral *wa*·tar
minute মিনিট *mi*·nit
mirror আয়না *a*·e·na
mobile phone মোবাইল ফোন *moh*·bail fohn
modem মোডেম *moh*·đem
money টাকা-পয়সা *ta*·ka·poy·sha
month মাস mash
morning (6am–1pm) সকাল *sho*·kal
mother মা maa
mother-in-law শাশুড়ি *sha*·shu·ṛi
motorcycle মটরসাইকেল *mo*·tohr·sai·kel
motorway (highway) মহাসড়ক *mo*·ha·sho·ṛok
mountain পাহাড় *pa*·haṛ
mouth মুখ muk'
movie (cinema) ছবি *ch'o*·bi
museum যাদুঘর *ja*·du·g'or
music মিউজিক *myu*·zik
musician সংগীত শিল্পী *shong*·geeţ *shil*·pi
Muslim (person) মুসলমান *mu*·sohl·man
my আমার *aa*·mar

N

nail clippers নেইল কাটার nayl *ka*·tar
name n নাম nam
napkin ন্যাপকিন *nạp*·kin
nappy ন্যাপি *nạ*·pi
nausea বমিভাব *boh*·mi·b'ab
near কাছে *ka*·ch'e
nearby কাছেধারে *ka*·ch'e·d'a·re
nearest সবচেয়ে কাছে *sob*·che *ka*·ch'e
necklace হার har
needle (sewing) সুই shui
Netherlands নেদারল্যান্ড *ne*·dar·lạnđ
new নতুন *noh*·tun
New Delhi নয়া দিল্লী *noy*·a *dil*·li
news খবর *k'o*·bohr
newspaper খবরের কাগজ *k'o*·boh·rer *ka*·gohz
New Year নব বর্ষ *no*·boh *bor*·shoh
New Zealand নিউ জিল্যান্ড nyu *zi*·lạnd
next (month) আগামি *aa*·ga·mi
night রাত raaţ
no না na
noisy হৈচৈ *hoi*·choi
nonsmoking ধুমপান নিষেধ *d'um*·pan *ni*·shed'
north উত্তর *uţ*·ţohr
nose নাক nak
notebook নোটবুক *noht*·buk
nothing কিছু না *ki*·ch'u na
now এখন *ạ*·k'ohn
number নম্বর *nom*·bohr
nurse n নার্স nars

O

off (food) বাশি *ba*·shi
oil তেল ţel
old (person) বৃদ্ধ *brid*·d'oh
old (thing) পুরানো *pu*·ra·noh
on অন on
once একবার *ạk*·bar
one-way ticket ওয়ান-ওয়ে টিকেট *wan*·way *ti*·ket
open a খোলা *k'oh*·la
orange (colour) কমলা *kom*·la
other অন্য *ohn*·noh
our আমাদের *aa*·ma·der
outside বাইরে *bai*·re

P

pacifier (dummy) চুশনি *chush*·ni
package (packet) প্যাকেট *pạ*·ket
padlock তালা *ţa*·la
pain ব্যাথা *bạ*·ţ'a

painkillers ব্যাথার ঔষধ *bq*·t̯'ar *oh*·shud'
Pakistan পাকিস্তান pa·kis·*t̯an*
palace রাজ প্রাসাদ raj *pra*·shad
pants (trousers) প্যান্ট pant
pantyhose প্যান্টিহোজ *pqn*·ti·hohz
panty liners প্যান্টি লাইনার *pqn*·ti *lai*·nar
paper কাগজ *ka*·gohj
paperwork কাগজপত্র *ka*·gohj·pot̯·roh
parents বাবা-মা *ba*·ba·ma
park n পার্ক park
party (entertainment/politics) পার্টি *par*·ti
passenger প্যাসেন্জার *pq*·sen·jar
passport পাসপোর্ট *pas*·pohrt
passport number পাসপোর্ট নম্বর *pas*·pohrt *nom*·bohr
past n অতিত *oh*·t̯it̯
path পথ pot̯'
pay v দাম দেওয়া dam *dq*·wa
payment দাম dam
pen কলম *ko*·lohm
pencil পেনসিল *pen*·sil
penis নুনু *nu*·nu
penknife পকেট ছুরি *po*·ket *ch'u*·ri
pensioner পেনশনার *pen*·shoh·nar
per (day) প্রতিদিন *proh*·t̯i·din
perfume পারফিউম *par*·fi·um
petrol (gas) পেট্রোল *pet*·rohl
pharmacist কেমিষ্ট *ke*·mist
pharmacy ঔষধের দোকান *oh*·shu·d'er *doh*·kan
phone book ফোন বই fohn buk
phone box ফোন বক্স fohn boks
phone card ফোন কার্ড fohn kard
photo ছবি *ch'o*·bi
photography আলোকচিত্র *a*·lohk·chit̯·roh
phrasebook ফ্রেজ বই frez *boh*·i
picnic পিকনিক *pik*·nik
pill ট্যাবলেট *tqb*·let
pillow বালিশ *ba*·lish
pillowcase বালিশের কাভার *ba*·li·sher *ka*·var
pink গোলাপি *goh*·la·pi
pistachio পেস্তা *pe*·st̯a
plane প্লেন plen
plate প্লেট plet
platform (train) প্লাটফর্ম *plqt*·form
play n&v খেলা *k'q*·la
plug n প্লাগ plag
police পুলিশ *pu*·lish
police station পুলিশ স্টেশন *pu*·lish *ste*·shohn
pool (swimming) পুল pul
postage পোস্টেজ *poh*·stej
postcard পোস্ট কার্ড pohst kard
post code পোস্ট কোড pohst kohd
poster পোস্টার *poh*·star
post office পোস্ট অফিস pohst *o*·fish
pound (money) পাউন্ড *pa*·und
pregnant গর্বভতি *gor*·b'oh·boh·t̯i
price দাম dam
private প্রাইভেট *prai*·vet
public telephone পাবলিক ফোন *pab*·lik fohn
public toilet পাবলিক টয়লেট *pab*·lik *toy*·let
pull টান tan
purple বেগুনি *be*·gu·ni

Q

queue n লাইন lain
quiet নিরব *ni*·rob

R

railway station ট্রেন স্টেশন tren *ste*·shohn
rain বৃষ্টি *brish*·ti
raincoat রেনকোট *ren*·koht
rare অসাধারণ *o*·sha·d'a·rohn
razor রেজার *rq*·zar
razor blades রেজার ব্লেইড *rq*·zar blayd
receipt রিসিট ri·*seet*
recommend সুপারিশ *su*·pa·rish
red লাল lal
refrigerator ফ্রিজ frij
refund v পয়সা ফেরত *poy*·sha *fe*·roht̯
registered mail রেজিস্ট্রি মেল *re*·ji·stri mayl
remote control রিমোট কন্ট্রোল *ri*·moht *kon*·trohl
rent n&v ভাড়া *b'a*·ṛa
repair v মেরামত *me*·ra·mot̯
reservation রিজার্ভেশন *ri*·sar·ve·shohn
restaurant রেস্তোরা *res*·t̯oh·ra

return v ফেরত *fe*·rohţ
return ticket রিটার্ন টিকেট ri·*tarn ti*·ket
right (correct) ঠিক t'ik
right (direction) ডান đaan
ring (call) v রিং ring
road রাস্তা *raa*·sţa
rock (music) রক rok
romantic রোমান্টিক ro·*man*·tik
room রুম rum
room number রুম নম্বর rum *nom*·bohr
ruins ধ্বংসস্তুপ *d'ong*·shoh·sţup
rupee রুপি *ru*·pi

S

safe a নিরাপদ *ni*·ra·pod
safe sex নিরাপদ সেক্স *ni*·ra·pod seks
sanitary napkins স্যানিটারি প্যাড *sạ*·ni·ta·ri pạd
scarf স্কার্ফ skarf
school স্কুল skul
science বিজ্ঞান *big*·gan
scientist বৈজ্ঞানিক *boyg*·ga·nik
scissors কেচি *ke*·chi
Scotland স্কটল্যান্ড *skot*·lạnd
sculpture মূর্তি *mur*·ţi
sea সমুদ্র *shoh*·mud·roh
season কাল kaal
seat সিট seet
seatbelt সিট বেল্ট seet belt
second (position) a দ্বিতীয় *di*·ţi·o
second (time) n সেকেন্ড *se*·kend
second-hand সেকেন্ড হ্যান্ড *se*·kend hạnđ
send পাঠান *pa*·t'a·noh
service charge সার্ভিস চার্জ *sar*·vis charj
service station পেট্রোল স্টেশন *pet*·rohl *ste*·shohn
sex সেক্স seks
share v সেয়ার *she*·ar
shave v সেভ shev
shaving cream সেভিং ক্রিম *she*·ving krim
sheet (bed) চাদর *cha*·dohr
shirt সার্ট shart
shoes জুতা *ju*·ţa
shoe shop জুতার দোকান *ju*·ţar *doh*·kan
shop n দোকান *doh*·kan
shopping centre সপিং সেন্টার *sho*·ping *sen*·tar
short (height) বেটে *be*·te
short (length) খাটো *kha*·toh
shorts সর্টস shorts
shoulder ঘাড় g'aṛ
shout চিৎকার *chiţ*·kar
show n সো shoh
shower n সাওয়ার *sha*·war
shut a&v বন্ধ *bon*·d'oh
sick অসুস্থ *o*·shu·sţ'oh
silk সিল্ক silk
silver রুপা *ru*·pa
single room সিঙ্গেল রুম *sin*·gel rum
single (unmarried) অবিবাহিত *o*·bi·ba·hi·ţoh
sister বোন bohn
size (clothes) মাপ map
skirt স্কার্ট skart
sleep n ঘুম g'um
sleeping bag স্লিপিং ব্যাগ *slee*·ping bạg
slide (film) স্লাইড slaiđ
slowly ধিরে *d'i*·re
small ছোট *ch'oh*·toh
smell n গন্ধ *gon*·d'oh
smile n হাসি *ha*·shi
smoke n ধুমপান *d'um*·pan
snack n নাস্তা *nash*·ţa
soap সাবান *sha*·ban
socks মোজা *moh*·ja
some কিছু *ki*·ch'u
son ছেলে *ch'e*·le
soon শিঘ্রি *shig*·ri
south দক্ষিণ *dohk*·k'in
souvenir সুভেনিয়ার *su*·ve·ni·er
souvenir shop সুভেনিয়ারের দোকান *su*·ve·ni·e·rer *doh*·kan
Spain স্পেইন spayn
speak কথা বলা *ko*·ţ'a *bo*·la
spoon চামুচ *cha*·much
sprain v মচকানো *moch*·ka·noh
spring (season) বসন্ত *bo*·shohn·ţoh
stairway সিড়ি *shi*·ṛi
stamp n স্ট্যাম্প stạmp
station স্টেশন *ste*·shohn

stockings স্টকিং *sto*·king
stomach পেট pet
stomachache পেট ব্যাথা pet *bq*·ţ'a
stop v থামুন *ţ'a*·mun
street রাস্তা *raa*·sţa
string সুতা *shu*·ţa
student ছাত্র *ch'aţ*·roh
subtitles সাবটাইটেল *sab*·tai·tel
suitcase সুটকেস *sut*·kes
summer গ্রীষ্ম *grish*·shoh
sun সূর্য্য *shur*·joh
sunblock সানব্লক *san*·blok
sunburn রোদে পোড়া *roh*·de *poh*·ŗa
sunglasses সানগ্লাস *san*·glas
sunrise সূর্য্যউদয় *shur*·jo·u·day
sunset সূর্য্যাস্ত *shur*·ja·sţoh
supermarket সুপারমার্কেট *su*·par·mar·ket
surface mail সারফেস মেল *sar*·fes mayl
surname সারনেম *sar*·nem
sweater সয়েটার *swe*·tar
sweet (dessert) n মিষ্টি *mish*·ti
sweet a মিষ্টি *mish*·ti
swim v সাতার *sha*·ţar
swimming pool সুয়িমিং পুল *swi*·ming pul
swimsuit সুয়িমস্যুট *swim*·sut

T

tailor দর্জি *dohr*·ji
taka (currency) টাকা *ta*·ka
take photographs ছবি তোলা *ch'o*·bi *ţoh*·la
tampons ট্যাম্পন *tqm*·pohn
tap কল kol
tasty মজা *mo*·ja
taxi ট্যাক্সি *tqk*·si
taxi stand ট্যাক্সি স্ট্যান্ড *tqk*·si stqnd
teacher শিক্ষক *shik*·k'ok
teaspoon চায়ের চামুচ *cha*·er *cha*·much
telegram টেলিগ্রাম *te*·li·gram
telephone n টেলিফোন *te*·li·fohn
television টেলিভিশন *te*·li·vi·shohn
temperature (fever) জ্বর jor
temperature (weather) টেমপারেচার
tem·pa·re·char

tennis টেনিস *te*·nis
theatre থিয়েটার *ţ'i*·e·tar
their ওদের *oh*·der
thirst n তেষ্টা *ţesh*·ta
this a এই ay
throat গলা *go*·la
ticket টিকেট *ti*·ket
ticket collector টিকেট কালেক্টার *ti*·ket *ka*·lek·tar
ticket office টিকেট অফিস *ti*·ket *o*·fish
time সময় *sho*·moy
time difference টাইম ডিফারেন্স taim *di*·fa·rens
timetable টাইমটেবিল *taim*·te·bil
tin (can) টিন teen
tin opener টিন ওপেনার teen *oh*·pe·nar
tip n আগা *aa*·ga
tired টায়ার্ড *tai*·ard
tissues টিস্যু *ti*·shu
toast (food) n টোস্ট tohst
toaster টোস্টার *toh*·star
today আজ aaj
together একসাথে *qk*·sha·ţ'e
toilet (city) টয়লেট *toy*·let
toilet (country) পায়খানা *pai*·k'a·na
toilet paper টয়লেট পেপার *toy*·let *pe*·par
tomorrow আগামিকাল *aa*·ga·mi·kaal
tomorrow afternoon আগামিকাল দুপুর
aa·ga·mi·kaal *du*·pur
tomorrow evening আগামিকাল সন্ধ্যা
aa·ga·mi·kaal *shon*·d'a
tomorrow morning আগামিকাল সকাল
aa·ga·mi·kaal *sho*·kal
tonight আজ রাত aaj raaţ
too (expensive) বেশি দাম *be*·shi dam
toothache দাতে ব্যাথা daa·ţe *bq*·ţ'a
toothbrush টুথব্রাশ *tuţ'*·brash
toothpaste টুথপেস্ট *tuţ'*·pest
toothpick টুথপিক *tuţ*·pik
torch (flashlight) টর্চ torch
tour v পর্যটন *por*·joh·ton
tourist n পর্যটক *por*·joh·tok
tourist office পর্যটন কেন্দ্র *pohr*·joh·tohn *ken*·droh
towel তোয়ালে *ţoh*·a·le
tower টাওয়ার *ta*·war

T

traffic ট্র্যাফিক *trq*·fik
traffic lights ট্র্যাফিক লাইট *trq*·fik lait
train ট্রেন tren
train station ট্রেন স্টেশন tren *ste*·shohn
tram ট্র্যাম trąm
transit lounge ট্র্যানজিট লাউঞ্জ *trqn*·zit *la*·unj
translate অনুবাদ *oh*·nu·bad
travel agency ট্র্যাভেল এজেন্সি *trq*·vel *q*·jen·si
travellers cheque ট্র্যাভেলার্স চেক *trq*·ve·lars chek
trousers প্যান্ট pant
try v চেষ্টা *chesh*·ta
tube (tyre) টিউব ti·*ub*
TV টিভি *ti*·vi
tweezers চিমটা *chim*·ta
tyre চাকা *cha*·ka

U

umbrella ছাতা *ch'a*·ţa
uncomfortable কষ্ট *kosh*·toh
underwear আন্ডারওয়ের *an*·dar·wer
university ইউনিভার্সিটি *yu*·ni·var·si·ti
up উপর *u*·pohr
Urdu (language) উর্দু *ur*·du
urgent জরুরি *joh*·ru·ri
USA আমেরিকা aa·*me*·ri·ka

V

vacant খালি *kh'a*·li
vacation ছুটি *ch'u*·ti
vaccination ইনজেকশন in·*jek*·shohn
vegetable n সবজি *shohb*·ji
vegetarian n&a ভেজিটেরিয়ান *ve*·ji·te·ri·an
video tape ভিডিও টেপ *vi*·di·o tep
view n দৃশ্য *drish*·shoh
village গ্রাম gram
visa ভিসা *vi*·sa

W

wait অপেক্ষা *o*·pek·k'a
waiter ওয়েটার *we*·tar
waiting room ওয়েটিং রুম *we*·ting rum
walk v হাটা *ha*·ta
wallet ওয়ালেট *wa*·let
warm a গরম *go*·rohm
wash (something) ধোয়া *d'oh*·a
washing machine ওয়াসিং মেশিন *wa*·shing *mq*·shin
watch n ঘড়ি *g'oh*·ŗi
water পানি *pa*·ni
wedding বিয়ে *bi*·ye
weekend উইকএন্ড *wee*·kend
west পশ্চিম *pohsh*·chim
wheelchair হুইলচেয়ার *weel*·che·ar
when কখন *ko*·k'ohn
where কোথায় *koh*·ţ'ai
white সাদা *sha*·da
who কে ke
why কেন *kq*·noh
wife স্ত্রী sţree
window জানালা *ja*·na·la
wine মদ mod
with সাথে *sha*·ţ'e
without ছাড়া *ch'a*·ŗa
woman মহিলা *moh*·hi·la
wood কাঠ kat'
wool উল ul
world বিশ্ব *bish*·shoh
write লেখা *le*·k'a

Y

yellow হলুদ *hoh*·lud
yes হ্যাঁ hang
yesterday গতকাল *go*·toh·kal
you inf তুমি *ţu*·mi
you pol আপনি *aap*·ni
youth hostel ইউথ হস্টেল *ee*·uţ' *ho*·stel

Z

zip/zipper জিপ zip
zoo চিড়িয়াখানা *chi*·ŗi·a·k'a·na

DICTIONARY > bengali–english

The words in this Bengali–English dictionary are ordered according to the Bengali alphabet (presented in the table below). Note that some Bengali characters change their primary forms when combined with each other – that's why some of the words grouped under a particular character may seem to start with a different character (for more information, see **pronunciation**, page 173). Bengali nouns are given in the nominative case (for more information on cases, see the **phrasebuilder**, page 180). The symbols n, a and v (indicating noun, adjective and verb) have been added for clarity where an English term could be either. If you're having trouble understanding Bengali, hand over this dictionary to a Bengali-speaking person, so they can look up the word they need and show you the English translation.

vowels										
অ	আ	ই	ঈ	উ	ঊ	ঋ	এ	ঐ	ও	ঔ

consonants										
ক	খ	গ	ঘ	ঙ	চ	ছ	জ	ঝ	ঞ	ট
ঠ	ড	ঢ	ণ	ত	থ	দ	ধ	ন	প	ফ
ব	ভ	ম	য	র	ল	শ	ষ	স	হ	

অ

অতিত *oh*·ţiţ **past** n
অন on **on**
অনুভব *oh*·nu·b'ob **feel**
অন্য *ohn*·noh **other**
অর্ধেক *or*·d'ek **half**
অসুস্থ *o*·shus·ţ'oh **ill • sick**

আ

আগামি *aa*·ga·mi **next (month)**
আগামিকাল *aa*·ga·mi·kaal **tomorrow**
আগে *aa*·ge **before**
আগে আগে *aa*·ge *aa*·ge **early**
আছে *aa*·ch'e **have**
আজ aaj **today**
আজ রাত aaj raaţ **tonight**
আন্ডারওয়ের *an*·dar·wer **underwear**
আপনি *aap*·ni **you** pol
আমার *aa*·mar **my**
আমাদের *aa*·ma·der **our**
আসুন *aa*·shun **come**

ই

ইকোনমি ক্লাস *ee*·ko·no·mi klas **economy class**
ইন্টারনেট *in*·tar·net **Internet**
ইন্সুরেন্স *in*·shu·rens **insurance**
ইমেইল *ee*·mayl **email**
ইলেকট্রিসিটি *ee*·lek·tri·si·ti **electricity**
ইংরেজি *ing*·re·ji **English (language)**

উ

উইকএন্ড *wee*·kend **weekend**
উইলচেয়ার *weel*·che·ar **wheelchair**
উকিল *u*·kil **lawyer**

উঁচা *u*·cha **high**
উত্তর *uṭ*·ṭohr **north**
উপহার *u*·poh·har **gift**
উর্দু *uṛ*·du **Urdu (language)**

এ

এই *ay* **this** a
এক্সচেঞ্জ রেট eks·*chenj* ret **exchange rate**
এক্সপ্রেস মেল ek·*spres* mayl **express mail**
এখানে *e*·k'a·ne **here**
এখন *ą*·k'ohn **now**
এটিএম *e*·ti·em **automatic teller machine**
এবং *e*·bohng **and**
এমার্জেন্সি e·*mar*·jen·si **emergency**
এয়ারকন্ডিশনার *e*·ar·kon·đi·shoh·nar **air conditioner**
এ্যাডাপ্টার ą·*đap*·tar **adaptor**
এ্যান্টিবায়োটিক *ąn*·ti·bai·o·tik **antibiotics**
এ্যান্টিসেপটিক *ąn*·ti·sep·tik **antiseptic** n&a
এ্যামবুলেন্স *ąm*·bu·lens **ambulance**
এ্যালার্জি *ą*·lar·ji **allergy • hay fever**
এ্যাসপিরিন *ąs*·pi·rin **aspirin**

ও

ওদের *oh*·der **their**
ওর ohr **her (possessive) • his**
ওয়ান-ওয়ে টিকেট *wan*·way *ti*·ket **one-way ticket**
ওয়ালেট *wa*·let **wallet**
ওয়েটার *we*·tar **waiter**

ঔ

ঔষধ *oh*·shud' **medicine (medication)**
ঔষুধের দোকান *oh*·shu·d'er *doh*·kan **pharmacy**

ক

কখন *ko*·k'ohn **when**
কথা বলা *ko*·ţ'a *bo*·la **speak**
কন্টাক্ট লেন্স *kon*·takt lens **contact lenses**
কন্ডম *kon*·dohm **condom**
কফি *ko*·fi **coffee**
কম kom **less**
কম্পিউটার *kom*·pyu·tar **computer**
কম্বল *kom*·bohl **blanket**
কলম *ko*·lohm **pen**
কাগজ *ka*·gohj **paper**
কাছে *ka*·ch'e **near**
কাজ kaj **job**
কাটা *ka*·ta **fork • cut** v
কারেন্ট *ka*·rent **electricity**
কালো *ka*·loh **black**
কালেক্ট কল *ka*·lekt kol **collect call**
কাশি *ka*·shi **cough** n&v
কাস্টমস *kas*·tohms **customs (immigration)**
কিছু *ki*·ch'u **some**
কিছু না *ki*·ch'u na **nothing**
কিন্তু *kin*·ţu **but**
কিলো *ki*·loh **kilogram**
কিলোমিটার *ki*·loh·mi·tar **kilometre**
ক্রেডিট কার্ড *kre*·đit karđ **credit card**
কে ke **who**
কেন *ką*·noh **why**
কেনা *ke*·na **buy**
কোথায় *koh*·ţ'ai **where**
ক্যান্সেল *kąn*·sel **cancel**
ক্যামেরা *ką*·me·ra **camera**
ক্যাশ kąsh **cash** n&v

খ

খবর *k'o*·bohr **news**
খবরের কাগজ *k'o*·boh·rer *ka*·gohz **newspaper**
খরচ *k'o*·rohch **cost** n
খাওয়া *k'a*·wa **eat**
খাটো *kh'a*·toh **short (length)**
খাবার *k'a*·bar **food**
খারাপ *k'a*·rap **bad**
খালি *k'a*·li **empty • vacant**
খুচরা *k'uch*·ra **coins**
খেলা *k'ą*·la **play** n&v
খোলা *k'oh*·la **open** a

গ

গতকাল *go*·toh·kal **yesterday**
গমন *go*·mohn **depart**

গরম *go*·rohm **hot • warm** a • **heat** n
গাইড gaiđ **guide (person)**
গাড়ি *ga*·ŗi **car**
গুরুত্বপূর্ন *gu*·ruţ·ţoh·pur·noh **important**
গোসল খানা *goh*·sohl *k'a*·na **bathroom**
গর্বভতি *gor*·b'oh·boh·ţi **pregnant**
গ্লাস glas **glass (drinking)**

ঘ

ঘড়ি *g'oh*·ŗi **watch** n
ঘুম g'um **sleep** n

চ

চশমা *chosh*·ma **glasses**
চাকা *cha*·ka **tyre**
চাদর *cha*·dohr **sheet (bed)**
চাবি *cha*·bi **key**
চামুচ *cha*·much **spoon**
চিঠি *chi*·ţ'i **letter**
চুশনি *chush*·ni **dummy (pacifier)**
চেক chek **cheque (bank)**
চেক-ইন *chek*·in **check in** v
চেক ভাঙ্গানো chek *b'ang*·ga·noh **cash (a cheque)**

ছ

ছবি *ch'o*·bi **cinema • movie • photo**
ছাত্র *ch'aţ*·roh **student**
ছাড়া *ch'a*·ŗa **without**
ছুটি *ch'u*·ti **holidays • vacation**
ছুরি *ch'u*·ri **knife**
ছেলে *ch'e*·le **boy • son**
ছোট *ch'oh*·toh **small**

জ

জরুরি *joh*·ru·ri **urgent**
জানালা *ja*·na·la **window**
জামা *ja*·ma **dress** n
জুতা *ju*·ţa **shoes**
জোরে *joh*·re **fast** a
জ্বর jor **fever • temperature**

ট

টয়লেট *toy*·let **toilet (city)**
টাকা-পয়সা *ta*·ka·poy·sha **money**
টাকা ভাঙ্গানো *ta*·ka *b'ang*·ga·noh
currency exchange
টায়ার্ড *tai*·ard **tired**
টিকেট *ti*·ket **ticket**
টিস্যু *ti*·shu **tissues**
টুথপেস্ট *tuţ'*·pest **toothpaste**
টুথব্রাশ *tuţ'*·brash **toothbrush**
টেমপারেচার *tem*·pa·re·char
temperature (weather)
টেলিগ্রাম *te*·li·gram **telegram**
টেলিফোন *te*·li·fohn **telephone** n
টেলিভিশন *te*·li·vi·shohn **television**
ট্যাক্সি *tąk*·si **taxi**
ট্রেন tren **train**
ট্র্যাভেল এজেন্সি *trą*·vel *ą*·jen·si **travel agency**
ট্র্যাভেলার্স চেক *trą*·ve·lars chek
travellers cheque
টর্চ torch **flashlight (torch)**

ঠ

ঠান্ডা *t'an*·đa **cold** n&a
ঠিকানা *t'i*·ka·na **address** n

ড

ডবল বেড *đo*·bohl beđ **double bed**
ডবল রুম *đo*·bohl rum **double room**
ডাইপার *đai*·par **diaper (nappy)**
ডাইরেক্ট *đai*·rekt **direct**
ডাক্তার *đak*·ţar **doctor**
ডান đaan **right (direction)**
ডায়েরিয়া *đai*·ri·a **diarrhoea**
ডিকশনারি *đik*·shoh·na·ri **dictionary**
ডিসকাউন্ট *đis*·ka·unt **discount**
ডেন্টিষ্ট *đen*·tist **dentist**
ড্রাইভ đraiv **drive** v
ড্রাগ đrag **drug (illegal)**

ত

তারিখ *ṭa*·rik' **date (time)**
তালা *ṭa*·la **padlock • lock** n&v
তুমি *ṭu*·mi **you** inf
তেল ṭel **oil • lubricant**
তেষ্টা *ṭesh*·ta **thirst** n
তোয়ালে *ṭoh*·a·le **towel**

থ

থাকার ব্যবস্থা *ṭ'a*·kar *bą*·bohs·ṭa **accommodation**
থামুন *ṭ'a*·mun **stop** v

দ

দক্ষিণ *dohk*·k'in **south**
দাঁতে ব্যাথা *daa*·ṭe *bą*·ṭ'a **toothache**
দাম dam **payment • price**
দামি *da*·mi **expensive**
দাম দেওয়া dam *dą*·wa **pay** v
দিন din **day**
দুটোই *du*·toy **both**
দূতাবাস *du*·ṭa·bash **embassy**
দুধ dud' **milk**
দুপুরের খাওয়া *du*·pu·rer *k'a*·wa **lunch**
দূর dur **far**
দূর্ঘটনা *dur*·g'o·toh·na **accident**
দেরি *de*·ri **delay** n&v • **late (not early)**
দেশলাই *desh*·lai **matches**
দোভাষী *doh*·b'a·shi **interpreter**
দোকান *doh*·kan **shop** n
দ্বিতীয় *di*·ṭi·o **second** a

ধ

ধিরে *d'i*·re **slowly**
ধুমপান *d'um*·pan **smoke** n
ধুমপান নিষেধ *d'um*·pan *ni*·shed' **nonsmoking**
ধোয়া *d'oh*·a **wash (something)**

ন

নতুণ *noh*·tun **new**
নম্বর *nom*·bohr **number**
নষ্ট *nosh*·toh **faulty**
না na **no**
নাম nam **name**
নাস্তা *nash*·ṭa **breakfast • snack**
নিচে *ni*·che **down**
নিরব *ni*·rob **quiet**
নিরাপদ *ni*·ra·pod **safe**
নির্দোষ *nir*·dohsh **free (of charge)**

প

পকেট ছুরি *po*·ket *ch'u*·ri **penknife**
পঙ্গু *pohng*·gu **disabled**
পছন্দ *po*·ch'ohn·doh **like** v
পথ poṭ' **path**
পরিচয় *poh*·ri·choy **identification**
পরিষ্কার *poh*·rish·kar **clean** a
পরে *po*·re **after**
পর্যটক *por*·joh·tok **tourist** n
পর্যটন *por*·joh·ton **tour** v
পর্যটন কেন্দ্র *pohr*·joh·tohn *ken*·droh **tourist office**
পশ্চিম *pohsh*·chim **west**
পয়সা ফেরত *poy*·sha *fe*·rohṭ **refund** v
পাঠান *pa*·t'a·noh **send**
পানি *pa*·ni **water**
পানিয় *pa*·ni·o **drink** n
পাসপোর্ট *pas*·pohrt **passport**
পাহাড় *pa*·haṛ **mountain**
পায়খানা *pai*·k'a·na **toilet (country)**
পায়ে হাটা *pa*·e *ha*·ta **hike** v
পিছন *pi*·ch'ohn **behind**
পূর্ব *pur*·boh **east**
পুরানো *pu*·ra·noh **old (thing)**
পুরুষ লোক *pu*·rush lohk **man**
পুলিশ *pu*·lish **police**
পেট ব্যাথা pet *bą*·ṭ'a **stomachache**
পেট্রোল *pet*·rohl **petrol (gas)**
পোস্ট pohst **mail (post)**
পোস্ট অফিস pohst *o*·fish **post office**
পোস্ট কার্ড pohst kard **postcard**
প্যাকেট *pą*·ket **package (packet)**
প্যান্ট pąnt **trousers**
প্রথম *proh*·ṭ'ohm **first**

প্রবেশ *pro*·besh **enter**
প্লেট plet **plate**
প্লেন plen **airplane**
প্লেনে ভ্রমন *ple*·ne *b'roh*·mohn **fly** v

ফ

ফল p'ol **fruit**
ফার্স্ট এইড বক্স farst ayđ boks **first-aid kit**
ফার্স্ট ক্লাস farst klas **first-class (ticket)**
ফিল্ম film **film (camera)**
ফেরত *fe*·rohţ **return** v
ফোন কার্ড fohn karđ **phone card**

ব

বন্ধ *bon*·d'oh **close** v • **closed** • **shut** a&v
বন্ধু *bohn*·d'u **boyfriend** • **friend**
বদল *bo*·dohl **change** v
বমিভাব *boh*·mi·b'ab **nausea**
বর্হিগমন *boh*·hir·go·mohn **departure**
বড় *bo*·ŗoh **big**
বাইরে *bai*·re **outside**
বাচ্চা *baach*·cha **baby** • **child**
বাজার *ba*·jar **market**
বাটি *ba*·ti **bowl**
বাতি *ba*·ţi **light** n
বাবা *ba*·ba **father**
বাস bas **bus**
বাহির *ba*·hir **exit** v
বাংলা *bang*·la **Bengali (language)**
বাংলাদেশ *bang*·la·desh **Bangladesh**
বিছানা *bi*·ch'a·na **bed**
বিপদজনক *bi*·pod·jo·nohk **dangerous**
বিমানবন্দর *bi*·man·bon·dohr **airport**
বিল beel **bill**
বীচ beech **beach**
বুকিং *bu*·king **book (make a reservation)**
বৃদ্ধ *brid*·d'oh **old (person)**
বৃষ্টি *brish*·ti **rain**
বোতল *boh*·ţohl **bottle**
ব্যাগেজ ক্লেইম *bą*·gej klaym **baggage claim**
ব্যাটারি *bą*·ta·ri **battery**
ব্যাথা *bą*·ţ'a **pain**
ব্যাথার ঔষধ *bą*·ţ'ar *oh*·shud' **painkillers**
ব্যান্ডেজ *bąn*·đej **bandage**
ব্যবসা *bąb*·sha **business**
ব্যাংক এ্যাকাউন্ট bąnk *ą*·ka·unt **bank account**
ব্লাড গ্রুপ blad grup **blood group**

ভ

ভরা *b'o*·ra **full**
ভাঙ্গা *b'ang*·a **broken**
ভাঙ্গানো *b'ang*·ga·noh **exchange (money)** v
ভাল *b'a*·loh **fine** • **good** a
ভালবাসা *b'a*·loh·ba·sha **love** n
ভাংতি *b'ang*·ţi **change (coins)** n
ভারত *b'a*·rohţ **India**
ভারি *b'a*·ri **heavy**
ভাড়া *b'a*·ŗa **hire** • **rent** n&v
ভেজিটেরিয়ান *ve*·ji·te·ri·an **vegetarian** n&a

ম

মটরসাইকেল *mo*·tohr·sai·kel **motorcycle**
মদ mod **alcohol** • **wine**
মহাসড়ক *mo*·ha·sho·ŗok **highway** • **motorway**
মহিলা *moh*·hi·la **woman**
ময়লা *moy*·la **dirty**
মা maa **mother**
মাঝখানে *maj'*·k'a·ne **centre**
মাথাব্যাথা *ma*·ţ'a·bą·ţ'a **headache**
মাপ map **size (clothes)**
মালপত্র *mal*·poţ·roh **luggage**
মাস mash **month**
মাংস *mang*·shoh **meat**
মিউজিক *myu*·zik **music**
মিনিট *mi*·nit **minute**
মিষ্টি *mish*·ti **dessert** • **sweet** a
মুসলমান *mu*·sohl·man **Muslim (person)**
মেরামত *me*·ra·moţ **repair**
মেয়ে *me*·e **daughter** • **girl**
ম্যেনু *me*·nu **menu**
মোবাইল ফোন *moh*·bail fohn **mobile (cell) phone**
ম্যাপ mąp **map**

য

যথেষ্ট *jo*·ţ'esh·toh **enough**
যান jan **go**

র

রাত raaţ **night**
রাতের খাবার *ra*·ţer *k'a*·bar **dinner**
রান্না ঘর *ran*·na g'or **kitchen**
রাস্তা *raa*·sţa **road • street**
রিজার্ভেশন *ri*·sar·ve·shohn **reservation**
রিটার্ন টিকেট ri·*tarn ti*·ket **return ticket**
রিসিট ri·*seet* **receipt**
রুপি *ru*·pi **rupee**
রুম rum **room**
রেজার ব্লেইড *rą*·zar blayd **razor blades**
রেজিষ্ট্রি মেল *re*·ji·stri mayl **registered mail**
রেস্তোরা *res*·ţoh·ra **restaurant**

ল

লম্বা *lom*·ba **long**
লন্ড্রি *lon*·đri **laundry (place)**
লস্ট প্রপার্টি অফিস lost *pro*·par·ti *o*·fish **lost property office**
লিফট্ lift **elevator (lift)**
লেখা *le*·k'a **write**
লেফট্ লাগেজ left *la*·gej **left luggage (office)**

স

সকাল *sho*·kal **morning (6am–1pm)**
স্কার্ট skart **skirt**
স্টেশন *ste*·shohn **station**
স্ট্যাম্প sţąmp **stamp**
স্ত্রী sţree **wife**
সন্ধ্যা *shohn*·d'a **evening**
সব shob **all**
সবজি *shob*·ji **vegetable** n
সময় *sho*·moy **time**
সমুদ্র *shoh*·mud·roh **sea**
সস্তা *sho*·sţa **cheap**
সংবাদ *shong*·bad **message**
সাইকেল *sai*·kel **bicycle**
সাওয়ার *sha*·war **shower** n
সাতার *sha*·ţar **swim** v
সাথে *sha*·ţ'e **with**
সাদা *sha*·da **white**
সাবান *sha*·ban **soap**
সার্ট shart **shirt**
সারনেম *sar*·nem **family name (surname)**
সাহায্য *sha*·haj·joh **help** n&v
সিগারেট *si*·ga·ret **cigarette**
সিট seet **seat**
সিঙ্গেল রুম *sin*·gel rum **single room**
সুখী *shu*·k'i **happy**
সুভেনিয়ারের দোকান *su*·ve·ni·e·rer *doh*·kan **souvenir shop**
সুন্দর *shun*·dohr **beautiful**
সুর্য্য *shur*·joh **sun**
সেক্স seks **sex**
সেভিং ক্রিম *she*·ving krim **shaving cream**
সেয়ার *she*·ar **share** v
সো shoh **show** n
স্বামি *shaa*·mi **husband**
স্যানিটারি প্যাড *są*·ni·ta·ri pąd **sanitary napkins**
স্লিপিং ব্যাগ *slee*·ping bąg **sleeping bag**

হ

হত *ho*·ţoh **injury**
হাটা *ha*·ta **walk** v
হার্ট কন্ডিশন hart *kon*·đi·shohn **heart condition**
হারিয়ে গেছে *ha*·ri·ye *gą*·ch'e **lost**
হাসপাতাল *hash*·pa·ţal **hospital**
হাসির *ha*·shir **funny**
হিন্দি *hin*·di **Hindi (language)**
হিন্দু *hin*·du **Hindu (person)**
হৈচৈ *hoi*·choi **noisy**
হোটেল *hoh*·tel **hotel**
হ্যাঁ hang **yes**
হ্যান্ডব্যাগ hąnđ bąg **handbag**
ক্ষুধার্ত *k'u*·d'ar·ţoh **hungry**

accusative	type of *case marking* which shows the *object* of the sentence – 'the couple's parents arranged the **marriage**'
adjective	a word that describes something – 'it was an **expensive** affair'
adverb	a word that explains how an action is done – 'inquiries were **discretely** made in the community'
affix	syllable added to a word to modify its meaning (can be *suffix* or *prefix*)
article	the words 'a', 'an', 'the'
case (marking)	word ending (*suffix*) which tells us the role of a person or thing in the sentence
direct	type of *case marking* which shows the *subject* of the sentence – 'the **families** had a meeting'
gender	the characteristic of a *noun* or an *adjective* that influences which *pronoun* ('he' or 'she') is used to refer to it – can be feminine or masculine
genitive	type of *case marking* which shows possession – 'the **bride**'s family prepared a large dowry …'
infinitive	the dictionary form of a *verb* – '… to **secure** a good match for her'
locative	type of *case marking* which shows location – 'the bridegroom went **to** their **home** on the wedding day'

nominative	type of *case marking* used for the *subject* of the sentence – '**friends** and **well-wishers** accompanied him'
noun	a person, thing or idea – 'a **band** played loud **music**'
object	the person or thing in the sentence that has the action directed to it – 'the guests had **great food**'
oblique	type of *case marking* used for all *nouns*, *pronouns* and *adjectives* other than the *subject* of a sentence – 'the bridegroom held the **bride's hand**'
possessive pronoun	a word that means 'my', 'mine', 'you', 'yours', etc
postposition	a word like 'to' or 'from' in English – in Hindi, Urdu & Bengali they come after the *noun*, *pronoun* or *adjective*
prefix	syllable added to the beginning of a word to modify its meaning – 'a priest **over**saw the ceremony'
pronoun	a word that means 'I', 'you', etc
subject	the person or thing in the sentence that does the action – 'the **crowd** cheered on the young couple'
suffix	syllable added to the end of a word to modify its meaning – 'the marriage was formalis**ed** …'
tense	form of a *verb* which indicates when the action is happening – eg past (ate), present (eat) or future (will eat)
transliteration	pronunciation guide for words and phrases of a foreign language
verb	the word that tells you what action happened – '… when they **walked** around the fire seven times'
verb stem	the part of a verb which doesn't change – 'the celebration **last**ed three days'

G

H

I

L

M

N

O

P

Q

R

S

T

V

W

Lonely Planet Offices

Australia
90 Maribyrnong St, Footscray,
Victoria 3011
☎ 03 8379 8000
fax 03 8379 8111
✉ talk2us@lonelyplanet.com

USA
150 Linden St, Oakland,
CA 94607
☎ 510 250 6400
Toll free 800 275 8555
fax 510 893 8572

UK
2nd fl, 186 City Rd,
London EC1V 2NT
☎ 020 7106 2100
fax 020 7106 2101

lonelyplanet.com